WALES AND THE FRENCH REVOLUTION

General Editors: Mary-Ann Constantine and Dafydd Johnston

EDWARD PUGH *of Ruthin*

1763–1813
'A Native Artist'

JOHN BARRELL

UNIVERSITY OF WALES PRESS

CARDIFF

2013

British Library Cataloguing-in-Publication Data

A catalogue record for this book is available from the
British Library.

ISBN (hb) 978-0-7083-2566-7
ISBN (pb) 978-0-7083-2567-4

The right of John Barrell to be identified as author
of this work have been asserted in accordance with
sections 77, 78 and 79 of the Copyright, Designs and
Patents Act 1988.

Typeset and designed by Chris Bell, cbdesign

Printed in Wales by Cambrian Printers Ltd,
Aberystwyth

To Clare Bond

WALES AND THE FRENCH REVOLUTION

The French Revolution of 1789 was perhaps the defining event of the Romantic period in Europe. It unsettled not only the ordering of society but language and thought itself: its effects were profoundly cultural, and they were long-lasting. The last twenty years have radically altered our understanding of the impact of the Revolution and its aftermath on British culture. In literature, as critical attention has shifted from a handful of major poets to the non-canonical edges, we can now see how the works of women writers, self-educated authors, radical pamphleteers, prophets and loyalist propagandists both shaped and were shaped by the language and ideas of the period. Yet surprising gaps remain, and even recent studies of the 'British' reaction to the Revolution remain poorly informed about responses from the regions. In literary and historical discussions of the so-called 'four nations' of Britain, Wales has been virtually invisible; many researchers working in this period are unaware of the kinds of sources available for comparative study.

The Wales and the French Revolution Series is the product of a four-year project funded by the AHRC and the University of Wales at the Centre for Advanced Welsh and Celtic Studies. It makes available a wide range of Welsh material from the decades spanning the Revolution and the subsequent wars with France. Each volume, edited by an expert in the field, presents a collection of texts (including, where relevant, translations) from a particular genre with a critical essay situating the material in its historical and literary context. A great deal of material is published here for the first time, and all kinds of genres are explored. From ballads and pamphlets to personal letters and prize-winning poems, essays, journals, sermons, songs and satires, the range of texts covered by this series is a stimulating reflection of the political and cultural complexity of the time. We hope these volumes will encourage scholars and students of Welsh history and literature to rediscover this fascinating period, and will offer ample comparative scope for those working further afield.

Mary-Ann Constantine and Dafydd Johnston
General Editors

CONTENTS

ACKNOWLEDGEMENTS

S ome time in the late 1990s Harriet Guest and I found and bought an unsigned and anonymous landscape watercolour in a picture gallery in Leominster, and a few years after that we set out to find the view it depicted, between Mold and Ruthin on the border of Flintshire and Denbighshire. Then, in 2008, Claire Connolly, then of the Department of English at the University of Cardiff, invited me to contribute to a conference on 'Ireland and Wales: Romantic Nations'. She invited me, I think, because I knew so little about Wales, Romantic or otherwise, and I accepted for the same reason, in the hope that I could put together a paper by researching our anonymous watercolour. I had pretty well roughed out the whole paper before I found out who the artist was. Trespassing in the grounds of Colomendy, looking for the place from where Richard Wilson had sketched his own version of the view, we were apprehended by the warden, if that was his title, Gareth Owen Ellis, who, after showing us Wilson's viewpoint, led us to a private museum of the area that he had assembled, loaded me with publications on the history of the locality, and showed me a photograph of a print clearly based on our watercolour. Thus we discovered that our anonymous artist was the almost forgotten Edward Pugh; and the more I found out about him, the more I wanted to write this book to resuscitate his reputation.

Starting from a position of complete ignorance I have needed a vast amount of help. C. J. Williams heard about my paper for Cardiff and invited me to submit it to the *Denbighshire Historical Society Transactions*, which he edits. He has helped me mainly on the history of lead- mining, but on every other issue I asked him about as well. I happened to be a member of the advisory panel on an ambitious research project at the Centre for Advanced Welsh and Celtic Studies of the University of Wales, on Wales and the French Revolution, led by Mary-Ann Constantine, and she and the members of the research team have been wonderfully generous with their knowledge and advice. Elizabeth Edwards led me to a wide range of material that turned out to be vital to this project; Marion Löffler, whose knowledge of political texts produced in and about Wales in the 1790s was invaluable; Ffion Mair Jones helped me with the history of the harp, and Cathryn Charnell-White with information about the London Welsh. Mary-Ann Constantine and Dafydd Johnston have been supportive throughout, and Mary-Ann was to first to read and comment on the completed manuscript in full. Alaw Mai Edwards, also of the Centre, told me about the poet Huw Jones and translated for me two of his poems which are quoted and discussed in Chapter 4. Also in Aberystwyth I've been helped by Hywel Davies, Geraint Jenkins and Peter Lord.

Elsewhere in Wales my gratitude is due to Ralph Griffiths, of the University of Swansea, and Abigail Kenvyn, of Brecknock Museum and Art Gallery, who helped me to match an engraving after Pugh to the scene it depicted, and to Ann Griffiths for information on a harp illustrated by Pugh. I have never met her, but Rhys Jones, himself a harpist and at the time of writing an MA student in the Centre for Eighteenth Century Studies at the University of York, got in touch with her, and on the basis of what she told him and what he already knew, put together a valuable dossier on early nineteenth-century harps, Welsh and otherwise, about which I knew nothing. My thanks also to Richard Aldrich, of the Old Ruthinian Association; to Neil Roberts, of the Ruthin-Pwllglas Golf Club, who pointed out to me the viewpoint of Pugh's image of Coedmarchan; to Cris Ebbs who gave me much information on the Loggerheads mines; to Jonathan Wilkins of the North Wales Geological Association, who attempted to give me, by email, a crash course on geology; to Nigel Young, who kindly checked what I had to say about Pugh's images of Monmouthshire, and to John Idris Jones, who alerted me to the volume of Pugh's drawings for his book *Cambria Depicta* in the National Library.

Over the last few years I have been lecturing on Pugh at universities and other institutions in England, Wales, Scotland, Poland, Switzerland, Canada, the USA and Australia, and on many occasions my thinking about Pugh has changed direction as a result of questions and comments from audiences. Many of those who helped in this way are unknown to me, but among the rest I especially valued the suggestions of Peter de Bolla, John Bonehill, Stephen Daniels, Christopher Dyer, Lucy Hartley, Paul Keen, Stephen Laird, Nigel Leask, Marcia Pointon, Alex Potts, David Solkin, Achim Timmermann, Anne Wagner and Andrew Wilton. At York I was helped and encouraged by Helen Cowie, Mark Hallett, Sarah Monks and Alison O'Byrne: the chapter on Pugh's London owes much to Alison's amazing knowledge of the history of the city. Others who have helped include Dennis Bailey, Matt Barrell, Helena Barrell, who helped compile the index, Michael Lewis, Morrigan Mason, Michael Phillips, and Margaret Ferguson, who translated for me Prince Hermann von Pückler-Muskau's account of his visit to Pont y Glyn Diffwys. Geoff Quilley and Nigel Rigby tried, in the event unsuccessfully, to track down a Hawaiian visitor to Britain painted by Pugh in 1796. As often before I have been helped greatly by Michael Rosenthal on questions to do with British art, by Tim Clark, with whom I thought I disagreed about place and landscape, but perhaps after all we agreed; by Keith Snell, on whose knowledge of rural history I have several times drawn; and by Jon Mee, whose knowledge and understanding of the 1790s in Britain has now left mine a long way behind. I owe a huge amount, also, to the ever-helpful staff of the Cheshire, Flintshire and Denbighshire Record Offices, as I do also to the staff of the National Library of Wales and to Felicity Myrone at the British Library. Working with the University of Wales Press has been a delight. Sarah Lewis has been as helpful, patient and encouraging a commissioning editor as I could have wished for. Henry Maas was an ever-alert, creative and good-humoured copy-editor; the press's editor and the press's production manager, Dafydd Jones and Siân Chapman, were always willing to forgive my occasional outbursts over layout, and to accommodate my anxieties. Thanks too to Catrin Harries of the marketing department, and to the designer of the book's beautiful cover.

A first version of Chapter 1 appeared as 'Edward Pugh at Carreg Carn March Arthur', in the *Denbighshire Historical Society Transactions*, 58 (2010), 23–55; some of Chapter 6 appeared as 'Topography v. Landscape', in the *London Review of Books*, 29 April 2010; and a shorter version of Chapter 7 appeared in the *London Journal*, October 2012.

While researching and writing the book I have also been involved in planning an exhibition of Pugh's work in his home town of Ruthin in 2013, the bicentenary of his death. At the time of writing it is too early to say what form this will take, but meanwhile I have been helped enormously both in my researches and my thinking about how to present Pugh to a modern audience by the participants in the 'Edward Pugh Project', as it has come to be known, in particular by Derek Jones, Philip Hughes of Ruthin Craft Centre, and Arnold Hughes, who was especially helpful on the history of Ruthin. The late Hafina Coppack was also an early supporter of the project. Together the Ruthin and District Civic Association and the Ruthin Local History Group put in a bid to the Paul Mellon Centre for British Art for a grant to employ a Curatorial Research Assistant, and we were incredibly fortunate in securing the services of the extraordinary Jill Piercy. She will be mainly influential on the exhibition, but I am aware of making numerous small decisions in revising this book which I would not have made had I not had the privilege of collaborating with her. The Paul Mellon Centre has supported this project from the outset with funds to support my research, and to help with the costs of publication, and I am immensely grateful for its help, and for the warm encouragement of Brian Allen.

Thanks, finally, to Iain McCalman, an early and very eager initiate into Pugh studies, and a vigorous and ever ready participant, and to Harriet Guest, who has walked every mile with me in Pugh's Denbighshire, has photographed all the sites of his six Denbighshire views of 1794, and has read every draft of this book. The book is dedicated to Clare Bond, in recognition of her unique contribution to the study of the eighteenth century over three decades.

John Barrell
Queen Mary University of London

LIST OF ILLUSTRATIONS

PICTURE CREDITS

I am grateful to have been granted permission to reproduce paintings, drawings and prints in the following collections, which own the copyright on the objects and/or photographs of the objects reproduced: the Ashmolean Museum, University of Oxford, for 1.6; the British Library Board, London, for 1.15, 1.20, 4.5, 4.7, 4.8, 5.4, 6.1; the British Museum, London, for 5.1, 7.6, 7.7, 7.12, 7.14, 7.15, 7.16, 9.5; City of London, London Metropolitan Archives, for 7.11; Denbighshire Record Office, Ruthin, for 6.3; Flintshire Record Office, Hawarden, for 1.27; the Museo Archeologico, Naples, for 2.6; the National Library of Wales, Aberystwyth, for 0.1, 0.2, 0.4, 0.12, 0.14, 0.16, 1.1, 1.3, 1.13, 1.16, 1.17, 1.18, 2.4, 2.9, 3.3, 3.6, 4.1, 4.2, 4.3, 4.4, 5.2, 5.3, 5.6, 5.7, 5.9, 6.2, 8.3, 8.5, 8.8, 8.9, 8.11, 9.3, 10.1, 10.4, 10.5, 11.3; the National Maritime Museum, Greenwich, for 7.17, 7.19; the National Museum of Wales, Cardiff, for 0.6, 0.8, 0.15, 1.8; the Tate, London, for 1.5; the Victoria and Albert Museum, London, for 0.9. The photograph reproduced as 11.1 and 11.2 was supplied by the Bodelwyddan Castle Trust. Plate 0.10 is reproduced by kind permission of Ian Cooke, and plate 3.11 by kind permission of his Grace the Duke of Bedford and the Trustees of the Bedford Estates. The remaining objects reproduced are privately owned.

Plate 5.4 has been enlarged beyond its actual size, to reveal topographical details otherwise hard to make out. Elsewhere, and for similar reasons, a few details of other images have also been enlarged beyond their actual size.

Plates 0.3 and 8.2 contain Ordnance Survey data © Crown copyright and database right 2012 (produced by www.themappingcompany.co.uk).

ABBREVIATIONS

CCh   *Chester Chronicle.*

CCo   *Chester Courant.*

CD   [Edward Pugh], *Cambria Depicta: A Tour through North Wales, illustrated with Picturesque Views. By a Native Artist* (London: E. Williams, 1816).

DRO   Denbighshire Record Office.

GM   *Gentleman's Magazine.*

ML   *Modern London; being the History of the Present State of the British Metropolis* (London: Richard Phillips, 1804).

NLW   National Library of Wales.

INTRODUCTION

I

In 1775, Richard Wilson issued, through the publisher John Boydell, six prints of his paintings of Welsh landscapes, engraved by various artists. The series covered a wide range of Welsh views, three in south Wales – Pembroke Castle and Town, Cilgerran Castle, and William Edwards's new bridge over the River Taff at Pontypridd (Plate 0.1) – and three in the north: Snowdon (Plate 0.2), Cader Idris, and Caernarvon Castle. The views chosen were among the grandest the country had to offer: three ancient castles, the two most striking mountains, and a modern bridge, built in 1756 by a local stonemason, then the longest single-span stone arch bridge in the world and considered the modern wonder of Wales. Some

Plate 0.1 *Pierre Charles Canot after Richard Wilson,* The Great Bridge over the Taaffe, *engraving (London: John Boydell, 1775), Aberystwyth, National Library of Wales.*

Plate 0.2 *William Woollett after Richard Wilson,* Snowden Hill and the Adjacent Country in North Wales, *engraving (London: John Boydell, 1775), Aberystwyth, National Library of Wales.*

I now speak of my native country, celebrated in our earliest history for its valour and tenacity of its liberty; for the stand it made against the *Romans*; for its slaughter of the legions . . . The spirit which the people shewed at the beginning, did not desert them to the last. Notwithstanding they were obliged to submit to the resistless power of the *Romans*, they never fell a prey to the enervating charms of luxury, as the other nations of this island did.[3]

In their different ways these are both instances of a new confidence about Wales and the culture of Wales, addressed to a wider British audience without apology or deference.

In 1794, Edward Pugh announced in the Chester newspapers his intention to publish *Six Views, in Denbighshire*, to be engraved in aquatint by William Ellis.[4] Pugh had the greatest respect and admiration for 'the inimitable Wilson', who had died twelve years earlier and was regarded as the greatest landscape painter that Wales or indeed Britain had produced.[5] He was especially impressed by his views of Wales: his Snowdon, engraved by William Woollett, 'by connoisseurs was esteemed one of the most excellent of his performances'; on Cader Idris, he made a point of standing upon the very spot 'where I thought Mr. Wilson must have sat, to sketch for that fine picture of his, which he afterwards published'.[6] For Pugh, Wilson was an 'incomparable artist': at a time when Claude Lorrain was almost universally regarded as the greatest landscape painter who had ever lived, 'this gentleman', wrote Pugh, 'rose to such a height of perfection in the arts, as to eclipse the (till then) unrivalled abilities of Claude himself.' He was also, Pugh added, 'the first who visited north Wales professionally as an artist: he unfolded its beauties,

of Wilson's six views had appeared previously, but the decision to issue them together as a series, a collaboration between two London Welshmen – Wilson was born in Penegoes in Montgomeryshire, Boydell brought up in Hawarden – was, as David Solkin has pointed out, a bold attempt to establish Wales as an ancient country and a sublime one,[1] as worthy to be depicted by an artist of high ambition as was the Roman Campagna. The claim is made with something of the same bravura as the grand opening with which Wilson's kinsman,[2] Thomas Pennant, three years later, began his *Tours in Wales*, as if he was a public orator addressing a formal assembly:

and, with his bewitching performances, enticed others to extend their visits to these inexhaustible resources of the arts.'[7] At a time when series of Welsh views by English artists were appearing nearly every year, there cannot be much doubt that Pugh's six landscape prints — the only such series to be produced by a Welsh-born, Welsh-speaking artist of the period — were issued in emulation of Wilson's. And though Pugh was too modest to think of himself as a rival — he was, he believed, an artist of 'moderate talent'[8] — at least one contemporary Welshman, the poet Richard Llwyd, claimed to believe that his close friend Pugh was worthy to be named alongside his great hero. 'Snowdon, Cader Idris, and other great features on the Cambrian countenance', wrote Llwyd in a note to his poem Beaumaris Bay, 'have been rendered familiar even to untravelled eyes, by the admired pencil of a Wilson; others will probably be so, by that of a native artist, Mr. Pugh.'[9]

Pugh's six landscape prints, however, were not images of the 'great features' of Wales. All were of views within a few miles of Ruthin (Plate 0.3), and there was nowhere in his native county that provided the sublime imagery of the counties further west. The nearest to a sublime landscape was the view of the falls under the new bridge at Pont y Glyn Diffwys near Llangwm, at that time one of the most visited, most depicted, most described views in Wales, though now made invisible by trees. There was a view of Moel Famau, the highest hill in the Clwydian range, too gentle and easy to climb to count as sublime. For the rest, there was a village scene, Llanfwrog from the west, looking past Ruthin to Foel Fenlli in the Clwydian range; a scene of quiet rural activity on the common at Coedmarchan, south of Ruthin, again looking eastward to the hills; and two images exemplifying

the celebrated beauty of the Dee valley: a country-house view of Pen-y-Lan near Ruabon, seen from across the river; and a view of the rapids near Llantysilio which Telford would later remodel as Horseshoe Falls. Together, these six aquatints offer a rich and fascinating account of rural life and scenery in Denbighshire in the early 1790s.

There are various possible reasons why Pugh should have chosen to announce himself as he did, with a series that both emulated Wilson and disclaimed any pretensions to the grand subjects that Wilson painted, or to the modified version of the 'grand style' which Wilson used for his Welsh views. First, there was simple loyalty to his home scenery, and the fact of course that by 1794 he was probably not at all widely travelled elsewhere in Wales; apart from Pen-y-Lan, which lay near one of the routes he may have taken between London and Ruthin, all of the views were comfortably within a day's walk of his home town, at any rate for an active pedestrian like Pugh. Secondly, there had been a slight shift in taste in the nearly twenty years since Wilson's views had appeared. Though sublime landscape never went out of fashion, the makers and consumers of landscape images were now interested also in the 'picturesque', an aesthetic category which concentrated on rough surfaces and broken lines that were more visible in relatively small-scale views than in grand panoramas.

Plate 0.3 *Map showing the locations of Pugh's Six Views, in Denbighshire.*

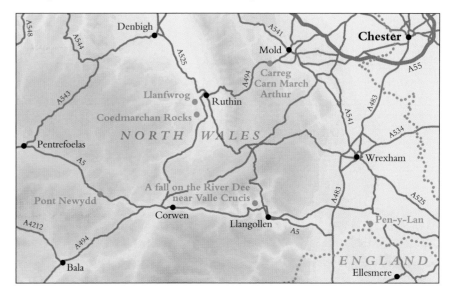

Finally, there were insidious issues of social class involved in the theory of the hierarchy of genres and of aesthetic categories. There were writers on the aesthetic who believed that, because painting was a liberal art, it could be produced and enjoyed only by men of liberal education: the rest, the 'mechanics', were capable only of a mechanical kind of art, making tame, dully accurate images of real places, not boldly imaginative and imaginary landscapes in the grand style of Claude or Nicolas Poussin. The abilities of women artists were thought to be different, but no less confined to a kind of servile copying. What is more, the sublime, and even the beautiful, were often held to be invisible except to men of private means. The relatively poor were (like women) creatures of appetite. They could admire in landscape only images of what could be consumed or sold: fields of thriving wheat, fat cattle. The pleasures of grand, wild, uncultivated landscapes were available only to those who were not worried about where their next meal was coming from.[10]

This theory could act of course to stimulate a taste for the sublime in those whom it declared to be incapable of it, but it could inhibit ambition as well, and it helped inscribe a social structure on the artistic culture of the late eighteenth century in which artists had to know their place or fight hard to escape it. With hopeful eagerness each of Pugh's six prints is 'respectfully dedicated' to a member of the local aristocracy or gentry from whom he no doubt hopes for patronage; with the deference due from the son of a country barber he describes Wilson, the son of an Oxford-educated country rector and related not only to Pennant but to the Mostyns of Mostyn, the Vaughans of Cors-y-Gedol, and the Wynns of Wynnstay,[11] as a 'gentleman'. This is matched in the other direction by Pennant describing the illustrations to his *Tours of Wales* by Moses Griffith, a labourer's son from Caernarvonshire, as 'the performances of a worthy servant, whom I keep for that purpose'; he patronisingly requests his readers to 'excuse any little imperfections they may find in them; as they are the works of an untaught genius, drawn from the most remote and obscure parts of *North Wales*'.[12]

All this helps explain the particular character of Pugh's six images, and in particular their rather hybrid character, carefully drawn images of 'the ordinary appearances of Nature', as the contemporary phrase had it, which have the air of being, in Henry Fuseli's phrase, 'delineations of given spots', but which nevertheless often rearrange the objects in the view in search of effects of structure and composition, occasionally of grandeur, in the manner of a more 'liberal' artist.[13] If he has neither the high ambition nor the cultural authority of Wilson, he is determined to be more than a mere mechanic, more than a servant-artist. He operates on both sides of the distinction, not yet fully developed, between 'landscape' and 'topography'; he is at once a metropolitan artist, anxious to cash in on the market for series of prints of Welsh landscape views, pioneered by Paul Sandby and by Wilson himself, and an intensely local artist, far more interested in the places he depicts in Wales, and what they would have meant to local people, than Sandby or Wilson or any of those, like Thomas Walmsley or John 'Warwick' Smith, who followed them to Wales. At home in Ruthin he was the son of a tradesman, a 'mechanic'; elsewhere in Wales, and in England especially, he could put on enough of the gentleman to be admitted as a portrait-artist to the houses of the gentry. It was this sense of Pugh as an artist of the in-between, of the both/

and, that particularly attracted me to him, and made me want to find out whatever I could about him.

I have not found out much. The artist and writer Edward Pugh was best known as a miniaturist, painting portraits in watercolour on ivory, mainly, it seems, of the Welsh gentry on their visits to London and Chester. But his true ambition was as an artist in landscape, and as well as the *Six Views, in Denbighshire* of 1794, he produced, ten years later, a striking series of urban views to illustrate a book called *Modern London* by Richard Phillips. Around 1810 he published two large coloured aquatints of scenes in Monmouthshire. His greatest achievement however was probably as a writer: his tour of north Wales, *Cambria Depicta*, was published in 1816, three years after his death at the age of fifty. This is the first tour of Wales by a writer whose first language was Welsh, and the only one published in the heyday of the 'Welsh tour', the late eighteenth and early nineteenth centuries, that was not written by an author with pretensions to gentility. It contained seventy-one illustrations aquatinted after drawings by Pugh himself, charming enough but, compared with Pugh's best work, not very memorable. The writing however is brilliant, and the book initiates a quite new style of travel writing about Wales, much more informal, and much better-informed, much more knowledgeable about and sympathetic towards the inhabitants of rural Wales than the numerous tours that came before it.

We learn a good deal about Pugh's character from *Cambria Depicta*, but very little about the events of his life. We have no real idea of what he looked like: he was as fond as Alfred Hitchcock of appearing in his own pictures, but always in the middle distance, sometimes turning away from us as if not wanting to draw our attention from the view.

The nearest to a likeness is probably the drawing he made of himself for *Cambria Depicta*, sitting on a turf bank at the source of the Severn, on Plynlimon, and looking at the black terrier that accompanied him throughout his tour (Plate 0.4). It is however fairly generic, as if Pugh was intending the detail to be added by an engraver in London who perhaps had never seen him in the flesh (Plate 0.5). As for Pugh's life, we have a few entries in parish registers and in exhibition catalogues; a collection of newspaper advertisements; a few, surprisingly few, autobiographical remarks in *Cambria Depicta*; three letters by him, two of them barely more than hasty notes, and one brief letter that mentions him; and a few miscellaneous titbits that tell us very little more. Until more is found, a 'life' of Edward Pugh has to be fashioned out of these.

Plate 0.4 *(above left) Edward Pugh, self-portrait with his dog Miss Wowski, detail from* The Source of the Severn, *grisaille watercolour for* Cambria Depicta, *between 1804 and 1813, Aberystwyth, National Library of Wales.*

Plate 0.5 *(above right) Thomas Cartwright after Edward Pugh, detail from* The Source of the Severn, *coloured aquatint from* Cambria Depicta, *dated June 1814.*

He was born in 1763 in Ruthin, a small country town in Denbighshire, in north-east Wales, where both his parents had also been born. They were members of the Church of England, as it then was — Pugh himself would remain loyal to the Church throughout his life — and were married at St Peter's at the north end of the town's central square. His father, David, was a barber, who would die when Pugh was twelve years old; his mother, Dorothy Jones, who was living, perhaps as a servant, at Llanbedr, a couple of miles to the north-east at the time of her marriage, would outlive Edward by three years: she was nearly 85 when she died in December 1815. The Pughs had six children, of whom the first two, both named John, died in infancy. Edward was the fourth child; his sister Mary was two years older than him; a third brother John was two and a half years younger than Edward, and his youngest brother Simon six years younger. Simon and the third John apparently survived childhood, but seem to have moved away from Ruthin: I have found no sign of their marriages, burials or offspring in the registers of Ruthin or the immediately surrounding parishes. Mary, however, stayed at home and outlived Edward: in March 1830, at the age of 69, she was buried in the neighbouring parish of Llanrhydd. Her address is given as Well Street, Ruthin, the street where Edward and his mother were living at the time of their deaths. She never married, and may well have lived with her mother all her life. In his few surviving letters, and in *Cambria Depicta*, Pugh never mentions his siblings, though on several occasions he writes, with great affection, about his mother.[14]

I have been unable to establish where Pugh went to school. He was extremely well educated, most likely at the famous grammar school at Ruthin, where the sons of poor tradesmen in the town could be educated at the expense of the tithes of the parish of Llanelidan. But a burst water-tank destroyed the school archives in the last century, and the only evidence that he was there is the mention of him, as a source for an anecdote about Ruthin schoolboys, in Keith Thompson's *Ruthin School: The First Seven Centuries*, where he is described as a 'Ruthin man', apparently Thompson's usual term for an old boy of the school.[15] His friend or acquaintance in later life, David Samwell, another Denbighshire man, son of a Welsh vicar, a poet and naval surgeon who had accompanied Cook on his third (and fatal) voyage to the Pacific, tells us a bit more. In 1795 he wrote to the poet Iolo Morganwg about their attempt to get Pugh to make a portrait of Thomas Edwards, stonemason, bricklayer and bard: Twm o'r Nant, 'the Cambrian Shakespeare'. Samwell and Edwards had grown up in the same parish, and Samwell was tirelessly plugging Edwards's reputation. 'I have wrote to the Nant,' he told Iolo, 'but shant be in town to receive his answer. The business we were talking about must be settled between Mr Pugh & him, but as P. cannot correspond in Welsh why cant you write to the Nant?'[16] We know Pugh was a native Welsh-speaker, but whatever education he received had taught him to write only in English. How well he read Welsh is not clear either. By the 1800s, at least, when he wrote *Cambria Depicta*, he was an urbane, witty, stylish writer in English with a knowledge of English poetry which would have been thoroughly impressive at the time in a university-educated literary man. In that book too he quotes a fair amount of Welsh poetry, but even for me, a non Welsh-speaker, it has not been hard to establish that most if not all of it is taken from books in English which quote and translate Welsh verse.

Somehow however Pugh got himself an education; somehow too he became an artist, and probably spent some of his twenties as an itinerant painter in Wales, calling at the houses of the gentry and offering to paint their portraits. One miniature attributed to him (it is not clear on what basis) has survived which probably dates from this period, a portrait of Margaret Jones Parry, identified on the backing paper as 'of Madryn Carnarvonshire and Llwyn Onn Denbighshire North Wales' (Plate 0.6), the wife of Thomas Parry Jones Parry. The portrait, tight, neat and careful in its depiction of Margaret Jones Parry's white lace and jet-black curls, its flat drapery, its textured but unvaried background, seems to suggest that Pugh, if this is by him, had taught himself to paint; but the conformity of the expression in her mouth with the set of her head and the way she returns Pugh's examination of her with a concentration equal to his, makes it clear that he (again, if it *is* he) has not mistaken his vocation.

In his first thirty years, the only trace I have found of Pugh is the record of his baptism. Then, as if out of nowhere, two of his portraits, displayed within a single frame,

were selected for display in the 1793 exhibition of the Royal Academy of Arts. There is no record of the sitters, but the catalogue entry shows that Pugh had now moved to London, and is lodging at 76 the Strand, a stone's throw from the Academy, then in Somerset House.[17] Three years later Pugh had another portrait accepted, this time of 'Wy, alias Brown, a native of Owyhee' (Hawaii). Who this man was I have been unable to discover. My guess is that he came to Britain on one of the trading ships the *Butterworth* or the *Jackal* of which a Captain Brown was master. In the early 1790s the British naval officer and explorer George Vancouver

Plate 0.6 *(above)* Attributed to *Edward Pugh*, Mrs Jones-Parry of Madryn and Llwyn Onn, *watercolour on ivory, ca. 1790, Cardiff, National Museum of Wales.*

Plate 0.7 *(left) J. Chapman after Edward Pugh,* The Cambrian Shakespeare *[Twm o'r Nant], stipple engraving (London: E. Pughe, 1800), private collection.*

Plate 0.8 Attributed to *Edward Pugh,* Lady Morris, *watercolour on ivory, ca. 1805, Cardiff, National Museum and Gallery.*

was repeatedly running into Captain Brown in the Pacific and especially around Hawaii. Perhaps the commission for this portrait too came via Samwell, through his connections with others who had seen the Pacific.[18]

In 1799 Pugh had no less than four portraits accepted by the Academy: 'a Lady of Quality'; what were probably once again two portraits in a single frame, 'Mr. Jackson of Holyhead, and an officer' and the portrait of Twm o'r Nant, which the *Public Advertiser* would commend as one of the 'most distinguished portraits' of the year (along with, however, about ninety others, equally distinguished).[19] In 1800 Pugh would publish an engraving of this (Plate 0.7) which he advertised for sale in the Chester newspapers.[20] The whereabouts of all these miniatures are now unknown; indeed I have found only three miniatures attributed to Pugh in public collections in Britain and Ireland. At the National Museum of Wales, along with the portrait of Margaret Jones Parry, there is another miniature said to be by Pugh of Lady Morris, the wife, presumably, of Sir John Morris, founder of Morriston, the early industrial village in Glamorgan (Plate 0.8). The latter portrait, signed but not apparently in Pugh's hand, is a much more polished and sophisticated effort than the image of Mrs Jones Parry, as is the much more spirited miniature in the Victoria and Albert Museum of an 'unknown lady', which according to a label on the back, was 'painted by Pugh the 28th April 1803' (Plate 0.9). This last, oval and framed to be worn from a chain, was in a style already becoming out of date when it was painted. A month after it was made, the up-and-coming Scottish miniaturist Andrew Robertson wrote that 'oval miniatures are, at best, but toys'; 'in the exhibition this year, oval miniatures have disappeared, as they are not so much

worn. Most of them are square' – as was Pugh's 'Lady Morris', which on stylistic grounds as well as on account of its format looks to be later than the miniature in the V. & A.[21]

The disappearance of the many hundreds of miniatures Pugh must have made in his career is not especially surprising. Many of them no doubt survive without its being known who painted them; many have no doubt been reattributed to artists whose names command higher prices than Pugh's. The same is true of his landscape drawings. Of the originals of the 'six views', only one is currently known to survive; and though more than sixty of the original drawings for *Cambria Depicta* are preserved in a bound volume in the National Library of Wales, it is unlikely that Pugh himself took any steps to preserve them, or even saw them again after he had dispatched them to London to be aquatinted. In short, I doubt if Pugh put much value on watercolours which were destined to be engraved. He generally made them *en grisaille*, in shades of grey, in order to guide the engravers on the relative tonalities he hoped to see reproduced in the aquatints. If he had hoped to sell them as original works, he would have painted them in colour, but other than his miniatures, only one coloured watercolour drawing definitely by Pugh is known to survive. It is a charming portrait of an unbreeched little boy, playing with a pet dog in what may be a rocky Welsh landscape (Plate 0.10), but exactly where is uncertain. The distant hill has reminded a number of people I have consulted of Moel Famau, and the obelisk or tower upon it is reminiscent of the first design for the tower built to celebrate the Golden Jubilee of George III's accession in 1810. The picture however is dated 1800, several years before there was any thought

Plate 0.9 *(above) Edward Pugh, portrait of an unknown lady, watercolour on ivory, 1803, London, Victoria and Albert Museum.*

Plate 0.10 *(right) Edward Pugh, Portrait of a little boy with his pet dog, 1800, watercolour, signed and dated on the rock in the right foreground, collection of Ian Cooke.*

of building the tower; and as there was no other hill with a tower at that date, in any place that we know of where Pugh worked, the view, and with it the family the boy belongs to, is a mystery.[22] There is also a coloured watercolour landscape, apparently the original for one of the illustrations to *Cambria Depicta*, in a private collection, where it is attributed to a very much more expensive artist. I have no desire to make trouble for myself by identifying it here. My hope, however, is that the publication of this book will lead to the discovery of other works by Pugh, at present unrecorded.

III

Pugh's success in having his portraits accepted for the 1793 Academy exhibition changed his prospects entirely. It probably brought him more customers in London and enabled him to charge more there for his work, though there is no evidence that this was the case. What it certainly did was encourage him to embark upon what became a rather stuttering career as a landscape artist, and, as a miniaturist, to open a seasonal practice nearer home, in Chester, effectively the metropolis of north Wales and a meeting place in the decades around 1800 for the north Welsh gentry.

Advertisements for the *Six Views, in Denbighshire* appeared in the *Chester Chronicle* on 24 January 1794 and in the *Chester Courant* a few days later (Plate 0.11). The images were proposed to be published by subscription, and the aim of the advertisements was to attract subscribers. The views were 'to be engraved in aqua-tinta, by a very eminent artist, from drawings made on the spot, by E. Pugh'. The engraver Pugh hired was William Ellis, who had indeed engraved the work of some very eminent artists, including Richard Wilson, Paul Sandby, Thomas Hearne, Francis Wheatley, and John Webber, who like Samwell had accompanied Cook to the South Pacific. The aquatints were to be sold uncoloured for a guinea, or coloured for two guineas, and each set would come with a list of subscribers, provided 'gratis'.

The advertisement tried to make it very clear that this was a list from which no right-thinking member of the Denbighshire gentry could afford to be omitted. For the venture was already 'patronized by the Right Hon. Lord Bagot, the Right Hon. Lord Bulkeley, Lord William Beauclerk, Ld. Kenyon, the Right Rev. Lord Bishop of St. Asaph, Sir W.W. Wynne, Bart, and Sir R.W.Vaughan, Bart.' The identity of this last patron, whose name Pugh had perhaps misremembered, will be discussed in Chapter 4; for the moment, what matters is that this was a list of the most prominent Tories in north Wales. Vaughan's estates were in Merionethshire, and Bulkeley's property was chiefly in Anglesey, where Pugh probably met him, but the others all had large estates in Denbighshire, or, in the bishop's case, a large income from Church lands. There is no room on the list for Whigs: no Thomas Pennant of Downing, though he had many good Tory friends; no Richard Myddelton of Chirk Castle, or Edward Eyton of Eyton Hall, above all no Robert Watkin Wynne, of whom more later. Aware of how much Britain's entry into the war with France has polarised the politics even of northwest Wales, Pugh sets up his subscription to ensure its appeal to the more numerous, and more influential party. His patrons, he claims, 'are of exquisite taste and judgment in the art', but the subscription, he seems also to be suggesting, is an opportunity to enrol your name in the best political company in the county; with the promise that it would be *seen* there, on the promised list, alongside 'many of the nobility and gentry of the first distinction'. Whether Pugh's courtship of the Tory gentry reflected his own politics at the time, or was simply a sensible commercial decision, we cannot know.

Pugh promised to deliver the sets to his subscribers before August; but on account, he would explain, 'of the many engagements, his engraver, Mr. ELLIS, has in hand', the deadline was missed and the publication plans altered. In the event, on September 30 he announced through the *Courant*, and a few days later in the *Chronicle*, that the first two views — *Llanfwrog, Ruthin and Llanbedr* and *View of Pont-Newydd over the Ceirw, near Corwen* — were now ready. Both are dated July 1794, the originally intended date. When the remaining four appeared, they were dated 'November'. The promise to provide a printed subscription list was quietly forgotten, to the disappointment perhaps of some of the minor gentry and the polite middle-class inhabitants of the county.

Meanwhile Pugh was pursuing his plan to establish a portrait practice in Chester. Already in September 1794 he had inserted another advertisement in the two Chester newspapers, announcing that 'E. Pugh, Miniature Painter, from London', had been 'solicited to make a short stay in Chester', and was therefore taking 'the earliest moment of acquainting the ladies and gentlemen of this city and its environs that he means (previous to his return to town) to stop there for a few weeks, for the purposes of painting likenesses in miniatures'.[23] These advertisements were followed up ten days later by two more. Now styling himself 'Mr. Pugh, Professor of Miniature Painting, and Exhibitor in the Royal Academy, London', he

most respectfully informs the Ladies and Gentlemen of Chester, and its vicinity, that he has engaged very suitable apartments at Mrs. Mousdale's, Bridge-street-row, near the Feathers; where he paints MINIATURES, from three to six guineas each; also BLACK PROFILES, not in the common manner but in a style properly his own, wherein the features are faithfully described, and a perfect semblance obtained in ten minutes.[24]

Pugh was not the only portraitist to advertise his services in the Chester press that year. In October J. Bunn in Princess Street, who was well established in Chester, was offering 'correct likenesses, painted in miniature', and earlier, in May, a Mr Prichard in Lower Bridge Street had guaranteed to produce 'striking likenesses' and 'perfect resemblances' of 'Ladies and Gentlemen', not miniatures but portraits in oils from small up to full-size.[25] Pugh's status however as an Academy-approved artist 'from London' meant that his rates, compared with those charged by Bunn (1 guinea) and Prichard (1–2 guineas, according to size), were reassuringly expensive. In May a paragraph in the *Chronicle*, apparently a news item but almost certainly inserted at Prichard's expense, announced that those who had seen his portraits were speaking of them 'in terms of the warmest admiration. The likenesses are allowed by all to be singularly STRIKING.' A few months later Pugh replied with a laconic paragraph in the *Chronicle*, no doubt also paid for. It read simply: 'Mr. Pugh's miniatures are spoken of, by connoisseurs, as the *ne plus ultra* in the art.'[26] Bunn and Prichard did not advertise again, or presumably practise, in Chester.

In London Pugh was a minnow in a lake; in Chester he would become a pike in a small pond. The following year, 1795, a man called Clarke — no initial, no 'Mr'[27] — offered his services to the 'ladies and gentlemen of Chester and its vicinity', inserting an advertisement of inordinate length in the *Courant*. He was not competing with Pugh in the miniature painting line, only in silhouettes; he made, in sittings of only 'FIVE MINUTES', black profiles to place in 'bracelets, lockets, rings, watch papers', or to frame and display. Like Prichard, he came to Chester one year and never again; he too may have made the mistake of competing on price, offering 'likenesses of a whole family' at the price 'generally given for one'.[28] In this year Pugh did not work in Chester,

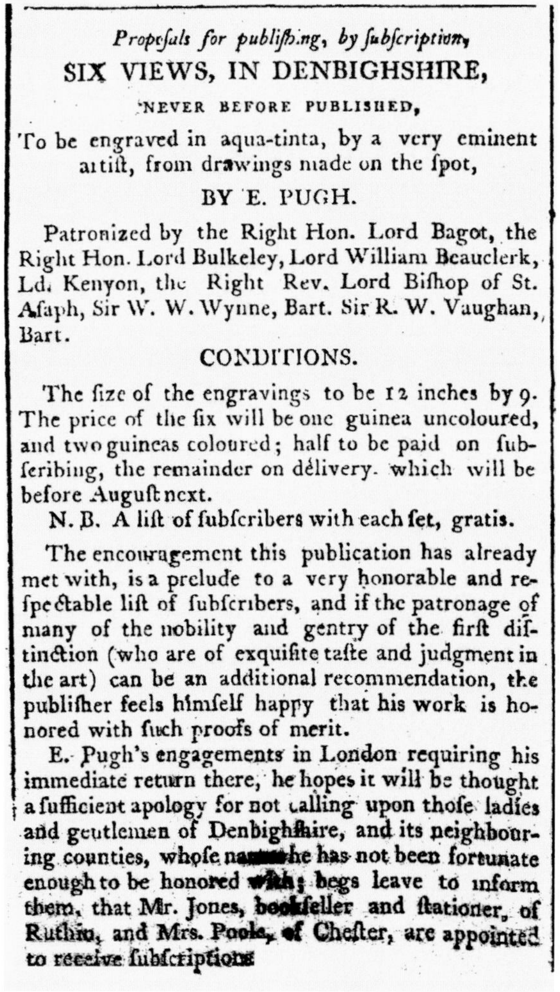

Plate 0.11 *Advertisement for the* Six Views, in Denbighshire, Chester Courant, *4 February 1794.*

instead spending his few weeks away from London in Ruthin. But he was still available to prospective clients; he still advertised his services in the Chester press, and was still charging six guineas for his best work, and making it clear that he was hugely in demand, both in London and Chester:

Many ladies and gentlemen having called at Mr. Pugh's lodgings last year (when he had quitted Chester for London) for the purpose of sitting to him for their portraits, he very respectfully informs them, wherever residing, that he will be happy to wait upon them, and shall pay due attention to any letters addressed to him at Ruthin, Denbighshire … His stay in the country will be three or four weeks, when an extended practice will call him to London.[29]

In 1796, it was the turn of a Mr. MacGavin to try to capture Pugh's Chester market. MacGavin may be been the competitor most likely to succeed: he felt able to charge prices similar to Pugh's, from one to five guineas according to size, because, like Pugh, he could advertise himself as 'of the Royal Academy, London'.[30] Indeed, since 1793 he had had more than twice as many miniatures accepted in the annual exhibition as Pugh, and had exhibited for four years running.[31] Pugh however had the advantage of prior possession, and of being a local man, or nearly so;

and probably the advantage too of an amiable and charming personality, as we shall see. MacGavin went the way of Prichard, Bunn and Clarke, and thereafter Pugh had only one competitor to deal with, a 'London Artist' who volunteered no name in his advertisements, and whose 'moderate prices' did not rise above two guineas for a miniature, even on ivory.[32] He too came to Chester once, in 1797, and did not try his luck there again.

In 1795 and 1796, Pugh issued four small line engravings of Welsh views, two landscapes in or near Ruthin, which we shall examine later, and two of Conway, one of them the Upper Gate, taken from the same viewpoint as Paul Sandby had used, the other the Conway ferry. These are puzzling prints. They are numbered Plates I to IV, as if intended for book-illustrations, but I have found no book in which they appear. They are published jointly by Pugh and W. Poole, who was probably connected with the Chester printing and publishing firm of that name which Pugh had already employed to receive subscriptions to the *Six Views*. Though the place of publication was given as London, the prints were probably produced to be sold in Chester, perhaps with Pugh's portrait-customers chiefly in mind. Poole was certainly not skilled enough to survive as an engraver in London, nor would these prints have been likely to find a market far from the views they recorded.

Pugh meanwhile, from 1796 onward, raised his game by ceasing to advertise like a mere tradesman in the classified columns of the Chester newspapers, instead paying (presumably) to insert paragraphs into the news sections, as if his comings and goings were a matter of general interest. He was still keen to give the impression of being overburdened by the demands of his clients. 'We hear', began the paragraph for 1796, as if written by the *Chronicle*'s sharp-eared news-gathering team, 'that Mr. Pugh is now in the Vale of Clwyd, for the recovery of his health, which was much injured by an extensive practice in Town. He means, we understand, before he goes to Dublin, to make a short stay in this city, to paint in oil and miniatures.'[33] It seems as though Pugh wishes it to be understood that he has also a short annual practice in Dublin, and though I have not succeeded in tracing him there it seems likely that he visited Ireland on several occasions. In *Cambria Depicta* he refers to having made frequent visits to Anglesey; and it emerges that by the 1800s he was on friendly terms with several gentry families on the island, including Jared Jackson of Holyhead, whose portrait he exhibited at the Academy in 1799.[33] He may have met his friend Richard Llwyd either there – he was a native of Beaumaris – or on the road to Anglesey, at Caerhun, near Conwy, where Llwyd was employed as steward and secretary.

Pugh went again to Chester in 1798 and 1800. 'We hear', announced the *Chronicle*, that he is on 'his annual visit'; 'we perceive', it reported two years later, 'that Mr. Pugh, whose Miniatures have given such universal satisfaction, has arrived in this city.'[35] He had now changed the season of his visit to April to coincide with the races and the assizes when the city was crowded with local gentry. 'During the race week,' he would write in *Cambria Depicta*,

> Chester is the centre of fashion and gaiety. The races commence the first Monday in May, and are attended by the first people in the country, when the theatre royal is open for a week.
>
> The higher ranks of the society, though in general not very opulent, are accomplished; the ladies are handsome, open, and unreserved in their conversation; the gentlemen free and communicative, and generally disposed to be friendly to the arts.[36]

In both years the supposed news items he inserted in the *Chronicle* and *Courant* are more or less identical, making it obvious that they are insertions paid for by Pugh himself. Perhaps he had already painted all of the richest gentry families in the region, for he had now reduced his top price to 5 guineas.[37] We do not know whether he visited Ruthin and Chester in 1797 and 1799, but otherwise his life from 1794 to 1800 had developed a regular routine. For some period every year he would leave London, travelling no doubt to see his mother in Ruthin, spending a period of a week or more in Chester or travelling in north-east Wales to visit clients in their country houses, and perhaps paying a visit via Anglesey to Dublin. Each time he left London he would give up his lodgings there, which suggests that his absences were lengthy, and take new lodgings on his return; a pattern facilitated by the fact that, as he tells us in *Cambria Depicta*, he was unmarried.[38] In 1793, as we have seen, he was living in the Strand; at the start of the following year he moved a hundred yards or so to 13 Bedford Street, south of Covent Garden, and by November was on the other side of the garden at Great Queen Street. From there Pugh moved to the edge of the West End, at 14 Cockspur Street, where we lose track of him until, in 1799, he is back in the Covent Garden area, at 28 Maiden Lane.

These addresses are not for the most part very respectable, and they suggest that Pugh visited his clients rather than their visiting him. Archibald Robertson, writing to his younger brother Andrew, who in 1799 was setting himself up as a miniature painter in London, advised him: 'you have no occasion to live in an expensive furnished lodging – but in a private and economical way – and if you have likenesses to take, you can take sittings in their own houses.'[39] It was an advantage to miniature painters that they did not need to live at addresses and in apartments suitable for the reception of genteel customers, and Pugh clearly felt exactly as Archibald Robertson did on this. Possibly the move to Cockspur Street, on the way between fashionable St James's and the luxury shops of the Strand, was an attempt to catch passing trade, but more likely Pugh's rooms were at the back of the house,

accessible by the narrow yard which is marked on Richard Horwood's large-scale map of London, and which his clients would have been loath to enter. In Chester, by contrast, Pugh's lodgings in Bridge Street Row and Watergate Street were advertised as 'very commodious' and 'very suitable' for the reception of the gentry. The first was attached to Mrs Mousdale's Circulating Library, a perfect place to attract polite inhabitants and visitors; the second at Richard Taylor's music shop, where Taylor probably also sold Pugh's prints and drawings.[40]

Two phantom sightings of Pugh in the historical record date from about this time. The amateur artist and wealthy partner in a house-painting business Henry Wigstead published his *Remarks on a Tour to North and South Wales in the year 1797, with Plates by Rowlandson, Pugh, Howitt &c*, in 1799 or 1800 (the book bears both dates), an account of a trip made in 1797.[41] It has generally been assumed, perhaps partly in the belief that Wigstead and the very metropolitan chums with whom he made this tour would need a guide as well as an auxiliary artist on their trip round Wales, that the 'Pugh' who made up one of this party was Edward, even though none of the illustrations bears his name or looks to be by him. More plausibly, Matthew and James Payne have suggested that the 'Pugh' in question was the well-known scene-painter Charles Pugh, whom they describe as a friend of Wigstead's.[42]

On 10 and 11 May 1799 Christie's held a sale of works by Gainsborough, following the death of his widow. Joseph Farington, landscape painter, pupil of Richard Wilson, royal academician and voluminous diarist, attended both days, and on the second day was probably hopeful of buying one of the sketchbooks on sale. But, he reports, 'they went for prices beyond my expectation – The eight books sold for 140-3-6. – Mr. Hibbert bought two, and He & Sir George Beaumont bought one to divide. – Mr. Payne Knight bought one. Mr. Pugh bought one.' A few days later Farington writes, 'Pugh & Barrow I called on to look at sketches by Gainsborough.'[43] In fact there were ten sketchbooks sold, and according to John Hayes, in his catalogue of Gainsborough's drawings, 'Mr. Pugh' bought three of them. The editors of Farington's diary have no suggestion to make about the identity of this Pugh, of whom Hayes says only that he was 'probably one of the artists of that name active in this period'.[44] It is certainly possible that this was Edward, just as it is possible that he was then living with the artist Joseph Charles Barrow: the two had in common at least the habit of taking lodgings around Covent Garden, and both were acquainted with the former engraver, publisher of Wilson's six views, and sometime Lord Mayor, John Boydell. But it is not easy to imagine Farington, self-consciously a gentleman, referring to Pugh as 'Mr. Pugh', nor to believe that at this period of his life Pugh had managed to accumulate sufficient savings to bid successfully, and for no less than three sketchbooks, against a room containing such amateurs of landscape painting as Sir George Beaumont, the rich landowner, connoisseur and amateur artist, and Richard Payne Knight, the probably even richer writer and collector. Perhaps 'Mr. Pugh' is Charles J. Pugh, who at this time was exhibiting landscapes, mostly of Welsh scenes, every year at the Academy from the same address, 7, The Terrace, Tottenham Court Road, and so perhaps lived a more settled and more affluent life than Pugh could enjoy.[45]

Pugh's last advertisements or paid-for news paragraphs appeared in the Chester newspapers in April 1800; and thereafter we have no reason to assume he practised there, though he seems to have visited the city again on the tour or tours that he wrote up as *Cambria Depicta*. Perhaps it no longer made economic sense to work there when his London practice may well have been taking off as never before. Between 1793 and 1799 he had seven miniatures accepted for the Academy exhibitions; between 1800 and 1807 he exhibited a further sixteen portraits at the Academy. To put these figures in perspective, however, Andrew Robertson, a phenomenally successful miniaturist and assiduous networker, between 1802, the year of his first exhibiting at the Academy, and 1807, when Pugh's last miniature was shown there, had no less than thirty-five portraits accepted to Pugh's ten, including those of Benjamin West (then President of the Academy), a bishop, a marquis, another 'Lord', an 'Hon.', two city aldermen (one of them knighted), various high-ranking militia officers, and His Royal Highness the Duke of Sussex (twice); by 1805 he had become Miniature Painter to the Duke, and in 1807 was painting the king's daughters at Windsor.[46] Robertson was fourteen years younger than Pugh. If that is what success looked like, Pugh had won second prize at best.

And in 1803 he did indeed win a second prize, £30, for the design of a vase in a competition organized by the Patriotic Fund, formed that year 'for the RELIEF and REWARD of the DEFENDERS of their COUNTRY, who may suffer, or by their Exertions merit, in the Public Service'.[47] In the following year the design was exhibited at the Academy. The tenor of the competition may be gauged from the account of the winning design, which featured Britannia on one side, and on the other a warrior fighting the Hydra, no doubt representing Napoleonic France, with which, after the

brief interlude of the peace of Amiens, Britain was once more at war.[48] As we shall see in Chapter 2, there is some possibility that at the start of the war with the French Republic Pugh had opposed it, but by this time he was a firm supporter of the war against Napoleon. On 22 August 1803, though he would later declare that his nature was 'unsuited to deeds of blood',[49] he signed up to be a member of an 'Armed Association of Artists' or 'A Corps of Artists … to offer its services to Government, under the Volunteer Act', organized by Robertson at the British School of Arts. Over 100 painters sculptors, architects and engravers signed up to join, and Pugh was one of forty-four who put his name to a declaration that, at a time when Britain was 'threatened by a most vindictive enemy', they were animated by a 'glow of patriotism' to form 'an armed association for the defence of our native land, of the liberty, independence, and even existence of that country, which has long been the Asylum of Literature, and the Fine Arts'. Three days later, however, Robertson reports that the 'Government has declined our offer as Volunteers, there being already too many . . . after we had lost so much time, and had 150 names, it is a great disappointment.'[50] Pugh's glow however was not entirely extinguished by the government's refusal, and the following year he exhibited at the Academy portraits of two unnamed volunteers, 'an Officer of the Yagers of the Hon. Artillery Company' and 'a Gentleman in the St. James's Corps of Volunteers'.

Very probably the greater frequency with which Pugh's works were now to be seen at the annual exhibition reflected an increasingly successful practice. His sitters, or those we know of, were not, like Robertson's, from the top drawer: they included the actor, and former manager

of the Theatre Royal, Chester, Joseph Austin, a Mr Munden, probably the famous actor Joseph Munden, one of the most frequently painted men of the age, and a number of other named sitters, men and women whom I have not been able to identify. But there are also several images of unknown, unnamed sitters which are exhibited as 'characteristic' portraits, portraits of children and adolescents represented as individuals but also as types: 'Portrait of a poor Orphan Boy'; 'Portrait of a Cadet'; 'Portrait of a Young Artist', probably William the son of Pugh's friend Hugh Jones of Beaumaris, who studied art in London and whom Pugh had helped there.[51] These may suggest that in his work as a portraitist Pugh was ambitious to be more than a mere miniaturist, a maker of likenesses for the middle classes; to be something more like a 'subject' painter or a 'genre' painter, of interest not simply for the sake of whom he painted, but by virtue of the quality of his observation. The same ambition may have made it particularly congenial to him to accept the commission from Richard Phillips to produce twenty views of 'modern London', many of them images of open spaces filled with bustling groups, busily moving through the metropolis or, equally busily, relaxing. This commission is the subject of chapter 7.

Though he was no longer apparently working in Chester, the pattern of giving up his London lodgings at the end of the season, visiting Wales and returning to find new lodgings in the autumn still continued. We left him in 1799 in Maiden Lane. The following year the Academy catalogue gives his address as Chester, and perhaps he stayed there and in Wales for a year. We next pick him up in London in 1801, 'at Mr. Fuller's, Charing Cross'; and the next year finds him in Charles Street, Westminster, a fashionable address a few streets south of Downing Street. This may well be an attempt to move upmarket, following his *annus mirabilis* when no fewer than five of his portraits had been accepted for the Academy exhibition, but, if so, it was probably a failure, for in 1803 he moved to the respectable but hardly fashionable New North Street, off Red Lion Square, High Holborn. He seems to have stayed here for two years, tied up no doubt with working on Phillips's illustrations, and he may even have missed his usual summer visit to Ruthin. In the summer of 1804, however, he may have begun the series of walks through north Wales that he would eventually illustrate and write up in *Cambria Depicta*. Back in London in autumn, he returns to New North Street, but to different lodgings a few doors from his previous lodging-house. Then, the following year, he moves to his most downmarket address so far, number 22 in the narrow, gloomy Bell Yard off Carey Street, south of Lincoln's Inn Fields. In 1807 the Academy catalogue gives his address as 22 Carey Place, which is probably the same building; he probably thought that 'Place' would sound better than 'Yard' to prospective customers.

This apparent decline may mean that Pugh found it hard to make a living in the years after the publication of *Modern London*: he had only one portrait a year in each of the exhibitions of 1805, 1806 and 1807. Or perhaps he was now happy to rent the cheaper lodgings because he had decided to retire and was saving as hard as he could. Either way, by 1808 he seems to have accumulated enough capital to leave London, perhaps to buy

a small annuity for himself and his mother, and to live with her in Ruthin. Already by the 1790s his native town had become a relatively bustling place, with a growing middle class to whom he might have hoped to sell his *Six Views* as well as his services as a portraitist. There were five clergymen, three surgeon-apothecaries, six attorneys, a schoolmaster, not to mention the numerous gentry in the Vale of Clwyd and the members of professions in other nearby towns: Llangollen, Corwen, Denbigh. There were two booksellers in Ruthin through whom he may have hoped to sell his prints.[52] His retirement was not especially comfortable, however: one of the factors that seems to have persuaded him to it was the fact that, as he calculated, the cost of living in Wales was 'two-fifths less than in London'.[53] In Ruthin he probably lived with his mother, probably in Well Street, which leads from the east uphill to St Peter's Square in the centre of town.[54] He would have preferred, he suggests in *Cambria Depicta*, to have retired to a respectable house in 'some Elysian vale', but in a 'state of poverty' as he was, 'it would have been the vainest arrogance to indulge' such a wish.[55]

One of the puzzles of Pugh's London years, which does as much as anything to bury him in obscurity, is his relationship with the London Welsh. As we have seen, he was a friend or acquaintance of David Samwell, and Samwell's letter suggests too that he knew Iolo Morganwg. He certainly knew William Owen, later William Owen Pughe, the lexicographer, grammarian, editor, antiquary and poet: one of the three letters by Pugh that I know

of shows him trying to arrange a sitting for Owen apparently in 1802 or 1803, and offering to shuffle his many engagements to accommodate him as soon as possible.[56] Through Owen he probably knew David Pugh, the antiquary, who wrote under the name David Hughson and probably compiled the long history of the metropolis included in *Modern London*.[57] It may have been through the good offices of one or both of these that he was introduced to Phillips; it was Samwell, as we have seen, who gave Pugh the commission for the portrait of Twm o'r Nant; and, as we shall see, it was another London Welshman, Boydell, who offered Pugh the publishing opportunity that eventually became *Cambria Depicta*. These connections might lead us to expect to find Pugh socializing busily with the London Welsh and joining one of the Welsh cultural societies and sociable charity organizations, the Cymmrodorion, for example, or the Gwyneddigion Society, or the Caradogion, or the Society of Ancient Britons, that were flourishing around 1800, and which left copious printed records to posterity – but his name never appears in them. Pugh was apparently a very amiable and sociable man, and no doubt had many friends, but the only close friend of his that we know of is the poet Richard Llwyd. Llwyd had moved to Chester in 1807, and no doubt he and Pugh saw a good deal of each other from then on. A letter of 1809 from Pugh to Thomas Lloyd of Tre'r Beirdd, near Mold (whom we shall come across again in a later chapter) is apparently written from Chester where Pugh was staying with Llwyd.[58]

V

'I'm sick of Portraits,' Gainsborough famously wrote to his friend William Jackson, 'and wish very much to take my Viol da Gam and walk off to some sweet Village where I can paint Landskips and enjoy the fag End of Life in quietness and ease.'[59] Released from what he had probably come to regard, as Gainsborough had, as the drudgery of face-painting, Pugh too saw retirement as an opportunity to focus on the art of landscape, though it is unlikely that he could afford entirely to refuse to paint portraits if asked to do so. In 1808 he exhibited for the last time at the Academy, but this time a landscape, *The Vale of Clwyd*, now of course lost or reattributed to a more marketable artist. In fact the catalogue gives his address as 21 Cecil Street, Strand, but this was an accommodation address that Pugh used in his later years in Ruthin, the house of his fellow-miniaturist Walter Henry Watts, whom in a letter Pugh described as his 'old friend'.[60] Robertson too had lived there for a year in 1801–2, at the start of his campaign to become rich and famous in London.[61] In the same year what looks to have been a small rural genre painting, *Gayton Wake*, illustrating a poem by Llwyd, was selected for exhibition at the British Institution. Colonel Maurice Grant suggests that Pugh had only just started painting landscapes in oils by this time, and though he does not give his source for this information, he is very probably right. Grant claimed to have seen several landscapes by Pugh in oil and watercolour, but where they were, and how secure the attributions, we do not know. He reproduces one, under the title *Welsh Landscape*, dated to 1811, and remarks that

Pugh's works in oil, judging by the few specimens we have seen, were actually superior to his aquarelles. They are quite rich and satisfactory little pieces, smartly and decisively touched, brightly tinted, and with considerable atmosphere. The figures are excellent, done in the neat manner of Paul Sandby, the sky bright and clever, the foreground most delicate and careful; whereas in his watercolours, neither colour nor care were distinguishing marks of Pugh's *pratique*.[62]

The photograph (Plate 3.1) is not clear enough to permit a comparison of Pugh's figures with Sandby's; but it is easy to see, in subject, composition and lighting, a considerable debt to Gainsborough's late paintings of families in woodland settings.

At one point in *Cambria Depicta*, Pugh writes of his various 'perambulations in different parts of Britain', but apart from a brief reference in that book to a trip he made to either Oxford or Cambridge, where he nearly fell victim to a student riot,[63] we know nothing of any of his travels except from London to Chester or Shrewsbury, around north Wales and possibly to Ireland. In the first year or two of his retirement, however, Pugh paid a visit to Newport in Monmouthshire, apparently in fulfilment of a commission from John Hodgkinson, an engineer in London. The trip resulted in two large and ambitious aquatints, published in London by T. Clay of Ludgate Hill and engraved by Thomas Cartwright, who would become the principal engraver of the plates for *Cambria Depicta*. The subjects are strikingly different: one predominantly an image of a proudly modern, the other of

ancient Wales, though that contrast is visible also within each image taken singly. They were apparently designed to be released as a pair, but in the event were published three years apart.

The first, which appeared in 1810, was a view of one of two new wonders of Wales, the 'Long Bridge' as it came to be known, stone-built, fifty feet high, thirty-three arches long, which carried the Sirhowy tram road across the valley of the river Ebbw at Risca, north-west of Newport (Plate 0.12). The bridge had been finished in 1805 and was demolished a century later. As the legend on the print explains, it linked the town and harbour at Newport with 'the extensive Iron works of Tredegar and Sirhowy, and the Intermediate Collieries: a distance of 24 miles'. Included in the view are the 'Works and Buildings of the Union Copper Company adjoining the Bridge'. These were built in 1807 and closed nine years later, and while they were open the company issued a copper token, depicting the smoking furnaces of the works, which was based on Pugh's aquatint (Plate 0.13). In the print three horses pull a line of carts full of ore or coal towards Newport, and a single-horse tram conveys passengers in the other direction, in what Dr Michael Lewis has suggested to me may be the first image of a railway-carriage ever made. The print is 'Dedicated to the Monmouthshire Canal and the Sirhowy Tram Road Companies. By their obliged and obed[t]. Humble Serv[t]. John Hodgkinson, Engineer London.'

The aquatint is in what we will recognize in the course of this book as Pugh's rather simplified, emblematic style of landscape, the trees based on a simple uniform pattern, the smoke similarly stylized, the buildings carefully ruled. What seems to have interested Pugh most in this subject is the sense of

how the bridge and works have suddenly appeared in this beautiful pastoral and woodland landscape. In the corner of a stony, unimproved foreground, two locals are inspecting these novelties at a distance, the young woman, smartly dressed, apparently explaining the benefits of improvement to an older man, probably her father, wearing appropriately Welsh costume. The bridge is rendered with an attention to detail which invites us to admire it as the harbinger of a new Wales, but there is an acknowledgement too of what is lost in the process of development without anything in the picture inviting us to adjudicate between them.

The aquatint was published as one of a pair with an even larger aquatint by Francis Jukes after J. Parry of another new wonder of Wales, also completed in 1805, the Pontcysyllte aqueduct by William Jessop and Thomas Telford, near Llangollen. The two prints were advertised together in the *Caledonian Mercury* on 7 January 1811 and in the *Chester Chronicle* four days later.[64] Despite the congruence of subjects, they are not truly 'companions', as the advertisements were claiming. Though they tried to conceal the fact, the Parry image was considerably larger than the Pugh; and the Pugh was available only coloured (at 26s.), whereas the Parry could be had either coloured or plain. Altogether it looks as if, removed as he was from London, Pugh could exert little control over how his drawings were treated by his publishers. We may suspect the same when, in Chapter 8, we turn to examine the plates for *Cambria Depicta*.

Of all Pugh's images, the other aquatint that originated from this trip to Monmouthshire, a view of the castle at Newport from across the Usk (Plate 0.14), is the closest in manner to his hero Richard Wilson, though perhaps not, as we shall

Plate 0.12 *(opposite) T. Cartwright after Edward Pugh, View of a Stone Bridge across the Valley and River at Risca in Monmouthshire, coloured aquatint (London: J. Hodgkinson and T. Clay, 1813), Aberystwyth, National Library of Wales.*

Plate 0.13 *(below) Risca Union Copper Company token, based on Pugh's* View of a Stone Bridge*, copper, 1811, private collection.*

see in Chapter 1, his most heartfelt act of homage. This is the true 'companion' of the image of the bridge at Risca, in terms of both size and subject, but it was not published until a few months after Pugh's death in 1813. The composition consciously recalls Wilson's painting of Caernarvon Castle (Plate 0.15),[65] except that in his subject, Pugh characteristically juxtaposes the antique and the modern, the picturesque decaying castle against the brand-new town bridge, designed by David Edwards, son of the architect of the bridge at Pontypridd, which replaced the rickety-looking wooden one that Sandby and Turner had depicted.[66] With this bridge or its later replacement, this aspect of Newport, from Pugh's viewpoint, has since featured in countless postcards of the town,

though with the angle shifted slightly to the left in order to lose the railway bridge that all but shears off what remains of the castle's northernmost tower. In an act of urban vandalism which has to be seen to be believed, the castle, long encroached upon by that railway bridge, is now crushed between the river and a partly elevated urban highway, on the concrete parapet of which Street View shows planters full of petunias attempting, in a ridiculous act of municipal contrition, to restore some amenity to what is now a wasteland.[67] If originally Pugh's view of the castle was intended to contrast the old Wales and the new, the place by itself now expresses perfectly the contempt of the present for the past.

Plate 0.14 *(opposite) T. Cartwright after Edward Pugh,* Newport in Monmouthshire, *coloured aquatint (London: T. Clay, 1813), Aberystwyth, National Library of Wales.*

Plate 0.15 *(below) Richard Wilson,* Caernarvon Castle, *oil on canvas, ca. 1762, Cardiff, National Museum and Gallery.*

VI

Apart from the two oil paintings Pugh exhibited in 1808, the two Monmouthshire aquatints and a book-illustration we shall glance at in Chapter 8, we know of no work definitely by Pugh, and produced in his retirement, other than *Cambria Depicta*. As I shall suggest later, though Pugh represents that book as the record of a single walking tour through north Wales, conducted in a single summer, it was more probably based on two or three journeys made between 1804 and 1806; so that the task of his retirement was to write up the walks, and to work up the sketches, that he had already made. His work on *Modern London* had apparently stimulated his desire to make a book all on his own, both text and illustrations.

Cambria Depicta is a wonderful book, but though it addresses us in a less formal, more personal tone than was often adopted by the authors of tours written for publication, it adds surprisingly little to our exiguous knowledge of Pugh's life. As we shall see in the chapters devoted to the book, we do however learn a good deal about his tastes and attitudes as we accompany him through 463 quarto pages, over 150,000 words, on a walking tour of some 700 miles. Wherever he goes, he seems always to be hankering to return to his home landscapes, at the southern end of the Vale of Clwyd. We learn of his anxiety to see the economy of north Wales developed; of his patriotism during the war against Napoleon; of his affection and respect for the Welsh peasantry; and of his love of poetry. At Holywell, on the Dee estuary, we learn of his horror at the 'disgraceful commerce' of the recently-abolished trade in African slaves, who, 'if but allowed to improve . . . might shine

as much in arts and sciences, as the most civilized people on earth'.[68] We learn that he was as hostile to Catholicism as a good member of the established Church was required to be, and that his own version of Protestantism, not unlike Wordsworth's, was a kind of natural religion, the landscapes he drew and described inspiring in him 'the strongest feelings of awe and admiration of the Author of all nature'; a 'reverential fear for the Author' of nature.[69] The book began life as a projected guide to north Wales, for the benefit of non-Welsh-speaking artists wary of wandering far from the high roads and tourist inns. It remained that, in part, but developed also into a vindication of the people of the region, whose character, Pugh believed, had been traduced by the legion of English travellers who had trooped into Snowdonia in search of the sublime.

The most personal document we have by Pugh is a long, three-page letter to Richard Llwyd, written in June 1811. It is the only relic of Pugh that allows us to get behind the meagre facts of his life in the public domain and to learn something about him as a private man. I do not mean that it divulges anything he might not have wanted to let out, anything about his interior life – we are no less shut out from that by this letter than by the catalogue entries and newspaper advertisements that otherwise make up his 'life'. What we learn from the letter is how he chose to represent himself to probably his closest friend, and that he put on much the same jovially masculine persona as other men did at the time when writing to their male friends. But he was also able to use the letter to ruminate on what price he should ask his publisher for the manuscript of

Cambria Depicta, and how much of his fee could be paid in ready money – half thinking aloud, half asking Llwyd's advice; to express frankly his satisfaction at what he had achieved in the book; to invite Llwyd to look through the MS in the clear expectation that he would agree, and would put his 'skilful fist' to the correction of any faults; to regret the assassination of the Prime Minister Spencer Perceval a month before, and to recount an anecdote connected with it; to pass on to Llwyd his mother's 'very best regards and good wishes'; and to give a circumstantial account of his health and the state of his bowels of a kind he would have given only to an intimate friend. 'My health', he writes, 'is but soso, having lately taken the advise of some, who never followed the profession of medicine, and taken Bark, which certainly had a happy effect for three days, but afterwards it locked me up for near three weeks. I am, however, recovering this slowly' (Plate 0.16).[70]

Bark was tried as a specific for so many ailments at this time that it is not clear how ill Pugh was or with what. But thirteen months later, on 17 July 1813, at the age of 50, he died in Ruthin of 'a paralytick stroke', according to the *Chester Chronicle*, and three days later at St Peter's the burial was registered of Edward Pugh, 'limner', of Well Street. In a brief but warm obituary notice, the *Chronicle* attested that he had been an 'honest and worthy man, and an ingenious artist, as the splendid work "Cambria Depicta", lately advertised in this and other papers, will amply prove. It is now the property of his venerable and affectionate mother, to whom Mr. Pugh was a most dutiful son.'[71] 'He was an amiable man,' wrote Richard Phillips in the *Monthly Magazine*, 'but lived in bad times, when the sword, directed by folly, devours the patrimony of the arts, and of all honest industry.'[72]

Some time after his death, and after the publication of *Cambria Depicta*, the *Six Views* were reissued, it is not clear by whom, or who was set to benefit from their republication. The second issue can be distinguished from the first only by their paper: the later printing is on smoother, Whatman paper, watermarked and dated. It is difficult to distinguish the issues otherwise: few enough copies seem to have been taken from the copper plates in 1794 for the later issue still to be clear and crisp, and (though not all the examples printed in 1794 were coloured) it is difficult too to distinguish the issues by colour. In some examples of course the colouring appears palpably later than the date of issue, but among the remaining prints it is more or less similar from one to another and from the first to the second issue, except for the clothing, where the colourists seem to have had a free hand. Also, there are examples of plates from each issue where the colour is lightly and partially applied, as if to highlight particular motifs, and after some hesitation I have become persuaded that such colouring is probably original, as if customers were being offered the options of no colour or of full or partial colouring.

There is at least one other publication that did not appear until after Pugh's death but in which he may have been involved. In the bound volume of his original illustrations for *Cambria Depicta* is a drawing – *en grisaille* like the rest – of fairies. It is the original of one of the nine coloured aquatints in Peter Roberts's book *The Cambrian Popular Antiquities* (1815), published, like *Cambria Depicta*, by Evan Williams (Plate 0.17).[73] The picture shows a pretty maidservant lying asleep, dreaming of fairies who are telling her when, so the accompanying poem explains, her lover will return. The plates all bear the name of

John Havell, who was responsible for many of the aquatints in *Cambria Depicta*, but the artist or artists who supplied the original drawings are not named. At least four of the illustrations are most unlikely to be by Pugh: they adopt a style of drawing which verges on the grotesque: heavy-jowelled, asymmetrical faces, unlike anything in his work. Of the rest, none seems obviously based on original work by him, and on their evidence alone we would probably not have suspected that he was a contributor to the book.

But he may well have been. That 'The Fairies' is bound into the NLW volume is not in itself proof of Pugh's involvement with Roberts's project, as we have no idea why the volume was made or for whom; the drawing may well have come to be associated with the *Cambria Depicta* illustrations simply because both books were going through the same printer's shop and the same publishing house at the same time, and John Havell was involved with both. But in Roberts's book the poem illustrated by 'The Fairies' is by Richard Llwyd, which certainly increases the likelihood that the original was by Pugh. It may not amount to much that it does not look like anything else he did. There are several images that could be Pughs, but their subjects, mainly popular rituals and celebrations, are new to him, genre-scenes which required much more concentration on the figures than even the views

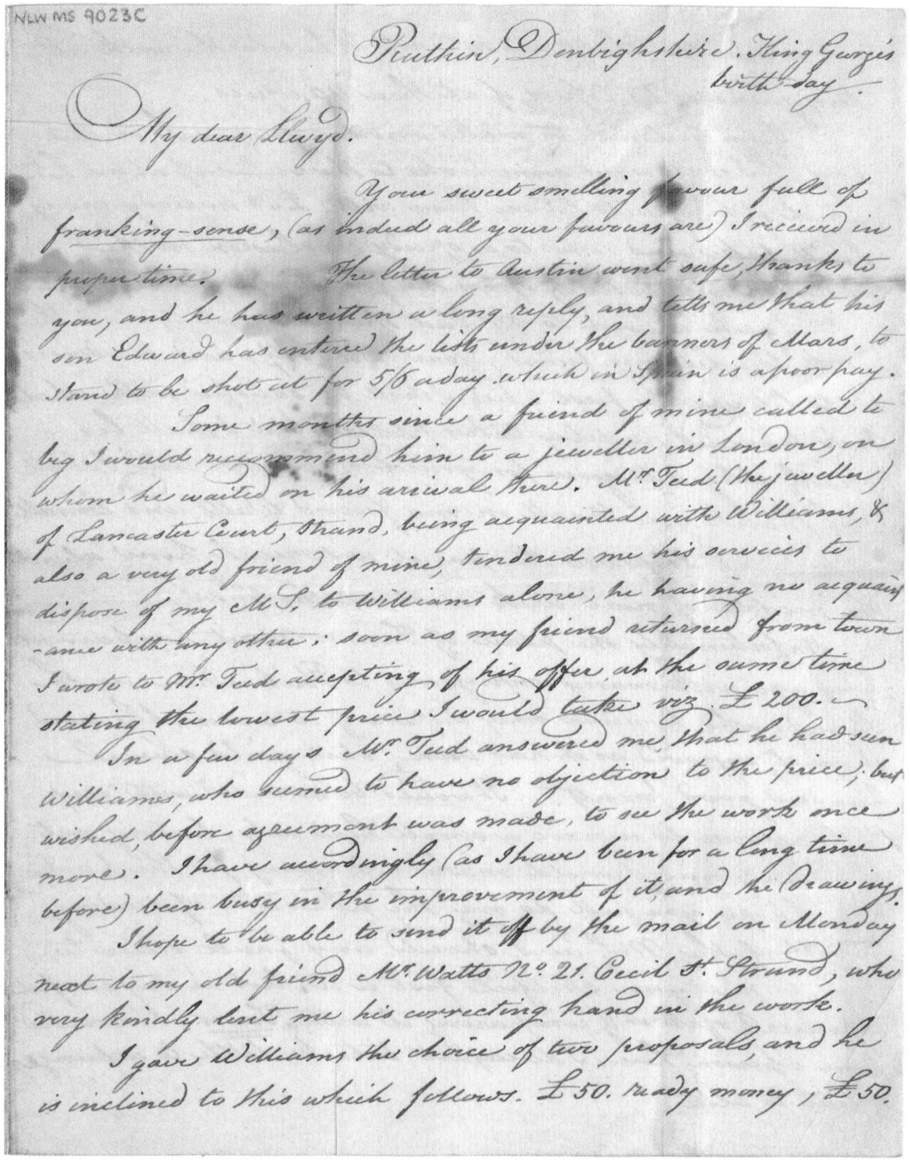

Ruthin, Denbighshire. King George's birth day.

My dear Llwyd.

Your sweet smelling favour full of franking-sense, (as indeed all your favours are) I received in proper time. The letter to Austin went safe, thanks to you, and he has written a long reply, and tells me that his son Edward has entered the lists under the banners of Mars, to stand to be shot at for 5/6 a day. which in Spain is a poor pay.

Some months since a friend of mine called to beg I would recommend him to a jeweller in London, on whom he waited on his arrival there. Mr. Teed (the jeweller) of Lancaster Court, Strand, being acquainted with Williams, & also a very old friend of mine, tendered me his services to dispose of my MS. to Williams alone, he having no acquaint-ance with any other; soon as my friend returned from town I wrote to Mr. Teed accepting of his offer at the same time stating the lowest price I would take viz £200. —

In a few days Mr. Teed answered me, that he had seen Williams, who seemed to have no objection to the price; but wished, before agreement was made, to see the work once more. I have accordingly (as I have been for a long time before) been busy in the improvement of it, and the drawings.

I hope to be able to send it off by the mail on Monday next to my old friend Mr. Watts No. 21. Cecil St. Strand, who very kindly lent me his correcting hand in the work.

I gave Williams the choice of two proposals, and he is inclined to this which follows. £50. ready money, £50.

Plate 0.16 *(right) Edward Pugh to Richard Lloyd, June 1811, Aberystwyth, National Library of Wales.*

at a month, £50 a 3 m°. and if he sold the work at two guineas 25 Copies, if at three 20 copies.

I am inclined to make another proposal in this way. I shall want some books to the value of about £5. which if he agree to let me have with £80 in ready money, I will take and come to a speedy conclusion in the business. I will take off from the first proposal £15—

I gave a hint to M' Ted that I meant to send the work to a literary friend, your noble self, and he advises me to let you try first: but I shall be satisfied with what I ask provided no delay takes place; but I shall be greatly obliged to you for your best advice: and I shall also thank you to call on my friend Watts and consult with him. I suppose the parcel will reach him about the middle of next week or about the 11th inst.

Unfortunately the plate of Twm or Nant has been sold long ago with many impressions, to Richardson in the Strand. who however may dispose of it reasonably, and it must, engraved as it has been, still yield several hundred good prints. It would be attended with very little expense to engrave a small head only, leaving out the hands and I would make a drawing for the purpose.

I hope you will do me the pleasure of reading a little of the M.S. and should any fault occur to you to put your skilful fist to it. but in my careful reperusal of it, & comparing it with a Tower, I borrowed from a person here, I do expect there be little to expunge, or little to alter,

The melancholy fate of poor M' Perceval will make a lasting impression on the mind of many people. An account was brought here three days ago, by the post boy from St Asaph of nearly a parallel case, but certainly more horrid in its execution. He said that one Rob' Jones, Butcher of that place had been murdered, his head cut off & thrown to a corner of the room, by a gang of seven men & now we hear that Jones's head is as firm upon his shoulders as ever. This boy is detested by all, as the lie has been invented by himself—

Recurring again to Williams. It strikes me that to take £15 from the price to which he seems to agree, might tend to throw cold water upon the business, and perhaps 'twould be better to propose to take Twenty pounds worth of such books as I may want, and that I do want them, is very notorious, my library's not worth £4. Whatever may lie in my power to promote the success of the publication, I shall do it with pleasure.

My health is but so so. having lately taken the advice of some, who never followed the profession of medicine, and taken Bark, which certainly had a happy effect for three or four days. but afterwards it locked me up for near three weeks. I am, however, recovering this slowly. My mother very earnestly desires her very best regards and good wishes.
I am Dear Lloyd with sincerity yours. Ed. Pugh

for *Modern London*. And because Havell aquatinted them after Pugh's death, he may have allowed himself far more freedom in interpreting the originals than he would have taken with an artist who was still alive and checking up on his work. The best of the possible Pughs are probably *Fives Playing and Singing to the Harp and Dancing* (Plate 0.18), a scene in which, after much mock-conflict between the friends and relations of bride and groom, the bride has finally been brought to the house of her new husband, and they dance together to the music of an aged harpist, watched by, among others, two fascinated little girls in their party-dresses.

Plate 0.17 *(above) John Havell after Edward Pugh (?),* The Fairies, *coloured aquatint from Peter Roberts,* The Cambrian Popular Antiquities *(London: E. Williams, 1815).*

Plate 0.18 *(right) John Havell after Edward Pugh (?),* Singing to the Harp and Dancing, *coloured aquatint from Peter Roberts,* The Cambrian Popular Antiquities.

VII

Pugh's career, at least the portion of it that we know about, fell entirely within the period of the French Revolutionary and the Napoleonic wars. He first exhibited at the Academy a few months after the execution of Louis XVI and Britain's entry into the war with France; when he died, the war still had two years to run, and Napoleon, driven from Russia, was enjoying his last victories on German soil before being beaten back into France. Phillips was right to call attention to this: whether or not Pugh's career would have been more successful and his profession more lucrative in a period in which some of the money raised to fight the war might have been spent instead on the fine arts, there is no question that the character of his work and its reception were in part determined by that apparently perpetual conflict. *Cambria Depicta*, in common with many other published tours of north Wales, was the production of a period in which the English, unable to tour on the continent of Europe, began taking their extended holidays in Britain: in Scotland, the north of England and Wales, north Wales especially. It was the war that created the market for such works, and though Pugh's book is far from preoccupied by the war, his tour lay through a land apparently depressed by its effects on the economy, more than usually suspicious of strangers – Pugh was twice suspected of being a spy, sketching likely places for a French landing on the coast[74] – but animated apparently by a cheerful patriotism, perhaps his own as much as that of those he met. In Llanidloes he was kept awake all night by the singing of 'noisy sons of Mars', a detachment of drunk English soldiers; but at Beaumaris, Dolgellau,

Corwen and Whitford he was delighted to witness reviews of volunteer and militia regiments;[75] near Criccieth he enjoyed a song in Welsh that mocked invasion-plans of Napoleon, or 'Mr. Bony-party (as the Welsh people call him), and at Llangynog he attempted to persuade 'a wrong-headed mountain politician', a critic of the war, of 'the necessity of opposing the Corsican', an attempt so successful that he left the 'old boy' shouting 'Confusion to Boney, confusion to Boney.'[76]

Modern London too may be understood as a wartime production. It was probably begun during the brief Peace of Amiens, but when it appeared it would have been seen among other things as a reference-book for out-of-town tourists unable to venture to Paris or Rome, and as a patriotic celebration of the metropolis of the British Empire, now challenged not by a republic but by the empire of Napoleon. And as we shall see, several of the *Six Views, in Denbighshire*, first announced when the war was less than a year old, would have been understood, to varying degrees, as images of Wales at war.

In the period of Pugh's career, the pace of social and economic change in north Wales was faster than anyone alive could remember, and it was above all the war that was the stimulus to economic development and what had come to be known as 'improvement'. Before the 1790s, as David Thomas put it, 'there were few improvers and little improvement',[77] even in the south Denbighshire landscapes that were Pugh's subject, where the influence of English farming methods was more apparent than further west. Many tenant farmers still paid rent in kind and in labour as well as in money, and landlords anxious to increase the income from their estates did not often invest in improvements.[78] They concentrated instead on forcing up the portion of the rent paid in money and on reclaiming the manorial rights on common land which had come to be regarded as open to be exploited by all, sometimes extending the boundaries of their estates into the commons and prosecuting others who had similarly encroached.[79] Tenant farmers were usually offered only yearly tenancies as opposed to leases, which might have given them the incentive and opportunity to improve their farms in the unlikely event of their having the capital to do so.[80] If they did manage to improve them, however, they might find their rent increased the following year to take account of the improvements they themselves had funded.[81] Where possible, landlords and their agents were looking for better-capitalized, English tenants, and were willing to aggregate farms together in order to attract them.[82] Many poor tenants and labourers eked out a living by following a trade as well as agricultural work, or by feeding stock on the commons, or by quarrying and burning lime or by mining lead when the price made it worthwhile, but in law mineral rights belonged to the lords of the manor, and increasingly through the century the lords of the manor were choosing to insist on the fact.[83]

The great stimulus to improvement was the huge rise in prices of foodstuffs.[84] The harvest of 1793 was poor enough for the duty on imports of corn, and the bounty on exports, to be suspended. The freak summer of 1794 shrivelled wheat and barley in the ear, and the spring harvest of 1795 was frozen to death by the coldest winter in memory. Prices rose and rose: in Denbighshire from 1794 to 1795 the price of barley, the primary bread corn of the county, almost doubled, and the price of wheat

more than doubled.[85] The army and navy increased hugely in size, which drew men away from agricultural work, increased the cost of labour, and added in various ways to the inflationary pressure on cereals. So also did the rising duties on commodities necessary to pay for the war, the shortage of European grain available to be imported, and later Napoleon's 'Continental System', the embargo against trade with Britain.

The expectation of high wartime prices for corn may have acted as a stimulus to increase the area of land under the plough by the enclosure of commons and wastes, but though during the war with France there was certainly a major shift in land use in the Vale of Clwyd from pasture to arable, there is little evidence that wastes, once enclosed, were used for anything but pasture and woodland.[86] Enclosures were achieved by acts of Parliament, and often to the detriment of the poorer inhabitants of an enclosing parish. The details of the enclosure were settled by commissioners who were, in the 1790s, often the stewards and agents of the rich landowners, who were themselves often virtual absentees; much of the business was done in London, out of reach and out of sight of local inhabitants. The cost of enclosure was often met by selling off portions of the land enclosed, which reduced the area available to be divided among rich and poor alike.[87] The cost of fencing the portions of land awarded to the poorer freeholders, and the access roads that led to them, was often too great for them to bear, so that they were forced to sell. The enclosure of wastes and commons effectively prevented the poor who claimed the right to graze animals on the common from continuing to do so if they had no documentary evidence of that right. It led to enforcing the rights of lords of manors over the mineral resources of common land, making it harder in particular for the poor to supplement their incomes by burning lime for fertilizer;[88] and it led to the widespread eviction, without compensation, of families of squatters, who may have lived for generations on the commons on land enclosed overnight from the common and in cottages built overnight, as the custom had been, and as they believed they had a right to do under medieval Welsh law. The less legal encroachments by wealthy landowners, or by tenants on their behalf, were treated as their legitimate property.[89] For many, enclosure meant they no longer had an independent stake in the parish of their birth: their supposed entitlement to quarry and graze the common taken away, they were left only with the entitlement to parish poor relief.[90]

In the 1790s, in the part of north Wales best known to Pugh, enclosures were moving westward from the border with England, and southward from the coastal marshland parishes around the mouth of the Clwyd.[91] In Flint, before the war began, acts had been passed for the enclosure of Hanmer and Hawarden before 1790, for Hope in 1791, and for Mold in 1792. The act for Cilcain was passed in 1793, and the same act provided for the enclosure of Llanferres in Denbighshire, a few miles east of Ruthin. Throughout 1794, when the *Six Views* were published, the Chester newspapers were full of advertisements inserted by enclosure commissioners detailing the progress of the division of the common land in these last three parishes. The act to enclose Llanfwrog, immediately south of Ruthin, was obtained in 1800, but it covered a useful stretch of common, believed to be rich in minerals, and the expectation and the rumour of its enclosure would have been abroad for several years before the act was obtained. By the time of Pugh's death,

acts had been obtained for the enclosure of land in a further eleven parishes in Flint and a further sixteen in Denbighshire.[92] In the medium term, enclosure must have led to the greater impoverishment of many who were already poor, though for some the work of fencing may have cushioned the blow for a year or two.[93] Other causes however were ensuring that the poor in Denbighshire, as elsewhere in north Wales, were getting poorer in the early and mid-1790s. Lead was mined in Llanferres, Cilcain and Mold, but the slowdown in the construction industry during the war greatly reduced its price, forcing some mines to close and leaving others barely profitable.[94]

Though the wages of agricultural labourers steadily increased through the decade, they could not catch up with the rapidly rising price of food.[95] Records of poor-rates in the parishes near Ruthin are very patchy, but for the parish of Llanfair Dyffryn Clwyd, a parish adjoining Ruthin to the south and featuring in the *Six Views*, they are complete, and show that the rate rose from 2s. 6d in the pound in 1788−9 to 3s. 6d in 1793−4 and to 5s. 6d in 1796−7.[96] There was no local workhouse − the poor were relieved in their own homes − but already in September 1794 some of the inhabitants of Ruthin were attempting to awaken interest in the building of a 'house of industry'. In the *Chester Chronicle* there appeared an advertisement headed 'Vale of Clwyd' which invited interested parties to a public meeting in the town hall at Ruthin to discuss measures for 'LESSENING the POOR'S RATES within the several parishes in this Vale'. Signed by four clergymen of Ruthin and Llanrhydd, as well as by two aldermen of the town and three lawyers, it proposed 'building an HOUSE of INDUSTRY in some convenient part of the Vale, for the accommodation of

the POOR belonging to the respective parishes'. Most of the twelve signatories had donated generously to the fund for augmenting the militia by signing up a hundred 'volunteers'; now they were apparently taking steps to clear up the problem of the families left behind.[97] Nothing came of this initiative, but the fact that it was advertised as a measure designed not to improve the lot of the poor but to reduce the cost of maintaining them suggests that the rise in poor rates was a cause of serious concern among the well-off.[98]

Unsurprisingly, then, in the part of north-east Wales best known to Pugh, there was evident an increasing hostility between the relatively poor and the relatively rich.[99] The Hope enclosure had led to serious rioting in the early months of the war, and the Vale of Clwyd, by reputation (at least among English tourists) a haven of rural peace, was the scene of riots over the price of food and more-or-less enforced recruitment into the militia and the navy. The response to these riots was the stationing of troops in Denbigh, Ruthin and Mold, and the formation by the gentry and 'middle orders' of volunteer forces to maintain order locally. From May to July the Chester newspapers carry lists of subscribers to the raising of these forces. They include many of the Flintshire and Denbighshire gentry, including, as we shall see, the three dedicatees of Pugh's *Six Views* who were normally resident in the two counties.

Many of the gentry, too, in the two counties, had joined the loyalist associations which in the winter of 1792−3 had sprung up all over Britain in imitation of the 'Association for the Preservation of Liberty and Property against Republicans and Levellers' established by John Reeves, a London magistrate and civil servant, at the Crown and

Anchor Tavern in the Strand in November 1792. It was dedicated to publishing propaganda criticizing the revolution in France and the proponents of parliamentary reform in Britain; to intimidating reformers in particular from meeting together; and to encouraging the prosecution of those who published supposedly seditious writings or who were reported as having spoken disrespectfully of the king or the constitution or in favour of the revolution. There were very few signs that the popular reform movement was spreading into north Wales in the 1790s, and the fear that it was may be better understood as a symptom of anxiety among the gentry about the spread of Methodism rather than of the influenza of French liberty. Nevertheless on December 18 an announcement in *Adam's Weekly Courant* announced that the magistrates for the district of Wrexham had met twelve days earlier and had proposed the establishment of an association to correspond with Reeves's association in London. On 14 January the association met to agree a patriotic declaration and to pass resolutions to the effect that they were united in opposing the spread in England of the 'levelling principles' adopted in France, and in their determination to assist in suppressing 'all riotous and disorderly assemblies', and 'all treasonable and seditious publications'. The signatories included Whigs and Tories alike: William Shipley, dean of St Asaph, who chaired the meeting, Richard Myddelton of Chirk Castle, Sir Watkin Williams Wynn of Wynnstay, Edward Lloyd Lloyd, soon to be of Pen-y-Lan, Philip Yorke of Erdigg, Earl Grosvenor, and Roger Kenyon of Cefn, to name only some of those whose names will appear again in this book.[100]

In Denbigh on 16 January a similar association, covering the western side of the county, was established, and declared its hostility to 'every design . . . to subvert or alter our invaluable constitution', whether originating in France or in Britain. It was chaired by Robert Watkin Wynne, MP for the county, whose political leanings will be discussed in Chapter 4, and among those present were the dean of St Asaph (again), the dissenting minister the Revd John Jenkins, and a number of those who would later support the scheme to establish a house of industry in the Vale of Clwyd.[101] A Flintshire association was established by Thomas Pennant of Downing at Holywell on 20 December 1792. It was aimed at 'the treasonable and seditious practices of a few disaffected persons, which are, to the best of their power, helping the French to ruin our trade and manufactures, to destroy our religion, our laws, and our king'. These people, Pennant warned, would 'leave the poor without any one able to give them bread' – that is to say, they would overthrow the rich gentry – 'or to protect them from wrongs from great or small' – they would destroy the magistracy. In short, they would 'bring confusion and destruction upon this now happy, and flourishing, kingdom'.[102] In Flintshire, unlike in Wrexham, the association was organized at parish level, as 'the best means of engaging the people' – the middle and lower ranks – 'in the loyalist cause': that is, of watching over them and intimidating them into supporting the views of the government.[103] Perhaps it tells us something about its success in doing this that the parishes that came together in Pennant's association were all in the north of the county, and that indisciplined Hope, as well as Mold and Hawarden, was not among them.

If the advent of the association movement appears to have prompted a show of unity among the loyalist Whig, radical Whig and Tory gentry against their greater enemies, popular radicalism and the French Republic, for Pennant – 'a *Whig*, Sir; a *sad dog*', according to the Tory Samuel Johnson[104] – it was a show only. In the early 1780s Dean Shipley had been the subject of a famous trial for seditious libel; he had read aloud at a public meeting a pamphlet published by the Society for Constitutional Information, a club dedicated to the radical reform of Parliament, and had been freed on the refusal of the jury to take direction from the judge. Though Shipley was no longer a great reformer, he had earned Pennant's inveterate hostility and not even his activism in both Denbighshire associations could conciliate the local Tories and loyalist Whigs. According to Pennant, soon after these meetings Lord Kenyon, as Lord Lieutenant of Flintshire, had refused an offer from Shipley to help raise a volunteer regiment, and he won Pennant's warm approbation for doing so. Pennant was an enemy also of Robert Watkin Wynne, chairman of the Denbigh association: notwithstanding the firmly loyalist resolutions he had carried through its inaugural meeting, Pennant described him as a supporter of the French Republic and 'a true democrat', about the worst insult in the loyalist book of curses.[105] Nor were the Denbighshire dissenters entirely at one with the Church of England clergy in their support of the loyal associations. The day after the Wrexham Association agreed its declaration, six of them met together to pass some resolutions of their own, declaring their attachment to the royal family and to the constitution, which contained within itself 'the means of exterminating corruption and reforming abuses', among which no doubt they particularly had in mind the Test and Corporation Acts which denied them the civil liberties enjoyed by members of the established Church.[106]

VIII

This then was the atmosphere in which Pugh's *Six Views* appeared, in the autumn and early winter of 1794, and part of my interest in them is to ask what it meant to publish landscapes of an area as troubled as Denbighshire at that time. I will not, except in the case of one of the views, be suggesting that Pugh set out to illustrate or comment upon the situation of the county. My point is rather that, unlike the English artists touring north Wales in search of the sublime, he knew and understood so well the landscapes he represented that the people and activities he depicted in them were bound to relate to, and to be understood in terms of, contemporary issues and conflicts: the exploitation of common land, the collapse of marginally profitable lead mines, the pauperization of the families of enlisted men, the survival or otherwise of customary rights and of the moral economy, the progress of improvement, and so on.

I am not trying to limit or reduce the value of the *Six Views* to how they might seem to participate in the tense atmosphere of the early years of the war with France. They belong within the visual culture of picturesque tourism far more obviously than within the visual representation of wartime Britain. In London, if they were seen there, they would have been received as examples of the now established genre of 'views', sequences of prints often depicting the rough, picturesque landscapes of Wales and Scotland now being explored by tourists in great numbers, and we in turn could understand them as images at once local and national, regional and metropolitan, the exactly appropriate expression of the hybrid character of Pugh's art, of Pugh himself, of a London Welshman. But were they seen in London? They were advertised only in Chester, and I doubt it they were much noticed outside the catchment area of the Chester newspapers. It seems unlikely, indeed, that they would have been sold in any numbers but to a local, Denbighshire, even south Denbighshire, audience, whose enjoyment of the images would have depended more on recognizing them, as depictions of places familiar to them, than on appreciating them as examples of aesthetic categories, the beautiful, the picturesque and so on.

When I had completed what I thought was the final draft of this book, I heard a lecture on Cézanne given by the distinguished historian of art T. J. Clark, which he called, not without some slight friendly mischief, 'The bright side of the landscape'. It began with a discussion of a poem by Elizabeth Bishop which she helpfully titled 'Poem' to distinguish it from the painting it describes. It is about looking at a very small oil-sketch of a rural landscape, which the 'gabled wooden houses' painted an 'awful shade of brown' immediately told her 'must be Nova Scotia'. Then, after several lines of careful description, careful enumeration of church, trees, cows, geese and so on, she suddenly exclaims: 'Heavens, I recognize the place, I know it!' For the three years that I had been writing this book, I had had what I thought was Bishop's line in my head. In fact, until Clark's lecture, I don't suppose I had actually read the poem for twenty years, and by a version of internal Chinese whispers my memory had whittled down that line to the faint and low-key echo that will appear, in a later chapter or two, as 'I know where *that* is.' Bishop's poem is primarily about the meanings that are generated, the knowledge that can be evoked, the feelings that are opened up, by landscapes of specific places that we know well. I did not know the neighbourhood about Ruthin at all when I started working on Pugh, and it is not my response to his pictures I have been trying to describe, but what they might have meant to those who lived around Ruthin when the aquatints were published, and whose first thoughts when they saw them must have been, 'I know where *that* is.' A pleased nod of recognition, but no great surprise.

But what is the point of looking at images of very particular places that we know well? This issue rarely seems of much concern to art historians, even to those who like to seek out the real originals of painted views, and it is hardly surprising, for two reasons at least. One I think is that, of all the disciplines of the humanities, there is something irremissively metropolitan about the history of art. Art history is largely written from, or *as if from*, the capital, where the great institutions of art are, the public and private galleries, the great auction-houses, as well as in many cases the leading centres of scholarship. In the capital, from the cultural centre, the individuality of places out there that get depicted in landscapes may not count for a great deal; in discussions of landscapes they are often abstracted, homogenized, into a category called 'place', which might pretend to subsume, but in fact seems to erase, the experience that Bishop seems to me to be talking about.

And inevitably the experience that Bishop describes cannot count for much in the history of art. In relation to pictures of any particular place, only a very few people will be able to make that exclamation. But perhaps when we look at landscapes we too easily forget how often, at least until the early nineteenth century, they were made to be looked at by individuals, by very little platoons, by people who *knew where that was*. Before that, in Britain at any rate, people who commissioned landscape images recognized the places they depicted not with the surprised recognition of Bishop, but with the nod of familiarity; they had got the picture they asked for of the place they knew. That didn't mean they didn't enjoy, collect, appreciate landscapes of other countries, of Italy or of the Low Countries, if they were British, but until landscapes came to be seen as examples of abstract categories, the sublime, the picturesque, and so on; until the market developed for collections of engraved views; and until élite landscape artists began producing landscapes on spec, for the market, and with an eye on exhibiting at the Academy or in the Salon, the chief point of landscape art was to show people images of places they already knew. The pleasure may have been simply that of happy recognition; it may have been in discovering that the most familiar places could be composed and re-presented as landscapes; or it may have been in seeing your very own acres displayed as if their value was as much aesthetic as economic; but in all cases the pleasure was, in part at least, about *knowing where that was*.

Pugh was a landscape artist who in his best works must have expected the scenes he depicted to be recognized by most of those who saw them. Though his real product is the reproductive print, not the original artwork made for a single patron, he is still making landscapes which will appeal mainly to a local audience, however much he would have hoped to sell them more widely. To different members of that audience, his pictures will mean different things, as the places they depict must certainly have done; but still most of those who saw them must have had in common that they *knew where that was*. When in *Cambria Depicta* Pugh looks for success by another route, by sketching throughout north Wales, seeking out the most unfamiliar places, and hoping to attract the more metropolitan audience that subscribed to collections of the kind of image, in Fuseli's phrase, 'that is commonly called Views', his pictures seem to lose all point. But in the *Six Views*, however few the people he could expect to be addressing, as a native and a local artist, sometimes a determinedly local one, he could address them, I think, in a way no English artist on a tour of Wales could have attempted. Unlike those other artists, Pugh's art was suggesting that what to other people were just landscapes were places to him and his neighbours. It was suggesting too, no doubt, more urgently in some images than in others, that what the inhabitants of Ruthin saw as places, *just* places, they could perhaps rediscover as landscapes too.

Notes

1 David Solkin, Richard Wilson: *The Landscape of Reaction* (London: Tate Gallery, 1982), pp. 94–9, 229.

2 See Thomas Pennant, *A Tour in Wales MDCCLXX*, 2 vols (London: Henry Hughes, 17778−81), vol. 2, p. 88.

3 Pennant, *Tour*, vol. 1, pp. 1–2.

4 *CCh* 24 January 1794, *CCo* 4 February.

5 *CD*, p. 323.

6 *CD*, pp. 136, 204.

7 *CD*, pp. 11–12, 345.

8 *CD*, p. vii.

9 Richard Llwyd, *Beaumaris Bay* (Chester: J. Fletcher, [1800]), p. 44.

10 See the essay 'The public prospect and the private view', in John Barrell, *The Birth of Pandora and the Division of Knowledge* (Philadelphia: University of Pennsylvania Press, 1992), pp. 41–61, and esp. p. 47. For a perfect exemplification of the supposed importance of class and gender in determining the capacity for aesthetic pleasure, see Ann Radcliffe's novel *The Italian* (1797), ed. Frederick Garber (Oxford: Oxford University Press, 1981), pp. 158–9, where three travellers, the genteel Vivaldi, his inamorata Elena and his servant Paulo, all stare enraptured at the same landscape, but all see different things: Vivaldi concentrates on the sublime mountains, Elena on the beautiful plain and valley, Paulo on some fishing boats which remind him of home.

11 See David Solkin's article on Wilson in *ODNB*.

12 Pennant, *Tour*, vol. 1, pp. iv–v; Geraint H. Jenkins, *The Foundations of Modern Wales 1642–1780* (Oxford: Oxford University Press and University of Wales Press, 1987), p. 423.

13 See for example *Monthly Magazine,* 48 (September 1819), 137; John Knowles (ed.), *The Life and Writings of Henry Fuseli, Esq., M.A., R.A.*, 3 vols (London: Henry Colburn and Richard Bentley, 1831), vol. 2, p. 217.

14 *CD*, p. 13. The first John Pugh ('John David Pugh') was baptized on 12 March 1757, and though I have found no further trace of him, he must have died before 4 January 1759, when a second John Pugh was baptized. He is the only sibling whose name appears again in the Ruthin parish register: he was buried on 11 May 1763, a fortnight or so before the birth of Edward.

15 Keith Thompson, *Ruthin School: The First Seven Centuries* (Ruthin: Ruthin School Quatercentenary Committee, 1974), pp. 97–8. I am grateful to Richard Aldrich, secretary of the Old Ruthinian Association, for the information about the meaning of the phrase 'Ruthin man' as used by Thompson.

16 Geraint H. Jenkins, Ffion Mair Jones and David Ceri Jones, *The Correspondence of Iolo Morganwg*, 3 vols (Cardiff: University of Wales Press, 2007), vol. 1: p. 745; for Pugh on Twm o'r Nant, see *CD*, pp. 388–9; for Samwell see E. G. Bowen, *David Samwell (Dafydd Ddu Feddyg) 1751–1798* (Cardiff: University of Wales Press, 1974).

17 Algernon Graves, *The Royal Academy of Arts: A Complete Dictionary of Contributors and their Work from its Foundation in 1769 to 1904*, 8 vols (London: Henry Graves and George Bell, 1905–6), vol. 6, p. 214. All references to Pugh's exhibits at the Academy and the addresses he exhibits from come from this volume and this page.

18 See W. Kaye Lamb (ed.), *The Voyage of George Vancouver 1791–1795*, 4 vols (London: Hakluyt Society, 1988), vol. 1, pp. 158, 170; vol. 3, pp. 797n., 818n., 1196n.; vol. 4, 1408n.

19 *Public Advertiser,* 30 April 1799.

20 *CCo* 22 April 1800, *CCh* 25 April.

21 Emily Robertson (ed.), *Letters and Papers of Andrew Robertson, AM, Miniature Painter* (London: Eyre and Spottiswoode, 1895), p. 99.

22 My thanks to Christopher J. Williams, Tony King, David Shiel and Heather Williams, all of whom plumped for Moel Famau, the last two suggesting that it was the view of Moel Famau from Eyarth Rocks. Thanks also to Ruth Williams of Denbighshire CC for seeking the opinion of Shiel, Area of Outstanding Natural Beauty Officer for the Clwydian Range. For the early designs for the Jubilee Tower, see King and Williams, 'The Jubilee Tower on Moel Fama', *Denbighshire Historical Society Transactions*, 58 (2010), 65–109.

23 *CCh* 19 and 26 September 1794, *CCo* 23 September.

24 *CCo* 30 September 1794, *CCh* 3 October.

25 For Bunn, see *CCh* 10 October 1794, *CCo* 14 October; Bunn had advertised previously in 1793, *CCh* 10 and 17 October. For Prichard, see *CCh* 2 and 9 May 1794; possibly he was the painter, Edward Prichard, who in 1851 was living in George Street, Chester, mentioned in Paul Joyner, *Artists in Wales c.1740–c.1851* (Aberystwyth: National Library of Wales, 1997), p. 96.

26 *CCh* 3 October 1794.

27 This is possibly John Heaviside Clark, b. 1771, which would make him about 24 in 1795; see Basil Long, *British Miniaturists 1520-1860* (1929) (London: Holland Press, 1966), p. 72.

28 *CCo* 3 March 1795.

29 *CCo* 6 October 1795,

30 *CCh* 9 September 1796.

31 Graves, *Royal Academy*, vol. 5, p. 139.

32 *CCo* 25 October 1797, *CCh* 28 October.

33 *CCh* 30 September 1796.

34 See *CD*, pp. 20, 79, 84.

35 *CCh* 6 April 1798, and see *CCo* 10 April; *CCh* 25 April 1800 and see *CCo* 22 April.

36 *CD*, p. 7.

37 *CCh* 6 April 1798, *CCo* 10 April.

38 *CD*, p. 249.

39 Robertson, *Letters and Papers*, p. 15.

40 *CCo* 30 September 1794, *CCh* 3 October; the 'London artist' who came to Chester in 1797 described the rooms he had taken at 'Mr. Taylor's musical shop, Watergate-street' as 'very commodious'; Pugh took the same rooms in 1798 and 1800: *CCh* 6 April 1798, and see *CCo* 10 April, *CCh* 25 April 1800 and *CCo* 22 April. See William Cowdroy, *The Directory and Guide for the City and County of Chester* (Chester: J. Fletcher, 1789), pp. 58, 63.

41 London: J. Bateson for W. Wigstead, 1800.

42 Matthew and James Payne, *Regarding Thomas Rowlandson 1757–1827: His Life, Art & Acquaintance* (no place: Hogarth Arts, 2010), pp. 221, 190–2.

43 Kenneth Garlick, Angus Macintyre, Kathryn Cave and Evelyn Newby (eds), *The Diary of Joseph Farington*, 17 vols (New Haven and London: Yale University Press for the Paul Mellon Centre for Studies in British Art, 1978–98), 4: 1222–3.

44 John Hayes, *The Drawings of Thomas Gainsborough*, text volume (London: A. Zwemmer, 1970), p. 96 and n.

45 Graves, *Royal Academy*, vol. 6, p. 214.

46 Graves, *Royal Academy*, vol. 6, p. 324; Robertson, *Letters and Papers*, pp. 136–43.

47 *Morning Chronicle*, 5 August 1803.

48 Graves, *Royal Academy*, vol. 6, p. 214; *Morning Chronicle*, 3 December 1803.

49 *CD*, p. 49.

50 Robertson, *Letters and Papers*, pp. 102–106.

51 *CD*, p. 91; Peter Lord, *The Visual Culture of Wales: Imaging the Nation* (Cardiff: University of Wales Press, 2000), p. 251n.

52 *The Universal British Directory of Trade, Commerce, and Manufactures*, vol. 4 (London: for the Patentees at the British Directory Office, and Champante and Whitrow, 1798), pp. 347.

53 *CD*, p. 447.

54 Pugh (in 1813) and his mother (in 1816) are both recorded, in the register of their burials, as living in Well Street, but I have not managed to trace them there. The surviving rate books for the Well Street division in Denbighshire Record Office (PD/90/1/154–6) show no one there by the name of Pugh in the three year lists that remain (1795–6, 1797, 1813), and the Church Rate book (PD/90/1/49) is similarly unhelpful. Probably Pugh's mother Dorothy was living with a relation, perhaps in one of the twenty-one households which in 1813, the year of Pugh's death, were headed by a Jones; or perhaps, by some error of the parish clerk, she is the 'Dorothy Jones' who appears in the poor-rate assessment in that year.

55 *CD*, pp. 447, 266.

56 NLW MS 13224B.

57 See the reference to 'an ingenious countryman of mine', 'Mr. William Owen of Barmouth', in *ML*, p. 2n. W. P. Courtney, '"David Hughson": Edward and David Pugh', *Notes and Queries*, n.s. 4 (22 July 1911), 70–2, suggest that David Pugh was Edward's cousin, but in fact we know too little about either Pugh to tell.

58 NLW MS 1562C.

59 John Hayes (ed.), *The Letters of Thomas Gainsborough* (New Haven and London: Yale University Press, 2001), p. 68.

60 Pugh to Llwyd, writing from Ruthin on 'King George's Birthday' (4 June 1812; letter franked 8 June), NLW MS 9023C. For Watts, see Algernon Graves, *The British Institution 1806–1807* (1875), (Bath: Kingsmead, 1969), p. 441, and Long, *British Miniaturists*, p. 455.

61 Robertson, *Letters and Papers*, p. 54; the following year he writes from 20 Cecil Street, which may or may not be a misprint for '21' (p. 86); after a trip home to Scotland at the start of 1803, he returns to London and lives at no. 16 (p. 93).

62 Colonel Maurice Harold Grant, *A Dictionary of British Landscape Painters from the 16th Century to the early 20th Century* [1952] (Leigh-on-Sea: F. Lewis, 1976), p. 154 and plate 414.

63 *CD*, pp. 340, 440.

64 My thanks to Dr Michael Lewis for bringing to my attention the advertisement in the *Caledonian Mercury*.

65 It may be that Clay reissued the Risca aquatint in 1813 as a companion this time to the castle view, for the earlier print exists in two differently coloured versions which may perhaps have been issued at different times, though the date of publication is the same on both. In one in which the foliage is predominantly brown, in the other green, with the clothes of the figures differently coloured also.

66 Sandby, *Newport Castle and Bridge*, watercolour, c.1773, Newport Museum and Art Gallery; J. M. W. Turner, *Newport Castle*, watercolour, 1796, British Museum. For more views of the bridge and castle, see the excellent website 'Newport Past', especially at *http://www.newportpast.com/gallery/prints/index.htm* and *http://www.newportpast.com/nmg/castle/nmg09.htm*.

67 Or so it did in the early summer of 2011. By August, Street View no longer showed the planters.

68 *CD*, p. 360.

69 *CD*, pp. 55, 275.

70 NLW MS 9023C.

71 *CCh* 23 July 1813.

72 *Monthly Magazine*, 36 (1813, part 2), 187. This obituary appeared also in the *Universal Magazine*, 20/118 (September 1813) p. 256. The briefer obituary in *GM*, 82 (November. 1813), 503 derives from the *Monthly Magazine*.

73   Peter Roberts, *The Cambrian Popular Antiquities; or, an Account of some Traditions, Customs, and Superstitions, of Wales* (London: E. Williams, 1815).

74   *CD*, pp. 135, 370.

75   *CD*, pp. 224, 90–1, 206, 296, 370.

76   *CD*, pp. 146, 195, 270–2.

77   David Thomas, *Agriculture in Wales during the Napoleonic Wars* (Cardiff: University of Wales Press, 1963), p. 181; David W. Howell, *The Rural Poor in Eighteenth-Century Wales* (Cardiff: University of Wales Press, 2000), p. 5.

78   Howell, *Rural Poor*, p. 41.

79   Howell, *Rural Poor*, pp. 119–20, 197–8, 7, 200–1.

80   Howell, *Rural Poor*, pp. 38, 40; David Jones, *Before Rebecca: Popular Protests in Wales 1793–1835* (London: Allen Lane, 1973), p. 40; John Wyn Edwards, 'Enclosure and agricultural improvement in the Vale of Clwyd 1750–1875' (unpublished MA thesis, University of London, 1963), 65–7.

81   Howell, *Rural Poor*, pp. 40–1, Edwards, 'Enclosure and agricultural improvement', 65–6.

82   Howell, *Rural Poor*, pp. 38–9.

83   Howell, *Rural Poor*, pp. 53, 197–8.

84   Thomas, *Agriculture in Wales*, pp. 181–2.

85   Thomas, *Agriculture in Wales*, pp. 3–4, 46, 46, 82; Jones, *Before Rebecca*, pp. 18–19; and see Edwards, 'Enclosure and agricultural improvement', 27.

86   Thomas, *Agriculture in Wales* pp. 7, 31,181; Edwards, 'Enclosure and agricultural improvement', 31.

87   See for example *CCh* 27 June, 17 October 1794 (Cilcain and Llanferres enclosure).

88   D. G. Evans, 'The Hope Enclosure Act of 1791', *Flintshire Historical Society Journal*, 31 (1983–4), 161–86.

89   Thomas, *Agriculture in Wales*, p. 60; Howell, Rural Poor, pp. 8, 200–1.

90   Jones, *Before Rebecca*, pp. 52–3.

91   John Chapman, 'Parliamentary Enclosure in Wales: Comparisons and Contrasts', *Welsh History Review*, 21/4 (December 2003), 761–9, esp. 764; Edwards, 140–1.

92   Calculated from John Chapman, *A Guide to Parliamentary Enclosures in Wales* (Cardiff: University of Wales Press, 1992), pp. 73–100, and including lands specified in acts which covered more than one parish.

93   See below, Chapter 1.

94   See below, Chapter 1.

95   Howell, *Rural Poor*, pp. 72–6.

96   DRO PD/55/1/43.

97   *CCh*, 3 October; 20 June 1794.

98   *CCh*, 3 October 1794, and see below, chapter 3.

99   Jones, *Before Rebecca*, p. 57.

100   *Adam's Weekly Courant*, 22 January 1793.

101   *Adam's Weekly Courant*, 5 February 1793.

102   Pennant, *The Literary Life of the late Thomas Pennant, Esq. By himself* (London: Benjamin and John White, and Robert Faulder, 1793), pp. 135–6; *Adam's Weekly Courant*, 18 December 1792. For an account of the associations in north-east Wales, see Hywel Davies, 'Loyalism in Wales, 1792–1793', *Welsh History Review*, 20/4 (December 2001), 687–716.

103   Davies, 'Loyalism in Wales', 700.

104   James Boswell, *Life of Johnson* (London: Oxford University Press, 1953), p. 933.

105   George T. Kenyon, *The Life of Lloyd, first Lord Kenyon, Lord Chief Justice of England* (London: Longmans, Green, 1873), pp. 324–5. Note however that the author of this book dates Pennant's reference to the refusal of Shipley's offer to January 1795, but that Kenyon did not become Lord Lieutenant until the following year.

106   *Adam's Weekly Courant*, 22 January 1793.

ONE *Foel-Famma, from Careg Carn-March Arther*

I

The *View of Foel-Famma, from Careg Carn-March Arther* (Plates 1.1, 1.2) is an image which aspires, modestly, to the sublime; to a gentle, feminine, Denbighshire sublime, well exemplified by Moel Famau, the highest hill in the Clwydian range but with nothing sharp or precipitous about it, and 'destitute', as Pugh described it in *Cambria Depicta*, 'of the terrific and melancholy'.[1] We are at the point on the road from Mold to Ruthin where travellers into Wales from Chester had their first sight of Denbighshire, and I have started my discussion of the *Six Views* with this image partly because, as an Englishman, it is by this route that I enter Pugh's home country; partly because it was the first image by Pugh that I came across; and partly because, as this chapter will suggest, it represents a limit case in the sequence, the view where the local seems to give most ground to an idea of landscape art which aspires to a more general appeal.

When Pugh was here Moel Famau was apparently visible on the western horizon, but from this viewpoint now it is obscured by trees even in winter. The arched monument covers Carreg Carn March Arthur, a stone 'with a cavity in it', Pugh tells us,

very like the impression of a horse's hoof. This has given rise to a traditional story, that King Arthur, when hunting on the hills, took a leap from the summit of Moel Famau, and his horse alighting upon this stone, impressed it with his hoof.[2]

The arch was built over the stone in the 1760s, to commemorate a decision of the High Court of Exchequer in 1763, which, following a protracted dispute, determined that the stone marked the boundary between the parishes of Mold and Llanferres, and thus between the counties of Flint and Denbigh.[3] The monument is now about ten feet high, but in 1974 when the A494 was widened its height was reduced by a course or two of stones and its position moved several yards to the east. The rhetoric of exactitude in Pugh's print, on display for example in the apparently meticulous (but probably factitious) marking of the boundaries of the old enclosures in the middle distance, may persuade us to take on trust the carefully enumerated stone courses in the monument, but in fact Pugh has nearly doubled its original height so that it towers above the men beneath.

The road from Mold to Ruthin, turnpiked in 1757, is heavily scarred by wheel ruts that mark it as a busy highway, but it was a difficult road for wheeled traffic, the way over the Clwydian hills 'being very precipitous, and near a mile to ascend'. In 1792 James Plumptre records that though the

Plate 1.1 *(opposite) William Ellis after Edward Pugh, Foel-Famma, from Careg Carn-March Arther, aquatint (London: E. Pugh, 1794), Aberystwyth, National Library of Wales.*

distance from Mold to Ruthin 'is but 9 miles, 10.6 [10s. 6d] is always charged for this stage, the roads being indifferent and up and down tremendous hills'.[4] Nor was it on the tourist route: for tourists and travellers, aiming for the beauties and antiquities of the Vale of Clwyd, the sublimities of Snowdon, or the Holyhead–Dublin packet, it ran the wrong way.[5] Those coming from Chester took what William Gilpin called 'the great Irish Road' through St Asaph and Conway;[6] those coming from Wrexham took what would later come to be known as 'the great Irish Road' through Llangollen and Corwen and past Pont y Glyn Diffwys, the subject of another of the *Six Views*. Nevertheless, the combination of the antiquarian interest of Arthur's stone, with its magical legend of the kind Romantic Wales was expected to provide, and the superb view once available from here of Moel Famau, three miles away, helps make this the most likely of the *Six Views* to appeal to a more than local audience.

In the National Library of Wales there is a version of this view by another local artist, John Ingleby, who was born in 1749 in Halkin, some five miles from this viewpoint, and died there in 1808 (Plate 1.3).[7] He was a semi-professional artist occasionally employed as an illustrator, at 5d a drawing, by Thomas Pennant, when his 'worthy servant' Moses Griffith was overburdened.[8] Ingleby,

Pennant remarked, patronizing as ever, was 'a very neat drawer', and this very neat drawing of Carreg Carn March Arthur was made in 1796 and probably intended for one of the private, extra-illustrated copies of his works that Pennant kept at Downing, his house in Flintshire. Pennant had come across the monument in his Welsh tour of 1773.[9] Ingleby makes more of the monument than even Pugh had done, nearly doubling the number of courses

Plate 1.3 (below) John Ingleby, The Stone under this Arch called Carreg Carn March Arthur, pen-and-ink and water-colour, 1796, Aberystwyth, National Library of Wales. Ingleby uses a 'v' mark to point out Moel Famau, and 'vv' to mark the position of the farmhouse Maes y Carn.

Plate 1.2 (opposite) William Ellis after Edward Pugh, Foel-Famma, from Careg Carn-March Arther, coloured aquatint (London: E. Pugh, 1794), first issue. Badly inked and much faded, this is the only example I have found in which the colour appears to be contemporary with the print.

Plate 1.4 *(above) Detail of plate 1.9.*

Plate 1.5 *(right) Richard Wilson,* View near the Loggerheads, *oil on canvas, ca. 1762, London, Tate Gallery.*

shown in Pugh's print. His viewpoint, as far as we can judge from the angle of the monument, is almost the same as Pugh's, but he has chosen to include more of the lump of limestone behind Arthur's stone known as Cefn Mawr, now decapitated by quarrying.

But there was still more to attract both artists, both born within two or three hours' walk of this spot of ground, than the gentle sublimity of Moel Famau and the antiquarian curiosity of the magic hoofprint. For landscape artists, above all for Welsh landscape artists, this spot was not only the viewpoint for a potentially saleable tourist print; it was

a place of pilgrimage. In Pugh's image, the road ahead branches: the downhill fork winds down to the Loggerheads Inn, the inn sign for which was by repute painted by Richard Wilson in exchange for ale; the uphill fork is a private drive, leading to Colomendy, the country house where Mrs Catherine Jones resided in the last decades of the eighteenth century.[10] She was the cousin of Wilson, who, in the last year of his life, short of money, his health 'greatly impaired by drinking',[11] fled London to live at Colomendy.

Wilson was 'a warm admirer of the scenery about this spot',[12] Pugh tells us, and when he died in 1782 he was buried at Mold. For Ingleby, it was so important to direct attention to the drive, and thus metonymically to Wilson himself, that he ends up producing a capriccio more than a view, squeezing monument, mountain and drive into a single prospect and sacrificing any topographical continuity between them. For Wilson himself, this spot may have been more the equivalent of the crossroads where in so many eighteenth-century paintings, operas and poems Hercules is shown pondering his next move, whether to take the easy road to vice – here, downhill to the pub – or the hard uphill path to virtue, to Mrs Jones and rehab.[13] We can imagine the elderly Wilson – but perhaps in Pugh's image we can actually see him, through the crook of the tree, a shadowy silhouette toiling up the drive, either avoiding the pub or returning from it early (it is not yet dark), so either way with a feeling of conscious virtue. He shows up best in the original watercolour of this print (Plate 1.4), of which more later.

And Wilson himself had also painted the scene. The painting is unfinished, but it is unique among Wilson's known paintings, because, as David Solkin puts it, 'it is the only known landscape by Wilson which he can be said to have painted for purely personal reasons'[14] – depicting a scene that meant something personal to himself and with no apparent intention to sell it. Wilson does not show the monument built over the boundary stone – indeed, the painting is now conjecturally dated to 1762, a year before the legal judgement recorded in the inscription. His *View near the Loggerheads* (Plate 1.5), as it has come to be known, is taken from a higher viewpoint, probably about a hundred yards up the drive to Colomendy: Pugh and Ingleby were probably constrained by fences

or shortage of time to remain on the public road, while Wilson could wander freely on his cousin's estate. Wilson looks north-north-west towards a more northerly peak in the Clwydian range, balancing Moel Famau, pushed to the far left, with Cefn Mawr much more prominent. His station allows him to look down along the land owned by his cousin in the valley of the river Alyn, and to trace the river as it winds from the Loggerheads around Cefn Mawr. But what interests me for the moment, in the painting and in the preparatory sketch in the Ashmolean Museum (Plate 1.6), is less what he sees down there than what he shows us at the top of the cliff, known as Pen-y-Garreg Wen, on the left side of Cefn Mawr.

Plate 1.6 *Richard Wilson,* A Welsh Valley, *pencil and black chalk, ca. 1762, Oxford, Ashmolean Museum.*

II

The cause of the boundary dispute, the resolution of which is recorded in the inscription beneath the arch, was mining rights. 'The Grosvenor family', explains a local historian, 'claimed the mineral rights under the common waste in the parish of Llanferres and the Lords of Mold those in Mold parish.' The bitter lawsuit, with much chicanery on Grosvenor's side, took eleven years to resolve.[15] In the period covered by these various pictures, to the north of the road that runs past the stone, was a long series of shafts running westward to Pen-y-Garreg Wen.[16] In the mid-eighteenth century, the mines from Cadole westward were being claimed by the Grosvenors, and leased out to individual miners. The lords of the manor of Mold, however, claimed the mining rights all along the north of the road as far west as the boundary stone.[17] In 1763 that claim was upheld.

The lead industry was booming in the 1760s, and in 1769 there began several years of heavy investment in the mines on this side of Cefn Mawr. The historian of the lead mines in this area, C. J. Williams, describes new shafts being sunk, new levels driven, a waterwheel installed to pump out the mines, wheeled wagons introduced underground;[18] the accounts of Catherine Jones indicate that she was supplying timber from the Colomendy estate to line the shafts.[19] All this investment came too late, however, to catch the tide: the mines did not come quickly into profit, and by the 1780s were being worked on a very small scale. By the mid-1790s they may have been barely open, and in the early 1800s, Pugh tells us, the 'once-great' mines in Llanferres were being worked by very few men,

'and the ore is hardly worth the expense of getting it up'. They were not fully opened again until the 1820s.[19] By the time of Pugh and Ingleby, therefore, there was very little mining in this area, but there must still have been very visible marks of mining on the landscape. The area behind Carreg Carn March Arthur was pierced with the adits, shafts and levels of lead miners, and scattered with spoil heaps left by their excavation, as well as by quarrying.[21]

Nowadays, the area of old mines north of the road, opposite Colomendy, is a well-known country park. It is covered in trees, with nature and mining heritage trails marked out along woodland paths. As the eighteenth-century images show, however, lime-burning and mining had left the area entirely treeless; but whatever evidence of mining was therefore visible, only Wilson, painting the view as the lawsuit moves from Ruthin to London and reaches its climax, gives us any definite indication that this area contained deposits of lead ore productive enough to be worth litigating about for eleven years. His painting, if not in the grand style of his earlier views

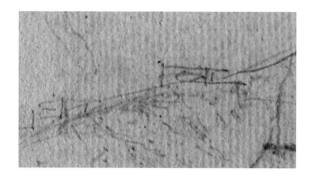

Plate 1.7 *Detail of plate 1.6.*

of the landscape near Rome, is in a far grander style than Ingleby or even Pugh aspires to. It has little of the topographical about it: even when finished, it would have had none of the neatness of Ingleby and none of the apparent exactitude of Pugh – except in one respect. The tiny structures Wilson shows on top of Pen-y-Garreg Wen – they show up better in the drawing – must be connected with the mine shafts there (Plate 1.7). Cris Ebbs, an expert on the mines of this area whom I have consulted about these images, has identified them as horse-whims, horse-powered winding-gear for raising lead ore (Plate 1.8).[22] They hardly insist on their presence, however, and except to those who knew the area well they would probably not be identifiable.

Uniquely among the six prints of 1794, for this aquatint Pugh's original artwork survives, in the form of a grisaille watercolour (Plate 1.9). Ellis is a fine aquatint artist, but in various small ways the two images differ, usually to the advantage of the original. The thin strip of light at the end of the road, which attracts the eye through the foreground figures and objects and gives the picture depth, is all but missing in the aquatint; the lines of the wheel-ruts and the hatching in the foreground of the print seem hard and out of keeping. In both images the gestures of the men who stand before it fasten our attention upon the monument, but the men give us no indication of its purpose. In the watercolour, the only legible words on the front plaque – from which the inscription, Pugh tells us in a passage of *Cambria Depicta*, written more than a decade later, was by then 'almost totally effaced'[23] – are 'This arch', 'Carreg Carn March Arthur' and 'Boundary between' (Plate 1.10). In the aquatint, the words 'Boundary between' have disappeared, and we are left to assume that the inscription tells an old antiquarian tale about

Arthur's horse rather than a modern story about a territorial dispute (Plate 1.11).[24] And Pugh chooses a viewpoint which allows a monument which is all about mining to obscure the remaining signs of the mines themselves. There is only, to the left of the monument, what may be a dark heap of spoil from a mine shaft – the position, says Ebbs, is 'perfect' for that[25] – but we would not suspect it to be so unless we already knew something about this area. Or the spoil may be from quarrying: the lime derived from this area was of the highest quality,[26] and there may well have been a limekiln where Pugh places it, by the side of the turnpike, convenient for the carriage of stone and barrels of burnt lime,[27] or he may have moved the limekiln that was certainly further up the hill and which the monument would otherwise have obscured.

Ingleby shows a limekiln roughly where Pugh positions his, and what I take to be another which gave its name to Limekiln Rake, a long vein of lead

Plate 1.8 *A horse-whim, in Paul Sandby,* Landscape with a Mine*, watercolour and gouache, ca. 1775, Cardiff, National Museum and Gallery.*

Plate 1.9 *(opposite) Edward Pugh,* Foel-Famma, from Careg Carn-March Arther, *grisaille watercolour, ca. 1794, private collection.*

ore on this side of Cefn Mawr – this upper kiln is still shown on nineteenth-century Ordnance Survey maps, but had disappeared by the time of the survey of 1912. But apart from this, Ingleby made no room at all for evidences of mining or quarrying, not even for the adit – the horizontal access level – that had been driven into the side of the rock at just this point.[28] A road known as the Green Path, or Pen-y-Garreg Wen Road, or Pen-y-bychan Road, ran just from the right of the arch to the upper limekiln and thence to the shafts depicted by Wilson (Plate 1.12). It still survives as a woodland path, setting off from

the left of the arch now it has been re-erected, but when Ingleby was active it served as the boundary between Mold and Llanferres. It had been important enough for provision to be made for its upkeep in the Llanferres enclosure award of 1801;[29] up until the mid-twentieth-century it connected the villages to the north with the road to Mold and Ruthin, and in the 1930s was even driveable, at least along some of its length.[30] But even this has been omitted from Ingleby's view. The rock is left bare and all but featureless, while instead he picks out for particular attention a farmhouse, Maes y Carn, fairly small today but in Ingleby's view a very substantial building, so that, together with the Colomendy drive, it helps make this a landscape of country houses more than of industry.

Plate 1.10 *(above top) Detail of plate 1.9.*

Plate 1.11 *(above bottom) Detail of plate 1.2.*

Plate 1.12 *(left)* Approach to Crosville Park, Loggerheads, with Ancient Boundary Monument in Foreground *(postcard, no publisher or postmark, c. 1930), showing the position of the boundary stone and arch before the widening of the A494.*

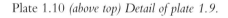

Plate 1.13 *John Ingleby,* View from the Loggerheads, *pen-and-ink and watercolour, 1796, Aberystwyth, National Library of Wales.*

traces of mining, which must still have been very apparent on Cefn Mawr, did not obtrude themselves too assertively on the landscape of the valley, but it is hard to believe that it could have been quite as remarkably unscarred as Ingleby's image suggests by the major capital investment in the mine which had taken place twenty years earlier.[33] Some years after Broster's visit Pugh also drew the Loggerheads, for *Cambria Depicta,* also as an entirely pastoral scene (Plate 1.14); by this time no doubt the scars had faded even further, and he gives no indication that this area had previously been more about mining than agriculture. Wilson had reduced the signs of mining to those two illegible marks on the cliff-top, so as not to attenuate the pastoral sentiment that suffuses his images of Wild Wales. But Ingleby, a practitioner in a more humble branch of the art, and so (we might expect) more concerned to produce images which imparted information about the places he depicted, ignored entirely the signs of mining in the area round the Loggerheads and the boundary stone, and Pugh shows us only that possible spoil heap, possibly the residue of mining, but so absorbed into the overall composition as not to put the aesthetic character of the landscape at risk. Partly, perhaps, both artists were responding to the changing nature of the place itself, but their reticence in depicting its residual industrial character must also have been a deliberate choice.

As we shall see, it was not entirely characteristic of either artist to conceal the evidence of mineral extraction which was so vital a part of the late eighteenth-century economy of north Wales. It *was* characteristic, however of the generality of views of Wales in the period, that the mining or quarrying of lead or copper or zinc, gold, calamine, iron, manganese or coal, or slate, building-stone and lime

In 1802 John Broster, a bookseller of Chester, passed along this road, and found at the foot of the hill, under Pen-y-Garreg Wen, by the Loggerheads Inn, 'a singularly beautiful valley, comprising wood, water, vale, mountain, with bridge, mill, and public-house, in a small space, highly picturesque'.[31] That is how Ingleby depicted the landscape there, on the same trip as his image of the view from the boundary stone (Plate 1.13): a few cottages, the overshot corn-mill fed by a leet, or small aqueduct,[32] in an entirely pastoral landscape. Probably by then the went, by and large, unrepresented. As Peter Lord has argued, though scenes of industrial Wales could be and sometimes were accommodated to the late eighteenth-century aesthetics of the sublime and the picturesque, and though some artists – Paul Sandby, John 'Warwick' Smith, Julius Caesar Ibbetson and others – occasionally produced striking images of industrial activity, in particular of the great Anglesey copper mines, the overwhelming impression of Wales developed in visual imagery of the late eighteenth and early nineteenth centuries was of a land 'essentially rural or mountainous . . . apparently unchanged in its form and the people unchanged in their behaviour since the mythic time of their creation'.[34] To those familiar with landscape images of north Wales, exceptions to this rule will come readily to mind – images of mills, mines, factories and so on – but these are relatively well known because they have been deliberately selected from out of the thousands of images made in conformity with Lord's account.

If that account is true of images of Wales in general, it is truer still of Clwyd, the heartland of Wilson, Pugh, Ingleby and his patron Pennant. In his *General View of the Agriculture of Flintshire*, published in 1794, George Kay wrote that 'the mineral productions of this county constitute the principal part of its commercial importance. Lead ore is raised in great quantities'.[35] At the close of the eighteenth century, wrote the poet and antiquary Walter Davies in 1810, Flintshire produced 'more lead than all of Wales besides'.[36] But if we were to judge by the titles at least, of the prints of Clwyd in the handlist compiled by Derrick Pratt and A. G. Veysey, there was no mining there at all. The print market, it appears from this list, could absorb an ever-flowing stream of sublime and pastoral landscapes, but there was virtually no demand for landscapes disfigured by

industry, particularly extractive industries. Of the 1,052 prints in the handlist, 'less than a dozen', write Pratt and Veysey, 'illustrate the early commercial and industrial development' of Clwyd.[37] Three show the elaborately ornamented bleach works, designed by Thomas Sandby, of the Hon. Thomas Fitzmaurice at Lleweni; two, by Ingleby, show the brass mills and smelting works at Greenfield; two more, by Griffith and Ingleby, show the copper works at Holywell; three more, by the same two artists, show cotton mills, and one shows a quarry.[38] Ten prints in all; the rest are overwhelmingly images of gentlemen's seats,

Plate 1.14 *Thomas Cartwright after Edward Pugh,* View near the Loggerheads, *coloured aquatint, from* Cambria Depicta, *dated April 1813.*

Plate 1.15 *John Hassell, drawn and engraved,* Shaft of a Lead Mine. View near Pont Aberglaslyn, Carnarvonshire, *coloured aquatint, 1798, London, British Library.*

buildings of antiquarian interest, and rural views sublime, picturesque or beautiful. West of Denbighshire, we do find a few prints of extractive industries; in 1798 John Hassell made an illuminating print of lead-mining near Aberglaslyn, with lumps of galena piled up by the shaft-entrance waiting to be carried away for smelting (Plate 1.15), a scene which allows us to imagine very clearly what the smaller-scale operations at the Loggerheads would have looked like.

On the basis of some of these images, commissioned by Pennant, and of his generally encouraging attitude towards industrial enterprise in Wales, Lord argues that Pennant 'identified wholeheartedly enough' with industrial development 'to commission pictures in which this new source of wealth was prominently celebrated'.[39] But though there is a handful of watercolours by Griffith and Ingleby, paid for by Pennant, to add to the tally of prints of industry in the handlist, in total such images are very few indeed. Of the 173 watercolours that Ingleby made for Pennant and that are preserved in the National Library of Wales, only four show any sign at all of industry – an image of the cotton mill at Mold, and the three images we shall look at shortly.

Contrary to Lord, I am more inclined to contrast than to compare the encouraging attitude to industry expressed by Pennant in his writings, with the paucity of images of it that he commissioned. Tourist writing found it relatively easy to accommodate an interest in the non-agricultural part of the Welsh economy, but overwhelmingly the demand of the print-market was for what Joseph Hucks went in search of in the pedestrian tour he made with Coleridge in 1795: 'romantic views', 'unmechanized by the ingenuity of man'.[40]

Ingleby however was not altogether shy of acknowledging the industrial character even of this corner of Flintshire, though it may well be that it was not he but Pennant who determined what he drew. His home, Halkin, was the centre of Flintshire lead-mining, and he was almost certainly related to Richard Ingleby, a successful mining entrepreneur who worked the wide vein of lead ore at Pen-y-Fron, on

Plate 1.16 *(above) John Ingleby,* Pen-y-Vron, *pen-and-ink and watercolour, 1796, Aberystwyth, National Library of Wales.*

Plate 1.17 *(left) John Ingleby,* View from Llyn-y-Pandy. Looking towards the Loggerheads, *pen-and-ink and watercolour, 1796, Aberystwyth, National Library of Wales.*

Plate 1.18 *John Ingleby,* Llyn-y-Pandy. Or the Black Valley, *pen-and-ink and watercolour, 1796, Aberystwyth, National Library of Wales.*

the north side of Cefn Mawr.[41] Ingleby drew the workings there with some attention to detail (Plate 1.16): according to C. J. Williams, the buildings in the distance, with their waterwheels, are lead smelting works, and halfway up the hill he identifies an engine-house, and below it a whim, part of the huge array of pumps, powered by horses, steam or water, by which Richard attempted to drain his shafts.[42] Nearer to us is a chute, a leet, a waterwheel, perhaps miners' cottages, but the viewpoint Ingleby has chosen keeps the heavy plant in the distance where it does not do much to compromise the picturesque atmosphere of the valley.

Ingleby also drew two views of the Alyn near Llyn-y-Pandy, one of the vast dispersed industrial interests of the great ironmaster John Wilkinson, a few miles downriver from the Loggerheads.[43] 'The scenery of this place', wrote the picturesque tourist and Foxite Whig Richard Warner, is 'wonderfully wild and romantick; a deep valley, rude and rocky, shut in by abrupt banks, clothed with the darkest shade of wood.' In one of these drawings (Plate 1.17), that is more or less what Ingleby sees, too, though I take it the two men in the bottom left are miners. From this viewpoint he chooses not to see, however, all else that Warner describes in the valley: 'stupendous' mine works, and four vast pumping engines by Boulton and Watt.[44] In the other view, however, he goes for broke (Plate 1.18): describing the subject as 'Llyn-y-Pandy. Or the Black Valley, with the Fire Engine and Great Promontory become perfectly black from the smoke'.

Throughout *Cambria Depicta* Pugh shows himself alert to and interested in the process of modernizing the Welsh economy, and though in his selection of views to illustrate, or in his treatment of them, he does not emphasize the importance of mining in north Wales, he does not avoid the issue as did the great majority of artists working there. In particular he included in that book two images of the famously sublime Mona copper mine at Parys Mountain on Anglesey.[45] He lamented that the mine was so little known to professional painters, and recommended 'those who are alive to, and know the value of, scenery so sublime, to spend a day or two there . . . the mine will afford the artist a variety, and if he be a man of taste, he will feel highly gratified with the sight.'[46] As we shall see, in another of the *Six Views,* he represents the contrast between the surface collection of limestone for burning and the extraction of harder-won minerals as an issue of importance to the economy of his local area. At Carreg Carn March Arthur, however, the mining industry is visible only in its erasure, and then only to those who have travelled this road and know what they might have expected to see here.

III

So why, at this border of Flintshire and Denbighshire, did both artists choose to efface the recent industrial history of the place? The most likely explanation seems to me to do with their desire to pay homage to their great predecessor at the place where he died. Such is the veneration of these humble artists for Wilson, that they take the opportunity of depicting at Colomendy an image of Wales, or rather of north Wales, as Wilson usually showed it, with whatever was unromantic hidden from view. Pugh in particular transforms a view which must have been scuffed with the detritus of an industry in recession into one entirely consecrated to Arthur,

to a gentle version of the sublime, and to Wilson himself; a Romantic island in time, sequestered from the economy of modern Wales. He rises above his usual artistic – and social – station to present himself as an artist in something approaching the tradition of Claude Lorrain, to which Wilson himself was affiliated. As if he is twiddling treble and bass controls, Pugh turns down the local to turn up the aesthetic; he is aspiring to project an aesthetic mood rather than mere local information.

Perhaps there is more to say, in this light, about the monument raised over the boundary stone in Pugh's version of the scene. In *Cambria Depicta*, the long eulogy of Wilson which I quoted from in the Introduction, and which culminates in the claim that he was, 'among artists, what a diamond is among gems, *a brilliant of the first water*', was occasioned by a visit to his grave in the churchyard at Mold, which was, Pugh was outraged to discover, nothing but 'a common table monument' (Plate 1.19). 'It is remarkable,' he exclaimed,

Plate 1.19 *The grave of Richard Wilson in Mold churchyard.*

> in a nation pretending to encourage and honour the polite arts, that his remains, for upwards of thirty years, should be so much disregarded as to have no national memorial, no monument of respect, to distinguish them from the ashes of the vulgar. – No! he lies under a plain stone, within the reach of a plebeian's purse.[47]

What would he have thought if it now? It stands isolated in a part of the churchyard converted to a car park, bringing to mind Joni Mitchell, paradise and parking-lots.

Plate 1.20 *S.F. Ravenet after J. Mortimer after Nicolas Poussin,* The Shepherds in Arcadia, *engraving (London: J. Boydell), 1763), London, British Museum.*

group standing before it evokes memories of the motif, familiar to eighteenth-century amateurs of art, 'Et in Arcadia ego.' In this version of the subject by Nicolas Poussin (Plate 1.20), which in Pugh's lifetime was at Devonshire House in Piccadilly and is now at Chatsworth, three shepherds and a river god are gathered before a tomb, one of whom reads out the famously ambiguous phrase inscribed upon it. Perhaps it is death who is imagined to speak: 'I am here, even in Arcadia, where time seems to be suspended.' Or perhaps it is the buried shepherd who warns those left behind: 'I too lived in Arcadia, where time seems to be suspended, but take it from me, it is not.' Either way, if Pugh invites us to understand the arch as a monument to the great painter of the Welsh pastoral landscape, the allusion is thoroughly appropriate, as is the absence of the marks of mining, which, as various Roman poets had explained, became necessary only when the Golden Age enjoyed in Arcadia gave way to the Iron Age. Then the earth ceased to bring forth its fruits spontaneously and had to be cultivated with tools of metal, 'rummaged', as Dryden put it in his translation of Ovid, from the very 'entrails' of the earth.[48]

Barber's son he may have been, but Pugh was perfectly capable of making allusions of this kind. In London the stores of the printsellers were open to him; an engraving of the Devonshire House painting had been published in 1763 by John Boydell, the publisher also of Wilson's six Welsh views, and would very likely have been known to Pugh. More recently, in 1789, John and Josiah Boydell had published another version of the subject, *Shepherds in Arcadia*, engraved by Thomas Kirk after Giovanni Battista Cipriani, in which the shepherds are rather more shocked to discover that death is present in Arcadia than Poussin's had been.

The aggrandizement of the monument in *The View of Foel-Famma*, the conveniently illegible inscription in the aquatint version, the familiar *topos* of travellers stopping to read an inscription, usually an epitaph ('Stop, traveller!'), all suggest that, whether consciously or not, Pugh was making the monument to the decision of the High Court of Exchequer stand also as the 'national memorial' which the nation itself had failed to raise, erected in the spot where Wilson had died. And once it occurs to us to see the arch as a funeral monument, the

Pugh was, as we saw in the Introduction, extraordinarily well read, especially in poetry, and in *Cambria Depicta* he quotes from Dryden's translations both of Ovid's *Metamorphoses*, in which the different ages of the earth were described, and of Virgil, from whom the story of the dead shepherd's tomb originally derived.[49]

But if Wilson is briefly imagined here as a shepherd, he was, to Pugh, a gentleman-shepherd, and it is not at all inappropriate therefore that the travellers standing before his imagined monument (Plates 1.21, 1.22), one reading the inscription, the other pointing at the stone, are themselves gentlemen, not the 'plebeians' from whom Pugh is so anxious to distinguish his great mentor. That the two men are to be taken as gentlemen is given by their dress, the powdered wigs they wear even when out for a walk, perhaps above all by that most conspicuous badge of gentility in the country, their white silk stockings: because the gentlemen men have the privilege of standing on the sunny side of the street, these are easily the whitest and brightest objects in the entire view. Their walking sticks, if not their wigs, suggest they may be on a tour through Wales, though travelling for the most part no doubt by coach – hence the absence of baggage – or they may be visitors at Colomendy. One way or another, they are strangers to the district; though Pugh may privately have intended one of them as himself. Now that he was a professional artist exhibited at the RA he would certainly be dressing as a gentleman, and, as I have already remarked, he liked to appear in his own pictures. Especially if he was thinking of the monument as a memorial, there could be no more appropriate traveller to answer its imagined plea that he should stop and contemplate the life of the man who died here.

Plate 1.21 *(top left)* Detail of plate 1.9.

Plate 1.22 *(bottom left)* Detail of plate 1.1

IV

The woman with the child and donkey, on the dark side of the landscape, is probably the local carrier (Plate 1.23), perhaps the same carrier, operating between Mold and Ruthin, who, in a letter of 1809, Pugh tells us was 'commonly called Jenny', probably by association with her ass.[50] And perhaps the gesture she makes, pointing so emphatically at the group around the monument, suggests a different reading of the conversation, one which might speak more directly to a local, Denbighshire public, and which would make this picture, for them, less an elegy to a dead painter than a satire on the tourists who had become so ubiquitous on the roads of north Wales. It may be that we are to assume that the travellers are Welsh-speakers, enquiring about the monument from a local man who could not at the time be expected to know English. But if the gentleman are taken to be interrogating this man in a language he does not understand, then perhaps Jenny, if it is she, is inviting us – though only if we are Welsh – to join her in ridiculing these overdressed English toffs and their failed attempt to communicate with a local 'plebeian'. In *Cambria Depicta*, Pugh himself sometimes shows a similar disdain for English tourists, especially when they are disdainful of the Welsh poor. This reading may explain why the plebeian himself is accorded a pose of thoroughly patrician dignity, an academy pose even, in what we can read as a riposte to numerous tourist accounts of the supposed slovenliness of the Welsh poor.

The satire, however, if it is there at all, must remain as unobtrusive as possible, so as not to disturb the pastoral mood of the picture, or to alienate potential customers in London and among the English-speaking Welsh gentry. Accordingly, this local man is as comforting in his demeanour as Solkin has suggested Wilson's peasants were. He knows his place, for he has pulled off his hat while the two apparent gentlemen remain covered. In the watercolour he can be seen to be wearing knitted woollen stockings, which point up the smoothness of their silk ones, though unlike them he is wearing buckled shoes, his unslovenly Sunday-best perhaps.[51] He also carries a bag of tools or of kindling on his back. If this man is anything in particular, he may be imagined as the lime-burner, collecting wood to fire his kiln, perhaps an employee of the lord of the manor, or perhaps working for himself but doomed, by the ongoing enclosure of Mold and Llanferres, to lose what he believes is his customary right to burn lime for himself on common land. Or we could think of him as one of the few remaining miners in the area, and an appropriate person therefore to inform the gentlemen about the dispute commemorated on the monument. Either way that bag of something, along with his dress and demeanour, identifies him as some kind of workman who has business in this place, some connection with it that the gentlemen-strangers evidently do not have.

In this man therefore we have found, after all, a *possible* acknowledgement of what had been until recently the main industry of this place: a *possible* miner. Of the Flintshire miners, the picturesque tourist Richard Warner wrote in 1798, 'the nature of their employment is obviously unwholesome . . . their appearance . . . pale, wan, and weakly.'[52] If this man *is* a miner, he looks extraordinarily well and very contented, surprisingly so considering that when the war with France began, the year before this drawing was engraved, the price of lead had crashed; in the first year of the war the export of smelted lead ore declined by 25 per cent.[53] The mines at Maeshafn, a mile to the south of Carreg Carn March Arthur, just about managed to stay open, and miners there who still had employment were earning between 2s. and 3s. a day all year round, as much or more than farmworkers at harvest time; according to Sir Frederic Morton Eden, in 1795 the poor tenant farmers of Llanferres could still sometimes depend on 'the carriage of ore' to make up the rent that they could not pay out of the sale of their produce.[54] But the mines on Cefn Mawr had closed or all but closed. The enclosure and appropriation of common land in the parish of Mold started in 1792, and in Llanferres the next year, and according to Walter Davies, the laid-off miners were saved from destitution only by taking up outdoor work, fencing and hedging the new enclosures.[55]

Many of them must have done this work with the respectful smile of Pugh's worker concealing the fist in their hearts. The enclosures initiated by the large landowners at the outbreak of the war with France met with violent resistance in parts of Flintshire and Denbighshire. Enclosure threatened not only the customary rights of the poor but the homes of squatters, who might be evicted from the homes they or their ancestors had built on common land no matter how long ago. In 1791 an act had been passed for the enclosure of some 4,000 acres of waste in and near the parish of Hope, less than five miles from Mold. The sharp practices of the major landowners and their agents in procuring and executing this act, described in detail by D. G. Evans, provoked in 1793 a popular revolt which began when a new enclosure fence was thrown down by Thomas Jones, a local labourer. He was arrested but soon released from

Flint gaol by protesters who over the next two days threw down all the fences newly erected on the common. Arrests and prosecutions followed, but those found guilty were never punished, and among the reasons for their release, suggests Evans, was the fear of provoking further revolts against the Mold enclosure, and in the forthcoming enclosure of common land in Cilcain and Llanferres. In Hope the enclosure further impoverished the poor, many of whom, like the lead-miners of Llanferres, probably came to be employed in fencing the wastes on which they had previously depended for fuel, lime and grazing.[56]

In March 1794 Sir Watkin Williams Wynn had begun forming a local regiment of fencible cavalry known as the Ancient British Fencibles, and in May the local gentry meeting at Ruthin voted to augment the county militia by one hundred volunteers, and began plans to establish a volunteer force of yeomanry cavalry. One announced aim of these decisions was to keep the poor and disaffected under control, as unemployment and food prices both increased. In Llanferres the amount spent on poor relief went up steadily each year, and by 1795 was 40 per cent higher than it had been in 1792.[57] In the atmosphere of suspicion in north-east Wales in those years, intensified as it must have been by the formation of the loyalist associations we glanced at in the Introduction, any working man keen to avoid trouble would have been well advised to behave towards his superiors as Pugh's does, and any artist courting the patronage of the great landowners of Wales would have been well-advised to show the workers smiling. Among the officers of the new cavalry corps were two of the six gentlemen to whom Pugh dedicated his six prints of Denbighshire, and Edward Lloyd Lloyd, the owner of Pen-y-Lan, the subject of another of the prints, would come

Plate 1.23 *Detail of plate 1.9.*

to command a troop in the Wrexham Yeomanry Cavalry, founded in 1795.[58] This print is inscribed to the Right Honourable Viscount Lord Bulkeley, whose local connections were with Anglesey more than with north-east Wales, and who may have been selected as a dedicatee for some reason to do with Pugh's connection with Anglesey, where he was a frequent visitor. Bulkeley too became the colonel of a volunteer regiment. He had also been proactive in Anglesey in the surveillance of suspected radicals, especially those who he alleged were guilty of listening to Methodist preachers recommending Thomas Paine's *Rights of Man*. He warned the Home Office of such people in October 1792, though he had later to report that in the event there was little evidence of Paineite preaching.[59]

V

Thanks in the first place, probably, to the advent of bicycle tourism, the viewpoint of Pugh's print had an afterlife in the late Victorian and early twentieth-century postcard industry, but with its character changed again. At this time Wilson was only beginning to be rediscovered and the mine-workings are now concealed by the trees which have also shut out the view of Moel Famau. Though some postcards show the monument erected over the boundary stone, it was now the drive to Colomendy, and in particular

the early nineteenth-century lodge, demolished in the 1960s, that was the principal attraction in the scene to tourists, who now came largely from Liverpool and other Lancashire towns and cities (Plates 1.24, 1.25, 1.26). Perhaps it is being read as the isolated, independent freeholder's cottage of Romantic dreams, though in fact it was an example of tied semi-feudal housing for estate-servants and more reminiscent of new housing in the suburbs than old-fashioned and inconvenient farmworkers' dwellings. And perhaps the attraction is also the

County Boundary-Stone, Nr Mold.

fork in the road, the choice, the public highway or the private drive, as it may also be in Pugh's image. My favourites among these cards are a series of autumnal views, probably all by F. H. Haines, a photographer from across the border in Tarporley, Cheshire, in which Pugh's donkey turns up again, I hope in a conscious tribute to his version of the view (Plate 1.27). The photographer hires one, I guess, to carry his equipment over the hills, with the boy as his driver, which is how the boy and his donkey happened to be photographed again, twice, in the same place on a later occasion (Plate 1.28, Plate 1.29), though by this time the boy, now a few inches taller, has a different coat and boots, and a smaller beast to manage.

Plate 1.24 *(opposite)* County Boundary Stone, Nr Mold, *tinted postcard (H. Haines, no postmark), private collection.*

Plate 1.25 *(top right)* The Lodge, Colomendy Hall, near Mold, *tinted postcard (Valentine's, postmarked 1907), private collection.*

Plate 1.26 *(bottom right)* Mold-Ruthin Road, Loggerheads, *postcard (Valentine's, postmarked 1933), private collection.*

The Lodge, Colomendy Hall, near Mold.

MOLD - RUTHIN ROAD, LOGGERHEADS.

"Autumn". Colomendy. Mold.

County Boundary Stone and Cadole. Nr. Mold. (Autumn.)

County Boundary Stone.
Nr The Loggerheads, Mold

Plate 1.27 *(opposite, top) F. H. Haines (?),*
"Autumn". Colomendy. Mold, *postcard, no*
publisher or postmark, Hawarden, Flintshire
Record Office.

Plate 1.28 *(opposite, bottom) F. H. Haines (?),*
County Boundary Stone and Cadole. Nr Mold.
(Autumn), *postcard, no publisher or postmark,*
private collection.

Plate 1.29 *(above) F. H. Haines, photographer*
and publisher, County Boundary Stone, Nr
The Loggerheads, Mold, *no date or postmark,*
private collection.

Notes

1 *CD*, p. 397.

2 *CD*, p. 11.

3 Tony King, 'The Boundary Markers of Llanferres', *Clwyd Historian*, 43 (Autumn 1999) 24–7; *The Boundary Dispute*, educational pamphlet containing primary source materials (Llanferres: Colomendy Centre for Outdoor Education, n.d.) p. 3.

4 [John Broster], *Circular Tour from Chester through North Wales* (London: printed for Crosby & Co. by Broster & Son, Chester, 1802), p. 159; Ian Ousby (ed.), *James Plumptre's Britain: The Journals of a Tourist in the 1790s* (London: Hutchinson, 1992), p. 50.

5 Those entering Wales from Chester are recommended to turn northwestward at Mold or just before for Holywell and St Asaph or Rhuddlan; those entering further south are advised to strike westward at Wrexham for Ruthin and then north to St Asaph or south to Corwen. See Daniel Paterson, *A New and Accurate Description of all the Direct and Principal Cross Roads in England and Wales*, tenth edn (London: Longman, 1794), pp. 121–2, 125–6; John Cary, *Cary's New Itinerary; or, an Accurate Delineation of the Great Roads, both Direct and Cross, throughout England and Wales* (London: John Cary, 1798), pp. 155–6, 645–6; J. Baker, *The Imperial Guide, with Picturesque Plans of the Great Post Roads* (London: C. Whittingham, 1802), vol. 1, pp. 9–10; Henry Penruddocke Wyndham, *A Gentleman's Tour through Monmouthshire and Wales, in the Months of June and July, 1774. A new edition* (London: T. Evans, 1781), p. 220; Edward Lloyd, *A Month's Tour in North Wales, Dublin, and its Environs* (London: G. Kearsly, 1781), pp. 9–21; Alun R. Jones and William Tydeman (eds), J. Hucks, *A Pedestrian Tour through North Wales, in a Series of Letters* (1795) (Cardiff: University of Wales Press, 1979), p. 108. See also the remarks on tourist routes by

D. Michael Francis in Donald Moore (ed.), *The Artist's Journey through North Wales: Clwyd: 18th and 19th century pictures from the National Library of Wales (Bodelwyddan Castle:* Clwyd Fine Arts Trust, n.d.), pp. 3–4.

6 William Gilpin, *Observations on Several Parts of the Counties of Cambridge, Norfolk, Suffolk, and Essex, And on Several Parts of North Wales; relative chiefly to Picturesque Beauty* (London: Cadell and Davies, 1809), pp. 115, 125, 131.

7 For more on Ingleby, see Paul Joyner, *Artists in Wales c. 1740–c. 1851* (Cardiff: University of Wales Press, 1997), p. 54, and the website of the National Library of Wales, *http://www.llgc.org.uk/index.php?id=inglebywatercolours*.

8 Peter Lord, *The Visual Culture of Wales: Imaging the Nation* (Cardiff: University of Wales Press, 2000), p. 135.

9 Pennant, *Literary Life*, 1793, p. 38; Pennant, *Tour*, vol. 1, p. 390. Pennant's tour was in fact made in 1773.

10 For Catherine Jones, see Rosa Baker, 'The Family of Richard Wilson, R.A., and its Welsh Connections', *Flintshire Historical Society Journal* 35 (1999), 85–114, and Rosa Baker and Rosemary Jones, 'The Park and Gardens of Colomendy Hall', *Flintshire Historical Society Journal*, 34 (1996), 33–52.

11 John Britton, *The Fine Arts of the English School* (London: Longman, Hurst, Rees, Orme, and Brown, 1812), p. 64.

12 *CD*, p. 12.

13 My thanks to Achim Timmermann of the University of Michigan for this suggestion.

14 Solkin, *Richard Wilson*, p. 229.

15 King, 'Boundary Markers' p. 25; for the law-suit, see *The Boundary Dispute;* C. J. Williams, 'The Lead Mines of the Alyn Valley', *Flintshire Historical Society Journal*, 29 (1979–80), 53–6, and Cris Ebbs, *Mines & Caves of Loggerheads Country Park* (Llanarmon-yn-ial: Cris Ebbs, 2008) unpaginated.

16 Information from the Metal Mines Survey of the Clwyd-Powys Archaeological Trust, home page *http://www.cpat.org.uk/projects/longer/mines/mines.htm*, accessed 14 July 2008; Williams, 'Lead Mines', and Ebbs, *Mines & Caves*.

17 C. J. Williams, 'The Lead Miners of Flintshire and Denbighshire', *Llafur*, 3 (1980), pt. 2, p. 88. The Lords of Mold had taken out leases on the mines of Mold Mountain from 1718 (see Clwyd Metal Mines Survey, Pantybuarth).

18 Williams, 'The Lead Mines', 64–5, Baker and Jones, 'The Park and Gardens,' 46.

19 Baker and Jones, 'The Park and Gardens,' p. 38.

20 *CD*, p. 429; W. J. Lewis, *Lead Mining in Wales* (Cardiff University of Wales Press, 1967), pp. 138–43; Richard Warner, *A Second Walk through Wales . . . in August and September 1798* (Bath: R. Cruttwell, and London: C. Dilly, 1799), p. 251 (on Llyn-y-Pandy mine, for more on which see below); Williams, 'Lead Mines', 68.

21 See Aubrey Strahan, *The Geology of the Neighbourhoods of Flint, Mold, and Ruthin* (London: HMSO, 1890) pp. 189–90.

22 Email to the author, 28 August 2008. For images of horse-whims, see C. J. Williams, *Metal Mines of North Wales: A Collection of Pictures* (Wrexham: Bridge Books, 1997), plates 7 and 8, and Lord, *The Visual Culture of Wales: Industrial Society* (Cardiff: University of Wales Press, 1998), pp. 27 (Sandby), 28 (Ibbetson), 35 (Hassell).

23 *CD*, p. 11.

24 The change in the wording of the inscription from watercolour to aquatint is an epitome of the story of the antiquarianization of the Welsh landscape told by Rod Jones in his essay 'Out of the Past: Pictures in Theory and History', in Tony Curtis (ed.), *Wales: The*

Imagined Nation. Studies in Cultural and National Identity (Bridgend: Poetry Wales Press, 1986), pp. 261–85.

25 Email to the author, 28 August 2008.

26 See Strahan, *Geology*, p. 225.

27 See Bryn Ellis, 'Limestone Quarrying in North-east Wales before 1900', *Welsh History Review*, 18/1 (June 1996), 130.

28 Ebbs, *Mines & Caves*.

29 See the map made in connection with the law-suit in *The Boundary Dispute*, p. 5, the enclosure map for Llanferres and Cilcain, Denbighshire Record Office DRO PD/57/1/99, and the enclosure map for Mold, Flintshire Record Office, QS/DE/9.

30 The noticeboard on the postcard 'Mold – Ruthin Road, Loggerheads (Plate 1.26), declares that 'motors can be taken to top of rock at owner's risk.'

31 Broster, *Circular Tour*, p. 159.

32 Williams, 'Lead Mines', pp. 79–80.

33 See Williams, 'Lead Mines', pp. 64–5.

34 Lord, *Visual Culture* (1998), p. 14.

35 George Kay, *General View of the Agriculture of Flintshire* ([Edinburgh: printed by John Moir, 1794]), pp. 23–4.

36 Walter Davies, *General View of the Agriculture and Domestic Economy of North Wales* (London: Richard Phillips, 1810), p. 55.

37 Derrick Pratt and A. G. Veysey, *A Handlist of the Topographical Prints of Clwyd (Denbighshire, Flintshire and Edeyrnion* (Hawarden: Clwyd Record Office, 1977), p. 7.

38 These are briefly discussed by Celina Fox, *The Arts of Industry in the Age of Enlightenment* (New Haven and London: Yale University Press, 2010), pp. 401–2.

39 Lord, *Visual Culture* (1998), p. 53.

40 Hucks, *A Pedestrian Tour*, pp. 70, 7.

41 Williams, 'Lead Mines', pp. 65–6. Pugh may have visited these mines briefly in the mid-1800s: see *CD*, p. 12.

42 Williams, 'Lead Mines', caption to plate I, opposite p. 64.

43 See Williams, 'Lead Mines', pp. 67–9, and for Wilkinson, see Norbert C. Soldon, *John Wilkinson 1728–1808, English Ironmaster and Inventor* (Lewiston NY, Queenston Ontario and Lampeter: Edwin Mellen, 1998); for Wilkinson's lead interests, see pp. 295–310. Ingleby's image is briefly discussed by Fox, *The Arts of Industry*, p. 402.

44 See Warner, *A Second Walk*, pp. 249–53

45 For Pugh on Parys mountain, see *CD*, pp. 46–7.

46 *CD*, pp. 47.

47 *CD*, p. 344–5.

48 See *Ovid's Metamorphoses in Fifteen Books. Translated by the most eminent Hands* (London: Jacob Tonson, 1717), p. 7.

49 See Virgil, *Eclogues* 5: 42–4, and *CD*, pp. 78 and 108.

50 This letter, from Pugh to Thomas Lloyd of Tre'r Beirdd, Mold, and dated 10 March 1809, is in a collection of MSS associated with Richard Llwyd at the National Library of Wales (NLW MS 1562C). I am grateful to Elizabeth Edwards of the Centre for Advanced Welsh Studies at the National Library for finding it.

51 I am grateful to Marcia Pointon for drawing my attention to this man's footwear. It is only in the watercolour that the workman wears buckled shoes, and the gentleman nearest to him wears laced shoes; in the print, though it is too ill defined for me to be certain, they appear to have swapped footwear.

52 Warner, *A Second Walk*, p. 218.

53 Soldon, *John Wilkinson*, p. 299.

54 Sir Frederic Morton Eden, *The State of the Poor: or, an History of the Labouring Classes in England*, 3 vols (London: B. and J. White et al., 1797), vol. 3, pp. 887–9.

55 Davies, *General View*, p. 58; Samuel Lewis, *A Topographical Dictionary of Wales* (London, S. Lewis, 1849), pp. 124–9.

56 Evans, 'The Hope Enclosure Act,' pp. 161–86.

57 Tim Jones, *Rioting in North East Wales 1536–1918* (Wrexham: Bridge Books, 1997), pp. 30–5; Colonel Ll. E. S. Parry and Engineer Lieutenant B. F. M. Freeman, *Historical Records of the Denbighshire Hussars Imperial Yeomanry* (Wrexham: Woodall, Minshall and Co., 1909), p. 5; Eden, *The State of the Poor*, vol. 3, p. 888.

58 Parry and Freeman, *Historical Records*, chs 1 and 2, and Appendix 4.

59 *CD*, p. 79 (Pugh and Anglesey); pp. 90–1 (Bulkeley and 'the volunteers of Beaumaris'); Davies, 'Loyalism in Wales', pp. 705–6.

TWO *Llanfwrog, Ruthin, and Llanbedr*

I

Llanfwrog, the subject of the next of the six Denbighshire views, is about three-quarters of a mile south-west of Ruthin, measured from parish church to parish church (Plate 2.1). With St Mwrog's conspicuous on its raised knoll, the village has retained a separate identity even though it has been linked to Ruthin, at least since Pugh's time, by a nearly continuous line of ribbon development. It seems however to have been invisible to late eighteenth- and early nineteenth-century artists and writers of travel diaries, and I have found no images or extended descriptions of Llanfwrog among the works of Pugh's contemporaries. For Pugh, it must have been his intense familiarity with a place so close to home – less than a mile from his mother's house in Well Street – that made it a subject worth depicting, of which more later. But in order to increase its interest for others he had slightly to distort the topography of the Vale of Clwyd. He has conflated the views from two different viewpoints. One was probably in the garden of Ty Gwyn, on the south side of the village street; the house belonged to Lord Bagot, to whom the print is 'respectfully inscribed'. Bagot was governor and guardian of a range of almhouses next door to Ty Gwyn, founded a century earlier by his ancestor Lady Jane Bagot; his family had owned nearby Pool Park, a mile or so south-west of Llanfwrog, since 1723.[1] From this position St Peter's at Ruthin, which Pugh shows just to the left of St Mwrog's, is

in fact entirely obscured behind St Mwrog's knoll; late Victorian and early twentieth-century postcard views, in order to include both churches, had to be taken from several hundred yards to the north (Plate 2.2). To see the hump of Foel Fenlli however rising high over the parish church as Pugh shows it, he needed a second viewpoint fifty or so yards further down the road from St Mwrog's, which is where the photograph of this view is taken (Plate 2.3). From either position, a lumberjack with a chainsaw would quickly reveal, all more or less where Pugh locates them, the site of the now disused church at Llanbedr, the old Llanbedr Hall, then the seat of Edward Thelwall, and the Bwlch Penbarras, towards which we can see the old road winding over the hill on its way to Carreg Carn March Arthur and Mold.

The village itself has changed little enough to be still clearly recognizable from Pugh's print. The Cross Keys Inn, now just across the road from the church, is shown by Pugh as at that time occupying a house known as Glan yr Afon on the north side of the street. A few yards to the right of the flat footbridge linking the front garden path of the pub to the village street is the confluence of two streams (they cannot both be seen in the print) into Ffrwd Arvon, 'the Rivulet

Plate 2.1 *(opposite) William Ellis after Edward Pugh,* Llanfwrog, Ruthin and Llanbedr, *aquatint (London: E. Pugh, 1794), first issue, private collection.*

that runneth through Mwrog Street', which meets the river Clwyd at Pont Howkin in Ruthin.[2] Pugh shows the stream getting wider and shallower as it passes between Ty Gwyn and Glan yr Afon, forming a watersplash across the street: a result no doubt of the fact that, as Arnold Hughes has pointed out to me, there are signs that the road was formerly a good deal lower than it is now. Whether or not this watersplash appeared only after heavy rain, and whether it survived the enclosure of 1800–5, is not clear: the enclosure map shows the watercourse confined to the north side of the street, but with a space on the south side which may have accommodated the occasional overflowing of its banks.[3] In front of the church the picturesque cottage of Brynffynnon is still there today, still in front of a fenced tract of pasture which

in Pugh's time was the property of Sir Watkin Williams Wynn, as was much of the land on the south side of the street. Two things in the landscape continue to puzzle me. One is the small cattle-pound or large water-tank or whatever else it is between Brynffynnon and the stream. In the 1826 map of Ruthin a smithy is shown as occupying this spot; but I have no firm opinion as to the function of the construction as depicted by Pugh. The other is the semi-rectangular shape, like a hand-basin in profile, that appears below what I take to be a footbridge crossed by the bent old man with a stick. I have no idea what it represents.

William, first Baron Bagot of Bagot's Bromley in Staffordshire, was 'a firm Tory, and ever a most zealous supporter of Church and King', so his son informs us. From 1754 until his ennoblement in 1780 he had been Tory MP for that county, which, according to T. H. B. Oldfield's contemporary analysis of parliamentary constituencies, was 'entirely under the direction of aristocratic influence', in the shape of Bagot himself and the Marquis of Stafford.[4] But 'though frequently and anxiously pressed' by Lords Bute and North, he 'invariably refused all offers of place and preferment' and left little mark on history.[5] In the Lords, his great zeal against the Whigs led him to break off his political connection with Lord North when the latter went into coalition with Charles James Fox, and, though initially suspicious of William Pitt, in his last years he evinced 'unbounded confidence in that wonderful Minister'.[6] Bagot had no great interest in his Pool Park estate: he regarded Blythfield in Staffordshire as his main residence, and Bachymbyd, a few miles north of Ruthin, as his principal seat in Wales. But he visited his Welsh properties rarely, and probably not at all in the years between the publication of this print and his death in 1798. The family's connection with Wales was chiefly

Plate 2.2 Ruthin from Llanfwrog, *tinted postcard (no publisher or postmark), private collection.*

20972   Ruthin from Llanfwrog.

maintained by Lord Bagot's position as one of the vice-presidents (along with Viscount Bulkeley and Sir Watkin) of the Welsh Charity school, which held its meetings in London, and by his brother Lewis, who was bishop of St Asaph from 1790 until 1802. Pugh probably caught up with Bagot, to secure him as a subscriber, in London; if in Wales, perhaps with the help of the bishop, who appears in Pugh's list of patrons in his original advertisement for the *Six Views*, but to whom no plate was inscribed.

Occasionally in the course of his political career events moved Bagot to the writing of enthusiastic anti-Whig verse. During the illness of George III in 1788–89, for example, he wrote a Horatian ode deploring the 'dark schemes' of the Whigs who were attempting to establish the Prince of Wales as Regent so that Fox could succeed Pitt as prime minister. He spatters their names with angry dashes, 'W—d—m', 'S—r—n', 'L—b—h', 'F—;' and, worst of all, 'B—ke', who, arguing in the Commons for the king to give way to his son, had 'impiously averr'd', Bagot snarled, 'That – "*God had hurl'd him down*."'[7] Four years later, following the execution of Louis XVI, he composed a longer, angrier ode, and a more explicit one, for so black were the crimes of the Jacobins that they had forfeited the right to have their names half-disguised with dashes: Robespierre, Marat, Egalité, Danton, Dumourier, Pétion, Dupont, Santerre and Condorcet suffer the indignity of having their names spelled out in full, and are denounced as monsters beyond any that history can show. Their teachers, Bagot sang or rather shouted, were no better – Voltaire! Rousseau! Helvétius! Raynal! Mirabeau! D'Alembert! Montesquieu! – each is provided by Bagot with his own individual mark of exclamation and infamy. For their 'New Philosophy' had sown the seeds of 'preposterous anarchy',

Which, bursting into monstrous birth,
Now shake the nations of the earth,
With universal War;

Plate 2.3 *Llanfwrog from one of the viewpoints used by Pugh, 2011.*

– but which, Bagot tells them, in an enjoyably ironic final stanza, have no chance of germinating on this side of the Channel. For 'you', he explains, 'are French Philosophers!' whereas in Britain we are kept secure by 'Paine, Priestley, Price and P—r!!!'[8] It adds much to the aristocratic loyalism enunciated in these verses that Bagot shows himself to be thoroughly, even affectedly conservative in pronunciation as in politics: 'war' rhyming with 'Parr', for example, or 'late' with 'seat', or (a Churchillian note, this) 'Montesquieu' with 'you'. In short, such were Bagot's politics that he was one of the last people to whom Pugh should have dedicated this print, or looked to for patronage; for, as we shall see, it was not at all likely to have pleased him. But probably he never so much as glanced at it, and it was as well for Pugh if he did not inspect it too closely.

II

The coloured versions of this print (Plate 2.4) are all blueish green and greenish blue, some with a pale violet, some with a sienna wash on the mountain, and the thinnest of light red washes on the roofs and road. The effect is as harmonious as life in this quiet village might be imagined to be, an effect which seems to mute even the melancholy image of the three figures in the foreground. By choosing a low viewpoint, from where almost nothing of the famous beauty of the Vale of Clwyd can be seen, Pugh was deliberately directing attention to those three foreground figures. The depth of their melancholy is more apparent in uncoloured versions of the print, closer to what would have been the grisaille of Pugh's original drawing, except that in the plate the acid has been allowed to bite deep enough to create stronger contrasts of black and white than in the other five views or in Pugh's surviving grisailles. In the uncoloured version especially, our eyes are drawn immediately to the nearly black, almost spectral figure in the centre, a near-silhouette but with soft edges, apparently a mother, wrapped in a shawl and clutching a baby (Plate 2.5). She looms out of a foreground in the deep shadow thrown by the dark cloud sweeping across Foel Fenlli.

The intensity of her suffering would have been apparent, to adepts in the theory of art, from the very fact that we cannot see her face – that she is turned away from us in the method recommended by some, but not all critics of art, in the late eighteenth century. The question of how to represent the extremes of grief was debated, by Sir Joshua Reynolds and Henry Fuseli among others, in relation to a lost painting of the sacrifice of Iphigenia by the ancient Greek artist Timanthes, of which a version, probably based on the original, was discovered in the House of the Tragic Poet at Pompeii (Plate 2.6). Timanthes, we learn from Pliny, chose to conceal Agamemnon's grief at the sacrifice of his daughter by veiling his face, and was praised by Pliny for thus acknowledging that it would have been impossible to paint Agamemnon's expression, that he was obliged to leave us to imagine his face contorted in grief. In veiling the father's face, Timanthes was veiling the limits of his art.[9] Not so, argued Reynolds; he was in fact revealing his own incapacity, for nothing was beyond the limits of art: a great painter would have known how to paint the father's grief in all its extremity.[10] But not, retorted Fuseli, in such a way as to compel our sympathy: Agamemnon's grief could certainly have been represented, but not with 'dignity', not with 'propriety'. 'Timanthes', he wrote, 'had too true a sense of nature to expose a father's feelings or to tear a passion to rags.'[11] Fuseli here was following the argument of the German critic and dramatist Gotthold Ephraim Lessing, in his essay on the limits of poetry and painting, the *Laocoon*. 'Timanthes', wrote Lessing, 'knew the limits within which the Graces had confined his art. He knew that the grief which became Agamemnon, as a father, must have been expressed

Plate 2.4 *(opposite) William Ellis after Edward Pugh,* Llanfwrog, Ruthin and Llanbedr, *coloured aquatint (London: E. Pugh, 1794), first issue, Aberystwyth, National Library of Wales.*

Plate 2.5 *Detail of plate 2.1.*

by contortions, at all times ugly.' In what he calls 'its disfiguring violence', Agamemnon's expression would have become 'horrible', something from which 'we gladly avert our eyes, for the sight of pain excites discomfort unless the beauty of the suffering subject changes that discomfort into the sweet emotion of compassion.'[12]

And for Fuseli, as for Lessing, it was the capacity of the image of suffering to arouse the sympathy, the compassion of the spectator that should give the rule here. Some years before Reynolds had discussed the painting of Iphigenia, the critic Daniel Webb had argued that Timanthes' decision to leave

Agamemnon's feelings 'entirely to our imagination' was more than a matter of tact; it was a 'stroke of ingenuity'. For it obliges us as spectators to fix our attention instead on the expressions of the other characters in the picture, and thus to rise 'from the real to a conception of the imaginary'.[13] This notion, as Webb called it, of a 'gradation in the expressions' by Timanthes,[14] was described rather more deftly by Fuseli: Timanthes, he argued, had communicated the depths of Agamemnon's suffering, by 'showing ... in the faces of the assistant mourners, *the reason why that of the principal* one, *was hid*'.[15] Fuseli believed that the rapidly mobile expressions of great suffering became grotesque when frozen into the synchronic imagery of the visual arts, and should be read only as reflected in the faces of those responding with less volatile looks of sympathy to the agony of the principal figure.[16] In accord with this notion we read this poor woman's unbearable anguish in Pugh's picture not in her own face but in the sympathetic expressions of Pugh's 'assistant mourners', the young gentleman-farmer (as he seems to be) and his wife, whose sympathy may be registered also by whatever it is she is holding – a handkerchief, to dry her tears? a purse, to offer alms? Following Fuseli, we know the mother's anguish is unbearable precisely *because* it is not directly exhibited to us.

Much more than any other figure in Pugh's six views, this woman will not let us see her as a mere figure in the landscape; she belongs in a narrative, she has a story to tell if she should choose to tell it, and her presence in the picture seems to challenge us to imagine what it might be. One possibility is that Pugh's image alludes to a fairy-tale collected by Elias Owen, the vicar of Llanyblodwel, a mile or so over the English border near Oswestry. He heard it from the curate of Clocaenog, some three miles from Pugh's viewpoint, who had it from Evan Roberts, 'an aged farmer' of Llanfwrog, and he published it in 1896 as the 'Llanfwrog Changeling Legend'. It told of a poor mother whose baby was stolen by the fairies while she was gleaning. 'At the time, the mother did not notice any difference between her own child and the one that took its place, but after awhile she observed with grief that the baby she was

Plate 2.6 *After Timanthes (?),* The Sacrifice of Iphigenia, *fresco, Naples, Museo Archaeologico, from the House of the Tragic Poet, Pompeii.*

nursing did not thrive, nor did it grow, nor would it try to walk.' Her neighbours advised her to try to recover it by a complicated procedure that involved brewing beer in an eggshell, but Roberts knew no more of the story than this, and in an attempt to give it some sort of an ending, Owen related it to 'a certain form of incantation' which, he tells us, 'was resorted to in Wales to reclaim children from the fairies'. The mother was to carry the changeling to a river in the company of a conjurer, and after uttering the brief incantation was to throw the child into the river. On returning home 'she would there find her own child safe and sound'.[17]

It might just be possible to read the picture as an illustration of this legend; the mother would be carrying the changeling to the watersplash, though it is hardly a river, where she will meet the conjurer, though the only available candidate for this role seems to be limping off towards Ruthin as if anxious to avoid her. But what makes this unlikely to be the story Pugh has in mind, even if he happened to know it, is that there is no apparent association between Llanfwrog and the part of the tale he would have been illustrating; and yet without such an association, the picture might not have made much sense even to anyone in the village itself who happened to see the print. To the enormous majority of those who saw it, the woman's story, if this was it, would have been entirely unknown.

As we saw in the Introduction, Pugh seems to have spent his summers in Ruthin, where he would have caught up with the news of the region disseminated in the Chester newspapers, in which he advertised his 'six views in Denbighshire' and announced his presence in the city when he stayed there in search of customers. Though the view of Llanfwrog was not delivered to those who had

made advance orders for the series until the first days of October 1794,[18] it was dated to July of that year, and must have been conceived at least a few weeks or months before that. On 14 March, probably about a week or so before Pugh reached Ruthin, with the war just over a year old and going very badly for Britain and her allies, the *Chester Chronicle* published a poem entitled 'The Horrors of War' by the United Irishman Thomas Russell, who would be executed by the British in 1803. The editor, William Cowdroy, introducing what he described as this 'beautiful and energetic fragment of a poem', informed his readers that it

wants no words to recommend it to the heart of sensibility. It is on a subject that demands no aid or embellishment from poetic fiction – the truth or the horrors which it delineates, setting all the romance of rhime, and the descriptive powers of the pen, at defiance.

'Too much of human carnage have I seen,' the fragment began, and after a few lines began to list the victims of the war with France:

Lo! Now methinks I see before mine eyes,
The ravages of war – . . .
I see the widow'd mother, frantic, wild,
Clasp to her throbbing breast her infant child;
I see the little prattling babe bewail,
He scarce knows what – in th' unnatural tale;
Who kill'd his father, asks – and is he dead?
He is – she cries . . .[19]

The previous summer, at a time when publishers were being intimidated all over Britain by prosecution and the threat of prosecution for seditious

libel, the intrepid Cowdroy had published two other poems protesting against the war, both by local writers. The self-effacing 'Bardulus' of Nantwich contributed some 'Occasional Stanzas' in which he asked:

what opiate balm can soothe the sigh
Of orphans mourning o'er a parent's bier?
Or who, while manly sorrow dims his eye,
Suppress the widow's agonizing tear?[20]

It was particularly brave of Cowdroy to publish 'War, A Fragment', by R. Jones of Altrincham. It concentrated chiefly on the innocent victims, civilians and unwilling combatants alike, whose death was as much worth lamenting – at least as much – as that of the 'guilty *Monarch*' who had ordained the war. It can have escaped prosecution as a seditious libel only because it managed deliberately to confuse George III and Louis XVI, so that it would have been just about possible to argue in court that the guilty king was Louis, not George. But like Russell's and Bardulus's poems it also lamented 'the helpless orphan's cry' and 'the widow'd matron's groan'.[21]

Early in January 1794, three weeks before Pugh advertised his six views in the *Chronicle*, an article by 'G. Burgess, B.A.' invited its readers to imagine the state of affairs 'at the conclusion of a spirited and long-contested war.' 'There is', he said,

scarcely a cottage to be met with that does not bear visible marks of its fruits. In one miserable hut you may behold, seated at their scanty meal, a mother and her circle of half-starved children; but father you will find none; Death met him in the field of battle, and, in a moment, made *his children fatherless, and his wife a widow*.[22]

And throughout the early months of the war, the *Chronicle* published stories of the victims of the war at home, in Manchester, in Norwich, and elsewhere. 'The ravages of war', began one, 'are not solely confined to those fields of blood where the death-awakening trumpet sounds to the charge.' Equally distressing are the sufferings of the 'starving poor' at home, thrown out of work and crammed into workhouses. 'The war has not yet raged *six months*; we defy it to last as many *years* – for long ere that period, unless its career be speedily checked, Britain (notwithstanding its vaunted constitution) will be an Orphan-house, and a Home for Widows!'[23] In short, by the time Pugh's print appeared, in the second year of a so far thoroughly unsuccessful war for the British, the poor woman dressed in black would almost certainly have been read as a poor war widow with her child, not least by those around Pugh's home town who regularly saw the *Chronicle*, and that was probably the great majority of those who read English.

So relentless was Cowdroy's opposition to the war that a month after the print of Llanfwrog was published, he received an anonymous threatening letter which he published in the *Chronicle*. Addressed to 'Mr. Cowdroy, at Mr. Fletcher's, printer, Chester', it read:

Knowing you to be a cursed Jacobin I beg to inform you that it is my intention to shoot you the first time I see you out at night therefore be careful of yourself.

I am,
Yours,
A Detester of all Democrats
Christlington, Nov. 5, 1794.   Julias Percian

I have been in your company frequently at Flookersbrook, where I have heard you discourse on politics.[24]

No doubt reckoning that a fanatic intent on assassination would not take such trouble to warn his victim, or give so broad a clue as to how he might be traced, Cowdroy responded by continuing to print anti-war propaganda, including, before the end of 1794, an essay by Anna Barbauld and a poem by the immensely popular love poet, now radical, Robert Merry.

In the same month, July 1794, as this print was originally intended to be published, the republican Joseph Hucks, touring north Wales with Samuel Taylor Coleridge, remarked on the poor women and children in the manufacturing town of Holywell who were 'half starving, whilst their husbands, fathers, and brothers, are gloriously signalizing themselves in the service of their country'.[25] Hucks, a member of Catharine Hall, Cambridge, was no doubt emboldened to include such a seditious notion in his published tour by the example of William Frend, a fellow of Jesus College, Cambridge where Coleridge was an undergraduate. Early in 1793 Frend had published a pamphlet entitled *Peace and Union recommended to the associated bodies of Republicans and Anti-Republicans.* It included, in an appendix, an essay entitled 'The Effect of War on the Poor', in which Frend focused on the plight of women wool-spinners in Cambridgeshire whose meagre wages had been reduced by a quarter in anticipation of a slump in demand occasioned by the imminent war, which would also, Frend argued, inevitably increase the price of bread.[26] For publishing this pamphlet, Frend was tried before a university court, and though the

charge against him alleged that he had impugned the established Church and its clergy (Frend was a Unitarian), the prosecution found occasion to make much of the essay on the poor, though irrelevant to the charge. In his summing-up at the end of the trial, Dr Isaac Milner, the vice-chancellor of the university, asked whether, 'at such a critical time as this' the author had taken care in his pamphlet to 'exhort the lower ranks of the people to be patient and submissive in bearing the additional burthens which might be necessary to repel by force, the unjust attacks of an outrageous and insolent enemy?'[27] It was a question expecting the answer 'no'. This controversy, which received wide publicity in the newspapers, is an important part of the context in which Pugh's image would have been interpreted.[28]

Two months before Frend's trial, the Treasury-funded newspaper the *Sun*, on hearing that Frend was considering issuing a second edition of his pamphlet, dared him to reprint the appendices, which had been removed from some copies of the first.[29] Unwilling to be intimidated by a paper always eager to sniff out sedition, Frend promptly obliged, and whether with or without his permission the appendix on the effects of the war on the poor also appeared as a clandestinely published three-page pamphlet.[30] At his trial, Frend, with the vocal encouragement of Coleridge in the gallery, defended himself bravely, even audaciously, but in May 1793, after refusing to sign a recantation written for him by the university authorities, he was banished from the university. 'The Rev. William Frend', expostulated Cowdroy in the *Chester Chronicle*, 'has been expelled the University of Cambridge, for writing a pamphlet called Peace and Union, on the horrid impolicy and injustice

of war!!'[31] Inevitably the case focused attention on exactly what the government would rather had remained obscure, the suffering of women victims of the war on the home front.

A Cambridge clergyman called William Firth now did his best to conceal it again – and to ingratiate himself at the same time with the Cambridge hierarchy – by publishing a sermon 'intended to have been preached before the vice-chancellor' on 28 February 1794. Four days earlier, a satirical contribution to the London *Morning Chronicle*, early in 1794, supposedly by a clergyman advising other clergy on how to discuss the war in their sermons without risking their chances of preferment, laid down as the very first rule that, 'whereas some pious and well-meaning Clergymen might (as Ministers of the Gospel of Peace) naturally be led . . . to lament the miseries of war . . . you must on the contrary carefully avoid touching on such topics.'[32] As if he had taken this advice thoroughly to heart, Firth warned against listening to so-called 'philanthropists', who 'stunned our ears with the suppositious cries of widows and orphans' when in fact, he assured the vice-chancellor, the evils of war were very much exaggerated.[33] This sermon may in turn have inspired Hucks's poem 'The Philanthropist', eventually published in 1798, in which he returned to the effect of war on poor womenfolk, and complained that 'The cries of orphans, and the widow's tears' were unheard by the rich and the powerful.[34]

The motif of the war widow and child would become increasingly common, in poetry though not in pictures, as the war dragged on. In the first two years of the war we find the motif for example in the 'Hymn for the Fast Day' of February 1794 by James Montgomery of the Sheffield Society for

Constitutional Information,[35] which was reprinted in the *Chester Chronicle* and partially translated into Welsh by Tomos Glyn Cothi, the radical Unitarian minister Thomas Evans.[36] We find it too in the publications of other notorious reformers like the Jacobin writers and booksellers Thomas Spence and Daniel Isaac Eaton, and the self-styled *sans-culottes* John Thelwall;[37] and it is not quite a coincidence, given the times, given the politics of the *Chronicle*, that in the column next to Russell's poem there appeared an account of the trial of Eaton for publishing a famous fable told by Thelwall of a game-cock, who tyrannized over the other fowl of the farmyard, and, like Louis XVI, had to be decapitated for the sake of the public safety.[38] Later in the decade we associate the motif with Wordsworth, in poems such as 'The Female Vagrant' and 'The Ruined Cottage'. If the woman was not always a widow, she had been left destitute when her husband had enlisted, or been balloted or pressed, into the armed services, was now God knows where, and, if alive, was without the possibility of supporting her or her children.

But the motif of the mother, widowed or left to fend for herself and her children, was found only in poetry and prose written in opposition to the war, and almost never appears, so far as I know, in the writings of loyalists at this time. I have found it only in loyalist publications produced at the very start of the war, mainly by writers in the provinces and perhaps out of touch with the government line, and before there had been any, or many, actual casualties.[39] Radical writers like Russell, and like this print by Pugh, contrast the violence and suffering of war with the supposed harmony, peace and plenty of the countryside before the war began, when, Russell continues,

— the rustic plow
Prepar'd the glebe, and golden crops of grain
Wav'd to the sickle of the reaper train.
The grateful peasant view'd his little hoard,
And pleasure crown'd his hospitable board(.)[40]

For loyalist writers in general, the effects of the war on country life seem to have been as invisible and inaudible as Hucks suggests, as if the countryside in the 1790s was to be preserved as an image of the peaceful life Britain was fighting to protect and restore, or of the contentment the poor supposedly enjoyed or should be taught to believe they enjoyed even in times of great hardship. Or it might remain the image of privacy and retirement, of a space and a life away from political conflict, but now with the implied suggestion that the life of its inhabitants remained entirely undisturbed by shortages, by high prices and the withdrawal they encouraged from the moral economy, by the organized political agitation that was becoming a characteristic not only of large towns and cities but of the country also, by recruitment into the army and the militia, and by the absence and death of men enlisted.[41]

When in January 1795 William Hodges, the artist of Cook's second voyage to the South Pacific, exhibited a pair of paintings, *The Effects of Peace* and *The Consequences of War*, the Duke of York, son of the king and the twice-defeated commander-in-chief of the British army that had just fled from northern Europe, demanded the closure of the exhibition and effectively ended Hodges's career (Plate 2.7).[42] In the same month the caricaturist James Gillray published a print that contrasted 'The Blessings of Peace', imagined as the comforts of a yeoman's family before the war, and 'The Curses of War' – the same family after a French raid on the coast, the

father bayonetted, his wife and daughter raped and distraught, an infant son bewildered (Plate 2.8). The loyalist Crown and Anchor Association, which had commissioned the image, seems to have refused to pay him.[43] For loyalists, the victims of war at home were not to be represented, just as the Bush administration prevented TV news from showing the arrival in the US of the coffins of soldiers who died in Iraq. It was not of course those flag-draped boxes that had to be hidden, but the widowed spouses, partners, orphans, parents, weeping inconsolably.

In the light of the evident support for the war against France on display in *Cambria Depicta*, it is perhaps surprising to find Pugh, in this aquatint, apparently identifying himself as an opponent of that war, and employing a motif used by Thomas Russell, and also by campaigners for universal manhood suffrage such as Eaton, already twice acquitted for publishing seditious libels, and Thelwall and Spence who, at the time this print appeared, were in prison awaiting trial for high treason. And it is no less surprising that he should dedicate the print to Lord Bagot, who, though he almost never spoke in Parliament, was well known to be a supporter of the war, and contributed loyally and generously to subscriptions for the clothing and arming of the militia.[44] By the time *Cambria Depicta* was published, however, most of those who had opposed the war against the French Republic were fervent supporters of the war against the French Empire – the invasion scare of 1798 had seen to that – and it is perfectly possible that in the mid-1790s Pugh had been more in sympathy with the position of the radicals and the Foxite Whigs, that Britain had no business interfering in the internal affairs of France, and no justification for fighting a war the aim of which was to restore the Bourbon monarchy apparently against the wishes

Plate 2.7 *Thomas Medland after William Hodges,*
The Consequences of War, *coloured aquatint
(no publication details, 1795?), private collection.*

of the majority of the French people. Even at the end of his life, in *Cambria Depicta*, Pugh professed his admiration for 'the worthy proprietor of the Chester Chronicle', John Fletcher, who had been responsible for the Foxite politics of the newspaper in the mid-1790s.[45] In publishing his six views of Denbighshire, however, he was appealing to the rich and uniformly loyalist landowners of Wales for their support and patronage; as a portrait-miniaturist he depended on the good will of the north Welsh gentry for many of his commissions, and can have had no interest in alienating them by what they might interpret as an expression of disloyalty.

So what was Pugh doing, publishing this view of Llanfwrog? Perhaps he did not realize that the *Chronicle* was treading a path that might end in a charge of seditious libel; after all, the Tory squirearchs and their lawyers were still apparently happy to insert in the paper notices of planned enclosures, of gatherings of the militia regiments, lists of those eligible to shoot game, and so on. There was no gentry boycott of the paper, no sign that Tory advertisers were abandoning it for the more loyal but less readable *Chester Courant*. Or perhaps Pugh did not realize, as a few months later Gillray and Hodges evidently did not, that an informal censorship of images was beginning to operate, not unlike the direct censorship by which pamphlets and newspapers were already being policed by the loyalist associations, which would brand images of the victims of war, of its 'curses' and violent 'consequences', as unpatriotic, or, as 'being of a political tendency', as Joseph Farington delicately put it of Hodges's paintings.[46] It may have been just as well that Pugh's print appeared before Hodges's did, and as one of a series in which, as we shall see, no other more radical sentiment appeared than support for the paternalist moral economy, and which represented itself as no more than a collection of rural views.

But just perhaps the image was intended to be read as having exactly the 'political tendency' I have attributed to it. In the countryside and small towns of Wales there was no great enthusiasm for the war with France, which threatened the male population with enlistment, more or less compulsory, in the militia, the army or the navy, and at a time of rapidly increasing food prices could take the chief breadwinner away from his family. By 1796 in north

Plate 2.8 *James Gillray,* The Blessings of Peace/ The Curses of War, *aquatint (London: H. Humphrey, 1795), private collection.*

Wales the militia amounted to 1,500 men, exclusive of officers, and militiamen were coming under increasing pressure to transfer to the regular army, which could mean active service abroad. Reluctance to enlist, sometimes downright resistance to enlistment, had been apparent in Wales from the earliest months of the war. In Denbighshire the high degree of the hostility to enlistment would become clear in April 1795, when by the terms of the Navy and Militia Acts, passed the previous month, the county was required to send seventy-five men to join the fleet, and to ballot additional men for the militia. This led to a riot at Denbigh in which the local magistrates were forced, under duress, to sign statements that they would not enforce the acts, now or in the future.[47] One JP, John Lloyd, even managed to persuade himself that the revolt was part of the supposed nation-wide revolutionary conspiracy master-minded by the popular radicals in London, who a few months earlier had been tried – and acquitted – on a charge of high treason.[48] The anti-enlistment riot soon turned into a food riot, as did a similar disturbance in Mold, and a sort of peace was not restored until the end of the month, when units of the Cardigan militia and of the Somerset Cavalry were stationed in Denbigh, Mold and Ruthin.[49]

Prominent among this and other revolts and disturbances in Wales in the revolutionary and Napoleonic wars were the artisans and tradesmen of country towns, the very class from which Pugh had sprung.[50] Even if Pugh believed that the war with France was just and necessary, he could hardly not have understood and sympathized with his friends and neighbours in Ruthin who knew that the augmentation of the armed services would plunge families into poverty, and would lead to the augmentation, also, of the number of widows and orphans. Perhaps in this aquatint he deliberately risked suggesting as much.

But then again – perhaps in the very local context of south Denbighshire in late 1794 the image was not as risky as it would have appeared to be in William Frend's Cambridge or Thelwall's London or even in Cowdroy's Chester; for perhaps we should read it in relation to the proposal, published in the *Chronicle* in September, to build a 'House of Industry', a workhouse, in the Vale of Clwyd. This, it was suggested in the Introduction, may have been prompted in part by the need to take care of war widows and of others left destitute by the departure of their menfolk to the war. The proposal was sponsored by four local ministers of the Church of England, one of whom, the Revd David Hughes, headmaster of Ruthin School, was definitely no opponent of the war. He had been writing belligerent anti-French, pro-war poetry, since the Seven Years War, when he was seventeen. Around 1794 he wrote, in particular, a jolly song which announced that 'old England' (which seems to have included Ruthin) had 'the sanction of justice, the fiat of God' to 'belabor Monseer', and to 'swinge the *soup maigres*', the French who never tasted roast beef. The same divine fiat would entitle the 'English' to hang Tom Paine, 'the chief of sedition', and consign him to 'Be'lzebub's shrine'.[51] However much I would like to read the print of Llanfwrog differently, Hughes and Pugh may well have been happy to sing from the same hymn-sheet.

III

Pugh's image of Llanfwrog is nevertheless unusually powerful, well beyond his usual range, for he is not an artist who usually seeks, in the words of the editor of the *Chronicle*, to 'recommend' his art 'to the heart of sensibility' in quite this fashion. Its power derives partly, no doubt, from the expressions of the gentlemanly farmer and his wife, which Ellis has managed with great tact and careful understatement. Beyond that, however, its ability to evoke how the war had reached into the remote villages of north Wales, instantly pauperizing poor families and wrecking their lives, must have depended, at least for its local audience in Denbighshire, on the fidelity with which the landscape of so ordinary a Welsh village is depicted. When the motif of the war-widowed mother appears in writings of the mid-1790s, it is never thus localized; she appears in a generalized landscape, not, as here, in a specific place.

It will seem hackneyed to say so, but the image approaches us with the power of what Freud described as the *unheimliche* – the 'uncanny' or the 'un-at-home' – here the appearance of the unfamiliar, ghostly presence in what would have been to Pugh's north Welsh customers a familiar street in a fully recognizable landscape. In his account of the uncanny, Freud leans particularly on the German philosopher Friedrich von Schelling's definition of the word as something 'that ought to have remained . . . secret and hidden but has come to light', which is exactly how the near-silhouette of this widow and orphan would have appeared to the imagination of loyalists; commanded to be absent from the imagery of the period, they return

as ghostly presences, haunting the imagination, and even the most peaceful scenes of rural life.[52] Their unhomeliness brings the war right home in a way no other version of the motif of widow and child that I can think of seems to do: the gentlemanly farmer and his wife, out for their usual evening promenade through their own village, suddenly encountering a woman in the extremes of despair. The meeting is reminiscent of Wordsworth's encounter with the blind beggar in *The Prelude*, which left him feeling 'As if admonished from another world'.[53]

In the story it tells, this picture differs from the five other views in Pugh's series. They are, I have argued, intensely local, in that they tell us something very specific to the places they depict. *Llanfwrog, Ruthin and Llanbedr* tells a story that could have been told anywhere, in any town or village in Britain, but it is no less local in its meaning, for its very point is that it tells that story *here*, in this actual, and recognizable place. Perhaps the point can be made more sharply if we compare this image with a much slighter image by Pugh, *Ruthin, Denbighshire*, engraved by William Poole and published in 1796 (Plate 2.9). The story could have been told here, too, and to no less powerful effect. In a scene that prefigures the happy families in Pugh's images of parents and their children in London parks, a particularly genteel gentleman, flourishing his cane like Uncle Toby in *Tristram Shandy* and showing off a style of walking so exaggeratedly elegant as to risk injury, is accompanying two women, again perhaps on their evening promenade beside the Clwyd. Ahead of them a gambolling young lad

is waving his hat in an attempt to stampede a couple of placid cows. A footbridge is still there and so is the path, which may have become an established place of promenade; early in the twentieth century it was still a point from which the makers of postcards liked to take a view of the town perched on its low hill (Plate 2.10). The print must have been sold very cheaply, and, though claiming to be published in London, is likely to have been sold, chiefly, in Ruthin itself, to just such people as it depicts. It would have elicited from them a response no more complex than the simple recognition – 'I know where that is' – of a place so familiar that it may have surprised them that Pugh saw it as the material for a landscape-print, however informal, however diffident the claim it made on their taste. But how unfamiliar the scene would have become if suddenly these carefree

Plate 2.9 *W. Poole after Edward Pugh,* Ruthin, Denbighshire, *engraving (London: E. Pugh and W. Poole, 1796), Aberystwyth, National Library of Wales.*

Plate 2.10 View from River, Ruthin, *tinted postcard (Valentine's, postmarked 1904), private collection.*

promenaders found themselves confronted, in their moments of quiet relaxation, with the image of tragic suffering the gentleman farmer and his wife had encountered, a few hundred yards away in Llanfwrog, two years before. What in the end is most intriguing, and most poignant, about the aquatint of Llanfwrog, is how it invites a nod of recognition, and then sets about making what is most familiar, most estranged.

Notes

1   See NLW Pool Park Estate Atlas, NLW Bachymbyd, vol. 1 139/2/6. 1813; terriers of the glebe land in Llanfwrog, DRO PD/59/1/15 (1793) and 16 (1801).

2   DRO PD/59/1/15.

3   DRO QSD DE 2 1805.

4   [T. H. B. Oldfield], *An Entire and Complete History, Political and Personal, of the Boroughs of Great Britain*, 3 vols (London: J. Debrett, 1792), vol. 2, p. 496.

5   [William, second Lord Bagot], *Memorials of the Bagot Family; compiled in 1823* (Blithfield: William Hodgetts, 1824), p. 90.

6   [Bagot], *Memorials*, p. 94.

7   [Bagot], *Memorials*, p. 95. The Whigs he denounces are Windham, Sheridan, Loughborough, Fox, and Burke. For an account of the occasion and consequences of Burke's claim that God had 'hurled' George from his throne, see Barrell, *Imagining the King's Death: Figurative Treason, Fantasies of Regicide 1793–1796* (Oxford: Oxford University Press, 2000), pp. 87–100.

8   [Bagot], *Memorials*, pp. 96–7.

9   Pliny, *Natural History*, Loeb edition, tr. H. Rackham, vol. 9 (Cambridge, MA and London: Harvard University Press and Heinemann, 1984), pp. 315–17.

10   Sir Joshua Reynolds, *Discourses on Art*, ed. Robert R. Wark (New Haven and London: Yale University Press, 1975), pp. 163–4.

11   Fuseli, *Life and Writings*, vol. 2, p. 52. For Fuseli's account of Reynolds's view, those of Pliny, Quintilian and Falconet, and of where he disagrees in particular with Reynolds, see pp. 45–58.

12   Gotthold Ephraim Lessing, 'Laocoon', in *Selected Prose Works of G. E. Lessing*, tr. E. C. Beasley and Helen Zimmern, ed. Edward Bell (London: George Bell, 1885), p. 17.

13   Daniel Webb, *An Inquiry into the Beauties of Painting; and into the Merits of the most Celebrated Painters, Ancient and Modern* (London: R. and J. Dodsley, 1760), pp. 192–3.

14   Webb, *An Inquiry*, p. 192.

15   Fuseli, *Life and Writings*, vol. 2, p. 55.

16   Pliny, *Natural History,* Book XXXV, sect. 36, § 73–4.

17   Elias Owen, *Welsh Folk-Lore: A Collection of the Folk-Tales and Legends of North Wales* (Oswestry and Wrexham: Woodall and Minshall, 1896), p. 51.

18   *CCo* 30 September 1794; *CCh* 3 October.

19   *CCh* 14 March 1794. My thanks, as so often, to Elizabeth Edwards of the Centre for Advanced Welsh and Celtic Studies, University of Wales, for drawing my attention to this poem.

20   *CCh* 5 April 1793.

21   *CCh* 21 June 1793.

22   *CCh* 3 January, 1794.

23   *CCh* 12 July 1793 (a few words in the last sentence are illegible and I have filled the lacunae); see also, for example, the issues for 10 May and 17 May 1793 and 23 March 1794.

24   *CCh* 21 November 1794; information supplied by the ever-generous Marion Löffler; and see her essay 'Serial literature and radical poetry in Wales at the end of the eighteenth century', in Michael Brown, Catriona Kennedy, John Kirk, and Andrew Noble (eds), *United Islands? Multi-Lingual Radical Poetry and Song in Britain and Ireland, 1770–1820*, vol. 2: *The Cultures of Resistance* (London: Pickering and Chatto, forthcoming). Flookersbrook and 'Christlington' (Christleton) are (now) suburbs of Chester.

25   Hucks, *A Pedestrian Tour*, p. 26.

26   William Frend, *Peace and Union recommended to the Associated Bodies of Republicans and Anti-Republicans* (St Ives: for the author, 1793), pp. 47–9. I am grateful to Michael Phillips for pointing out the relevance of the Frend controversy to Pugh's picture.

27   See *A Complete Collection of State Trials*, 30 vols, ed. William Cobbett and T. B. Howells (London: Longman et al., 1816–22), vol. 22, col. 635, and see also 551–5.

28   On this topic generally, see Patricia Lin, 'Caring for the nation's families: British soldiers' and sailors' families and the state, 1793–1815', in Alan Forrest, Karen Hagemann and Jane Rendall (eds), *Soldiers, Citizens and Civilians: Experiences and Perceptions of the French Wars, 1790–1820* (Basingstoke: Palgrave Macmillan, 2009).

29   *Sun*, 20 March 1793.

30   Frend, *Extract from the Appendix of a Pamphlet entitled Peace and Union* (London: no bookseller credited, 1793).

31   CCh 17 June 1793.

32   *Morning Chronicle*, 24 February 1794.

33   [William Firth], *Christian Warfare defended and recommended in a Sermon intended to have been preached before the Vice-Chancellor and the University at St. Mary's Church, Cambridge, on 28th of February, 1794, the Day appointed for a General Fast* (London: C. and G. Kearsley, 1794), p. 1.

34   *Poems, by J. Hucks, A. M. Fellow of Catharine Hall, Cambridge* (Cambridge: Benjamin Flower, 1798), p. 36.

35   *Fast Day, as observed at Sheffield . . . February 28, 1794. Being the Day appointed for a General Fast; to which are added a Hymn and Resolutions* ('London Reprinted': 1794), pp. 10–11.

36   *CCh* 28 March 1794; for the information about Tomos Glyn Cothi my thanks to Marion Löffler of the Centre for Advanced Welsh and Celtic Studies, University of Wales, who writes: 'Three Welsh adaptations of the hymn were made by three Welsh Dissenters and poets in south Wales who knew each other. Thomas Evans (Tomos Glyn Cothi), Brechfa, published an adaptation in his radical Welsh periodical *The Miscellaneous Repository*, vol. 1 (Haf 1795), pp. 16–18;

Edward Evan, Aberdare, published a translation with facing English text in his collection of poems *Afalau'r Awen* (Merthyr Tydfil, 1804), pp. 56–7. Since he died in 1798, it must be assumed that he translated the hymn in the 1790s. The translation made by David Davis, Castell-hywel, was not published until 1848, when the Welsh Unitarians founded their periodical, *Yr Ymofynnyd*, I/9 (1848), 216, but then it shed light on the two other versions, because they were mentioned in the paratext introducing it. There was clearly a connection between all three. For the text of the satirical anti-fast day hymn by Jac Glan-y-Gors, which was probably inspired by the English hymn and its Welsh echoes, see *CCh*, 4 and 11 March 1796.'

37 See 'To the Printer of the Sheffield Register', in *Pig's Meat, or, Lessons for the Swinish Multitude*, 3 vols (London: Thomas Spence, 1794), vol. 2, esp. p. 10; John Harrison, *A Letter to the Rt. Hon. Henry Dundas, MP* (London: J. Smith and D. I. Eaton, 1794), p. 20; *Politics for the People, vol. II, Number XV* (London: D. I. Eaton, 1794), pp. 232–7; *The Evidence Summed Up; or a Statement of the Apparent Causes and Objects of the War* (London: D. I. Eaton, 1794), p. 37, and see *Considerations on the Causes and Alarming Consequences of the Present War* (London: J. S. Jordan, 1794), p. 46; John Thelwall, *Political Lectures (No. I.) on the Moral Tendency of a System of Spies and Informers* (London: D. I. Eaton, 1794),

p. 18. See also J. Edwards, *A Discourse delivered on Friday, April 19, 1793) being the Day appointed by the King for a General Fast* (Birmingham: J. Thompson, 1793), p. 14; [Michael Nash], *Gideon's Cake of Barley Meal. A Letter to the Rev. William Romaine, on his preaching for the Emigrant Popish Clergy*, 2nd edn (London: J. S. Jordan, 1793), p. 109; Thomas Scott, *An Estimate of the Religious Character and State of Great Britain* (London: J. S. Jordan et al., 1793), p. 8; *Thoughts on the Present War with France* (London: J. Debrett, 1793), pp. 39–40.

38 For an account of this fable and the trial it occasioned, see Barrell, *Imagining*, pp. 103–16.

39 See for example *Annual Register. . . for the Year 1793* (London: G. G. and J. Robinson, 1794), p. 7; *The Country Spectator* (Gainsborough, Lincoln and London: Mozeley & co. et al.), 35 (1793), 197–204; Mrs Darwall, *Poems on Several Occasions*, 2 vols (Walsall: F. Milward, 1794), vol. 2, pp. 100–3; W. R. Wake, *Two Sermons preached in the Parish Church of St. Michael, one on the Fast Day, April 19* (Bath: Bull and Co. et al., [1793]), p. 1.

40 *CCh* 14 March 1794.

41 For more on this, see the chapter 'Cottage politics' in my book *The Spirit of Despotism: Invasions of Privacy in the 1790s* (Oxford: Oxford University Press, 2006), pp. 210–46.

42 For a full account see Harriet Guest, *Empire, Barbarism, and Civilisation: Captain Cook, William Hodges,*

and the Return to the Pacific (Cambridge: Cambridge University Press, 2007), pp. 169–98.

43 See Draper Hill, *Mr. Gillray the Caricaturist: A Biography* (London: Phaidon Press, 1965), pp. 54–5; and on the caricature more generally, Diana Donald, *The Age of Caricature: Satirical Prints in the Age of George III* (New Haven: Yale University Press, 1996), esp. pp. 156–7, and Guest, *Empire*, pp. 193–7.

44 See for example the *Oracle*, 12 June 1795; *True Briton* 11 April 1795.

45 *CD*, pp. 2–3.

46 See Guest, *Empire*, p. 170.

47 Jones, *Before Rebecca*, pp. 51–3; Tim Jones, *Rioting*, pp. 32–4.

48 W. Lloyd Davies, 'The riot at Denbigh in 1795', *Bulletin of the Board of Celtic Studies*, 4 (1927), 62, 68–70.

49 Tim Jones, *Rioting*, pp. 33–4.

50 Jones, *Before Rebecca*, pp. 31–3, 64–5.

51 David Hughes, *Poems, on Various Subjects, in English and Latin* (Denbigh: W. Morris, 1865), pp. 57–8, 153–5.

52 Sigmund Freud, 'The "uncanny"', in *Art and Literature*, tr. James Strachey, The Penguin Freud Library, vol. 14 (Harmondsworth: Penguin Books, 1985), pp. 339–76, and especially p. 345.

53 Wordsworth, *The Prelude* (1805 version), Book VII, l. 623.

THREE *Bathafern Hills from Coedmarchan Rocks*

I

In 1808 Pugh exhibited, for the first and only time at the Royal Academy, a landscape painting, *The Vale of Clwyd*. It was probably in oils, no doubt of a modest size in accordance with his lowly status in the profession, and it is now lost. It would have been fascinating to see what he had made of painting his native vale, which, in *Cambria Depicta*, he describes as 'unrivalled', and to which, as the climax of that book, he devotes four pages of detailed description and praise.[1] Did he attempt such a panoramic view of the vale in the painting, or a small picturesque subject within it? Quite likely the picture resembled the small lost painting by Pugh referred to in the introduction, and reproduced by Maurice Harold Grant. Grant dates it to 1811 and names it *A Welsh Landscape*. It shows a more or less occluded, not a panoramic view (Plate 3.1), in which a mother, her children and three cows are set in a foreground hemmed in by trees, but with glimpses here and there of an illuminated middle ground, and a path winding past a church tower towards a looming mountain.[2] Apart from that mountain it is very much in the manner of the woodland scenes of late Gainsborough.

Plate 3.1 *(left) Edward Pugh,* A Welsh Landscape, *oil on canvas, 1811, reproduced in* Colonel Maurice Harold Grant, A Dictionary of British Landscape Painters from the 16th Century to the early 20th Century *(1952).*

Plate 3.2 *(opposite) William Ellis after Edward Pugh,* Bathafern Hills, from Coedmarchan Rocks, *aquatint (London: E. Pugh, 1794), first issue, private collection.*

Plate 3.3 *(opposite) William Ellis after Edward Pugh,* Bathafern Hills, from Coedmarchan Rocks, *coloured aquatint (London: E. Pugh, 1794), first issue, Aberystwyth, National Library of Wales.*

But whatever Pugh had made of the Vale of Clwyd, it is intriguing to hear of him, in 1808, probably now retired to Ruthin from the London art world, taking on a subject which, remarkably, he had not attempted in his first, attention-seeking statement, the *Six Views.* The two best-known Denbighshire subjects, arguably the only ones that amateurs of landscape and topography who had never visited Wales were likely to have heard of, were the Vale of Llangollen and the Vale of Clwyd. Pugh included the first in the series, but not the second. He might have taken the opportunity of depicting it in *Llanfwrog, Ruthin and Llanbedr,* but chose there a viewpoint so low that nothing of the vale appears. The nearest he came was in *Bathafern Hills, from Coedmarchan Rocks* (Plate 3.2), but in that image, as we shall see, his main interest was focused on something altogether different.

Coedmarchan is a long, low hill, south of Ruthin, stretched out between Llanfwrog and Pwllglas and forming for a mile or so the western rampart of the Vale of Clwyd at what is nearly its southernmost point. Along its western edge runs a vertical cliff of dark red limestone, the remains of quarrying; on the ridge above is the Ruthin–Pwllglas golf course, east of which, running downhill towards the river Clwyd and the A494 Ruthin–Corwen road, is a mixture of woodland and meadow, and of pasture scattered with loose stones and trees – 'limestone grounds, and rocky', as Walter Davies described them in 1810 in his survey of the agriculture of north Wales.[3] Here and there are low grey-white limestone outcrops, some incorporated into hedges, others overgrown with less formal vegetation. In 1794 this was common land, grazed by sheep and perhaps by goats, quarried by lime-burners, and criss-crossed with roads, one of which, running over the south-eastern shoulder of the hill, was the old Ruthin–Corwen turnpike. It survives now as a

steep tarmac road from Pwllglas which terminates at a gate and stile by the farmhouse called Pen-y-mynydd, but a hundred yards or so further on it reappears as a green lane running between low hedges. The common, amounting to just over 400 acres exclusive of a few old enclosures and encroachments, was shared between the parishes of Llanfwrog and Efenechtyd.[4] The boundary between the parishes, running northwest from Eyarth bridge, was marked at one point, near the southern end of the turnpike, by a hefty boulder, a glacial erratic to which we will return, for it will emerge as vital to an understanding of this place.[5]

Thomas Pennant, travelling this road in 1773, described Coedmarchan as 'a large naked common'.[6] It was clearly regarded by tourists as a dreary place, devoid of picturesque or antiquarian interest; and though many of them passed over it, or skirted its foot when the turnpike was redirected eastward to the lower, flatter ground beside the Clwyd, few of those who wrote up their travels bother even to mention it. *Bathafern Hills from Coedmarchan Rocks* is the only late eighteenth- or early nineteenth-century image I have found of it. Revisiting Coedmarchan ten or more years after the drawing for this aquatint was made, Pugh himself described it, in *Cambria Depicta,* as 'a barren rocky mountain', from the summit of which, however, there was 'a delightful view of the vale'.[7] This double aspect, the dreary foreground giving way to the beauties of the vale beyond, is indeed what the aquatint shows us – or just about. The top of the common is depicted as 'naked' as it then was, with no trees obscuring, as they do now, the sight of Eyarth bridge, the river Clwyd and the church tower of Llanfair Dyffryn Clwyd. Beyond and below, in the narrow 'v' between the dark coulisse of trees on the right and the answering trees behind the outcrop on the left, is a sliver, for it

is no more than that, of the famously fertile fields of the Vale of Clwyd, bounded by an accurate profile of the southern end of the Clwydian range.

Pugh has chosen to show us the scene not from the summit of Coedmarchan, but from a lower viewpoint, hard to locate precisely but apparently just below the turnpike. This decision greatly increases the area of the picture devoted to a foreground which, picturesque perhaps in its rough and broken surfaces, is still conspicuously unprepossessing. This area nowadays is attractively verdant at all times of the year, but even in the coloured versions of the print (Plate 3.3) Pugh shows it as dark, perhaps as if overgrazed. According to George Kay in his *General Views* of the agriculture of the counties of north Wales, goats were regarded as so destructive of trees, and even of the roughest pasture, that landlords in Merionethshire banned their tenants from keeping them; in Anglesey, he reported, 'the whole race are nearly extirpated.'[8] Kay does not seem to have visited the Vale of Clwyd, where, on the evidence of this picture, they would seem to have found a refuge on common land, though, as we shall see, they may have found their way there from a landscape in Italy.

To repeat, this scene is the only opportunity Pugh gave himself to include in his series of Denbighshire views the Vale of Clwyd itself, the pride of the county, famous throughout Britain for its beauty. That there is something out there worth seeing is teasingly made clear by the man on the summit with his telescope, whom I take to be Pugh himself, who habitually carried one, at least on his walks described in *Cambria Depicta*.[9] As it is, Pugh has produced what would seem to be an almost deliberately unmarketable image: not an ideal landscape, nor a topographical subject with antiquarian interest, not an image of the abundance of nature, not beautiful, not very picturesque, not anything much. So why this meagre glimpse of the vale, and why did this barren, dreary common earn a place among the *Six Views*?

That question is made more pertinent by the fact that the aquatint is inscribed to the Right Hon. Lord William Beauclerk, the second son of the Duke of St Albans, who in 1816 would himself succeed to the dukedom on the death of his nephew, the infant seventh Duke. Beauclerk's patronage, like Bagot's among those listed as among Pugh's patrons in the advertisement for the six views, was probably secured in London, not in Wales, for Beauclerk was a newcomer among the Denbighshire squirearchy, a habitual absentee who, if he ever visited the county, alighted there briefly only to take off again almost immediately. In 1791 he had married Elizabeth, the daughter of the Revd Robert Carter, a Lincolnshire squire, who had become Robert Carter Thelwall as a condition of his inheriting the Bathafarn estate. When he died in 1787 he left Elizabeth as his sole heiress: along with Bathafarn, a paltry 972 acres and a similarly sized estate at Pickworth, north of Stamford, she inherited the huge estate at Redbourne, near Scunthorpe, consisting of about twenty farms and two villages. It was here, not at Bathafarn, that the Beauclerks made their home.

Lady William Beauclerk 'was a lady of most amiable manners,' writes Pugh in *Cambria Depicta*, 'and well taught in the school of honour and humanity; she trod in the steps of her good father and mother, but died a few years after her marriage' in 1797.[10] She left all these lands to her husband, who two years later would marry her distant relation, the heiress Maria Janetta Nelthorpe, daughter of Sir John Nelthorpe of Lincolnshire, now famous if at all as the subject of a portrait by George Stubbs, which shows him posing with dogs and shotgun on the plump estate that Maria would one day feed to her land-hungry husband. Beauclerk's inheritance of Bathafarn was contested: there was evidence to suggest that Elizabeth's will was written under duress, and that a later will was suppressed by Beauclerk. He won, however, the subsequent law-suit, and sold Bathafarn to the Revd Butler Clough in 1805, by which time the estate amounted to 1,900 acres.[11]

So: if a more commercially minded artist would have found a way to show more of the famed beauty of the Vale of Clwyd, one more determined to keep hold of Beauclerk's patronage would have made sure to include Bathafarn Hall in the view. Instead, from the viewpoint Pugh has chosen, the vale was largely hidden, and the house concealed by the long limestone crag, and it would anyway be so far away as to be almost invisible except to the man with the telescope.[12] In short, the choice of Beauclerk as dedicatee was perhaps especially odd when there were apparently two much more appropriate candidates, Richard Myddelton of Chirk, owner of the Ruthin Castle estate and lord of the manor of Ruthin in which Coedmarchan was situated, or his son, MP for Denbigh and its contributory boroughs of Holt and Ruthin. But the Myddeltons had a long history as Whigs,[13] and Pugh may have feared that their presence on the list of his patrons and dedicatees would have lost him some of the rest, all, so he probably believed, firm Tories.

Pugh based his composition on an engraving after Antonio De Bittìo, who had assisted John Strange, the British Ambassador to the Venetian Republic, in his geological researches. The engraving illustrated an article by Strange on basalt rock formations, published in the *Philosophical Transactions of the Royal Society* for 1775 (Plate 3.4).[14] It shows the basalt columns on Monte Rosso, in the Eugenaean Hills, south of Padua, and suggests that Pugh's decision to depict this scene, and to devote so much space to the foreground, arose from an interest in its geology, the same interest as that of the few others who wrote about Coedmarchan. For when Coedmarchan does briefly engage those who traversed it in the 1790s and the decades around them, it is almost invariably on account of its geology and the mineral resources thought to lie beneath it.

Some thought there might be iron and lead, though in 1849 Samuel Lewis reported that 'an attempt was made to obtain lead-ore, for which purpose some works were erected at Coedmarchan, but they were not attended with any success.' By the mid-nineteenth century, Lewis noted, barites was being extracted in abundance, and a mill had been established to process it, but in Pugh's period this is never mentioned.[15] There was known to be marble there, or rather some fairly acceptable substitute for it, according to Edward Lhuyd; it was 'coarse red and white' according to Pennant and Thomas Walford; 'really handsome, and of a purple hue', according to Pugh, 'with variegated marks or vestiges of marine productions'. And, loyal as ever to his home turf, he adds 'that there is coal in the vale is demonstrable: iron, its never-failing attendant, is visible: that there may be lead, is probable: that there is slate is likely to be true.'[16]

He would turn out to be wrong on all counts, but it was, anyway, the marble that interested him most, though exactly what he and others meant by marble is unclear. In *Cambria Depicta*, for example, he describes a blue-black 'marble' near Mallwyd, which, he says, 'were it capable of a polish, would be very valuable for its great beauty.'[17] A couple of hundred yards from the scene of this print he writes of the 'marble' at Eyarth rocks, which, though a handsome and serviceable building-stone – it may be seen on the façade of the County Offices at Ruthin – is hardly a marble in the sense we understand today.[18] Unsurprisingly therefore it has been hard to locate the marble Pugh admires at Coedmarchan, but it is possibly the strata of red carboniferous limestone, visible now as a quarried cliff along the road that forms the western boundary of Coedmarchan.[19] Perhaps more likely it has been worked out, and may be found only in scattered remnants like the outcrop that breaks the surface of the old turnpike road just north of the turning to Pen-y-mynydd, more or less in the area from where Pugh's view of Coedmarchan is taken (Plate 3.5). But whatever it was, of this supposed marble he reported that 'many of the old houses in the vale have chimney-pieces made of it.' With Britain at war with France throughout Pugh's career as an artist, the importing of marble from Europe had come to a stop, and this substitute might have come to seem a valuable commodity. But though a Liverpool firm, Pugh tells us, was 'making a trial' to see if quarrying it would

Plate 3.4 *Antonio De Bittìo*, Monte Rosso, *engraving, from* Philosophical Transactions of the Royal Society, *vol. 65, part 1, 1775.*

be an economic proposition, the marble was barely exploited by the local inhabitants.

The main reason was probably the difficulty of transporting any heavy minerals to market in the absence of a canal running the length of the Clwyd. According to the *Universal British Directory*, it had 'oftentimes been in agitation to make this river navigable', but every scheme had come to nothing, 'either through penury, or disagreements among the land-owners'. According to Pugh, the Hon. Thomas Fitzmaurice of Lleweni had proposed building such a canal around 1780, in consultation with some merchants of Liverpool, but for whatever reason – Pugh did not know why – the scheme had foundered.[20] Three years before the publication of this aquatint, however, the idea of a canal through the vale had been proposed again by a correspondent who called himself 'Navigator', writing to *Adam's Weekly Courant* early in 1791, and calling upon the gentry with property along its proposed route – 'a Myddleton, a Fitzmaurice, a Mostyn, a Pennant, a Davies, &c. … to step forward, and foster this darling child'. But this proposal too went nowhere, perhaps as a result

of a discouraging reply to this letter published in the *Courant* a few weeks later.[21]

Pugh particularly regretted the absence of a canal, not only because of the facility with which the minerals of the upper vale might have found a market, but on account of the 'energy of mind' and the increase in population as well as in trade that the canal would have occasioned: the Montgomeryshire canal, he believed, had transformed the economy of north Wales all along its route. But Pugh believed there were other reasons too for the neglect of the Coedmarchan marble. There was, he said, a want of ability among 'the country stone-cutters', who 'either have not the skill or the patience to prepare this stone for more general use'. There was also 'want of a spirit of adventure in the vale' among the gentry. In his remarks on Coedmarchan, Pugh looks forward to a time when Wales 'will display an energy of mind which may produce as much local commerce, as any trading part of Great

Plate 3.5 *An outcrop on the unmade road near Pen-y-mynydd, by Coedmarchan, 2011.*

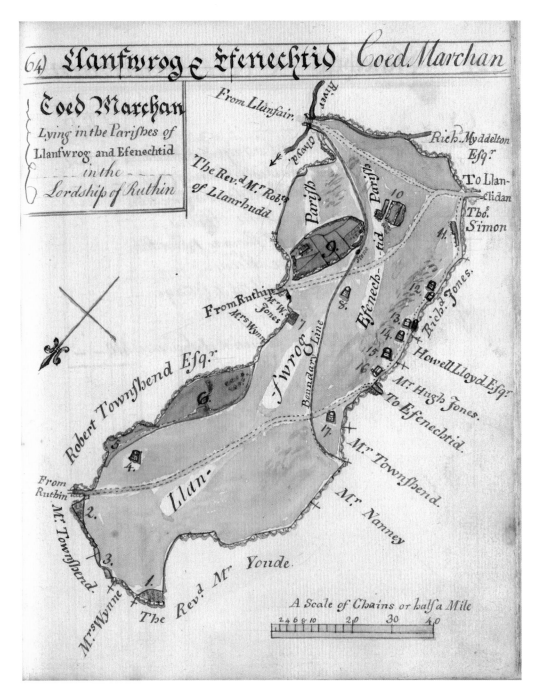

Plate 3.6 *S. Minshull,* Llanfwrog & Efenechtid Coed Marchan, *map 64 in* A Survey of Lands enclosed from the Waste in the Lordship of Ruthin, *1779, Aberystwyth, National Library of Wales.*

Britain'; but in the meantime he laments the fact that in north Wales generally, but in the Vale of Clwyd in particular, the gentry prefer 'to hug themselves in the security of five per cent', obtainable presumably in wartime from government securities, rather than to speculate in extractive industries which would be likely, from the nature of the local geology, to lead to 'the enriching of the local proprietors, as well as to the benefit of the poor labourers'.[22]

As a result, the Revd J. Evans tells us, though Coedmarchan was 'known' to contain lead, 'the procuration of lime, for agricultural purposes, is considered much more profitable, or expedient, than adventures for subterraneous treasures.'[23] In 1779, Richard Myddelton commissioned from S. Minshull an atlas of the waste lands in the lordship; the map for Coedmarchan shows no less than eight limekilns scattered across the common, in the possession of six different owners (Plate 3.6), helping to confirm the claim that in north-east Wales 'nearly every farmer had a limestone quarry and lime kiln.'[24] Along with the goats, the need for fuel to feed these kilns no doubt accounts for the nakedness of the common as Pugh and Pennant saw it. Vast amounts of lime, usually mixed with dung and sometimes soil – the 'clearings of ponds, roads, drains' – were used on arable land in Denbighshire at this time. Walter Davies recorded quantities of up to 165 bushels per acre on one farm, twenty tons per acre on another. Evans regarded farmers who used lime in such quantities as 'fatally bounti-ful', their practice justified less by good husbandry than by 'the strength of prevailing custom', and somehow all the more reprehensible in that lime, in Denbighshire, was so easy to procure.[25] Pennant however had taken a different view: 'the detached rocks of … *Coed Marchon* beyond *Ruthyn*', he wrote, 'yield to the industrious farmer, by their excellent lime, a manure more certainly produc-tive of wealth, than the precarious search after the deep-hid minerals.'[26] Pugh's view of Coedmarchan responds directly to this debate, this opposition between modernizers in favour of exploiting the supposed subterranean resources of the common, and those like Pennant who recommend the com-moners to scratch the surface for a living.

In *Cambria Depicta* Pugh usually places him-self on the side of those self-conscious modern-izers who wish to see the common more profitably exploited, and who associate with 'unimproved' common land a lack of know-how and entrepre-neurial energy. The image however is more divided, as it was bound to be at a time when no landscape or topographical artist could avoid working, to some degree at least, under the regime of the pic-turesque. For though, as we shall see, Coedmarchan gives him the opportunity to stage, to dramatize the opposition between subterranean enterprise and superficial idleness, it is no doubt also the fact that the place is, in Hucks's phrase, 'unmechanized by the ingenuity of man',[27] not pierced with mines or too much heaped with spoil, that makes this scene appropriate for inclusion in his series.

To some theorists of the picturesque, notably the most influential, William Gilpin, scenes con-taminated with the 'vulgarity … of employment' were unworthy of representation;[28] 'even the peas-ant cannot be admitted, if he be employed in the low occupations of his profession: the spade, the scythe, and the rake are all excluded';[29] he is wel-come in images of landscape only if he leaves his tools behind, and seems to have no need to work hard for a living. 'In a moral view,' writes Gilpin,

the industrious mechanic is a more pleasing object, than the loitering peasant. But in a pic-turesque light, it is otherwise. The arts of industry are rejected; and even idleness, if I may so speak, adds dignity to a character. Thus the lazy cow-herd resting on his pole; or the peasant lolling on a rock, may be allowed in the grandest scenes; while the laborious mechanic, with his imple-ments of labour, would be repulsed.[30]

These words appeared in 1789, five years before Pugh's series was published, and it is very likely that Pugh knew them: Gilpin's works were required reading for landscape artists. Pugh how-ever was not aspiring to depict 'the grandest scenes'; and he could afford to derogate just a lit-tle from Gilpin's rules, as indeed did many artists. His view of Coedmarchan is rather more ambiva-lent about the propriety of depicting hard manual labour, but it is more ambivalent, too, about the virtues of improvement than his prose description of the place.

III

The figures chatting to each other on the left, presumably examples of the 'poor labourers' who would benefit from a large injection into the landscape of capital and enterprise, exhibit all the easygoing inertia associated with pastoral, the picturesque and the common, at least for those who appear to work there for themselves and in their own time (Plate 3.7). The loose stones to be collected and burnt are retrieved from the surface so easily that the lime-burner has time to 'loll on a rock', giving every indication that his time is not bought and paid for, at least not overseen, by anyone else. The stones for burning lie conveniently at the side of the road that runs uphill behind him; he will not have to lift them far to the wagon that will bear them to one of the kilns that then lined the crest of the hill. He treats his spade as a footrest, not as an implement

Plate 3.7 *Detail of plate 3.2*

of labour, and the still more 'lazy' goatherd rests on his pole in the manner approved by Gilpin, but in a sitting position. They won't get rich this way, but neither will they get tired. A lunch basket is waiting nearby. This left-hand side of the picture is Claude or Gilpin translated into Welsh. Still more it is Virgil; for not only the composition but the figures in this image, the goats, even that basket are apparently borrowed from the view of Monte Rosso, which itself could be a rococo illustration to Virgil's pastorals (Plate 3.8).[31]

In the right foreground, in the darker side of a dark landscape, is a laborious miner or quarryman, who seems to stand for the kind of industry associated with the full exploitation of the mineral resources of the common. With his back to the audience as if too busy to acknowledge us, he appears to have been searching for what Evans called 'subterraneous treasures', and has thrown up another pile of spoil like that in *Careg Carn-March Arther.* Just to his left, in the centre foreground, is a large lump of stone, an erratic boulder (Plate 3.9), presumably the boulder now to be seen on Coedmarchan a field's width to the east of the hedged track that was once the turnpike road (Plate 3.10). Pugh and those who knew Coedmarchan would have recognized this boulder as the main boundary stone, clearly shown on the 'Boundary Line' on Minshull's map, marking the border of Llanfwrog parish, on the right, from Efenechtyd, on the left. And as J. W. Edwards has pointed out, Minshull's map shows a clear difference between the character of the common as it falls within one parish or another. Minshull's atlas was made to show the encroachments on the commons, the lands enclosed without title from the waste throughout the lordship of Ruthin. In Llanfwrog, those encroachments on the common had been made by the lord of the manor

Plate 3.8 *Detail of plate 3.4.*

himself, Myddelton, in the form of two very small plantations, and by the tenant farmers of substantial local landowners, to one of whom the single lime-kiln in Llanfwrog parish may also have belonged.[32] In contrast, on the Efenechtyd side of the boundary the only encroachments were a cottage with three small enclosures, amounting in all to barely more than an acre, and two 'crofts', or squatters' cottages, built on the same crest as six of the seven limekilns on this side of the common, which apparently belonged to local men living in part by burning lime. 'Presumably', writes Edwards, 'different common rights existed on either side of this boundary . . . and it is possible that in Efenechtyd the poor were encouraged to build cottages for themselves on the common, whereas this

Plate 3.9 *(right) Detail of plate 3.3.*

Plate 3.10 *(below) The large boulder near Bron Eyarth Farm, east of Coedmarchan, 2011.*

practice was discouraged in Llanfwrog.'[33] Presumably too, therefore, a moral economy that respected customary rights was in a more flourishing state on the west side of the boundary stone than on the other, and that too may help explain the difference between the easygoing commoners on the left of Pugh's landscape, working for themselves at their own pace, and the laborious excavator on the right.

As we saw in the introduction, the rights to the mineral wealth lying on or under common land belonged to the lord of the manor, and as Bryn Ellis has pointed out, in some places, for example where the mineral rights were controlled by the Grosvenor estates – an instance would be the quarries and kilns near Carreg Carn March Arthur – the right to collect stone for burning appears to have been tightly controlled. Elsewhere, however, the lord of the manor may have been prepared to wink at such small-scale exploitation of surface stone as our lime-burner is engaged in, especially if the local inhabitants believed they had a strong customary right to burn lime, a belief that it might have been troublesome to contest.[34] On the Llanfwrog side of the boundary, however, things were evidently different: the map suggests that Myddelton was able to exert much more control there than in Efenechtyd, and our excavator therefore may have been read as working hard because he was working for someone other than himself, or because, as often in the extractive industries, this is 'bargain-work', let to him as the highest bidder by Myddelton's steward.

It is not exactly clear why Myddelton was so keen to have Minshull produce a carefully drawn, coloured and annotated atlas of the common lands in the Manor of Ruthin, with the exact acreages of the encroachments upon them: according to Edwards, it is the only known example of such an atlas in England and Wales. Very likely, however, Myddelton commissioned it with the idea that he could extract more income from the wastes, whether by charging rent for the encroachments or by enclosing the common, which would mean extinguishing the supposed rights of the commoners and clearing out the squatters. When Pugh's image was published, the inevitable enclosure, if not yet a concerted plan, may already have been the subject of troubling rumours; rumours that would probably have begun in the late 1770s, when Minshull and his assistant arrived with theodolite and chain and began their survey.[35] In 1794 when Pugh published this image, the threat posed by enclosure to the moral economy, active or imminent in the now enclosing parishes of Mold, Llanferres and Cilcain, Upper Kinnerton and Hope, was still held back from Coedmarchan by the bulwark of the Clwydian Hills. It would be too fanciful, I suppose, to suggest that the man with the telescope, Pugh I believe, is watching the horizon for signs of its arrival in his native vale, but there, I *have* suggested it.

Richard Myddelton died in 1795, and when his son Richard followed him to the grave a year later, the family estates were divided between his two sisters, the Ruthin Castle estate, and with it the lordship of the manor, passing to his sister Harriet. Only now were steps taken to enclose the common. But the act of Parliament, obtained in 1800, provided for the enclosure of the waste lands in Llanfwrog only, not in Efenechtyd; probably the land in the latter parish was simply not then thought susceptible to improvement or therefore worth enclosing. The principal allottees of the Llanfwrog enclosure included the Myddeltons, the Wynns of Wynnstay, and Lord Bagot; but the cost of obtaining the enclosure would be so high that, to pay for it, 'the best of the waste' was sold off, 'to the prejudice of the poor ffreeholders'.[36] The tithe map of about 1840 suggests that the division between the right and left halves of the landscape depicted by Pugh had been reinforced in the intervening years. The enclosed land in Llanfwrog parish had become improved pasture and woodland, while Efenechtyd remained 'open common', as it had been on Minshull's map and in Pugh's aquatint. It remained so until the Ruthin enclosure of 1852–61, which took in many of the wastes shown in Minshull's atlas of the lordship, mainly to the benefit of the Bagots.[37]

IV

Perhaps more than any of Pugh's *Six Views, Bathafern Hills, from Coedmarchan Rocks* speaks to a local audience, for the realization of its structure and meaning depends so much on local knowledge, in particular on the function of the great boulder. A wider audience however would very likely have recognized from other eighteenth-century landscapes that the meaning of the picture depended upon the division between georgic and pastoral; from Gainsborough's *Landscape with a Woodcutter courting a Milkmaid*, for example (Plate 3.11), made forty years earlier for the Duke of Bedford, though here the relation between the division of labour and the division of space is much more evident than in Pugh's image. That landscape, as Keith Snell was the first to point out, is unmistakably divided between the arable land in the middle distance, enclosed, fenced, evidently private property; and, in the right foreground, the common wasteland where the milkmaid can keep her cow, the woodcutter can collect firing and others can turn out their asses to graze.[38] On the arable, a dingy ploughman follows his team and, subject as he is to the disciplines of wage labour, he is hard at work. On the common there is time to relax: the commoners are freer to mix their work, of the fruits of which no landlord or employer can claim a share, with self-chosen pursuits. The sense that their dalliance is a temporary but welcome interruption in their labours is given by the fact that the woodcutter manages his courtship without even laying down his billhook or bundle of sticks. The painting, however, may not be quite as open-hearted as first appears: the milkmaid, as she turns to scoop a dish of milk

to give the woodcutter, foolishly allows her cow to kick over the second bucket, and there is more than a hint here of those genre paintings which warn of the moral and economic cost to children, servants and the poor of diverting their attention from work and duty. If the image were a little less light-hearted we could almost read this painting as one which reminds the Duke of Bedford, improving landlord that he was, of the dangers to the well-being of the poor themselves in the survival of commons.

Pugh's aquatint, like Gainsborough's painting, is also available to be moralized. It represents this corner of Denbighshire as reassuringly underdeveloped, a place where the poor can enjoy all the advantages of the moral economy and the freedom offered by their access to common land, but also as reassuringly capable of development, for those prepared to dig till they gently perspire, or to pay someone to do it for them. Perhaps the image would have been read as suggesting that, at Coedmarchan, the moral economy could still be found alongside the beginnings of a more commercial economy: that the pastoral, with its promises of a life of only light labour, could coexist with the georgic, with its warning that only by toil and sweat can life, and civilization, be sustained. Or perhaps it would have seemed to suggest that these two alternative ways of organizing land and labour are ineluctably in conflict, and that, as the man with the telescope can see, looking towards England and the enclosing parishes to the east, only one of them can win.

Finally, however, the point I want to make about this image is that its unprepossessing character, its refusal to be particularly sublime, particularly beautiful, particularly picturesque, is the sign of its uncompromising commitment to the local. That refusal is its way of announcing that it is chiefly addressed to those who will respond by saying, 'Oh I know where that is,' but who, in recognizing the place from its topography – the boulder, the configuration of river, bridge and church, the profile of the Clwydian range of hills, as accurate as a coastline charted by Captain Cook – recognize it also as a place, well known to them, where the conflict between the commercial and the customary, modernity and tradition, georgic and pastoral, was especially visible. Twiddling the controls again, this time Pugh turns down the aesthetic interest to turn up the local; in doing so he vastly diminishes the number of those to whom it will appeal, but offers the remainder an opportunity to meditate on what is happening to their locality that never could be offered by all the views produced by the metropolitan watercolourists who piled into north Wales every summer in search of the sublime.

Plate 3.11 *Thomas Gainsborough,* Landscape with a Woodcutter courting a Milkmaid, *oil on canvas, 1755, Duke of Bedford, Woburn Abbey.*

Notes

1 *CD*, pp. 432, 445–8.

2 See Colonel Maurice Harold Grant, *A Chronological History of the Old English Landscape Painters (in Oil) from the XVIth Century to the XIXth Century*, new revised and enlarged edition, 8 vols (1957–61), vol. 5 (Leigh-on-Sea: F. Lewis, 1959), plate 414. Grant gives the painting's dimensions as 21cm x 28cm.

3 Davies, *General View*, p. 273.

4 See 'A Summary of Lands enclosed from the Waste in the Lordship of Ruthin Richard Myddelton Esqr. of Chirk-Castle in the County of Denbigh Lord of the Manor. Taken 1779 by. S. Minshull', NLW MS Maps vol. 20: the Coedmarchan map is no. 64, and the computation of the acreage enclosed and unenclosed is on the preceding and following pages.

5 A line of stones marking the parish boundary is shown on the 1805 enclosure map of Llanfwrog DRO QSD DE 2, and possibly those other than the large erratic may have been put in place at the enclosure. For the erratic, see Strahan, *Geology*, pp. 146–8.

6 Pennant, *Tours*, vol. 2, p. 58.

7 *CD*, p. 441.

8 Kay, *General View of the Agriculture and Rural Economy of Merionethshire* (Edinburgh: John Moir, 1794), pp. 8, 15; *General View of the Agriculture and Rural Economy of Anglesey* (Edinburgh: John Moir, 1794), p. 28. My thanks to Christopher Dyer for calling my attention to this issue.

9 *CD*, p. 14.

10 *CD*, p. 435.

11 See J.Y.W. Lloyd, *The History of the Princes, the Lords Marcher, and the Ancient Nobility of Powys Fadog*, vol. 4 (London: Whiting, 1884), p. 315; Pugh, *CD*, p. 435; and especially Donald Adamson and Peter Beauclerk Dewar, *The House of Nell Gwyn: The Fortunes of the Beauclerk Family 1670–1974* (London: William Kimber, 1974), pp. 105–10. I do not know whether the Revd Butler Clough, as Pugh calls him, was the same man as the Revd Roger Clough of Bathafarn, a banker who was declared bankrupt in 1817: see *The European Magazine and London Review*, 71 (January 1817), 77. The identity of Clough, or rather, whether this Revd Roger Clough was the same as the Revd Roger Butler Clough, is confused further by the articles by J. B. Lewis, 'The Cloughs in the North West', *Clwyd Historian*, 27 (Autumn 1991), 16–20, and by the editors, 'The Cloughs in the North West–Corrections', *Clwyd Historian,* 47 (Autumn 2001), 2 8. The corrections are themselves confusing in that, while suggesting that Lewis conflated two generations and two pairs of Richard and Roger Cloughs into one, they do not sufficiently clarify who was who. The corrections are surely wrong however in suggesting that no 'Butler Clough' existed at the time that Pugh places one in Bathafarn Hall. For the extent of the estate at the 1805 sale see *CCh* 18 October and 29 November 1805.

12 It is possible that, in defiance of the geography of the area, one of the tiny white shapes in the centre distance, which under a magnifying glass turn out to be houses, is in fact intended to be the hall. Like these houses Bathafarn is situated just where the hills begin to rise steeply, though considerably further north. It is most unlikely, however, that Beauclerk, if he did ever glance at the print, would have recognized in it his at most very occasional residence, or, if he had, that he would have been flattered by the representation.

13 Peter D. G. Thomas, 'Wynnstay versus Chirk Castle: Parliamentary Elections in Denbighshire 1716–1741', *National Library of Wales Journal*, 11/2 (Winter 1959), 105–22.

14 John Strange, 'An account of two giants causeways, or groups of prismatic basaltine columns, and other curious vulcanic concretions, in the Venetian state in Italy; with some remarks on the characters of these and other similar bodies, and on the physical geography of the countries in which they are found', *Philosophical Transactions of the Royal Society of London*, LXV/1 (1775), 5–47, Tabula I, opposite p. 6. For the authorship of the plate, see Maria Toscano, '"Nature Catched in the Fact": sperimentalismo e collezionismo antiquario-naturalistico nel regno di Napoli, Veneto, Gran Bretagna tra XVIII–XIX secolo', Ph. D. thesis, no date, Università degli Studi di Napoli 'Federico II', pp. 212–13, *http://www.fedoa.unina.it/777/1/Tesi_Toscano.pdf*.

15 Samuel Lewis, *A Topographical Dictionary of Wales*, 1849, pp. 147–57, and 328–32.

16 'Unpublished Letters of Edward Llwyd, of the Ashmolean Library, Oxford', *Cambrian Quarterly Magazine and Celtic Repertory*, 3/10 (April 1831), 211; Pennant, vol. 2, p. 58; Thomas Walford, *The Scientific Tourist through England, Wales, & Scotland*, 2 vols (London, J. Booth, 1818), vol. 2, unpaginated; Pugh, *CD*, pp. 441–2.

17 *CD*, p. 199.

18 *CD*, p. 441.

19 For this outcrop, see Strahan, *Geology*, p. 15, and for more on the 'marbles' of the Mold/Ruthin region, see p. 27.

20 *Universal British Directory*, vol. 4, pp. 346–7; *CD*, p. 442.

21 'The Vale of Clwyd', Navigator had written, 'produces a superabundance of grain and timber; the hills are replete with valuable minerals; these, for want of a market, are unprofitable to the owners of the land, and useless to the public: by means of a navigable canal

alone, these rich gifts of nature might become useful, and be dispersed thro' distant regions, which now stand in need of such blessings.' Such a canal, he argued, running from the head of the vale up to St Asaph and round to the Dee estuary, would be cheap to construct, as it would run on a 'dead level' (*Adam's Weekly Courant*, 8 March 1791). Navigator's arguments were questioned in a letter of 29 March, to which Navigator replied on 12 April. My thanks to Marion Löffler for bringing this correspondence to my attention.

22 *CD*, pp. 231, 442–3.

23 [J. Evans], *The Beauties of England and Wales . . .* vol. XVII, part I (London: J. Harris, et. al.), 1812), p. 513; on the marble industry in Wales during the wars of 1793–1815, see A. H. Dodd, *The Industrial Revolution in North Wales* (Cardiff: University of Wales Press, 1951), pp. 223–4.

24 Quoted in Ellis, 'Limestone quarrying', 126.

25 Davies, *General View*, p. 301; Ellis, 'Limestone quarrying', 128; J. Evans, *Letters written during a Tour through North Wales, in the Year 1798, and at Other Times*, 3rd edn (London: C. and R. Baldwin, 1804), p. 373.

26 Pennant, *Tours*, vol. 1, pp. 416–17.

27 Hucks, *A Pedestrian Tour*, p. 7.

28 Quoted in C. P. Barbier, *William Gilpin* (Oxford: Oxford University Press, 1963), p. 112.

29 Gilpin, *Observations, relative chiefly to Picturesque Beauty, Made in the Year 1772, On Several Parts of England; particularly the Mountains and Lakes of Cumberland, and Westmoreland* (1789), 2 vols, 3rd edn (London: R. Blamire, 1792), vol. 2, pp. 43–4; and see 'the picturesque has nothing to do with the affairs of the plough and the spade', in his *Remarks on Forest Scenery, and other Woodland Views, (Relative chiefly to Picturesque Beauty)*, 2 vols (London: R. Blamire, 1791), vol. 1, p. 298.

30 Gilpin, *Observations, relative chiefly to Picturesque Beauty*, vol. 2, p. 44. For a fuller discussion of these issues, see the essay 'Visualising the division of labour', in Barrell, *The Birth of Pandora*, pp. 89–118.

31 See Toscano, 'Nature Catched in the Fact', p. 213.

32 It is entered by Minshull as 'John Dale's Widow a Lime Kiln', but other encroachments involving Mrs Dale are entered as 'Lands belonging [to] Robert Townshend Esqr. in Widow Dale's Tenure'.

33 Edwards, 'Enclosure and agricultural improvement', pp. 107–9, and see p. 121.

34 See Ellis, 'The History of Quarrying in the Maeshafn-Llanarmon Area', *Denbighshire Historical Society Transactions*, 43 (1994), 45–65, esp. 45–6; Ellis, 'Limestone quarrying', 133–4; D. G. Evans, 'The Hope Enclosure Act', 167, 170, 183. See also Jones, *Before Rebecca*, p. 41 on restrictions on access to lime quarries following enclosure. I am most grateful to C. J. Williams for his help on this matter.

35 On rumours of enclosure, see Evans, 'The Hope Enclosure Act', p. 167.

36 Chapman, *Guide*, p. 80; Jones, *Before Rebecca*, p. 41; for examples of such sales, see *CCh* 11 July 1794, 20 March 1801.

37 Edwards, 'Enclosure and Agricultural Improvement', pp. 109, 192; Chapman, *Guide*, p. 86.

38 K. D. M. Snell, *Annals of the Labouring Poor: Social Change and Agrarian England, 1660–1900*, Cambridge (Cambridge University Press, 1985), p. 172n.

FOUR *Pont-Newydd over the Ceirw near Corwen*

I

In late August 1793, a Shropshire gentleman, Plowden Slaney, was returning home to Shifnal by a circuitous route after a month's holiday in the new sea-bathing resort of Barmouth. On the road between Cerrig-y-Drudion and Corwen, he stopped to admire the gorge and waterfall of Glyn Diffwys. He wrote:

> [we] passed by the side of a vale called the troubled vale, over which from rock to rock, there was being erected a bridge of one arch. This bridge will be a second Devil's bridge: the height from the water to the arch is very great; and a roaring river of about six or seven yards broad, almost hid with trees and precipices, entirely fills the vale, and forms a very pleasing scene.[1]

The bridge was being built across the river Ceirw and had been commissioned the previous November, at the Quarter Sessions at Denbigh, from John Parry, a stone-mason of Llansanffraid Glynceiriog, who bound himself to construct it on the same design as one over the river Alwen at Betwys Gwerful Goch, three miles away; on more or less the same design, indeed, as dozens if not hundreds of other bridges in north Wales, including, among famous ones, Pont Aberglaslyn. It was apparently intended to join the road from Ruthin to Bala with the road from Llanrwst,[2] though there were as yet no roads running up to the site of the bridge on the south side of the river. Once the bridge had been built, however, Parry entered into another agreement, in May 1794, this time to raise the level of the road over the bridge in order to marry it up with a renewed stretch of the turnpike on the north side, and two proposed new roads on the south side, one running due south, the other heading off to the south-west towards the village of Llangwm.[3]

At a time when, as A. H. Dodd put it, the state of the roads there was so 'deplorable' that 'a "Welsh journey" became a byword',[4] the works at Glyn Diffwys were part of a major upgrading of the infrastructure of north Wales in general, and of Denbighshire in particular. Throughout Denbighshire in the 1790s, according to Sir Frederic Morton Eden, the county rate was unusually high, 'owing chiefly to the great number of bridges'.[5] In Llangwm parish new bridges were constructed and old ones improved, six in total, between the late 1770s and the end of the century, from Pont Maesmor in the east to Pont Arddwyfaen in the north-west.[6] The most significant part of this upgrading involved the road between Cerrig-y-Drudion and Corwen, which had been turnpiked following a comprehensive act

Plate 4.1 *(opposite) William Ellis after Edward Pugh, Pont-Newydd over the Ceirw near Corwen, aquatint (London: E. Pugh, 1794), first issue, Aberystwyth, National Library of Wales.*

of 1777, piloted through the Commons by Sir Watkin Williams Wynn among others,[7] which aimed at improving the state of numerous roads across Merionethshire and into Denbighshire, from Llangollen to Traeth Mawr, from Aberdovey to Llanrwst.[8] A part of the aim of the act was to make a new road to Holyhead, avoiding the half-mile ferry crossing over the Conwy estuary – 'bad boatage', as John Byng described it[9] – by which travellers on the coastal route from Chester were frequently delayed. The new Great Irish Road would run from Shrewsbury, through Llangollen and Corwen, along the edge of Glyn Diffwys, and then, from Betws y Coed, either up through Llanrwst to join the old Irish Road on the west bank of the Conwy estuary, or along the Llugwy valley and Nant Francon to join it at Bangor.

The turnpiking of the new Holyhead Road did not however eliminate the dangers it presented to coach traffic in particular. 'From Ty Nant through the rocky pass of Glyn Duffws,' in the words of a parliamentary report on the road in 1817, 'the road is confined between steep rocks and a precipice, in places only 12 feet wide, with quick turnings.'[10] This was a part of the road particularly in need of the attention of Thomas Telford, who began re-engineering the Holyhead road from 1819. When he came to Glyn Diffwys, wrote Charles G. Harper, he found

the uplands on the right presently culminating in the crags of Cader Dinmael, and the valley of the Geirw on the left gradually deepening and contracting into a profound and narrow gorge; the road running round cornices of rock, fenced by breast-high masonry on the one side, and overhung by rocky cliffs on the other. With

boring-tools, pickaxe, and blasting-powder, Telford forced a way for his road round this shoulder of the mountain and converted what had been a narrow and dangerous track into a smooth highway, thirty-six feet in width.[11]

Pugh visited Glyn Diffwys in late 1793 or the early summer of the following year,[12] and William Ellis's aquatint, *The View of Pont-Newydd over the Ceirw near Corwen* appeared in October 1794, though dated July (Plate 4.1). I have never seen a version of this print with its original colouring. Along with the view of Llanfwrog it was one of the first two of Pugh's Denbighshire series to be published, and the scene had an obvious attraction for him in his project of modestly emulating Richard Wilson's six views in Wales. For we may think of this aquatint as an act of homage to Wilson's *The Great Bridge over the Taaffe*, the image of an engineering achievement still known, in Pugh's day, as the 'Pont Newydd' or 'Newbridge' (see Plate 0.1). Appropriately of course the bridge in Wilson's image was far grander than the little Denbighshire effort depicted by Pugh, but both images recorded and celebrated the modernization of the transport infrastructure of Wales, as, later, would Pugh's grand pair of images of Monmouthshire, discussed in the Introduction.

Pugh might have dedicated this print to Lewis Bagot, bishop of St Asaph, who had been one of the patrons mentioned in Pugh's original advertisement for the *Six Views*, and who was also the sinecure rector of Llangwm parish. In the event however he inscribed it with 'the greatest respect' to Robert Watkin Wynne, by 'his obedient and obliged servant'. We came across Wynne in the Introduction, chairing the inaugural meeting of the Denbigh Loyal Association in January 1793. Of the five estates he owned in north Wales,[13] Wynne resided most frequently in Garthmeilio, in Llangwm, two miles from the new bridge. Along with his relation Watkin Edwards Wynne of Voylas (ten miles further west along the turnpike), he had been one of the JPs who had commissioned the bridge at Glyn Diffwys, partly perhaps in order to obtain, at the expense of the county, a short-cut to Garthmeilio from the east.[14] It appears from Pugh's first advertisement for his *Six Views* that he had originally secured the patronage of Sir Robert Williams Vaughan, of Nannau, Tory MP for Merionethshire. In the event, however, none of the views was dedicated to Vaughan, who had no particular connection with Denbighshire, and it is likely that Pugh had confused R. W. Vaughan with R. W. Wynne – in *Cambria Depicta* he would misremember the same Sir Robert Williams Vaughan as 'Sir Robert Williams'.[15] But for a man hoping to keep in with the great Tory squires of north Wales, to confuse Vaughan with Wynne was quite a blunder.

In 1789, on the death of Sir Watkin Williams Wynn of Wynnstay, the Wynn family began to look round for someone to succeed him as MP for Denbighshire. The seat was understood, by the Wynns at least, to be their hereditary property – they had first represented the county in the reign of Henry VIII[16] – and they wanted someone who would agree to be a caretaker only, keeping the seat warm until the next general election when the next Sir Watkin Williams Wynn, a minor, would be of age. According to the not unbiased Whig landowner Edward Eyton, they offered the seat first to Philip Yorke of Erddig, then to Robert Wynne of Garthewin and then to Thomas Grenville, who owned no property in the county. All refused a position they no doubt regarded as humiliating, and the honour eventually fell to the man who was fourth choice.[17] 'Alas! Poor Denbighshire!' groaned Eyton, '— thou didst get a representative' – Robert Watkin Wynne of Garthmeilio.[18]

Eyton's objection to Wynne, however, was not that he was just another obedient Tory, just lobby fodder, but that he was too radical for the mainstream Whigs. John Jones, Jac Glan-y-Gors, who had been born in the next parish to Llangwm, Cerrig-y-drudion, claimed that in the 1790s the MPs for Denbighshire sat for many years, 'without uttering one word, bad or good, nor doing anything else but lifting their hands to please other people'.[19] Jones was a follower of Tom Paine and a political associate of John Thelwall, and perhaps he exaggerated, but I can find no record of Wynne speaking in Parliament. He did vote, however: in April 1792, he voted with the minority, led by Charles Grey, against Pitt's threatening belligerence towards Russia during the Ochakov crisis, and in the same month he supported the repeal of the Test Act in Scotland. In May 1793 he was again in the minority in supporting the Sheffield petition for parliamentary reform. He seems to have become increasingly radicalized by Pitt's attack on the reform movement, and after the summer of 1794, when the Whig party split and the majority of them, led by the Duke of Portland, entered a coalition with Pitt, Wynne is repeatedly found voting with the minority of Whigs, led by Charles James Fox, against Pitt and his new allies. In December, and again in January and February 1795, he voted against the coalition and in favour of motions for peace with France proposed by Wilberforce and by Grey, and in February again he voted against Pitt's plan to lend a huge sum to Austria to persuade the emperor to continue the war against the French Republic. He also opposed the coalition's attempts to suppress the reform movement, voting

against the continued suspension of Habeas Corpus in January 1795 and in November against the Seditious Meetings Bill, one of the notorious 'two acts' (strongly supported by Pennant) intended to prevent public political meetings promoting reform.[20] This voting record cannot have been anticipated at Wynnstay when he was chosen, with whatever degree of reluctance, to nurse Sir Watkin's future seat.

If Wynne had been enough of a loyalist to act as chairman of the short-lived Denbigh Loyal Association, he was also enough of a radical Whig to send his son John to be educated by Samuel Parr, 'the Whig Dr. Johnson', who had educated and radicalized some of the most prominent members of the leading reform group, the London Corresponding Society. In 1797 John eloped with Parr's daughter, Sarah Anne.[21] Shortly after their marriage Parr went down to Denbighshire to visit Robert Watkin Wynne, and the two must have had much in common. 'The squire', Pennant claimed, passing on to Lloyd Kenyon a piece of gossip he had probably invented himself, 'is a true democrat, and is said even to threaten to join the French';[22] while Parr was known as 'the Jacobinical parson', and was a supporter of the revolution in France at least through the 1790s. We came across him briefly in Chapter 2, in a song by Bagot, where he featured alongside Paine, Richard Price and Joseph Priestley in an alliterative quadrumvirate of pro-revolutionary scoundrels.

Sir Watkin himself entered Parliament as MP for Beaumaris in November 1794, at the age of twenty-two – the seat was a pocket borough controlled by Viscount Bulkeley, the dedicatee of Pugh's print of Carreg Carn March Arthur – and claimed the Denbighshire seat from Wynne at the general election of 1796.[23] Unlike Pennant, however, he did not hold Wynne's politics against him. When in May 1794 the local gentry led by Sir Watkin established a volunteer force of fencible cavalry intended to keep under control the disaffected poor of Denbighshire, Wynne, who had served as captain in the Royal Denbighshire Militia during the war with America, was rewarded by being appointed second-in-command.[24] When he relinquished his seat in the Commons he was further rewarded by Sir Watkin with a sinecure appointment, deputy steward of Bromfield and Yale. Wynne died in 1806. A year after the publication of the *Six Views*, he must have looked an unlikely addition to the list of dedicatees, the sole Whig among five Tories, and a radical Whig at that. When Pugh originally solicited him to accept a dedication, however, he would have been aware no doubt that Wynne had supported the loyalist associations and the fencibles, but of course quite unaware of how radical he would be revealed to be by the events of late 1794 and 1795. He probably thought of him simply as another Tory among the many Tory squires whom he needed to propitiate in order to prosper as an artist in north Wales.[25]

II

In 1771 the famous poet Huw Jones, who also lived in Llangwm, composed 'A New Song to the Honourable Esquire Robert Watkin Wynne of Garthmeilio and Many Other Places', probably in anticipation of Wynne's coming of age, and coming into the large inheritance which, by the time of his death, he would mostly have lost. 'God, let the rightful heir succeed,' prayed Jones, dutifully confident that the happiness of the inhabitants of Llangwm and the tenants of the Garthmeilio estate was now assured:

> He is our tree in foliage, our royal tree and
>   our ridge-tree,
> A beam to his tenants in adversity, a cheerful man …
>
> Justice is what Robert Watkin Wynne wishes
>   for …
>
> He's thoughtful towards his country through
>   our caring Father,
> Always doing goodness and offering charity …
>
> Young and old, God will love him and his
>   fair smile,
> He is kind towards his tenants …[26]

In another, undated ballad, however, 'The Complaint of the Irritated Father', Jones speaks as one in despair as his landlord, presumably Wynne himself if we are to take this 'irritated farmer' as Jones himself, keeps raising his rent:

> … the rent through the parish has been raised
>   twice more,

> Many weak farmers are sick because of the strain,
> Ploughing the hard land until they fell on their
>   arses,
> So that the masters can spend time drinking
>   punch and wine. …
> A big fat steward will arrive, we have to bow to
>   the ground …

In addition, there is the constant drain on his income by way of taxes and tithes: the king, his officers and soldiers, the bishop, 'who could feed a hundred with the money I pay him', the parson, who earns his share of the tithe for 'sitting and lounging and reading prayers', even the curate. Finally, there is the grasping turnpike trust:

> A wasted part of today's bread
> Goes to senseless, foolish, faithless men
> For making along the mountains new roads for us,
> Such an endless pressure on a farmer are these
>   persuasive men;
> They've mentioned now that they'll empty the
>   Traeth Mawr,
> And the Berwyn Mountains will be destroyed
>   or levelled;
> And it's the farmer himself who supports every man
> So that they can extend their arms and grab more
>   money,
> They are so fat and ugly, very unsightly;
> I have to feed the man by the post with bread
>   and roast meat,
> For opening gates I offer him pennies,
> We've been paying the old man quite a sum for
>   some time.[27]

In short, Jones represents himself, or his 'irritated' farmer, as the epitome of everything that the squirearchy, and English travellers in Wales, regarded as 'backward' about Welsh tenant farmers and farmworkers. He fails to see how repeated increases in his rent work to his advantage, as a stimulus to greater productivity. He cannot understand how much he gains from the new turnpikes, all at the trifling cost of a few pence for taking his livestock or his wagon through the turnpike gate; and he turns away from the civilizing religion of the Church to grumble in the chapel. And yet his discontents do not quite persuade him into disloyalty to his squire: the fat steward arrives in time to divert his attack from the 'masters', just as the fat keeper of the turnpike gate – he probably has in mind the gate at the staging-post at Cernioge Mawr, a few miles west of Llangwm – attracts some of the anger at first directed against the trust.

By contrast with Jones's 'Complaint', Pugh's image stands for modernity, or seems at least sympathetic to the efforts of those who thought of themselves as hauling Denbighshire into the late eighteenth century and the modern world of commerce. Pugh was the first of the many artists who were attracted to this location to depict the new bridge, though not the first to depict the falls at Glyn Diffwys. Before the bridge was built, J. G. Wood, in a fine aquatint made by the versatile Maria Prestel, published in 1793 (Plate 4.2), had taken a viewpoint apparently a few yards further down the gorge than Pugh, peering through thick foliage

Plate 4.2 *M. C. Prestel after J. G. Wood*, Part of Glyn Dyffwys near Corwen, *coloured aquatint (London: J. G. Wood, 1793), Aberystwyth, National Library of Wales.*

towards the waterfall where the bridge was about to be built. There is also an enigmatically titled watercolour by John 'Warwick' Smith, entitled 'Falls of the C---- on Monday, North Wales' (Plate 4.3), one of a number of watercolours he made of waterfalls in north Wales, this one on a river the name of which he had either forgotten or could not spell.[28] Among north Welsh rivers beginning with 'C', there are substantial falls on the Conwy (which Smith drew) and the Crafnant, but to me this looks most like the first two drops at Glyn Diffwys on the river Ceirw (hard to spell for an Englishman), above which the bridge would soon be built. As in other images of the fall, Smith shows it surrounded but not obscured by trees, these more convincingly stunted and spindly than the trees in the images illustrated later in this chapter. He is positioned, or draws as if positioned, much closer to the fall than other artists, and whatever sense of the power of the water he sacrifices by being unable, from this viewpoint, to show its whole descent, he makes up for by greater proximity. Other images of Glyn Diffwys communicate much more quietly than the rushing falls and plunge pool as Smith shows them to us. The shape taken by waterfalls changes, of course, with every variation in rainfall, besides which topographical drawings were in the habit of taking too many liberties with landscape for us to be sure beyond any doubt that the C---- was indeed the Ceirw. If it was, the picture would probably date from 1792, just before the bridge was built, when Smith is known to have been touring the area.

Pugh draws the new bridge in such a way as to acknowledge its newness, and with an attention to detail that those who followed him here had no interest in emulating. He shows the bridge as it was and still is, with a very slight suggestion

of a peak at the centre, with splayed ends which terminate in square piers, and a string course on the spandrel just below a parapet with a coping of flat stones. The picture is no doubt dedicated to Wynne not only as the local squire but as the projector of the bridge; he earns Pugh's 'greatest respect' by virtue not only of his rank but of his philanthropic concern for the improvement of his parish and his county. A few months before Pont y Glyn was commissioned, at the May Quarter Sessions at Denbigh, two stonemasons, one from Llangwm, one from Llangynhafal, contracted to carry out large-scale repairs on the massive bridge over the Clwyedog at Bontuchel, a few miles west of Ruthin. As soon as these repairs were complete and the bridge renewed, Pugh went to draw it, and with his engraver Poole published a print of it in 1795. He shows the bridge at Bontuchel as no more quaint or picturesque than Pont y Glyn: it stands square, solid, and entirely functional, another testament to the new spirit of improvement (Plate 4.4).[29]

The point is underlined by comparing Pugh's picture of the bridge at Glyn Diffwys with the English artist Thomas Walmsley's *Pont y Glen, Corwen, North Wales*, aquatinted by R. and D. Havell

Plate 4.3 *John 'Warwick' Smith,* Falls of the C---- on Monday, North Wales, *watercolour, circa 1792–3, National Library of Wales.*

Plate 4.4 *(right) W. Poole after Edward Pugh*, Pont Ychel Ruthin, *engraving (London: E. Pugh and W. Poole, 1796), Aberystwyth, National Library of Wales.*

Plate 4.5 *(opposite) R. and D. Havell after Thomas Walmsley*, Pont y Glen, Corwen, North Wales, *coloured aquatint, in* Miscellaneous British Scenery *no. 2nd, plate first. (London: James Daniell: 1810), London, British Library.*

and published in 1810 (Plate 4.5).[30] For Walmsley it seems the idea of a modern bridge is incompatible with the version of the picturesque he has come to Wales in search of; and so he has chosen to gothicize Pont y Glyn by dilapidating it and by giving it a pointed arch, a stepped parapet, and a gradient which would be impractically steep for wheeled traffic if the bridge were not obviously too narrow to admit any. The efforts Parry made to protect the bridge from the effects of the weather – the coping, the string course, the voussoirs recessed beneath a

projecting regulating course – have all been wished away. Foliage trails from between the stones, hurrying the structure to its imminent ruin; some entirely imaginary crags make up the distance. In a view of Llangollen bridge, Walmsley's determination to pitch Wales into a Gothic past had led him grotesquely to sharpen the only slightly pointed arches of that bridge too.[31] To Pugh, his fashionably romantic predilections must have seemed as 'backward' as he perhaps would have regarded the complaints of Jones's irritated farmer.

III

In the years following the building of the bridge Glyn Diffwys became a major tourist site, as it had not been before: the only place on the Holyhead Road that the English tourists now crowding into Wales thought worth stopping at between the home of Owain Glyndŵr at Glyndyfrdwy and Betws y Coed. When Telford rebuilt the road here, he set into the wall two viewing refuges: from one, travellers could stare down into the depths of the glen; from the other they could admire the bridge and waterfall. He built another elsewhere on the road, by the river Llugwy at Capel Curig, which came to be illustrated by David Cox (Plate 4.6).

Pont y Glyn became a magnet for artists, and the description of it became a set piece of published and unpublished tours: you can almost imagine authors rolling up their sleeves and licking their pencils before taking it on. If it was the bridge that called attention, however, to the gorge and waterfall, no other artists or writers saw it quite as Pugh

Plate 4.6 *William Radclyffe after David Cox*, Bridge over the Llugwy, *engraving, from Thomas Roscoe,* Wanderings and Excursions in North Wales *(London: C. Tilt; Simpkin and Co., 1836), private collection.*

saw it, as something worth representing with some exactitude, as an example of the modern spirit of improvement.

In 1798 the Revd Brian Broughton, a youngish Fellow of New College, Oxford,[32] published a volume of *Poetical Reflections* on leaving Wales, including some lines on Pont y Glyn:

> flung from rock to rock,
> Pont y Glyn Dyffid, 'neath whose lofty arch
> The loud wave rages, whitening with his foam
> Tall oaks of vivid green, or paler ash,
> The craggy banks concealing.[33]

The volume included a drawing by Broughton of the bridge, aquatinted by Samuel Alken; another version, in a smaller format, appeared in a second edition of the poem two years later, and the larger version, now coloured, was reissued in 1801 (Plate 4.7).[34] This is an attractive engraving, enhanced by the restraint of its colouring, grisaille with a hint of late autumn tints in the foliage. But though Broughton captures well the shape of the arch, he makes the parapets improbably long, as if he did not know how to bring them to an end, and he has to rely on the contours of the hills to come to his aid. Something similar is true of J. Warren's more highly coloured aquatint of the scene, published in 1814 (Plate 4.8);[35] as a structure Warren's bridge is more plausible than Broughton's but not more like the actual bridge. My point is not, however, to suggest anything inept in Broughton's or Warren's work, merely that whatever they were doing their interest in the bridge was very different from Pugh's.

Richard Warner, who visited the scene in the summer of 1797, described the bridge as 'a simple arch of lofty construction', but returning the following year he saw it as a 'curious specimen of modern

masonry', a strange phrase to use of a structure so resolutely functional, and simple.[36] But apart from Slaney he is the only writer I have found who pointed out that the bridge was a new bridge, as if, for the others, to acknowledge that would be to detract from the Romantic character of the scene. Others describe it as 'bold', 'curious', 'lofty',[37] and admire the energy, almost, with which it 'springs' from the rocky bastions on either side of the narrow river, or 'bestrides' the chasm.[38] The Londoner William Eade, writing a travel journal to be read by his younger sister, described it as 'rudely simple according well with the wild scenery in which it stands'.[39]

These artists and authors of tours needed to represent the bridge as if it were a 'natural' part of a natural landscape, not a recent addition to it: just there, not just put there. As Edmund Burke had pointed out,

Plate 4.7 *Samuel Alken after the Rev. Brian Broughton, Pont y Glynn Dyffis, near Corwen, coloured aquatint, in Broughton,* Six Picturesque Views in North Wales *(London: J. Mawman, 1801), London, British Library.*

Plate 4.8 *Henri Merke after J. Warren,* Pontnewydd, near Corwen, Merionethshire, *coloured aquatint (London: T. Macdonald, 1814), London, British Library.*

in his *Philosophical Enquiry into the Origin of our Ideas of the Sublime and Beautiful* (1757), the 'rudeness' of a structure increases its 'grandeur', 'as it excludes the idea of art, and contrivance';[40] and if those who drew or described Pont y Glyn did not all represent it as 'rude' or 'simple', all of them except Pugh took care not to emphasize the human skill that had brought it into being. They were looking at Glyn Diffwys not as a place but as a landscape, and so had to represent it in terms not of a narrative of human intervention but of the aesthetic vocabulary that had been developed to characterize the varieties of natural landscape. To them, Glyn Diffwys and its bridge offered the kind of scenery that asked to be understood as sublime or picturesque or some indeterminate combination of the two. The tourists describe the scene as 'wild' and 'bold', as 'grand', as 'romantic' and 'picturesque',[41] but, when they focus on the waterfall itself, they represent

it in the vocabulary of the sublime. The sublime, as defined by Burke, was related to feelings of extreme fear or terror, 'the strongest emotion which the mind is capable of feeling' for it was 'an apprehension of pain or death'.[42] Natural landscapes that appeared to threaten our instinct for self-preservation were productive of such feelings, which however could only be experienced as aesthetic pleasure or delight when they did not 'press too nearly', 'when we have an idea of pain and danger, without actually being in such circumstances'.[43] To be in the vicinity of a precipice, near the edge, is the kind of experience Burke had in mind; to stand close to a high waterfall, especially one rushing among protruding rocks, would be another; provided in each case we were near the edge, but safe from falling.

Richard Warner, on his first visit to the glen, was delighted and awestruck by the contrast in the river Ceirw above and below the bridge. 'Hitherto', he wrote, 'this stream has winded quietly and peaceably thro' the valley, but now entering suddenly a bed of disjoined crags, it boils fiercely over them, and rushes between steep, stupendous rocks.' Once under the bridge 'it discharges itself by a fall of many feet into a deep, rocky gulley, so obscured by over-hanging woods, and dark from its profundity, that the eye cannot trace the torrent through all its madness and horror.'[44] The Revd John Evans, despite his name and his education at Jesus College, Oxford, had been born in Gloucestershire, went to school and later taught in Bristol, and appears never to have lived in Wales. In his much-reprinted *Letters written during a Tour through North Wales* (1800), he describes (in terms borrowed from Warner as well as Burke) travelling eastward along the turnpike from Cerrig-y-Drudion and coming suddenly upon 'a scene as grand as it was unexpected. PONT LLYN DYFFWS'.

A bridge of one arch, about fifty feet in the span, is seen bestriding a deep and dismal chasm, through which the hoarse-sounding torrent, the Glynn, rushing down into a deepened bed, roars over the disjointed rocks beneath, and, lashing the rocky sides that check its impetuosity, rolls its angry waters to the Dee. The stupendous fissure, full two hundred feet deep, is overhung by large forest trees, whose spreading branches, intermingling from the opposite side, throw a darkened shade over the awful scene, and the eye dreads to follow the maddened torrent through the profundity of its horrible bed.

A bold cataract, above the bridge, gives you sufficient notice that you are near, and the hoarse rumblings of the water, heard in distant murmurs down the dark and wooded glen, give an additional effect in this truly sublime scene.[45]

Altitude, especially when we look down, and experience it not as height but as 'profundity'; darkness, with only a 'dismal' light; the impetuous violence of a 'maddened torrent', 'its madness and horror' as it were transferred to us as a feeling of losing self-control, as if stupefied by something 'stupendous' – this is the true sublime, and the kind of scene, the kind of thrill, that brought many tourists to Wales. Depending on their route Glyn Diffwys was for many the first or the last sublime experience of their holiday.

The more sublime the thrill they experienced here, the deeper they reckoned the glen to be. William Bingley, who thought the scene 'picturesque and elegant' rather than sublime, thought that the 'cataract' was 'not very lofty', and reckoned the bridge to be 'at least fifty feet above the bed of the stream'; though from there the view down the hollow 'was grand and tremendous'.[46] Bingley's estimate was about right; but to Richard Warner the bridge was 'one hundred feet above the water', and to Evans the glen was 'full two hundred feet deep'. To John Henry Manners, the fifth Duke of Rutland, who described the 'irresistible violence' of the Ceirw as, 'half concealed amongst the thickening foliage', it 'foamed . . . through the massy rocks, that everywhere presented their rugged faces', the glen was 'at least *an hundred yards* in depth' (my emphasis).[47]

For both Broughton and Warren, like these literary tourists, Glyn Diffwys was a landscape rather than a place. This is made especially clear by the figures in their images. Broughton places two gentlemen (to judge by their clothing), no doubt imagined to be tourists in search of the sublime and the picturesque, standing on a rock in the right foreground, evidently admiring and discussing the character and merits of the scene before them. Warren provides two more gentlemen spectators of the scene, but more engagingly he shows them struggling over the rocks, one of them using the branch of a dead tree as a handhold, trying to gain a station from which the bridge and waterfall can be seen to best advantage. Probably they have read Warner's first tour, where he tells us that 'the best point from which to view this grand *spectacle* is a little to the south-east of the arch,'[48] the point these gentlemen are endeavouring to occupy. There are other people in both scenes, on the bridge itself, as there almost always are in pictures of bridges at this period, and they appear to be either locals or travellers as opposed to tourists: Warren shows a man with a pack a few steps ahead of a weary, bonneted woman; Broughton shows an encounter between a horseman and a pedestrian. But the character of the

view, as a landscape, is given by the more genteel figures closer to our own viewpoint; as we register these aesthetic tourists, so we become aesthetic tourists as well; they indicate to us in what spirit the images are to be enjoyed.

Something similar is true of the image of Glyn Diffwys after J. G. Wood (Plate 4.2), which has an artist in the foreground with, apparently, a local

PONT Y GLYN.

NEAR CERIC Y DRUIDIAN

DENBIGHSHIRE.

man standing behind him, who is watching him at work and learning to see the place as landscape. The remarkable etching, published in the *Gentleman's Magazine* in 1816 by J. B. Knight (Plate 4.9), a Dorset land surveyor and painter, has a single figure on the bridge and two in the right foreground, so indeterminate as to repel any attempt to interpret them. The detail of the bridge makes it unmistakably Pont y Glyn, but the image as a whole is so boldly, and so explicitly, an exercise in the picturesque – in the contrast of textures between rocks and foliage, in the chiaroscuro – as to rule out the possibility of reading it as anything else, and Knight's commentary, in the *Gentleman's*, on his image of this 'romantic scene', is all about its aesthetic character: 'The beauties of Pont y Glynn are of a softened kind, compared to the native grandeur and sublimity of Pistyll Rhaidr', and so on. Thomas Walmsley needs no foreground figures to establish the aesthetic character of his thoroughly idealized version of the view. Henry Gastineau, the friend of J. M. W. Turner, also produced a version of the glen, in *Wales Illustrated in a Series of Views* which appeared in two volumes in 1830–1, but by this time a good deal more topographical accuracy was expected in such views. The bridge, now weathered by more than thirty-five years' exposure to the frosts and rains of upland Wales, already extensively repaired[49] and looking less than brand new, is shown with the same fidelity to its architecture as Pugh had demonstrated (Plate 4.10). This image, like the others in the same volume, seeks to combine a degree of topographical accuracy with a picturesque appetite for highly textured appearances, and does without the foreground figures that might have propelled our understanding of it in one direction or the other.

Plate 4.9 *(above) J.B. Knight,* Pont y Glyn, near Corwen, Merionethshire, *etching, in* Gentleman's Magazine *Vol. 86, part 2 (1816), frontispiece.*

Plate 4.10 *(right) Henry Gastineau,* Pont y Glyn: near Ceric y Druidian, Denbighshire, *engraving (London: Jones & Co., 1831), private collection.*

IV

For the figures in the foreground of Pugh's *Pont Newydd* the glen is a place to fish rather than an experience of the sublime. For all that, it is not exactly clear who they are imagined to be. In the centre is a gentleman wearing a waist-length spencer, with his breeches informally unbuttoned at the knee, and a box for flies slung by a strap over his shoulder (Plate 4.11). He has caught a fish, presumably one of the trout which were so abundant in the Ceirw,[50] and is holding it out in one hand while another man, probably his servant, appears to be carefully removing the hook from its mouth. This second man wears not breeches and stockings but the trousers that mark him

as less than genteel, as does the fact that he appears to be wearing no shirt, but that will remain unclear until a version of the print with its original colouring turns up. The rod he leans against his shoulder may suggest that his master allows him to fish; equally likely it is his master's spare. On the right, another man, possibly a gentleman but less well dressed than the central angler, is making heavy weather of the difficult descent from the road: he seems trapped on a dangerous rockfall – this was not, as Pugh explains

Plate 4.11 *Detail of plate 4.1.*

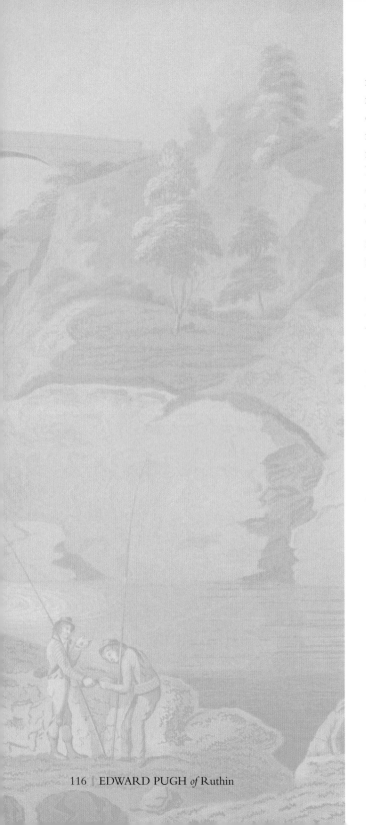

in *Cambria Depicta*, the best way into the glen. The fourth man may be pointing out the danger he is in, or attempting to show him a safer way of descending; or (as we shall be more inclined to believe later in this book, when we have looked more deeply into Pugh's attitude to rocky landscapes) he may be asking, or pleading with the man descending, not to loosen the stones and send them tumbling on top of him. The central angler too is pointing to the man on the rockfall, as if calling the attention of his servant to his friend's predicament.

This central figure may be a local squire – we can imagine him, in the context of Pugh's dedication, as Robert Watkin Wynne himself – or he may be on a fishing tour, for north Wales was becoming established as a place for gentlemanly recreational angling. Sir Watkin Williams Wynn fished at least as far west as Bala Lake, Llyn Tegid, where as we shall see he claimed all the fish belonged to him. Richard Colt Hoare of Stourhead frequently visited this area to fish, and left a list of the lakes he had fished, the fish he had killed, and what they had weighed.[51] By the early years of the next century, according to William Mavor, he had set up, with 'Sir J. Lister, a joint establishment for the purpose of fishing' on Llyn Tegid, where 'one of the fishermen had attended Sir R.C. Hoare … to almost every remarkable spot in Wales'.[52] When Hoare visited Pont y Glyn in 1801, however, there was so little water in the river that for a trout fisherman it was not worth making the difficult descent to the bed of the gorge. 'I satisfied myself with a view of it from above,' he wrote; 'but after hard rains I should think would amply repay the inquisitive traveller and lover of fine scenery for his trouble.[53]

Pugh's fishermen happen to be fishing in a sublime location; they are not there because the location is sublime. Images of sublime landscapes around 1800, when they are not entirely unpeopled, still emphasize the solitude necessary to an appreciation of the scene: a local peasant beneath a beetling cliff could be useful to give the scale, and, as we have seen, a tourist or two could serve to point out that this was a landscape, not just another place. Pugh's figures, while they certainly give the scale, also socialize the view; they invite us to see the glen as a place to meet and do things, as having a more than simply aesthetic character. But that does not mean that for Pugh Glyn Diffwys is a site simply of improvement and human activity, and not also a place with the power to astonish, as Burke says the sublime astonishes us.[54] Indeed, more than any of the other artists whose images we have looked at, Pugh seems to have been fascinated by the waterfall – the uneven stages of its descent, the rocks that interrupt its flow, the resting places where the waters briefly repose before tumbling further down the glen, all help create the sense, even by brief moments of contrast, of a dangerous violence. In *Cambria Depicta* he produced a description of what he calls the 'wild romantic hollow' of Glyn Diffws, as he encountered it on his second visit there in the 1800s, which captures the sublime power of the waterfall better than any other description of it that I have read. On leaving Corwen, he writes:

I made directly west, to the fall at Pont-newydd, alias Pont-y-Glynn, of the river Ceirw. I had seen this magnificent picture some years before, and could not resist the alluring temptation of visiting it once more. The river winds softly and quietly along a mountain-valley, till, meeting with this abrupt and craggy descent, the waters are poured down, under a single-arched bridge, in a volume, which becomes instantly convulsed by the resistance of the massy black crags, over which the bridge is seen pensile from rock to rock: then forcing its way, and foaming over other rude precipices and dislodged rocks, it at last finds temporary ease in a deep, large, circular basin in the bottom, from whence it starts again, over a rough bed of stone, through a deep woody dingle, which, for a quarter of a mile, is almost denied the light of day, from its vast depth, and its confinement between two high woody hills. The river, at a place called Pandy, finally finds repose, and steals along the quiet vales till its union with the Alwen.[55]

The second sentence here is constructed in such a way as to enact the movement of the water in its strife with the rocks. Especially artful is the way the sentence is deliberately protracted beyond the point where it seems ready to come to an end, where the waters have at last found 'ease' in the 'circular basin' depicted in the bottom right of Pugh's image. But we have been forewarned by the word 'temporary': the water's energy is not yet expended, and off it starts again, through the dark, profound gorge, finding repose only when it reaches the 'quiet vales' and the confluence with the Alwen. This is descriptive writing of a very high order, and demonstrates a knowledge of the discourse of the sublime, and a sensibility to sublime experience, which is also evident in the engraving.

Pugh's fascination with the uneven descent of the waterfall is no doubt partly the product of his willingness, on his first visit, to find a way to somewhere near its foot, daring to venture where even Evans's eye 'dreaded' to follow 'the maddened torrent'. 'The great road,' writes Pugh,

from London, through Shrewsbury, to Holyhead, is brought to the verge of this scene, and is cut through the solid rock; a work of great labour. From the road this chasm is seen to advantage, but the artist will rather chuse his points from the bottom. There are difficulties that present themselves to him in descending, but, if he has had a little practice in this way in Wales, he will know how to accomplish the task. When I was here before, I was advised to use a long pole, which I did, and it proved very useful in leaping from one rock to another; by these means I was enabled to follow the river, and see the noble scenery from the fall to the end of the glen.[56]

Pugh is the only literary tourist I have found who took the time and trouble to descend into the glen; most examined it from the road, or the bridge, or, in the case of Henry Eyre in 1796, from the inside of the coach on a rainy day.[57] Broughton tells us of his image that 'the spot from whence this view was taken is on the great road running from Shrewsbury to Holyhead';[58] and Warren's appears to be taken from pretty much the same viewpoint.

It would be possible to argue that the absorption of Pugh's two central figures in the job of fishing directs attention away from the sublimity of the scene by the suggestion that to them it is so familiar as to cease to astonish. We could even imagine Coleridge, in *Biographia Literaria*, adducing Pugh's picture to reinforce his attack on Wordsworth's claim in the 'Preface' to the *Lyrical Ballads* that 'men in rustic life' are improved, in mind, soul, sensibility, language, by living in sublime landscapes. 'Among the peasantry of North Wales,' claimed Coleridge – and he had been there for a couple of weeks, about twenty years earlier, so he knew all there was to know about them – 'the ancient mountains, with all their terrors and all their

Plate 4.12 Pont-y-Glyn, near Corwen, *postcard (no publication details or postmark), private collection*

HEN FFORDD TELFORD

YN Y MAN HWN
SAFODD GEORGE BORROW YN 1854
I FWYNHAU " .....UN O'R GOLYGFEYDD HARDDAF
A MWYAF DI DRAMGWYDD Y GELLIR EU DYCHMYGU...."*

" CYFIEITHIAD O'R GWAITH " WILD WALES, ITS PEOPLE LANGUAGE AND SCENERY "
GAN GEORGE BORROW

THE OLD TELFORD ROAD

AT THIS PLACE
GEORGE BORROW STOOD IN 1854
AND ENJOYED " ....ONE OF THE WILDEST AND
MOST BEAUTIFUL SCENES IMAGINABLE... "*

" FROM " WILD WALES, ITS PEOPLE LANGUAGE AND SCENERY " BY GEORGE BORROW

Plate 4.13 *Plaque near Pont y Glyn Diffwys, erected in 1996, 2011.*

glories, are pictures to the blind, and music to the deaf.'[59] But how we read the picture, whether we see it as privileging place above landscape, or landscape above place, or as at ease with its own hybridity and so managing to show the two as coexisting without obliging us to favour one or the other – that depends on us; on our assumptions about the relative value of 'landscape' and what would come to be called 'topographical' art; perhaps too on whether we are looking at Pugh's image in London or in Denbighshire.

The scene that attracted so many artists and writers, from those of the period I have been discussing

through to Prince Hermann von Pückler-Muskau, who spent more time there flirting with a pretty tourist in another coach than admiring the landscape,[60] and the evolutionist Alfred Wallace, no longer exists.[61] Glyn Diffwys has become a Site of Special Scientific Interest, by virtue of the presence there of the limestone woundwort, transplanted to the glen in 1998, and growing in what Conwy Council describes as 'rare semi-natural ancient broadleaved woodland'.[62] This woodland has been allowed to grow up to the point where even in winter the bridge and the waterfall are invisible from Telford's viewing refuges, but for the odd glimpse of white water; in summer nothing whatever can be seen. The literary record on Glyn Diffwys in the years around 1800 rather qualifies that phrase 'semi-ancient'. Writers at that period suggest that the glen below the waterfall was thickly wooded, as it is shown to be in the Wood–Prestel image of 1793, but that in the 1790s and the early decades of the nineteenth century the fall and bridge, though here and there concealed by foliage, were nevertheless clearly visible from along the Holyhead Road. Why else should Telford have built his refuges, from which Borrow enjoyed a clear view of the scene,[63] but which now has trees growing up densely around it, denying a view of anything but themselves? Even making allowance for artistic licence, the pictorial record suggests that when Pugh

was drawing the glen, there was not so much wood growing in the bowl of the waterfall as to conceal the view. It is of course likely that many trees were felled at the time of the bridge-building, but only by the time of Gastineau's image, in the early 1830s, had they grown back to fill up the bowl, and still not to the extent that they spoiled Borrow's view three decades later.

But by the beginning of the twentieth century, if that is the rough date of the only postcard I have found of the bridge, the waterfall had disappeared behind the trees, and has never been seen in summer since (Plate 4.12). A plaque, unveiled in 1996 by the parliamentary under-secretary of state, and commemorating Borrow's enjoyment of what he described as 'one of the wildest and most beautiful scenes imaginable', seems a very bad joke indeed (Plate 4.13). This view is surely as much part of the heritage of Wales as the transplanted woundwort, and it is impossible to believe that to make it visible again would have any very adverse effect on the flora of the glen. Of a similarly 'lost' waterfall at the head of Nant y Bache, a few miles south-west of Llangollen, Pugh writes: 'from the profusion of young wood about it, it is barely seen: but it would make a show, if a few saplings were cut away.'[64] That is all that is required, too, at Pont y Glyn Diffwys: to open a narrow passage from the nearer refuge, across Pugh's 'deep, large, circular basin', to the waterfall and bridge, it would be enough to lop a few branches, to fell a handful of scrawny trees, and to ensure, year by year, that new branches and saplings did not grow up to obscure the view.

Notes

1 [Plowden Slaney], 'A Short Journal of a Tour through the Counties of Denbigh, Merioneth, Cardigan, and Carnarvon, and the island of Anglesea in 1793' (NLW MS 9854C), p. 67.

2 [Evans], *Beauties*, vol. 17, Part 1, p. 939.

3 Denbighshire Quarter Sessions Records QSD/AB/1/428(A); *CCh* 9 May 1794.

4 A. H. Dodd, 'The Roads of North Wales, 1750-1850', *Archaeologia Cambrensis*, 80/1 (June 1925), 121.

5 Eden, *The State of the Poor*, vol. 3, p. 889.

6 See *Llangwm, Conway (part)*, (Cardiff: CADW, Welsh Historic Monuments, 1998), pp. 4, 8, 18, 21, 24, 26, and QSD AB/1/187, 205, 258, 260, 264 (Pont Arddwyfaen); 264 (Pont Ty-Gwyn); 316, 341, 374 (Pont y Capel); 420(e), 428 (A) and 430 (Pont y Glyn). For the repair of various bridges in Llangwm and elsewhere in the county in 1778, see 258.

7 See *Journals of the House of Commons*, 10, 21, 25 February, 7, 11 March 1777. The petition for the bill was presented to the Commons on 10 February, and it received the royal assent on 27 March.

8 See R. T. Pritchard, 'Denbighshire Roads and Turnpike Trusts', *Denbighshire Historical Society Transactions*, 12 (1963), 97, 108–9.

9 John Byng, *The Torrington Diaries,* ed. C. Bruyn Andrews, 4 vols (London: Eyre & Spottiswoode, 1934), vol. 1, p. 169.

10 Pritchard, 'Denbighshire Roads', 98.

11 Charles G. Harper, *The Holyhead Road: The Mail-Coach Road to Dublin*, 2 vols (London: Chapman and Hall, 1902), vol. 2, p. 220.

12 Pugh's first visit is alluded to in *CD*, pp. 297–8.

13 See P. R. Roberts, 'The Decline of the Welsh Squires in the Eighteenth Century', *National Library of Wales Journal*, 13/2 (1963), p. 163.

14 QSD/AB/1/420 (E).

15 *CD*, pp. 176, 183–4.

16 Oldfield, *Entire and Complete History*, vol. 3, p. 22.

17 *CCh* 21 August 1789, and see Eric Griffiths, *Philip Yorke I (1743–1804) Squire of Erthig* (Wrexham: Bridge Books, 2005), p. 118.

18 Edward Eyton, *A Letter, addressed to Sir W.W. Wynne, Bart.* (Chester, Shrewsbury and Wrexham: [John Fletcher, 1794]), pp. 13–14. For the progress of Robert Watkin Wynne's candidature, first announced in the same issue of the *CCh* as the death of Sir Watkin, see that newspaper, 7, 14 and 21 August 1789.

19 J. B. Edwards, 'John Jones (Jan Glan-y-Gors): Tom Paine's Denbighshire Henchman?', *Denbighshire Historical Society Transactions*, 51 (2002), 104. For Jones's association with Thelwall, see John Barrell and Jon Mee (eds), *Trials for Treason and Sedition 1792–1794*, 8 vols (London: Pickering & Chatto, 2006–7), p. 32, and the *Hereford Journal*, 10 December 1794. My thanks to Marion Löffler for identifying this John Jones as Thelwall's associate, and for supplying the last reference. For more on Jones, see Middleton Pennant Jones, 'John Jones or Glan-y-Gors', *The Transactions of the Honourable Society of Cymmrodorion. Session 1909–1910* (1911), 60–94.

20 *http://www.historyofparliamentonline.org/volume/1790-1820/member/wynne-robert-watkin-1755-1806*; *Correct List of the Minority on Mr. Grey's Motions, moved in the House of Commons, Tuesday April 12, 1791, on the Approach of a Russian War* (London: J. Debrett, 1791); *The Parliamentary History of England*, 36 vols (London: R. Bagshaw, T. Longman, 1806-20), vol. 31, cols 1062, 1192, 1248; *The History of Two Acts* (London: G. G. and J. Robinson, 1796, p. 466. The debates of January 1795 to renew the Habeas Corpus Suspension Act,

first passed in the early summer of 1794, became a debate on the notorious treason trials of 1794 in which leaders of the societies for parliamentary reform had been acquitted of high treason. To vote against the continued suspension of the act was in effect to acknowledge their innocence, which Pitt's government and supporters continued to deny. For the Seditious Meetings Bill and the two acts generally, see Barrell, *Imagining the King's Death*, pp. 551–603; for Pennant's support of the bill, see Kenyon, *Life of Kenyon*, p. 324.

21 Mary Shelley, 'Life of William Godwin', ed. Pamela Clemit, in *Mary Shelley's Literary Lives*, gen. ed. Nora Crook, 4 vols (London: Pickering and Chatto, 2002), vol. 4, p. 95n.

22 Kenyon, *Life of Kenyon*, p. 325.

23 See *CCh* 7 November 1794, 31 May 1795.

24 See *The Cumberland Chronicle and Whitehaven Public Advertiser*, 2 July 1778; Parry and Freeman, *Historical Records*, chs 1 and 2, and especially the letter from R. W. Wynne in Appendix 4. pp. xxiv–xxv.

25 Wynne died in 1806, heavily in debt. John and Sarah Wynne (née Parr) separated soon after.

26 Huw Jones, 'Cerdd Newydd i'r Anrhydeddus Ysgwïer Robert Watgyn Wynne o Garthmeilo ac Amryw Fannau', dated 14 January 1771, MSS NLW 2068, 81. I am most grateful to Dr Alaw Mai Jones of the Centre for Advanced Welsh and Celtic Studies at University of Wales, for calling Jones's ballads to my attention and for translating some of them for me.

27 Jones, 'Cwynfan yr Hwsmon Trafferthus'; printed in ballad book number 249b (at Chester by Thomas Huxley, undated). Also in manuscript NLW Cwrtmawr 39, p. 260 (*c.* eighteenth century); translated by Alaw Mai Jones, but I take responsibility for substituting the word 'arses' for her more polite 'behind'.

28 See the collection of Smith's watercolours of Wales digitised at *http://www.llgc.org.uk/index.php?id=5752*.

29 For Pugh's account of Bontuchel, see *CD*, p. 427.

30 Thomas Walmsley and R. and D. Havell, *Miscellaneous British Scenery no. 2nd, plate first. Pont y Glen, near Corwen, North Wales* (London: James Daniell, 480 Strand, 16 April 1810).

31 Walmsley and Jukes, *Llangollen Bridge–on the River Dee, Jan 30 1800* (London: Jukes, 30 January 1800).

32 For Broughton see his obituary in *GM* (February 1838), 216.

33 *Four Picturesque Views in North Wales, engraved in Aquatinta by Alken, from Drawings made on the Spot by the Rev. Brian Broughton, M.A. Fellow of New College, Oxford: with Poetical Reflections on Leaving that Country* (folio; London: printed for the author, B. Broughton, Oxford. To be had of W. Clarke, Bookseller, New Bond-Street, 1798), pp. 21–2. 'Dyffid' became 'Dyffis' in the edition of 1801 (see next note).

34 The image in its various versions appeared first as *Pont y Dyffid* [sic], *Corwen, Merionethshire*, in *Four Picturesque Views*; then as a single sheet (London: F. Jukes, 1 July 1800); and finally as *Pont y Glynn Dyffis, near Corwen*, in *Six Picturesque Views in North Wales, engraved in Aquatinta by Alken, from Drawings made on the Spot: with Poetical Reflections on Leaving that Country, by the Rev. Brian Broughton, M.A. Fellow of New College, Oxford* (quarto: London: for J. Mawman, in the Poultry, by T. Bensley, Bolt Court, Fleet Street, 1801).

35 Henry Merke, after J. Warren, *Pontnewydd, near Corwen, Merionethshire* (London: T. Macdonald, Poets Gallery, 39 Fleet Street, 14 May 1814).

36 Richard Warner, *A Walk through Wales, in August 1797* (Bath: R. Cruttwell, and London: C. Dilly, 1798), p. 163; Warner, *A Second Walk*, p. 192.

37 Henry Skrine, *Two Successive Tours through the Whole of Wales* (London: Emsley and Bremner, 1798), p. 237; Richard Colt Hoare, 'Journal of a Tour in 1801', in M. W. Thompson (ed.), *The Journeys of Sir Richard Colt Hoare through Wales and England 1793–1810* (Gloucester: Alan Sutton, 1983), 178; John Henry Manners, Duke of Rutland, *Journal of a Tour through North and South Wales, the Isle of Man, &c. &c.* (London: J. Triphook, 1805), p. 322.

38 W. Hutton, *Remarks upon North Wales, being the Result of Sixteen Tours through that Part of the Principality* (Birmingham: Knott & Lloyd, 1803), p. 38; Skrine, p. 237; Warner 1, p. 163.

39 William Eade, 'Journal of a tour through North Wales', Spring 1802, NLW MS 22190B, f. 26 (obverse).

40 Burke, *A Philosophical Enquiry into the Origin of our Ideas of the Sublime and Beautiful* (1757), ed. J. T. Boulton (London: Routledge and Kegan Paul, 1958), p. 77.

41 Henry Eyre, 'Tours in Wales', vol. 1. NLW MS 62B, p. 9 (2 January 1796); Warner, *A Walk*, p. 162; Henry Wigstead, *Remarks on a Tour to North and South Wales in the Year 1797* (London: W. Wigstead, 1800), p. 21; William Bingley, *A Tour round North Wales, performed during the Summer of 1798* (London: E. Williams, 1800), pp. 437–8.

42 Burke, *A Philosophical Enquiry*, pp. 39, 57.

43 Burke, *A Philosophical Enquiry*, pp. 40, 51.

44 Warner, *A Walk*, p. 163.

45 Evans, *Letters*, p. 290.

46 Bingley, *A Tour*, p. 438.

47 Manners, *Journal*, p. 322.

48 Warner, *A Walk*, p. 163.

49 See QSD/AB/1/743 (1820).

50 Lewis, *Topographical Dictionary*, article 'Llangwm'.

51 See Richard Colt Hoare, 'Diary of a Fishing Tour in North Wales June 1799' (NLW MS 5370C).

52 [William Fordyce Mavor], *A Tour in Wales, and through several Counties of England, including both the Universities, performed in the Summer of 1805* (London: Richard Phillips, 1806), p. 128. 'Lister' is Sir John Leicester, Bt., who shared with Hoare an interest in fine art as well as in fishing.

53 Richard Colt Hoare, 'Journal', in Thompson (ed.), *The Journeys*, p. 178.

54 Burke, *A Philosophical Enquiry*, p. 57.

55 *CD*, pp. 297–8.

56 *CD*, p. 298.

57 Henry Eyre, 'Tours in Wales' (NLW MS 62B), p. 9.

58 Broughton, *Six Picturesque Views*, p. 31.

59 S. T. Coleridge, *Biographia Literaria*, ed. James Engell and W. Jackson Bate, 2 vols (London: Routledge & Kegan Paul, and Princeton: Princeton University Press, 1983), vol. 2, p. 45. For Coleridge's account of his tour of Wales, see Earl Leslie Griggs (ed.), *Collected Letters of Samuel Taylor Coleridge*, 6 vols (Oxford: Clarendon Press, 1956), vol. 2, pp. 85–95.

60 Hermann Fürst von Pückler-Muskau, *Briefe eines Verstorbenen. Ein fragmentarisches Tagebuch aus England, Wales, Irland und Frankreich, geschrieben in den Jahren 1828 und 1829*, 4 vols (Stuttgart: Hallberger 1831) *http://194.64.252.38/index.php?id=5&xid=2108&kapitel=48&cHash=4a5e87b9cd2#gb_found*. I am most grateful to Margaret Ferguson of the University of York for translating for me the Prince's account of his trip to Glyn Diffwys.

61 Wallace visited Pont y Glyn in August 1867. He wrote: 'In about five miles we reached Pont-y-glyn, where a farm-road crossed a very deep ravine. This

we descended and found the bottom full of curious hollows, with vertical rocks damp or dripping, overshadowed by trees and shrubs. Here the yellow Welsh poppy grew luxuriantly, as well as the globe-flowers and the subalpine *Rubus saxatilis*. But what delighted Mr. Mitten on this his first walk in Wales was the abundance of mosses and hepaticas, and for a full hour he explored every nook and cranny, and every few minutes cried out to me, "I've got another species I never gathered before," till I thought he would never tear himself away; and during several other visits to Wales in the Snowdon and Cader Idris districts, and in the Vale of Neath, I do not think he ever came upon a richer spot for his favourite group of plants.' A. R. Wallace, *My Life: A Record of Events and Opinions.* 2 vols (London: Chapman and Hall, 1905), vol. 2, pp. 401–2.

62 *http://conwy.leadpartners.co.uk/docs.asp?doc=colwyn &sec=chapter8*

63 George Borrow, *Wild Wales: The People, Language and Scenery* (1862) (London: J. M. Dent, and New York: E. P. Dutton, 1906), p. 131. The first viewing refuge that Borrow came to, walking westward, now has a plaque recording his enjoyment of the scene from a point where the bridge was always invisible. He discovered the second refuge, from where the bridge *was* visible (but is not now) a few hundred yards nearer to it, northwestward.

64 *CD*, p. 310, and see also p. 295, where Pugh describes a waterfall on the Trystion, a couple of miles south-west of Corwen, where 'some young ash-trees have, very injudiciously, been suffered to grow in front of the fall, thus precluding a sight of it from those points, where it would best make a picture.'

FIVE *A Fall on the Dee, near the Vale of Crucis*

I

Among tourists at the end of the eighteenth century, the Vale of Llangollen, especially the first few miles west of the town towards Corwen, was widely agreed to be the most beautiful part of north Wales. Some travellers still preferred the variety and plenitude of the Vale of Clwyd, but, as we shall see in a later chapter, the reputation of that vale was beginning to be tarnished, at the end of the eighteenth century, by the sense that its beauty was more a matter of fertility and productivity than of its purely aesthetic character. To the taste of late eighteenth-century landscape hunters the qualities of Llangollen Vale were becoming more congenial. It was, wrote the house-painter and amateur artist Henry Wigstead, 'the most beautiful valley I ever saw'.[1] It was 'unrivalled', claimed Richard Warner, 'in point of beauty and variety'; it presents scenes of such richness and romantic beauty', declared Aikin, 'as are scarcely ever beheld in union'; 'there is no place in Wales', exclaimed John Ferrar, 'where the refined lover of picturesque views, the sentimental or the romantic, can give a fuller indulgence to his inclination.'[2] 'Nothing less did it call to mind', according to an anonymous and very poetical tourist of 1808, 'than the fabulous region of Arcadia, where Spring ever smiled, and where Peace and Happiness held perpetual reign,' and, as he would do often on his short tour, he pulled out his pocket edition *The Seasons* to find the quotation that would clinch the point.

'Here surely might the lover of retirement realize the words of James Thomson, and

> . . . far from public rage,
> Deep in the vale, with a choice few retired,
> Drinks the pure pleasures of the Rural Life.'[3]

In *Cambria Depicta*, Pugh was no less enthusiastic. This 'verdant valley', he wrote, 'with its vast profundity, and its profusion of wood, in which the Dee is frequently buried, and as often seen undulating in one broad sheet, is of itself great and fine, even passing description; and every circumstance in the view seems to hold it out as a paragon of beauty'.[4]

In his immensely influential *Philosophical Enquiry*, Burke had defined the characteristics of the beautiful as smoothness and gradual variation, where these coexist on a relatively small scale: 'smooth slopes of earth in gardens, smooth streams in the landscape'; 'the variety of the surface, which is never for the smallest space the same'.[5] These were exactly the characteristics that tourists found in the Vale of Llangollen, at least above the rapids that run under the chain bridge at Berwyn. John Evans and William Mavor were particularly responsive to the feminine, indeed the coquettish idea of beauty to be found in Burke. Evans thought the river's 'capricious turns' and 'whimsical vagaries' produced 'a diversity of combinations . . . well deserving pictorial representation', and Mavor remarked that

the river serpentines round hills and knolls in a style at once novel and enchanting: its banks are everywhere fringed with woods; and sometimes it appears from the road in reaches, sometimes makes a sudden bend and partially disappears, but in every form and every turn it is calculated to please.'[6]

As the river twisted its way between hills and meadows, the various elements in the ever-changing views spontaneously coalesced in arrangements that of themselves formed 'pictures', as Pugh would put it, needing no rearrangement or composition. 'From the winding of the river, and the turnings

Plate 5.1 *John Warwick Smith, view of Llantysilio Hall seen from across the Dee on the Road to Corwen, pen-and-ink and watercolour, date unknown, London, British Museum.*

of the vale,' wrote William Bingley, 'almost every step presented a new landscape.'[7] Something of what tourists found so enchanting on this bank of the river is communicated in an undated watercolour of the valley around Llantysilio by Pugh's near-contemporary John 'Warwick' Smith (Plate 5.1). The view is taken from the south bank a few hundred yards west of the viewpoint Pugh wold choose, on the road from Berwyn to Llangollen, above Rhysgog Farm. We are looking across the great loop of the Dee – see the flash of white where the road dips and disappears – towards Llantysilio Hall, which Smith has transmuted from brick to stone and placed on a slightly more elevated position than it actually occupied.[8] The mountain skyline, though not exactly imaginary, compresses a very wide horizon into a much narrower arc, but beneath it the drawing captures well the smooth undulating fields, sprinkled over with trees, with the river winding between them, which enchanted those tourists who took the same road as Smith's weary peasant women.

The views in the vale were recognized as 'picturesque', not in the sense that they were highly textured, with broken lines, in the newly technical sense of the word being pioneered by writers on aesthetics, but in the older sense of 'suitable for representation in a picture'. 'Few spots', wrote Corbet Hue, who had been so disappointed by the Vale of Clwyd, were equal to 'the picturesque windings of the valley in the first three miles from Llangollen', on the road to Corwen.[9] 'Few rides', wrote the Chester printer John Broster, excel the ride from Corwen to Llangollen: 'the picturesque views of the Dee are justly allowed to be equal, if not superior to any river in Britain.'[10] 'From Llangollen', wrote Evelyn Shirley,

we proceeded to Corwen, by a Road, winding at the Foot, and along side of the Berwyn Mountains; on the right, is a beautiful Vale, watered by the Dee, whose serpentine convolutions, now presenting a broad and polished Surface, now, suddenly concealed, by the pendent foliage of the Trees, which overshadow its Banks, form a most pleasing, and prominent feature, in a Landschape where all is picturesque.[11]

William Gilpin, the theorist of landscape beauty and the picturesque, was particularly impressed by the vale, and wrote a long, considered account of what made it so (nearly) perfect. There was, he decided, 'nothing striking from one end of it to the other; no peculiar feature; nothing that could give it form *in description*.' It was however

varied into so pleasing a combination of parts; the ground so beautifully thrown about; the little knolls, and vallies so diversified, and contrasted; the trees so happily interspersed; and the openings, and windings of the river displayed to such advantage; in a word, the whole formed into such a variety of pleasing, natural scenes, that we scrupled not to call this valley one of the most interesting we had seen.

The source of its beauty, he explained, was 'the harmonious combination' of its elements. 'Composition is the life of scenery. It is not trees, it is not rocks,

Plate 5.2 *(opposite) William Ellis after Edward Pugh,* A Fall on the Dee, near the Vale of Crucis, *coloured aquatint (London: E. Pugh, 1794), second issue, Aberystwyth, National Library of Wales.*

Plate 5.3 *(opposite) William Ellis after Edward Pugh, A Fall on the Dee, near the Vale of Crucis, aquatint (London: E. Pugh, 1794), first issue, Aberystwyth, National Library of Wales.*

it is not varied ground . . . that makes a beautiful scene,' but the manner in which all these are brought together.

Nature, Gilpin believed, had less talent for 'picturesque composition' than had artists: we almost never see in nature a scene as well organized as we find in pictures. 'Sometimes however we do; as in the valley we are now admiring; in which nature has given us a succession of sylvan scenery, as correct in the whole, as it is elegant in it's [*sic*] parts.'[12] But even this valley was something of a rough diamond, for nature was quite incapable of producing a '*polished gem*', and so Gilpin proposed a few improvements: perhaps Velvet Hill, separating the vale from the valley in which the abbey of Valle Crucis was situated, could be bulldozed away, and the two valleys 'united . . . in one plan'; 'a little rubbish . . . might be cleared away'; a few openings made; here and there perhaps a new building, 'if it were truly sylvan, might appear to advantage'.[13] By and large however nature had done its best, and had done unexpectedly well; not quite an A, perhaps, but certainly an A minus.

The road from Llangollen to Corwen ran along the south bank of the river, and it was the 'amazing fine view' of the opposite bank,[14] especially in the parish of Llantysilio with its tiny church and handsome secluded hall, that travellers especially admired. At this point, wrote Mavor, the far side of the river 'exhibits a variety of the most exquisite charms of nature, embellished by the works of art. Llandysilio hall, and its environs, possess almost unrivalled beauty of situation: wood, water, hills, vales, all contribute to render this situation one of the most delightful that can be conceived.'[15] The north bank, Plowden Slaney rhapsodized, was

> ornamented . . . with a range of lofty trees, which hang over, and cast a pleasant gloom upon the water. The meadows, through which it flows, are of a lovely green; and mountains peeping behind mountains, inhabiting the regions of the clouds, and opening, at every step, to the delighted traveller, a new and more distant prospect, bound a ravishing and enchanting scene.[16]

It is this scenery of the north bank, with its 'birchen shades, That sweep o'er Landysilio's sheltered glades', as the poet William Sotheby described them,[17] that Pugh represents in his *View of a Fall on the Dee, near the Vale of Crucis* (Plates 5.2, 5.3).

II

Pugh's viewpoint can be identified precisely, for the 'fall on the Dee' in the centre of the picture is what would be replaced, in 1806, by the weir known as Horseshoe Falls, designed by Thomas Telford as a means of channelling water into the Llangollen Canal that from here runs alongside the Dee and acts as a feeder to the Ellesmere Canal. Pugh's print was published a year after the act of Parliament which authorized the construction of the feeder canal, but it would be ten years before work on the weir was begun. It involved removing the rocky projection on which, in Pugh's picture, the angler is standing with his rod; all that is now visible of those projecting rocks is a stump on the river bank, apparently sawn off in a straight line. The remodelled falls are first illustrated in a tiny engraving, probably by William Havell, which appeared in an almanac of 1815 (Plate 5.4).[18] It shows how the river was widened when Telford's horseshoe was constructed, and redirected to flow round two newly created islets, which now, two hundred years later, have coalesced and are thickly wooded.

At this point the Dee makes a sudden turn southwards, so that Pugh's picture looks more or less north–north–west, towards, in the far horizon on the right, the rounded outline of the southernmost

Plate 5.4 *John Pye [?] after William Havell [?],* Llantysilio Hall, Denbighshire – Seat of T. Jones Esqr, *from* Peacock's Polite Repository; or Pocket Companion, *engraving (London: Peacocks and Bampton, 1815), unpaginated. This is from the opening for 'June', and has been enlarged from the original.*

summit of Maesyrychen mountain, rising just to the north of the village, and, on the left and nearer, the more serrated shape of Moel y Gamelin, which in nature is a good deal less serrated, and is in fact the more distant of the two hills. Pugh has also made them both much more imposing: from his viewpoint they are visible nowadays only in winter, through the leafless branches of the trees that clothe the river-bank. The effect of this rearrangement is to increase the sense of the valley's enclosure, and to help shep-herd our eye backwards and leftwards round the next bend of this famously winding river. Ahead of us, at the end of that avenue of what appear to be elms, are three small white buildings. We can iden-tify them by their positions relative to each other rather than by their architecture. Furthest to the left, as those familiar with this spot would have recog-nized, is the tiny limewashed church of St Tysilio,[19] indicated by the gable end with its apex projecting higher than the ridge of the roof, and by the lean-to which Pugh has eased off the north transept and attached to the east end (Plate 5.5). Of its other most recognizable characteristics, however, the bellcote at the west end has been omitted, and the porch to the south door is hidden by the trees. Immediately to its right is the now demolished cottage marked on William Vaughan's map of about 1780 as 'the House and Quillets by the Church-Yard' (Plate 5.6).[20] A quillet is a slip of land, and on the quillet adjoin-ing the house we can see a fully formed rick, sug-gesting that the hay has recently been taken off the riverside meadows. The furthest and most substantial building is presumably the farmhouse also shown on Vaughan's map, on the far side of the lane leading to the hall, and known as Tyn-llan.

The first edition of the Ordnance Survey six-inch map, of about 1870, shows an ornamental

avenue running from near the falls to the church, in a position apparently close to Pugh's elms, but as this avenue does not appear on the late eighteenth-century maps, his row of tall trees may be intended as lining the Llangollen–Llantysilio road. On the same map, all the land on this bank in Pugh's pic-ture is shown as parkland, belonging to the hall, but when Pugh and Slaney were there it seems to have been meadowland, perhaps still divided by hedge-rows (as it is in William Griffiths's map (Plate 5.7))[21] into two principal fields, which in Vaughan's map are named the Field under the Church Yard, and, nearer to us, Henddwfrdu, and as Cae tan Fynwent and Yr hen dwr dy in a sale map of 1867.[22] Pugh's image suggests however that these fields were planted with

Plate 5.5 *Henry Adlard after Henry Gastineau,* Llantisilio Church, Vale of Llangollen, Denbigh-shire, *engraving (London: Jones & Co., 1831), private collection.*

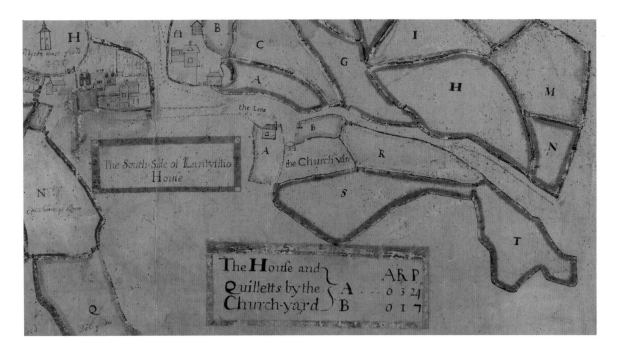

Plate 5.6 *William Vaughan,* A Map of an Estate: lying in the Parish of Llantysilio *(detail), ca. 1780, National Library of Wales. The river is not shown, but flows along the southern edge of the fields marked 'S' and 'T'. Pugh's viewpoint is somewhere in 'T'.*

specimen trees, and it may well have been their dual character, both working farmland and pleasure-ground, which so delighted tourists looking at them from the road across the Dee. The 1815 image even shows the further of the two fields ploughed into ridges and grazed by sheep, so presumably lying fallow. Given its low-lying riverside situation, however, it is not very likely to have been ploughed, and more probably the artist has taken a licence in order to vary the texture of the middle distance.

As the almanac image shows, Pugh's choice of viewpoint was critical to the making of his picture. In *Cambria Depicta* he would observe that it is 'an allowable liberty' for an artist 'to compose a fore-ground of his own'.[23] A predecessor on this spot, an artist called Evans who had drawn the hall in the late 1780s, did exactly that (Plate 5.8); from a view-point on the south bank of the river, he uses for

a *coulisse* to his right a steep hill which, as we can tell from the course of the river in the print, would have been well to his rear. It may be that Pugh has used his 'allowable liberty' to narrow the river, and to use the thick clump of trees he shows on the south bank as a *coulisse* to conceal from our view Llantysilio Hall, presiding over its beautiful demesne. Nowadays the trees in this spot do still mask the hall from Pugh's viewpoint, but whether or not they did in Pugh's time is uncertain: Smith's watercolour suggests they did, while the 1815 image shows the land there as treeless, divided into small fields, with cattle lying in the one nearest the fall. But as we have seen repeatedly in this book, the topographi-cal 'evidence' offered by supposedly topographi-cal art in the eighteenth century cannot be trusted where it comes into conflict with the exigencies of picture-making. What seems clear, however, is that there would certainly have been positions a few yards away – a little further forward, a few yards up the slope – from which Pugh would have been able to include the hall. Why did he choose not to? Per-haps, having decided to include Pen-y-Lan in his set of six prints, he did not want another country-house portrait; perhaps he felt that, in this of all scenes, the 'paragon' of beauty among the landscapes of north Wales, he did not want to include the hall, though plenty of commentators saw it as adding to the beauty of the scene, not detracting from it. So indeed did Pugh himself, in *Cambria Depicta*, where he describes the hall as contributing to the sense of comfortable seclusion expressed by the landscape as a whole: 'It is situated on a gentle rise,' he wrote, 'hardly perceptible, on the verge of the Dee, nearly surrounded by a profusion of wood, and by huge mountains above, which shelter it from the chilling effects of the northern and easterly winds.'[24]

But for whatever reasons Pugh chose to conceal the hall, they must have been reinforced by considerations of the patronage he hoped to secure from the gentry of Denbighshire. Had he depicted the hall, convention would have obliged him to include in the title of his print the words that appear beneath both Evans's and the almanac image: the 'seat of Thomas Jones. Esq.' There is no reason to suppose that the omission of the hall was intended as a slight against a man who two years previously had been high sheriff of the county, was a leading figure in local affairs as a member of the Llangollen Association for the prosecution of felons, and whom Pugh would describe in *Cambria Depicta* as 'an amateur, and a friend of the arts'.[25] But to include it, with the appropriate legend, would have deprived him of his best opportunity to inscribe one of his six views to the richest of all potential patrons, Sir Watkin Williams Wynn III of Wynnstay. Though the Wynns owned only a few small parcels of land in this southerly part of the parish, and had recently sold the ruins of the nearby abbey and the lands adjoining it, they had remained lords of the manor of Valle Crucis: thus the mineral resources of those distant hills, lime and especially slate, were theirs to exploit.[26] Wynn was also the impropriator of the tithes of the parish, and the patron of the living, with the right to nominate the incumbents of what was, for a perpetual curacy, an unusually comfortable berth, reckoned by Samuel Lewis in 1849 to be worth £112 per annum:[27] hence perhaps Pugh's choice of a viewpoint which, in the absence of the hall, made the church a chief focal point in the distance, the last thing we see on the bend of the river as it glides behind the trees.

Sir Watkin, unlike Jones, and unlike his father the second Sir Watkin, had no interest in the arts,

but such was the position of the Wynns of Wynnstay among the gentry and aristocracy of north Wales that in no selection of half-a-dozen dedicatees for his prints could Pugh possibly have ignored him. And least of all in 1794, when the young baronet, having come of age the year before to elaborately orchestrated illuminations, ox-roastings and

Plate 5.7 *William Griffiths,* A Plan of Llandysilio Demesne, *ca. 1740?, National Library of Wales. Pugh's viewpont is by the rapids shown in the river flowing past the field marked 'K'.*

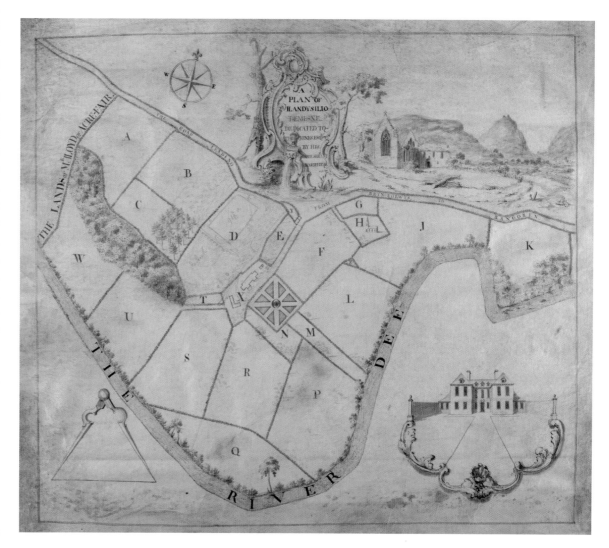

Plate 5.8 *Walker after Evans,* Llandillio, in Denbighshire, the Seat of Thos Jones Esq., *engraving [1788], second edition (London: H.D. Symonds, et al., 1796), private collection.*

distributions of free beer at Wynnstay, Ruabon, Wrexham, Oswestry, Bala, Ruthin, Much Wenlock and elsewhere,[28] was busily reasserting the Wynns' position of dominance. When this print was published, in November of that year, he had just been chosen, as we saw in chapter 4, MP for the pocket borough of Beaumaris, where the right of election was confined to the twenty-four members of the town corporation, under the sole influence and direction of Viscount Bulkeley, the dedicatee of Pugh's image of Carreg Carn March Arthur.[29] Wynn was occupying the seat at Beaumaris while waiting for the 1796 general election, when he would, by the consent of the county squirearchy,

assume, as if it was his birthright, the seat for Denbighshire.[30] In the spring of that year, he had just raised his personal cavalry regiment, the Ancient British Fencibles, officered by many of the local gentry and intended to suppress unrest among the poor of the county; these would play an active part in the suppression of the Irish rising in 1798, earning the title of the 'bloody Britons' mainly in acknowledgement of the atrocities they committed at Newry.[31] In 1794 he moved centre stage; and we can read the composition of this image as an emblem of that move: as Sir Watkin's emergence inevitably had the effect of throwing the rest of the gentry some way into the shade, so Pugh's homage to Sir Watkin requires him to mask the presence in this landscape of the gentleman whose demesne it portrays. The very name of Llantysilio, the immediate location of the view, is excluded from the title of the print; instead we are told that this 'fall on the Dee' is 'near the Vale of Crucis', replacing the name of Jones's lands with that of Wynn's manor, perhaps also to attract the interest of the antiquarian market, though only to disappoint it, for the abbey is nearly a mile away. The little church of St Tysilio, controlled by Sir Watkin, would have cut a poor figure in the landscape beside Llantysilio Hall; but with the hall eclipsed, it can, like Sir Watkin himself, take a position at the centre of things. This little drama of inclusion and exclusion is played out of course entirely to a local audience: to those who do not know this valley there is no missing hall, and the church is simply a focal point in the middle distance, unrecognizable as a church, and so with no iconographic meaning, no suggestion for example that the beauty of this landscape is to be understood as in some relation to religion.

III

If the young baronet was not much devoted to art, he did have interests more private and more peaceable than politics and military matters, and was especially fond of fishing. On the Dee above Llangollen, according to W. T. Simpson in his topographical account of Llangollen and its vicinity, the trout were 'as fine as any in the kingdom, and very plentiful', and there were still many salmon, despite 'the new inventions' erected downstream 'to intrap them on their way from the sea'.[32] A prospectus drawn up in 1886 when the hall was to let promised also pike and 'grealing'.[33] It is tempting to believe that, in a picture inscribed to him, we are invited to identify the elegant young gentleman in breeches and buckled shoes, standing centre stage and elevated above the less politely dressed men around him, as Sir Watkin himself. He looks perhaps too boyish for a twenty-one-year-old, but no more boyish than others of Pugh's young men – the lime-burner for example at Coedmarchan or the angler descending the scree at Pont Newydd. The identification may be rather less likely, however, in view of the company he is keeping, of which more later.

The anglers are most likely fishing for trout: they have no reels to their rods, their lines are short, and so they are not equipped to play salmon.[34] Unlike the fly-fisherman at Pont Newydd, the central young gentleman man appears to be using bait: that may be a minnow on his hook, a bait recommended by various fishing manuals in the late eighteenth century for catching 'great trouts'.[35] According to William Augustus Osbaldiston, for example, 'the minnow is the most excellent of all baits for the trout.'[36] According to Charles Bowlker,

an expert angler from Ludlow, the minnow 'was a most excellent bait, very destructive, of strong exercise, being always in motion, and affords the angler variety of sport.' With it could be taken 'the best and largest of fish', whether salmon or trout. It was best used 'in rapid streams, which helps give the minnow a brisk motion'.[37]

What of the other men? It is not clear to me what the two men are doing who are not angling. The man on the right, apparently making for the shore, has a net over his shoulder containing a trout. He may be the young gentleman's servant, in which case the fish may be one caught by his master. The square front edge of his net, however, is characteristic more of a shrimp net than a landing net, and is apparently designed for scraping over the river bed. Perhaps his main job is to catch minnows for his master's bait;[38] or perhaps he has been using the net to try and catch trout as they pause, gather themselves and prepare to leap the fall. The man nearest us seems to be using a net as well, whether attempting to net trout on his own account, or minnows for use by his master, is again unclear.[39] As for the two other anglers, one seems to be the young gentleman's trousered, ungenteel companion, but the other has turned his back on us to fish upstream of the fall, and seems to have no likely connection with the young gentleman. He appears to be one of the 'many men' who, according to Simpson, 'obtain a livelihood during the season by fishing in this beautiful river',[40] and the same may at least be true of the men with nets.

A hundred years after this aquatint was published it would have seemed an unusually

democratic image of trout fishing, though to Pugh it was simply how things were. In law, a river could be fished above its navigable portion only by, or with the permission of, its riparian owners.[41] In fact, however, until about 1860, the fishing between Corwen and Llangollen was entirely unreserved. Below Llangollen, and as far downstream as Bangor Is Y-Coed, the public right of fishing remained, until in the late 1870s it came to be challenged by the fifteen or so gentlemen-members of the Mid-Dee Club, who had leased from the riparian owners, 'for the sum of one shilling a year if demanded', all the fishing on both sides of the river from Newbridge, just below Llangollen, to Eyton on the far side of Overton Bridge, a stretch of some ten or a dozen miles.[42] They allowed other gentlemen to fish this water for sport even without their express permission; their aim was to drive from the river those who looked to it for at least part of their living. In 1880 a committee was formed to take up the case of the 'poor persons living on the banks of the Dee, who earned their living by fishing in its waters' and whose livelihood had now been taken from them.[43]

The committee denied that the riparian owners had a right to grant the leases, and set out to engineer prosecutions in order to prove in court what everyone knew to be the truth, that until the club was formed, no one, whether or not they owned land bordering the river, had been prevented from fishing there.[44] The fishermen, they claimed, whether anglers or net-fishers, 'had been allowed to fish from time immemorial'; 'they had actually made a trade of it,' and in the burial registers in parishes along the length of the Dee many people were described as having been fishermen for a living.[45] At a hearing at the petty sessions in

Llangollen, George Burton, seventy-two years old, gave evidence that he had fished the river all the way down from Corwen to Erbistock since he was ten, and 'was never interfered with, and no one had told him not to fish'. He had fished on the Chirk Castle Estate and the Wynnstay estate, 'and had never been interrupted. He had seen scores of other people fishing there. The farmers used to make stiles to enable them to get to the river.'[46] Though the case was about fishing the river below Llangollen, at the sessions in Ruabon another septuagenarian came forward to claim that he had fished without interference as far upriver as Corwen, at Glyndyrdwy for example, before the fishing there had been reserved.[47] For the Mid-Dee Club, Arthur Mostyn Owen of Woodhouse, West Felton, did acknowledge that 'until a recent period', three of four years ago, 'people had fished' in the water since leased by the club, but there was now, he declared, 'not an inch of free fishing'.[48] Richard Myddelton Biddulph of Chirk Castle stood down from the bench in order to give evidence on behalf of the riparian owners, and he testified in the true spirit of the new Welsh squirearchy. 'He had heard something about the public claiming to have a right of fishing in that river,' he told Lord Trevor and the other remaining magistrates. 'The fish had been preserved by his family. The public might insist as much as they liked, but it was all nonsense.'[49]

Pugh's image of the fall on the Dee at Llantysilio, where 'poor persons' are apparently shown exercising and enjoying their immemorial right, is a good answer to the nonsense of Biddulph. And it throws an interesting light on to the dedication to Wynn, and the missing dedication to Thomas Jones. Jones was the riparian owner, and these poor fishermen are there with his tacit, perhaps even with his express permission. Unnamed though he is, the print invites those who know him to be the owner of this fishing to see him as acquiescing in an aspect of the local moral economy and the immemorial but increasingly fragile rights of the poor.[50] To those who know nothing of Jones, the print will impute a similarly generous or at least acquiescent spirit to Wynn, for the dedicatee of the image of an estate would usually be supposed the owner of that estate. This however was not the spirit of Sir Watkin, at least as far as fishing was concerned. His vast inheritance included the fishing-box Glan-y-Llyn, on Llyn Tegid or Bala Lake, and he claimed absolute ownership of the fishing rights on the lake, continuing the practice of his father in banning fishing with nets and in forbidding boats on the lake except by his permission, which he granted only to other gentlemen.[51]

Those who fished the rivers and lakes of north Wales for a living or primarily to feed their families frequently used nets, whether hand nets as in this picture, or stretched across the river, as at the famous salmon leap at Aberglaslyn bridge, or stretched between two coracles, as in Thomas Walmsley's image of fishermen at Erbistock church (Plate 5.9), published in the same year as Pugh's six views of Denbighshire. To forbid fishing with nets was bound to have the effect of greatly reducing the amount of fish they could take.[52] The Wynns' aim on Llyn Tegid does not seem to have been the conservation of fish stocks, but, as so often when customary rights were extinguished, to reduce the independence of the poor, the degree to which they had access to the means of survival outside the discipline of wage-labour. This picture might be read, therefore, as an attempt at once to attract the patronage of Sir Watkin and to admonish him.

It is in effect an act of very qualified obeisance, once again whether we think of Wynn as actually appearing in the picture or merely as its dedicatee. The young gentleman angler is shown benevolently coexisting with a group of poor men exercising what they regarded as a customary right, and apparently consenting in their doing so. Should that tacit consent be withdrawn, however, as it had been on the lake, the respect for Sir Watkin declared below the image might have been more qualified, and Pugh might have become rather less his 'very obedient humble servant'.

Plate 5.9 *Francis Jukes after Thomas Walmsley, Erbistock Church, coloured aquatint (London: F. Jukes, 1794), Aberystwyth, National Library of Wales.*

Notes

1 Wigstead, *Remarks*, p. 22.

2 Warner, *A Walk*, p. 165; Arthur Aikin, *Journal of a Tour through North Wales and Part of Shropshire; with Observations in Mineralogy* (London: J. Johnson, 1797), p. 183; John Ferrar, *A Tour from Dublin to London, in 1795* (Dublin: no bookseller named, 1796), p. 19.

3 'Journal of an Excursion made in the Summer of 1808 through several Counties of North Wales' (DRO DD/DH/228/78), pp. 47–8, quoting James Thomson, *The Seasons*, 'Autumn', lines 1236–8.

4 *CD*, p. 302.

5 Burke, *A Philosophical Enquiry*, pp. 14–15.

6 [Evans], *Beauties*, vol. xvii, pt. 1, pp. 561–2; Mavor, *A Tour*, p. 132.

7 Bingley, *A Tour*, p. 431.

8 BM 1958,0712.373. The date is unknown. According to Basil Long, Smith visited Wales a dozen times between 1784 and 1806, but none of the itineraries he gives include the Dee valley between Llangollen and Bala; see Long, 'John Warwick Smith (1749–1831)', *Walker's Quarterly* (1927), 24. Smith had however visited the area before 1794, for in that year a view by him of Llangollen appeared in William Sotheby's *A Tour through Parts of Wales, Sonnets, Odes, and other Poems* (London: R. Blamire, 1794). For a description of the old, brick-built hall, see for example Evans, *Beauties*, vol. xvii, pt. 1, pp. 561–2.

9 Corbet Hue, 'Journal of a Tour through North Wales' (NLW MS 23218), p. 106.

10 [Broster], *Circular Tour*, p. 14.

11 [Evelyn Shirley], 'Cursory Remarks made in a Tour through different Parts of England and Wales in the months of August and September 1797' (NLW MS 1613.3C), Part the third, p. 5.

12 Gilpin, *Observations on Several Parts*, pp. 173–5. Gilpin's tour had been made in 1773.

13 Gilpin, *Observations on Several Parts*, pp. 176–7.

14 Joshua and Elizabeth Hawker, 'Tour of Jos. Hawkins & Elizabeth his Wife through North Wales anno 1812' (NLW MS 64B), p. 6.

15 Mavor, *A Tour*, p. 132, and for a similar opinion, see Bingley, *A Tour*, p. 431.

16 Slaney, 'A Short Journal', p. 9.

17 Sotheby, *A Tour through Parts of Wales*, p. 116, and see too Skrine, *Two Successive Tours*, p. 238.

18 The only attributed illustration in the 1815 volume of *Peacock's Polite Repository; or Pocket Companion*, (London: Peacocks and Bampton, 1815) is an engraving by John Pye after William Havell. As that is of Telford's great aqueduct a few miles from Llantysilio, it seems likely that Havell also made the drawing of Llantysilio Hall in the same volume.

19 See the photograph of the church prior to its Victorian restoration in Gordon Sherratt, *An Illustrated History of Llangollen* (Llangollen, Ceiriog Press: 2000), p. 66.

20 NLW Harrison 74 139/4/3.

21 NLW Harrison 76 139/4/3; dated to the 1740s by the NLW, but the style of its decoration looks several decades later.

22 *Particulars of Sale . . . 26th Day of September, 1867 . . . the Mansion House and Demesne Lands known as "Llantysilio Hall"*, NLW Long. 095 Filing Cabinets.

23 *CD*, p. 113.

24 *CD*, pp. 302–3.

25 *CCh* 7 March 1794; *CD*, p. 302.

26 For the lordship of the manor, see 'Manor of Llangwst, otherwise Valle Crucis, Coed Herddyn Common, in the township of Maes-yr-uchain, in the parish of Llantysilio, Denbighshire, shewing the old enclosures' (1858), NLW Longueville Deposit,

vol. 22 028/7/5; for the sale of Valle Crucis to John Lloyd of Trevor Hall, see *http://www.coflein.gov.uk/pdf/CPG104/*; and for the mineral resources, see Samuel Lewis, *A Topographical Dictionary of Wales* (1849), *http://www.british-history.ac.uk/report.aspx?compid=47857#s14*.

27 Lewis, *Topographical Dictionary*. For the Wynns' patronage of the living, see the person record of the incumbent in 1794, Revd Edward Jones, at *http://ccedb.cch.kcl.ac.uk/jsp/persons/CreatePersonFrames.jsp?PersonID=112395*

28 *CCh* 8 November 1793.

29 [Oldfield], *An Entire and Complete History*, vol. 3, p. 4.

30 See [Oldfield], *An Entire and Complete History*, vol. 3, p. 22, and CCo, 31 May 1795.

31 Parry and Freeman, *Historical Records*, ch. 1; John Askew Roberts, *Wynnstay and the Wynns: A Volume of Varieties* (Oswestry: Woodall and Venables, 1876), pp. 19–20. My thanks to Hywel Davies of the University of Aberystwyth for his help on this point.

32 W. T. Simpson, *Some Account of Llangollen and its Vicinity* (London: C. B. Whittaker, 1827), pp. 139–41.

33 DRO DD/LH/40.

34 See William Augustus Osbaldiston, *The British Sportsman, or, Nobleman, Gentleman, and Farmer's Dictionary, of Recreation and Amusement* (London: J. Stead for Champante and Whitrow, n.d.), p. 315; [Thomas Shirley], *The Angler's Museum; or, the whole Art of Float and Fly Fishing* (London: John Fielding, [1784?]), p. 58; Samuel Taylor, *Angling in all its Branches, reduced to a Complete Science* (London: T. N. Longman and O. Rees, 1800), p. 110. On 'the separation of salmon and trout fishing into different disciplines' during the eighteenth century, see Andrew Herd, *The Fly* (Ellesmere: Medlar Press, 2003), pp. 119–62.

35 *The North Country Angler, or the Art of Angling as practised in the Northern Counties of England*, second edn (Leeds: D. Smith, 1788), p. 14.

36 Osbaldiston, *The British Sportsman*, p. 315, and Thomas Best, *A Concise Treatise on the Art of Angling*, fouth edn (London: B. Crosby, 1798) p. 35.

37 [Shirley], *The Angler's Museum*, p. 23, and Charles Bowlker, *The Art of Angling; and Compleat Fly Fishing* (Birmingham: M. Swinney, and London: G. G. J. and J. Robinson, 1786), pp. 105–6. Similar accounts (often in the same words) of the use of minnows as a bait for trout are found in other angling treatises, often in the same words, for they copy one from another continually. See for example R. Brookes, *The Art of Angling* (London: W. Lowndes, 1793), pp. 168–9; J. Fairfax, *The Complete Sportsman; or, Country Gentleman's Recreation* (London: 'the Booksellers', 1795) p. 23; The Gentleman Angler (London: G. Kearsley, 1786) p. 42; *The North Country Angler* has a useful chapter on the matter, pp. 66–70, and see pp. 73–4.

38 See *The North Country Angler*, p. 80.

39 An engraving however by John Hassell and W. Nicholls after Philip Reinagle, *Fishermen* (London: J. Hassell and Thomas Rickards, 1814) shows similar square-front-ended nets which must have been used simply as landing nets, for the mesh is too wide for them to be used for catching bait. In other engravings of the period, landing nets seem always to be round.

40 Simpson, *Some Account*, p. 140.

41 John Burn, *The Justice of the Peace, and Parish Officer*, eighteenth edn, 4 vols (London: T. Cadell, 1793), vol. 2, §§381–3.

42 *Montgomeryshire Mercury*, 8 December 1880, preserved in DRO DD/WY/7121.

43 *North Wales Guardian*, 27 November7 1880, DRO DD/WY/7121.

44 *North Wales Guardian*, 27 November 1880.

45 *Montgomeryshire Mercury*, 8 December 1880.

46 *North Wales Guardian*, 4 December 1880, DRO DD/WY/7121.

47 *Montgomeryshire Mercury*, 8 December 1880.

48 *Montgomeryshire Mercury*, 8 December 1880.

49 *North Wales Guardian*, 4 December 1880.

50 For some thoughtful paragraphs on the privatization of fishing and the division between game and coarse fishing as it began to develop in the eighteenth century, and the relation of this to enclosure and the law of trespass, see Herd, *The Fly*, pp. 121–2.

51 See Mavor, *A Tour*, p. 127–8; Evans, *Letters*, p. 71; *CD*, pp. 280, 286; and the MSS at DRO DD/WY/5596.

52 For a fascinating account of struggles between 'the gentry rod and line men' and 'fishermen whose livelihood was dependent on their netting',   involving, as on the Dee, 'a private right being re-imposed against customary   practices', see J. H. Porter, 'Net fishermen and the salmon laws: conflict in late Victorian Devon', in Barry Stapleton (ed.), *Conflict and Community in Southern England: Essays in the Social History of Rural and Urban Labour from Mediaeval to Modern Times* (New York: St. Martin's Press, 1992), pp. 240–50.

SIX *Pen-y-Lan, across the Dee*

I

One of the offenders prosecuted at the Ruabon Petty Sessions had been caught fishing in the Graig Pool at Pen-y-Lan, four or so miles upstream of Erbistock, and a mile and a half south-east of Wynnstay. In the last of Pugh's six prints of Denbighshire, *Pen-y-Lan, across the Dee*, the pool is to the right, downstream, concealed by the trees clothing the river bank (Plates 6.1, 6.2). The picture is dedicated to the Right Honourable Lord Kenyon, who had been attorney-general in three different administrations, Master of the Rolls, and, since 1788, Lord Chief Justice. A strong opponent of the French Revolution, Kenyon, when this print was published, had just presided, with something less than complete impartiality, in a series of political trials, including those of Thomas Paine in 1792 for publishing the second part of *Rights of Man*, and, in 1793, of the radical publisher Daniel Isaac Eaton for publishing the same work, and of John Frost, for announcing in a London coffee-house, 'I am for equality and no king.' Kenyon was not a Denbighshire man – his seat was Gredington Hall, near Hanmer in Flintshire, seven miles from Pen-y-Lan – but Pugh took this opportunity to inscribe a print to the fabulously rich lawyer on the strength of the fact that, according to the prefatory note to the Pen-y-Lan records in the Denbighshire Record Office, his younger brother Roger, of Cefn near Wrexham, had purchased the Pen-y-Lan estate two years earlier. In 1796 it would pass to his son Edward Kenyon, who would then change his name to Edward Lloyd Kenyon, and who would change it again as occasion and testators dictated to Edward Lloyd Williams and to Edward Lloyd, sometimes with an extra 'Lloyd'. Under that last name, in 1794, he would contribute to a fund organized in Flintshire by Sir Roger Mostyn to raise the Ancient British Fencible Cavalry in which he would serve as a captain, as he would a year or so later in the Wrexham Yeomanry Cavalry. On 28 June 1805, according to the *Shrewsbury Chronicle*, he would give 'an elegant entertainment to the whole Corps' at his 'deservedly admired villa Pen-y-lan'.[1]

Pugh's viewpoint is a field on the Shropshire side of the river, reached by a partly sunken lane which now forms a portion of the Llwybr Maelor Way, between Sodylt Hall and Plas-yn-y-Coed farm. Here, looking west-north-west across to Ruabon mountain, he had the advantage of a full view of the late seventeenth-century front of Pen-y-Lan house, but at the cost of being a good three-quarters of a mile distant; as a result the house cuts a very small figure in the landscape, though a larger one than appears in photographs taken from the spot. Almost all the records of the estate were lost in a fire at an

Plate 6.1 *(opposite) William Ellis after Edward Pugh,* Pen-y-Lan, across the Dee, *aquatint (London: E. Pugh, 1794), first issue, London, British Library.*

attorney's office in Wrexham in the very year this image was published, which is one reason why it has been difficult to write about this print at the same length as the others. But we are fortunate that two

contemporary estate plans have survived, one in a survey of 1778, the other by J. Bennion in 1799.[2] These both show the parkland, the field boundaries and the plantations in some detail, and demonstrate that Pugh has taken, as usual, a good degree of artistic licence, preserving the boundaries of the parkland and of the fields nearest to him, but hacking away a plantation to make the house more visible, displacing some small fields further west in order to articulate the space to the left of the house more clearly,

Plate 6.2 (opposite) *William Ellis after Edward Pugh, Pen-y-Lan, across the Dee, coloured aquatint (London: E. Pugh, 1794), first issue, Aberystwyth, National Library of Wales.*

Plate 6.3 *Anonymous,* Pen-y-Lan, *lithograph (no publication details, [1851–4?]), Ruthin, Denbighshire Record Office.*

Plate 6.4 *Detail of plate 6.2.*

and either demolishing what is the most prominent building from this viewpoint, Graig farmhouse, or masking it with the trees on the right. The topography nevertheless seems to be displayed with an air of verisimilitude: nothing looks imaginary, and so every apparently meticulous detail is received as exact.

After it had been remodelled and gothicized in 1830, a lithograph was made of the house (Plate 6.3), probably in connection with the sale of 1851-4, from more or less due south, the nearest point to it on the opposite bank of the Dee. This brings the house far closer to us, and presents it less as the centre of a working estate than as a family house with fields now converted to parkland and with sporting amenities: the sale brochure made much of the covers that 'ABOUND WITH GAME' and the 'EXCELLENT FISHING in the River Dee',[3] though as we saw in the last chapter it would be some time before that fishing was secured for the exclusive enjoyment of the riparian owners. In a sense, Pugh's image is an advertisement also, and this may help explain why it seems so much less interesting, so much more conventional than the others in the series. More than the others this image seems to serve as an example of what he could do for prospective patrons and customers. In contrast with the anonymous artist of the lithograph, Pugh was not advertising himself as an architectural draftsman. What he is offering prospective customers is in the sub-genre known as

the estate portrait, showing how a house belonged within its local landscape, how it presided over its demesne. He sees those customers, who might commission future images of their own estates, as the country gentlemen of north-east Wales, whereas the lithograph seems to be pitched at those who have made their money elsewhere and are now looking to buy not so much a rural business as a country retreat. A few years before the sale in the early 1850s, Pen-y-Lan had become accessible, via Wrexham, by railways which, if the changes worked smoothly, could speed you there from Manchester, Liverpool or Birmingham in a few hours. Life in the country house no longer meant life: it could be enjoyed for summers, or for weekends.

We may be intended to recognize the smartly-dressed foreground figures (plate 6.4) from *Careg Carn-March Arther.* The artist is presumably to be imagined as Pugh himself; but his companion holding the umbrella or parasol, and wearing riding boots like the artist, is more likely in this picture to be an imaginary servant than an imaginary friend. This pair too, I take it, are part of the advertisement: if you commission me to draw your house, Pugh is suggesting, you will be commissioning an artist with the air, if not the pedigree, of a gentleman, and it is a part of his supposed genteel credentials that he employs a gentleman's gentleman, though almost certainly he did not.

The 'estate portrait' belongs within the category of landscape art that at some point in the history of British art came to be described as 'topographical' as opposed to landscape proper. This opposition has a complicated and tendentious history, one which we need to come to terms with if we are to understand how the *Six Views* would themselves have been understood, first when they were published and then in the subsequent history of the art of landscape. By reputation, Pugh has come to be categorized as a 'topographer', a 'topographical artist',[4] and the terms, as they are now usually used, though apparently descriptive cannot help but be taken as pejorative: topographers are landscape artists second-class. When the *Six Views* were published, however, it is not clear that there was any such stable category as topographical art, and when the term came to be used more frequently in the early nineteenth century, it was not always with the aim of putting a lower valuation on one kind of landscape art as opposed to another.

Nowadays historians of art by and large use the words 'topography', 'topographical' to refer to views of named places in graphic media – prints, drawings, watercolours – which apparently cannot be claimed to be somehow *more* than topographical. It seems that in using these terms they believe they are following eighteenth-century practice: that in the heyday of what is now called the 'topographical tradition', which includes Pugh, Paul and Thomas Sandby, Thomas Walmsley, John 'Warwick' Smith among the artists mentioned in this book, views of real places were distinguished from ideal landscapes by being described as 'topographical'. I believed

this myself until I began researching the uses of the word on various on-line databases which reproduce a huge selection of eighteenth-century books, pamphlets, newspapers and periodicals. Of between two and three thousand hits on 'topographical' covering the years 1750–1810, I had, after stripping out the repetitions (repeated advertisements in newspapers, reprintings of books) only thirty-three results – barely one every two years – in which the adjective 'topographical' qualified a noun that had anything to do with picture-making.[5] A few of these referred to military drawings of fortifications or profiles of contours.[6] Most of the time the adjective was used in connection with images of old buildings of antiquarian interest. In a very few cases it is possible, though on the whole unlikely, that the word refers to views of 'real' landscapes which are not, primarily, the setting for some kind of ancient monument. Only once – in an entry in the *Encyclopaedia Britannica* which I will quote shortly – did it clearly do so. Advertisements for books of engraved 'views' frequently promised 'topographical *descriptions*' of places to accompany the prints, but I did not find such an advertisement that described the *views themselves* as topographical.[7]

These searches confirm that in the eighteenth century 'topography' was a genre of literature, at least of writing, not of visual art, but opinions on what it was and should be about differed sharply. Some writers championed a more expansive sense by which it comes close to many of the modern meanings of the 'geography' of a place, including its natural features, its settlements, its agriculture, mineral resources, communications, industry and commerce, its institutions, its history as expressed in the relics of its past, old buildings in particular but also surviving legends and customs, and so on: more or less the agenda, as we shall see in Chapter 8, of *Cambria Depicta*.[8] In practice, however, many of those who claimed to be 'topographers' worked with a much narrower brief, concentrating very largely on archaeological and architectural remains and the genealogies and the houses of the nobility and gentry families, 'those great men', wrote the radical poet John Thelwall, who in return for such 'servile adulations' can 'recompense them with sinecure places and pensions'. Both Thelwall and John Stockdale, in his preface to John Aikin's *Description of the Country ... round Manchester*, protested about this: what we find, they complained, in the writings of most topographers is a kind of antiquarianism designed to flatter 'the great men who have proud mansions in those neighbourhoods they describe'. What we should find instead are 'circumstances more universally interesting': descriptions of 'the real condition of the people'.[9]

We shall return later to this more expansive notion of topography; my point, in the meantime, is that when we describe a certain kind of late eighteenth-century landscape art as topographical, we probably think we are meeting it upon its own terms, or in the terms of its own time; but in fact we are using the word in a sense in which it was then barely used, and which, when it came to be generally used in the later nineteenth century, was intended not simply to identify a genre but to indicate its supposed limitations. If we still choose to refer to the landscape images of Pugh or Sandby as 'topographical', and to see them as belonging to a 'topographical tradition', we need to be careful of importing into the discussion assumptions about the nature of landscape art which, if they were made more explicit, we would probably choose to disown.

So how did it happen that there had emerged, by 1870 or so, a settled distinction between landscape art proper and (mere) topography? We can approach the answer through a letter, written in the 1760s, by Thomas Gainsborough to the Earl of Hardwicke. The Earl had attempted to commission Thomas Gainsborough to paint a view for him; the artist replied:

> Mr Gainsborough presents his Humble respects to Lord Hardwicke; and shall always think it an honor to be employ'd in any thing for His Lordship; but with regard to real Views from Nature in this Country, he has never seen any Place that affords a Subject equal to the poorest imitations of Gaspar or Claude Paul Sanby is the only Man of Genius, he believes, who has employ'd his Pencil that Way – Mr G. hopes Lord Hardwicke will not mistake his meaning, but if His Lordship wishes to have any thing tollerable in the name of G. the Subject altogether as well as figures &c must be of his own Brain.[10]

In this intriguing response, Gainsborough, who was still far from establishing himself among the elite painters of late eighteenth-century Britain, nevertheless makes it clear to Lord Hardwicke that he wishes to be regarded as a candidate for promotion to the premier league. He is not a servant painter; he has no eagerness to cater to the mistaken taste of a patron whatever the title he bears or the price he offers. He demands respect for the quality of his imagination, of his invention, and wishes to be compared with the great names of Italian landscape art, an ambition that would be compromised if he were to agree to paint subjects unworthy of him: views of *real* places in a country where the landscape is so obviously second-rate. Gainsborough of course loved the English countryside, as a place to walk in, to sketch in, perhaps to retire to – but not as a subject for painting. Individually the hills, the trees, the roads, the ponds of England might be perfectly paintable, but only when reorganized into structures imagined by the artist's 'own Brain'. The name for an artist who would agree to paint the real places, however tame or scruffy, that Hardwicke's ignorance might lead him to admire, was 'Mr Sanby'. Sandby, Gainsborough concedes, is nevertheless a man of genius, but he seems to be saying so only in order to claim the same status for himself: among us men of genius, he implies, only Sandby is sufficiently obedient or mercenary to do what no man of genius should ever do. Though he does not use the term 'topography', he clearly associates the willingness to depict 'real Views' with the same servile posture towards 'great men' as did Thelwall.

By the end of the century, the cultural cringe towards France and Italy that led Gainsborough to claim that the landscape of Britain, or at least of England, was unworthy of representation, was a thing of the past. But that did not stop theorists of high art disparaging artists who painted 'real Views from Nature' in this or any other country. The (to me unknown) author of a long article on painting published in the *Encyclopaedia Britannica* in the 1790s wrote of the seventeenth-century Dutch landscape painters – he is thinking apparently of artists such as Hobbema, or Jacob van Ruisdael – that they have

> no rivals in landscape painting, considered as the faithful representation of a particular scene; but they are far from equalling Titian, Poussin, Claude Lorrain, &c. who have carried to the greatest

perfection the ideal landscape, and whose pictures, instead of being the topographical representations of certain places, are the combined result of every thing beautiful in their imagination or in nature.[11]

And a few years later Henry Fuseli, speaking in his capacity of Professor of Painting at the Royal Academy, told the students in the Academy schools that included among the 'uninteresting subjects' of art which they should take care to avoid was

> that kind of landscape which is entirely occupied with the tame delineation of a given spot; an enumeration of hill and dale, clumps of trees, shrubs, water, meadows, cottages, and houses, what is commonly called Views. These . . . may delight the owner of the acres they enclose, the inhabitants of the spot, perhaps the antiquary or the traveller, but to every other eye they are little more than topography. The landscape of Titian, of Mola, of Salvator, of the Poussins, Claude, Rubens, Elzheimer, Rembrandt, and Wilson, spurns all relation with this kind of map-work.[12]

Fuseli did introduce a small saving clause in defence of painters of 'Views': their 'enumerations' of the objects in a scene become 'little more than topography' only if they are not 'assisted by nature, dictated by taste, or chosen for character'. But this does little to protect them from the charge of being more cartographers than artists, for every 'view', in the opinion of whoever is making a picture of it, is chosen with taste and chosen for character. Obviously the only proper option for a landscape painter of ambition is to make it up. Equally obviously, to the writers just quoted, *Pen-y-Lan, across the Dee*, however inexact it might be when compared with the place

itself, would look like 'map-work': the 'topographical representation' of a 'particular scene', 'entirely occupied with the tame delineation of a given spot', and calculated primarily to 'delight the owner of the acres' it displays.

From one point of view, opinions like these look like the last gasp of a notion that art must represent an idealized nature if it is to take us above and beyond the quotidian, the commonplace, the merely 'real'. Was there ever an artist more devoted to English views than Constable? Had there ever been an artist more intent on painting them with all the minute fidelity that would appeal, according to Fuseli, only to the landowners and inhabitants of those places? In 1809, in an essay on Richard Wilson, John Britton rode to the defence of the representation of 'particular scenes', apparently in direct contradiction of the *Encyclopaedia Britannica* essay and Fuseli's lecture. Wilson, he pointed out, sometimes 'delineated views of certain places', yet 'many of his pictures, which are strictly "topographical," are replete with merit, and are now fully appreciated and valued by the impartial connoisseur'. Why? – because 'truth is preferable to falsehood; reality is more valuable than fiction; the works of nature are more worthy of regard than the inventions of man.' Thus

> the artist who, like Wilson and Turner, after having chosen a scene for pictorial representation, can portray all the local features of that scene, and at the same time embellish them with the most favourable effects of light and shade, sun, mist, cloud and varied colours of the seasons, is entitled to our admiration and praise. It speaks a language to be understood by all persons of every nation and every situation in life; because the scenery of nature is unfolded to all eyes, and he "who runs may read."

Britton's rejection of those who had attacked the representation of real views sounds a good deal more thoroughgoing than it was. His agenda was apparently modern and democratic, as if he wanted to curtail the reverence of rich collectors for the artists their ancestors had admired and collected on their grand tours, and believed that the best way to nurture a landscape art open to be enjoyed by everyone was to depict those 'romantic views', 'unmechanized by the ingenuity of man' that Joseph Hucks had sought out. Such scenes appeared to speak of an unmediated nature in a universal language, whereas all views of nature modified by 'man' – perhaps especially 'estate portraits' like *Pen y Lan, across the Dee* – speak of the power of one class, the labour of another, and mean different things to different observers.

To Britton, the notion that landscape artists should invent the scenes they painted would look like a recipe not for 'high art' but for snobbery, misguided anthropocentrism, idleness and cheating. Landscapes were to be painted as nature (supposedly) had designed them, with a better taste and more invention than any artist could pretend to; the artist's imagination, Britton suggested, was to be looked for in the ability to make views atmospheric, poetic, by capturing the 'effects' on places of light, weather and season. But just because he was proposing the 'faithful representation' of particular scenes as the modern categorical imperative of landscape painting, it became especially important to him that

'topographers' should be zealously distinguished from true artists concerned with 'effects'. Britton himself was as dismissive as Fuseli of 'the tame and tasteless painter who attempts to delineate every commonplace scene that is presented to his view, or copies each object indiscriminately'. Such artists, though as applied to them the word was clearly a misnomer, were 'unworthy of approbation'; indeed 'almost beneath the notice of criticism'.[13]

A more radical critique of the views of Fuseli and Britton alike appeared in an immensely influential series of essays by the artist and writer William Pyne, and published in his own short-lived periodical, *The Somerset House Gazette*, in 1823 and 1824. Pyne was attempting in part to reorganize the theory of landscape painting to make room, alongside oil painting, for the fast-developing, increasingly popular and much cheaper medium of watercolour. At its simplest, the story Pyne told in 'The Rise and Progress of Watercolour Painting in England' was of a major shift in the use of the medium at the end of the eighteenth century. Earlier makers of landscape in watercolour made 'tinted drawings', first drawing their outlines, shading them through in black or grey, and finally 'staining' or 'tinting' them. The most distinguished practitioner of this method, for Pyne, was Sandby, 'whose memory is regarded with veneration by the present school'. His importance now, however, was that he had laid a foundation for a practice of watercolour *painting* that had made his method obsolete. The modern school,

Turner, Girtin and their followers, had worked like painters in oils, 'laying in the object with local colour, and shadowing the same with the individual tint of its own shadow'. 'It was this new practice . . . that acquired for designs in watercolours upon paper, the title of paintings.'[14]

In the same series of essays, Pyne distinguished between the 'topographical' and 'landscape', whether in tinted drawings or in true watercolour paintings. For him, whether the views represented by artists were 'real' views of particular places was of no particular importance, and though he presumed that 'topographical' images were of real places, it did not follow that 'landscapes' were expected not to be. Topographical images were pictures of 'abbeys, castles, ancient towns, and noblemen's seats' and suchlike[15] that when represented in 'tinted drawings' appealed especially to those with antiquarian tastes. Landscapes were images where the main interest was in rural scenes in which buildings were incidental or at least not the primary object of attention. For Pyne, both landscape and antiquarian topography were equally worthy subjects, and he took to task those who mistakenly believed that topographical subjects 'did not afford sufficient scope for the display of much talent'. Girtin, and especially Turner, had shown that they could be treated with the same degree of 'original feeling . . . beauty of detail, variety of tones, elegant touch, breadth of effect, and general harmony' as landscape subjects.[16]

III

Perhaps it was in part a response to the invention of photography, but by the end of the third quarter of the nineteenth century, a firm distinction seems generally to have been agreed between true landscape and topography, which was nothing to do with whether a view was real or imaginary, but was useful as a means of distinguishing the most effect-ful paintings of landscape from the soulless images photography could be accused of providing. In a fascinating essay on the changing reputation of Paul Sandby which appeared in the catalogue of the exhibition of that artist's works at the Royal Academy and elsewhere in 2009–10, Felicity Myrone, curator of topography at the British Library, shows how the label attached to the images she is charged with curating was fastened to Sandby even by his admirers, a term that managed to appear at once innocently descriptive and a mark of inferiority. Samuel Redgrave, in his biographical dictionary of artists first published in 1874, remarked of him that he 'did not get beyond topography and the mere tinted imitation of nature'; of Frances Jukes, on the other hand, Sandby's friend and the engraver of some of his works, Redgrave wrote that he 'began art as a topographical landscape painter, but by great perseverance raised himself to much distinction as an aqua-tint engraver'. Better to be an engraver than a mere topographer; better to copy (with distinction) the works of other artists than to copy, supposedly no doubt without 'effects', those 'real Views from nature'. Even Sandby's great-great-nephew William Sandby described Paul as an artist 'struggling to free himself from tradition, which was topographical', whereas an artist like Tom Girtin or

J. M. W. Turner had 'got free, and was turning his wings in the open, which was landscape'. For all this, he continued, Sandby 'contributed much to the reputation of English landscape, and paved the way for his illustrious successors'. For Martin Hardie, writing in the 1940s, Sandby was 'the last, as he is the greatest, of the topographers':

> he was not an original artist like Turner or Cozens; he was of his age and gave it what it liked and could understand . . . The rapid development of watercolour . . . left no longer any room for such an art as Sandby's. The antiquarian and the connoisseur, topography and landscape art, were cast as opposed and incompatible.[17]

These accounts of the place of topography in the history of watercolour all appear to derive from, and yet all misread, Pyne's essay on watercolour painting. Whether by inattention, or deliberately and with their own agendas, Redgrave, William Sandby, Hardie and numerous others who took over Pyne's distinction between 'tinted drawings' and 'watercolour painting', conflated it with a division between topography and landscape which they presumed to be his but was in fact their own. This enabled them to associate topography – by which they meant landscape short on 'effects' – with tinted drawings and the followers of Sandby, and to represent them as all obsolete, second-rate, and now fortunately superseded by landscape, watercolour painting and the followers of Turner. As Myrone points out, it was then, when supposedly topographical art came to be generally thought of as 'mere' topography, that the vast collection of views and landscapes in the British Museum was split: what the late nineteenth-century keepers decided was 'art' went into the Department of Prints and Drawings at the Museum; what they branded as 'topography' was relegated to a kind of *salon des refusés* in the library, where, exactly as Fuseli would have wanted, it is now kept with the maps in what has become, in spite of all, a thoroughly fascinating and enriching collection of images.[18] It is here that we find *Pen-y-Lan, across the Dee*, and with it the rest of Pugh's *Six Views*.

In spite of all I have said, I do not think they are in the wrong collection. It seems appropriate to me that they should be regarded as 'topographical', though not for any reason that Fuseli, or Britton, or Pyne would recognize, though Aikin and Thelwall might. The Sandby exhibition was dedicated to a way of thinking about topographical art similar to one that I have been working with in this discussion of Pugh's *Six Views*. Its curators, Stephen Daniels and John Bonehill, advocate what Myrone calls a more 'expansive sense' of what topography meant in the eighteenth century, not much to do with whether a view displays 'effects' or not, or is focused primarily on old buildings or on the natural landscape, but one in which the places depicted are able to be understood, to some degree or other, as contested sites, places over which different interests assert incompatible claims, where the past and present compete for attention, where the local may be at odds with the national, where values are affirmed because somewhere else they are being called into question, where different versions of what Britain should be grind against each other. In this way of reading them, images of landscape do not have anything so reassuring as a 'meaning'; their disparate elements are just about – or not quite – held together by a visual rhetoric that invites us to believe that these antagonisms might somehow be balanced or blended by composition, by the harmonious arrangement of colours, or by that relation of near and far that artists called 'keeping'. A topographical art that appears to respond to this meaning of the term will be far from the wholly 'natural' landscapes favoured by Britton, and will not necessarily be concerned with the kinds of effects, poetic or otherwise, that he and Pyne saw as essential to make landscapes into art. They will be views of places that have been modified by who has owned them and who has worked them, by who inhabits them and who visits them. As such they will inevitably set us thinking about the conflict and coexistence of the various – the word that comes to hand is 'stakeholders' – in the landscape and in its representation, including those whose interest in a view is primarily aesthetic and those for whom its interest may also be in the view as a *place*. Five of the *Six Views*, to varying extents, prompt such reflections. The difficulty of saying much about *Pen-y-Lan, across the Dee* is that it barely does so at all.

Notes

1   Parry and Freeman, *Historical Records*, pp. 32–3; *CCh* 11 July 1794; DRO, preface to the index of Pen-y-Lan records. A different history is given in Arnold Neobard Palmer's *A History of the Parish of Ruabon* (Wrexham: Bridge Books, 1992), p. 54, by which, on the death of Roger Kenyon's widow (Roger himself having predeceased her), her eldest son Edward Lloyd Kenyon became owner of Pen-y-Lan. For the purposes of this chapter the disagreement is immaterial. Edward Lloyd Lloyd is very likely the Edward Lloyd who in 1794 contributed £50 to a fund organized in Flintshire by Sir Roger Mostyn

2   DRO DD/PL/143; NLW Maps, vol. 69 094/9/4; and see also the-mid nineteenth-century *Map of Pen-y-Lan Mansion, Park & Lands* (Chester: J. Evans, n.d.[1853?]), DRO DD/PL/165.

3   NLW Sale Catalogue, Denbighshire 399.

4   See Peter Lord's very useful article on Pugh in the *Oxford Dictionary of National Biography*.

5   The only periodical I searched online was *The Gentleman's Magazine*, the general-interest periodical most hospitable to readers with an interest in 'topography'. It was searched between 1750 and 1810, as were the newspapers. The invaluable ECCO – 'Eighteenth Century Collections Online' – containing books and pamphlets, runs only up to 1800. These on-line searches can be irritating because from one day to another the results they throw up can be oddly different. Maybe there is a way of regulating them so that they do not duplicate results or omit results one day that they had included the day before, but I am not a very sophisticated user of such databases, and cannot do it.

6   'Topographical drawings being frequently required by a commanding officer, it will be found useful, not only to take the ground plans of a country, but its profils. By profils, I mean sections made on different lines, in order to discover the inequalities of ground …'; Lieutenant Christian, *Military reflections addressed to the generals and field officers of the British Army* (London: printed for J. and T. Egerton, at the Military Library, Whitehall, 1786), p. 29.

7   See for example the advertisements for Joseph Farington's *Picturesque View and Scenery of Edinburgh*, *Public Advertiser*, 17 March 1789; for John Walker's *Picturesque Scenery of Scotland*, *Morning Chronicle*, 25 June 1794, or for (Clérisseau's?) *Antiquities of the South of France*, *Morning Chronicle*, 30 April 1794.

8   See for example Percival Barlow, *The General History of Europe* (London: printed by and for W. and J. Stratford, [1791?]), p. ii.

9   Thelwall, *The Tribune*, 3 vols (London: D. I. Eaton et al., 1795–6), vol. 2 (1796), p. 326; Aikin, *A Description of the Country from Thirty to Forty Miles round Manchester* (London: John Stockdale, 1795), p. v.

10   John Hayes (ed.), *The Letters of Thomas Gainsborough* (New Haven and London: Yale University Press, 2001), p. 30.

11   *Encyclopaedia Britannica; or, a Dictionary of Arts, Sciences, and Miscellaneous Literature*, 20 vols (Dublin: James Moore, 1790–8), vol. 18 (1797), pp. 604–5.

12   Fuseli, *Life and Writings*, vol. 2, p. 217.

13   Britton, *Fine Arts*, pp. 65–6.

14   'Ephraim Hardcastle' [William Pyne], in *Somerset House Gazette and Literary Museum; or, Weekly Miscellany of Fine Arts, Antiquities, and Literary Chit Chat*, ed. Ephraim Hardcastle, 2 vols in 1 (London: W. Wetton, 1824), vol. 1, pp. 65, 66–7.

15   *Somerset House Gazette*, p. 65.

16   *Somerset House Gazette*, p. 98.

17   See Felicity Myrone, '"The Monarch of the Plain": Paul Sandby and topography', in John Bonehill and Stephen Daniels (eds), *Paul Sandby: Picturing Britain* (Nottingham, Edinburgh and London: Nottingham City Museums and Galleries, National Gallery of Scotland and Royal Academy of Arts, 2009), p. 58, where all quotations by Redgrave, William Sandby and Hardie appear, except for the remark about Jukes, from Samuel Redgrave, *A Dictionary of Artists of the English School: Painters, Sculptors, Architects, Engravers, and Ornamentists*, 2nd edn (1878; reprinted in facsimile, Bath: Kingsmead Reprints, 1970), p. 244.

18   Myrone, 'Monarch', pp. 62–3.

SEVEN Modern Leisure in *Modern London*

I

The drawings that Pugh provided to be engraved as 'embellishments' to *Modern London*, published by Richard Phillips in 1804, represented an entirely new departure for him, and the commission was probably the biggest artistic challenge of his career. It required him to develop two skills, one that he had hitherto deployed only occasionally, another that he had had no occasion to acquire. It is clear from the explanatory notes that accompanied the prints that for Phillips the main function of the plates was to show off the architecture, and in particular the modern architecture, of eighteenth-century London. Of the few buildings that appear in Pugh's earlier landscape images, some drawn freehand, some (particularly those engraved by Poole) with a ruler, none required great skill in geometry or perspective. Architectural drawing was a skill that many excellent artists involved in book illustration managed to do without. When in 1808–10 Rudolph Ackermann published the three volumes of the immensely popular *Microcosm of London*, he hired Auguste Pugin, father of the great architect A. W. N. Pugin, to draw the streets and buildings, and Thomas Rowlandson to add the figures. For Phillips, however, Pugh took on both jobs, and this obliged him to develop also the skill of observing and sketching people in what were called 'characteristic groups'. With so much to learn it would be small wonder if he did neglect to visit Wales, as was

suggested in the Introduction, in the years when he was making these drawings.

Ten years before the publication of *Modern London* he had animated most of the *Six Views* with characteristic groups, but with the possible exception of the figures in *Careg Carn-March Arther*, they had a pastoral, not the comic character that, as we shall see, was appropriate for Phillips's commission. The nearest he had produced to an image in which a comic 'characteristic group' appeared before a range of carefully drawn buildings was the view of Ruthin we glanced at briefly in chapter 2. Here the jolly boy trying to scare the cows, and the man flourishing his cane, are conceived more in the spirit of the later drawings for *Modern London*. But for those Pugh had to learn to use a pair of compasses as well as a ruler, and to invent dozens of such expressive little narratives. Thomas Rowlandson was the acknowledged master here (Plate 7.1), but in comparison with what he would achieve in the *Microcosm*, Pugh's groups show more animation, are more various, more imaginatively conceived, and reveal an idea of how social life was conducted in modern London which is considerably more sophisticated than Rowlandson's.

Plate 7.1 *(opposite) [Thomas Rowlandson], untitled page of characteristic groups (Brighthelmstone: M. Lay, and London: H. Brookes, 1790), private collection.*

Pub.d June 1 1790 by M. Lay Brighthelmstone & H. Brookes Coventry Street, London.

Plate 7.2 *Joseph Thomson after Edward Pugh,* The Houses of Parliament, with the Royal Procession, *etching and engraving, from* Modern London *(London: Richard Phillips, 1804).*

book claimed as its unique selling point that it was a description, for the visitor and for the interested foreigner, of 'the actual present state' of 'this great Metropolis', as distinguished from John Stow's *Survey of London* of 1598, William Maitland's *History of London* of 1739, and Thomas Pennant's recent *History of London*, published in 1790. Such works, Phillips thought, were of interest only to antiquaries, whereas he wanted to address those looking for 'accurate, ample, and pleasing' information about the political and cultural life and institutions of *modern London*.[3] He included, nevertheless, an opening chapter, over a hundred pages long, on the history of London, probably written by the London Welsh antiquary David Hughson;[4] much of the rest of the book was transcribed from Feltham's handbook. Phillips was himself a Londoner who as a young man had moved to Leicester, set up as a bookseller, founded the *Leicester Herald*, and, in January 1793, had been imprisoned for eighteen months for selling Thomas Paine's *Rights of Man*. On his release Phillips returned to London and founded the semi-radical *Monthly Magazine*, and in an extraordinary process of rehabilitation, and without ceasing to be a 'dirty little jacobin',[5] as the Tory journalist John Wilson described him, he became a reforming sheriff of London in 1807 and was knighted the following year.

Phillips himself is often named as the author of *Modern London*, and though much of the text was borrowed from Feltham, it shows plenty of

Modern London; being the History of the Present State of the British Metropolis was published in September 1804 by Richard Phillips. It had been developed from John Feltham's handbook, *The Picture of London*, published by Phillips in 1802 and annually thereafter. The 'great approbation' that had greeted Feltham's work, Phillips claimed in the 'advertisement' with which he prefaced its 1805 edition, had 'induced the proprietor to print an enlarged and extended edition, under the title of MODERN LONDON, in one elegant volume, quarto'. With 'sixty copper-plates', this was no less than 'the most splendid work in the English language', as well as being 'worthy of the great City which it describes'.[1] At three guineas[2] it was an expensive production, including in the event fifty-four engraved copperplates, of which thirty-one, by William Marshall Craig, were hand-coloured versions of London Cries, set in recognizable London locations. Twenty of the remaining illustrations were by Pugh. The

evidence of his radical leanings. Following Feltham, it professes a great admiration for the controversial painter James Barry, Irish, pro-French revolutionary, and recently expelled from the Royal Academy.[6] Phillips's political hero is Sir Francis Burdett, the radical baronet, who is praised for his campaign, begun in 1798, to expose the harsh regime at Cold Bath Fields prison.[7] At the time of the publication of *Modern London* Burdett was fighting a battle to be reinstated as MP for Middlesex after being cheated out of his seat by corrupt and reactionary local officials. The preface announces the intention to describe, in italics, '*London as it is*'; the conclusion claims that it has shown 'things as they are; leaving things as they have been to a different kind of work', phrases which, taken together, remind us of the titles of so-called 'jacobin' novels by Robert Bage and William Godwin.[8]

It is clear however from the book as a whole that if Phillips was still in some sense a jacobin, he was certainly not a Bonapartist. He does not want Britain to become part of the French Empire, and in his support for the war he is now a good loyalist. This is particularly obvious in his decision to include among the 'embellishments' supplied by Pugh a view of *The Houses of Parliament, with the Royal Procession* – to the State Opening of Parliament – engraved by Joseph Thomson (Plate 7.2). Its significance would not have been lost on his contemporaries. In 1795, nine years before *Modern London* was published, and a year of great scarcity, this place, Old Palace Yard, had been the

scene of a riot, when the state coach was pelted by an angry crowd shouting 'Peace, peace!', 'Bread, bread!', 'No famine!', 'No War!', 'No Pitt!', 'Down with George!', 'No king!', 'No George!' A missile of some sort – a marble or an air-gun pellet according to some, a bullet according to the terrified king – shattered the window of the coach.[9] The incident was treated by the government as a full-blown assassination attempt, and as an opportunity, therefore, to introduce the repressive 'two bills' designed to crush the popular movement for the reform of Parliament which it blamed for the riot. Now, however, those who have waited outside the House of Lords for a sight of the leader of the free world, as they believe George to be, are shown loyally waving their hats to him, even tossing them in the air; but the legacy of nine years ago is apparent, perhaps, in the drawn swords of the 'strong detachment of the horse-guards' accompanying the carriage and keeping back the crowd.[10]

Radical though Phillips remained in his belief in the necessity of parliamentary, social and economic reform, he was committed also to a more politically safe idea of modernity, one appropriate to the go-getting businessman he had become. It emerges perhaps most clearly in the very positive account, again taken over from Feltham, of the beneficial effect of the 'genius for gain' which animates the commerce of London, and directs every aspect of the life of the metropolis 'to its own purpose, though not to the exclusion, yet to the subjugation, of all other objects'. It emerges too in the text's

confidence that though 'commerce has many selfish and consequently injurious propensities', the merchants of London have learned 'the divine maxim, that honesty is the best policy', the best for their own interests as well as for the general interest of the commercial world. In this spirit, Pugh's illustrations are declared to 'exhibit the very soul of the Metropolis in a way which has never before been attempted. Most of the busy haunts of the inhabitants, whether for the gratification of ambition, avarice, or pleasure, have been exactly pourtrayed.'[11] What could be more *modern* London than that? The modern commercial world, structured by the division of labour, had been authoritatively described by Adam Smith as one in which public spirit, public virtue, were quite unnecessary to the cohesion and unity of advanced economies. We all pursue our own interests and concentrate on whatever money-making activity we do best, whether as butcher, baker, candlestick-maker, porter, philosopher or politician, and social cooperation and cohesion are the certain but quite unintended result of our need to exchange the goods and services we can provide for those we cannot. If you make my candlesticks, I will do your philosophizing. Public spirit, public virtue were, like Stow's or Pennant's histories of London, of interest only to the antiquary: in the capital of the world's commerce, all we do, and all we are required to do by this new commercial version of the social contract, is to gratify 'ambition, avarice, or leisure'; they are our 'very soul' – or at least what we have in place of a soul.

II

Pugh contributed twenty images to *Modern London*; the job of engraving them was shared out between no fewer than twelve engravers, which suggests that the illustrations may have had to be prepared in a hurry: maybe the commission came to him late, or it took him longer than anticipated. Pugh chose to populate the streets and buildings with men and women on the edge of caricature, as Rowlandson did later, as if the inhabitants of the modern world, absolved of any need to strive for the public good, and in quest only of wealth, place or pleasure, could be represented only in the comic mode. But Pugh's figures seem to have been conceived more generously than that would suggest, especially when they showed Londoners in moments of leisure. *The Entrance to Hyde Park on a Sunday* (Plate 7.3), engraved by John Pass, a 'bustling scene' as the book describes it,[12] is divided between the mildly satirical and the genially comic. A number of horsemen of mixed ability and social class are exercising their horses in Rotten Row, which stretches from the middle-ground away into the left distance, skirting the edge of the Serpentine Lake. According to the commentary on the plate, probably written by Phillips himself, the 'persons ambitious of equestrian fame' who ride in the park on Sundays range from 'the highest quality to the apprentice and shopman, who hire their hacks at a livery stable, for half a guinea a day'.[13] Most of the riders are evidently competent, but at least one is having serious problems controlling his mount; another has been thrown and his horse is rolling on its back; yet another horse may have leapt the fence into the grassed area, and

is being chased by two men towards a semicircular plantation of trees. Perhaps in jovial anticipation of such accidents, a large number of spectators have arranged themselves along the length of the fence that divides Rotten Row from the footpath leading to Kensington Gardens, and are amusing themselves by watching the horsemen and chatting animatedly.

Between us and Rotten Row, however, are two friezes of characters. The further one is mainly made up of the presumably very well-off, riding mainly in closed coaches; but on the right is a sporty open carriage, managed by a gentleman who flourishes a whip over his four impeccable greys in an attempt to impress a young lady on the perch beside him. These are 'the quality', 'people of fashion', taking the air without effort and without the risk of unexpected encounters with those they would rather avoid.[14] That they are here in the park at all, rather than on their estates in the country, suggests that the time of year is late May or June: the leaves are on the trees and the Season is nearly but not quite over. These carriage-folk are in sharp contrast to the people in the frieze nearest us – a friendly parade of pedestrians, mostly families with, between them, at least a dozen young children. For them, Sunday is a family day, a day to be spent in the park, kids and all; and they are making the very most of it – enjoying being families together in a crowd rather than showing themselves off to others, welcoming chance encounters with friends and acquaintances, and delighted to have time to play, in some cases quite rumbustuously, with their children.

Alison O'Byrne has shown that in the middle and late eighteenth century there was much anxiety, at least on the part of those who regarded themselves as 'the quality', about social mixing in the London parks, as the inhabitants of the city who had made their wealth from trade, and even artisans and their families, trekked to the West End to join the quality in performing the *passeggiata*, dressed in their best clothes, making judgements about the dress and deportment of others, and trying to pass themselves off as something better than they were. She quotes Priscilla Wakefield, however, to show that 'on fine Sundays' in Hyde Park, 'the foot-paths are equally full of persons of all ranks; but all rivalling each other in taste and fashion.'[15] *Modern London* too remarks that here 'people of fashion' are 'mingled with a great multitude of well dressed persons of various ranks'; indeed, it reports, 'the different ranks of people' who crowd the public promenades on a Sunday 'are scarcely distinguished either by their dress or manners'.[16] Though hard to tell apart, the pedestrians in Pugh's *Hyde Park* do indeed appear to be a mixture of the gentry and the commercial middle class, and their jovial expressions suggest that their social differences are less important to them than what they may have come to the park to enjoy in common: a relaxation of the rules of deportment which allows them to enjoy being in such mixed company.

The striking informality of these pedestrians may not suit the imperiously benign naval officer on the left and his nose-in-the-air wife, with their young son and a liveried black footman in tow: the couple are a little too conscious of feeling above the mêlée and have veered aside in the hope of avoiding it. For someone else too the informality may go too far: the young woman on the right, perhaps a servant, looks taken aback to find her

Plate 7.3 *J. Pass after Edward Pugh,* The Entrance to Hyde Park on a Sunday, *etching and engraving, from* Modern London.

hand seized by an importunate army officer. But nowhere else in the comedy of the front row is there any real hint of social anxiety or of satire. The key figure here is the chubby man to the right of centre with a chubby toddler in a romper-suit clinging to him. He has a delightfully friendly air, the air not of a gentleman but of someone who is not one and doesn't much care. He is just breaking off his chat with a seemingly more gentlemanly acquaintance to greet a young couple advancing towards him, the husband carrying a little boy on his shoulders. Behind this group, a young father has swept up his little son and daughter, one under each arm, and is playfully charging their mother;[17] another toddler has turned to watch the impending collision, which seems destined to end in a general hug (Plate 7.4). On the extreme right, behind two boys playing marbles, an army officer bows as he

is introduced by a male friend to a young woman of marriageable age, and to a widow, who may be her mother or sister; perhaps another war-widow, for by now the war with France is popular and it is safe to acknowledge that war-widows exist. Further left again, a young man and his dog are tangled up in their lead, and the dog, barking in frustration, is being threatened with a blow which surely, in this happy atmosphere, will never be landed. And there are more of these playful mini-narratives, together suggesting that modern London is a place of happy sociability, at least for those content to mingle indiscriminately and with no wish to ape the formality of the carriage-folk.

Hyde Park becomes especially interesting when compared with Pugh's image of *The Promenade in St. James's Park*, engraved by Edward Edwards (Plate 7.5). The description of this plate explains that

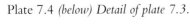

Plate 7.4 *(below) Detail of plate 7.3.*

The Mall used formerly to be much frequented by company, great part of which was often of the highest fashion . . . It is still a Sunday promenade, but its visitors are comparatively few; the fashionable walk at present being the Green-park of an evening, and Hyde-Park and Kensington-gardens in the morning.[18]

It is not entirely apparent to me that in this image Pugh has followed the lead given by Phillips. According to John Trusler in 1790, the Mall was then, at least, still thronged with 'people of fashion' in the early afternoons in May and June; while on summer evenings 'the walks are covered with the trading sort of people.'[19] As we have seen, it was difficult, according to Phillips (here again following Feltham), to distinguish rank by dress alone. Compared with the informality of Hyde Park, the promenaders in Pugh's *St. James's Park* are relatively stiff, as if on their best behaviour: this may be because they are more socially insecure, as the text would suggest, and are adopting a formal manner in the mistaken belief that it will make them appear more genteel; or they may be 'people of fashion' enjoying an afternoon walk in no expectation of having to rub shoulders with their social inferiors. Either way, the 'active part of the scene',[20] to use the text's term to distinguish the people from the places, is relatively inert, sedate. This is partly the result of the near-absence of children. Apart from the babe-in-arms, there are only two in the foreground, the elder of them posing formally to have his picture taken with his dog.

If we came across Pugh's image of St James's Park in isolation from his other scenes of public spaces, this would not seem remarkable: children do not usually make much of a figure in outdoor scenes of sociable intercourse in London, and when they do, they are generally seen but not heard. In 1793 Edward Dayes found room for eight children in his view of the Mall, but apart from a toddler-in-arms, they are all little adults, their behaviour as polite as that of the parents who pay them so little attention

(Plate 7.6). Even Henry Bunbury, a gentleman-caricaturist, who ten years earlier had also managed to include at least eight children in a scene in St James's Park, did not allow them to engage in horseplay, or to demand the slightest attention from their parents (Plate 7.7). A black page stands isolated in the centre; the only child being noticed by an adult is a beggar-boy on the right, threatened with a whipping by an irritated gentleman with his hand in his pocket, perhaps in search of a halfpenny, perhaps making sure his pocket has not been picked. But the near-absence of children from Pugh's image of the Mall is noteworthy only in comparison with his other images of London open spaces, not just of Hyde Park but of Greenwich Park and Horse Guards, where we find raucous children all over the place.

Plate 7.6 *(above) François David Soiron after Edward Dayes,* The Promenade in St James's Park, *etching and stipple engraving (London: Thomas Gaugain, 1793), London, British Museum.*

Plate 7.7 *(right) Henry Bunbury,* St James's Park, *etching and engraving (London: J. Wallis, 1793), London, British Museum.*

III

Phillips generally appears to have given Pugh a free hand in designing his figures. Though the preface to *Modern London* tells us that the images will focus equally on 'places which interest from their celebrity, and . . . scenes which characterise the manners of the people',[21] the commentary on the images has vastly more to say about the architecture of modern London than its inhabitants. Its account, for example, of a view of the Bank of England and the Royal Exchange, devotes almost all its attention to the buildings and almost none to the 'active part' of the scene (Plate 7.8), and even then, though it notices the vehicular traffic – a carriage, a stagecoach, a brewer's dray – the commentary ignores the wonderful variety of the tradesmen and

Plate 7.8 *Unknown engraver after Edward Pugh,* The Bank, Bank Buildings, Royal Exchange & Cornhill, *etching and engraving, from* Modern London.

on the right, the WAR-OFFICE in the centre, and THE ADMIRALTY on the left.'[23] For the author, in short, this image is of the most important institutions of modern London considered as the metropolis of an empire at war.

For Pugh, modern London in general, and Horse Guards in particular, are something else entirely. He draws all these public buildings with the clarity and detail no doubt required by his employer, but for him, once again, the modernity of modern London is in its people, not in its buildings, and in the new informal manners that have developed in the open spaces of the city. On the far side of the parade ground the Foot Guards are, to be sure, doing their stuff, their massed ranks marching metronomically forward, watched by a thin sprinkling of spectators. For most of those, however, who have made the journey to the Horse Guards, or stepped aside on to the military parade ground from the civilian parade grounds of the Mall, watching the soldiers drilling, even in wartime, is not the real point of their visit. For them, the parade ground is just another public space, a place to stroll, to chat, to meet people, and for their children and dogs to play. All the animation of the scene derives from them; the 'very soul' of modern London, to misappropriate Phillips's phrase, is in the relaxed sociability of its inhabitants.

Thus an off-duty guardsman has taken the opportunity to meet up with his wife and young child; another man converses more intimately with a young woman, perhaps making a suggestion to her that he would rather we did not hear. Two more

tradeswomen, the businessmen, the gentlemen and ladies who throng Cornhill, Threadneedle Street and Poultry.[22] But in no picture is it more apparent that Pugh is working with quite different priorities from the written text than the view of the Horse Guards engraved by John Pass and entitled *The Admiralty, the War Office, and the Treasury* (Plate 7.9). The commentary is entirely about the mainly government buildings that line the far side of the parade ground. The author carefully enumerates the War Office, Lord Melbourne's House (formerly, he

tells us, the Duke of York's), the Treasury, the house of the first Lord of the Admiralty, and beyond them in the left distance St Martin-in-the-Fields. When he comes, briefly, to consider the foreground – the parade ground of the Foot Guards – he tells us that it is very spacious, is laid with gravel, and is altogether excellently adapted to its purpose. 'The *coup d'oeil*', he concludes, 'of the public buildings on this spot is one of the finest about the metropolis. It contains in one view the three principal offices connected with the government of the country; THE TREASURY

Foot Guards are considering buying a cup of milk from the woman who keeps a cow in St James's Park, and has wandered over here in search of brisker trade. A lady and her companion seem determined to ignore a man with a peg-leg, (to use the term of the period) a wounded veteran no doubt, at the same time as one of them drops a coin in his hat. Behind the two foremost gentlemen, politely conversing, we can just make out the bottom of a little boy dragging a little horse on wheels; his elder sister is dragging their mother leftwards, or perhaps is trying to dance with her and another woman. Another little girl in a fashionable hat is being drawn over the gravel in an ornate baby-carriage like one of the people of fashion in the Hyde Park picture. A teenage boy seems to be showing off the tricks he has taught his dog; other dogs chase over the ground.

Plate 7.10 *(above) Isaac Taylor after Edward Pugh,* The Society of Arts distributing its Premiums, *etching and engraving, from* Modern London.

Plate 7.11 *(left) John Bluck after A.C. Pugin and Thomas Rowlandson,* Society for the Encouragement of Arts, & c. Adelphi, *coloured aquatint, from* The Microcosm of London *(London: R. Ackermann, 1809), City of London, London Metropolitan Archives.*

Beyond these various social encounters and mini-narratives of sociability in the foreground, there are others dispersed across the parade ground right to the back. On the far right, the long wall, so the commentary tells us, encloses the gardens of the Prime Minister, but for Pugh it is mainly the background for a vigorous game of catch.

Whether or not Pugh's images were as original and unprecedented as Phillips suggests, they were certainly influential on the much better-known *Microcosm of London*. Compare for example Pugh's image of the annual distribution of premiums in the Great Room of the Society of Arts, engraved by Isaac Taylor, with Rowlandson's and Pugin's version of the same subject (Plates 7.10, 7.11). Even granted the limits to originality imposed by the occasion and the geography of the room, the imitation is clear: perhaps clearest in Rowlandson and Pugin's determination *not* to imitate, to do, so to speak, the same as, but the opposite of, what Pugh had done. In Pugh's version a man is being rewarded, in Rowlandson's a woman; Pugh's principal usher has turned away from the president, Rowlandson's towards him; Pugin and Rowlandson show the same view as Pugh had drawn but from the opposite side of the room, which obliged them to forgo the rhyme that Pugh had taken advantage of, between the actual prize-giving and the painting of prize-giving in the top right-hand corner, the fifth in the great cycle of paintings on the progress of civilization with which Barry had embellished the Great Room, and which are described at length in *Modern London*.[24]

Rowlandson and Pugin also devoted a print to the Horse Guards (Plate 7.12), which, compared with Pugh's, is altogether less striking and innovative. In the distance, once more, the Foot Guards are drilling; so they are too in the divided foreground, encouraged by a boy in a soldier-suit with a toy sword, at the head of a small crowd of women, citizens and soldiers. Two dismounted Horse Guards are chatting with a young lady in a straw bonnet; two more young ladies are chatting with an elderly alderman; on the far left is a woman with a large basket, a pie-seller perhaps. It is a pleasant and polite gathering of people at ease with themselves and each other, but it has none of the sense that Pugh offers of a new world of manners, based not just on informal conversational exchange between the sexes, but on a new kind of affectionate family life, one in which the duties of parenthood have become the greatest pleasure, in which children are allowed to be children, and play is no longer seen as a waste of time but, up to a certain age, the very best way to spend it.

Plate 7.12 *J. Bluck after A.C. Pugin and Thomas Rowlandson,* Mounting Guard, St James's Park, *coloured aquatint, from* The Microcosm of London *(London: R. Ackermann, 1809), London, British Museum.*

IV

We associate this new attitude to children with the emergence in increasing numbers through the eighteenth century of a polite, educated middle class. In his view however of *Greenwich Park with the Royal Observatory on Easter Monday*, engraved by Pass (Plate 7.13), Pugh turns to examine a different stratum of London society. For once, he and Phillips are in tune: the commentary on the image is much less concerned with the grand architecture of Greenwich, which Pugh depicted elsewhere in *Modern London*, than with the Greenwich as the scene of a mixing of classes to a degree that could not possibly have occurred in the parks of the West End. 'In the Easter and Whitsuntide holidays', writes the commentary on Pugh's plate, Greenwich Park 'presents a very gay, busy, and festive scene . . . At such times, it is supposed that from ten to thirty thousand . . . holiday keepers have been collected in this Park in a single point of view.'[25]

Pugh's image is one of a century-long series of images of the Easter and Whitsun merry-making that accompanied the fairs held in Greenwich on those festivals. The earliest I have found dates from the mid-eighteenth century; the latest is by Phiz, published in the *Illustrated London News* in 1853, four years before the fairs and their associated roistering were suppressed. The motifs in these images are for the most part permed from a very standard set of characteristic groups (Plates 7.14, 7.15, 7.16). Young men, many of them sailors in trousers made of Holland or ticking, dance or play 'kiss in the ring' with young women in dresses with or without aprons or pinafores, according to their station, or in white muslin dresses, when these became fashionable. The music is provided in

one print by a hurdy-gurdy man, but usually by a fiddler, most often a '*Timber Toe*',[26] a man with a peg-leg, a former sailor perhaps, perhaps now a pensioner of Greenwich Hospital. After hearing one such peg-legged Greenwich sailor-violinist 'murder "Black-eyed Susan"', William Hone wrote that 'if the man at the wall of the Fishmongers' almshouses were dead, he would be the worst player in England.'[27] Sometimes a hawker is selling fruit or drink or pies; in one image, published by John Marshall in the same year as Pugh's (Plate 7.17), she is a woman, so preoccupied by the gentleman chucking her under the chin that she notices neither the dog peeing on her skirt nor the pilferer who is emptying her basket. In the middle distance, there is often a small crowd formed in a ring, to watch a boxing-match, or to listen to a man who may be preaching, selling ballads or making a political speech. And invariably young couples indulge in 'tumbling', the sport for which the Observatory Hill and One Tree Hill in Greenwich Park were most famous. Of the former, the hill depicted by Pugh, the commentary explains:

> The hill . . . is the principal attraction to the merry-making folks. It is extremely steep, and usually thronged; and, every now and then, a group of young men and women, locked hand in hand, rush down this path at full speed; the grand jest and enjoyment of the scene consisting in the falls that happen to the females as well as males in this slippery enterprise.[28]

It was certainly slippery in a moral sense, leading, in the case of the 'females', to much teasing exposure

Plate 7.13 *J. Pass after Edward Pugh*, Greenwich Park, with the Royal Observatory, on Easter Monday, *etching and engraving, from* Modern London.

and touching that could be passed off as accidental and therefore blameless. In *Contrariety*, a short comedy by J. Tomlinson describing a 'Greenwich Park adventure', a jovial sailor blurts out, 'See how that jolly lass rolls down the hill! Hold up black stockings; – Split me if ever I see such a pair of legs!'[29] A rhapsodic poem accompanying a print of Whit Monday in the park exclaimed:

> Heels over head! Away they go!
> Tumbling to the vale below!
> In vain the rolling fair-one tries
> To hide her charms from vulgar eyes;
> The stocking black, or blue, or white,
> The lovely legs expos'd to sight,
> The pretty foot in neat-made shoe,
> Nay, e'en the sacred garter too![30]

There is tumbling in every image I have found of Easter or Whitsun in Greenwich Park. For the great comic artist Thomas Rowlandson, tireless in his search for opportunities to draw women's bottoms, it was the only thing in Greenwich Park worth portraying, the downmarket equivalent of his much more famous *Exhibition Stare-case* (Plate 7.18).

Opinion was divided about the tumblers. Hone, the tireless defender of popular festivals and festivities, thought that 'the far greater number were, in appearance and manners, devoid of that vulgarity and grossness from which it might be inferred that the sport was any way improper.' For Rowlandson and others caricaturists, this completely missed the point: it was precisely 'the joyous vulgarity, the freedom, variety, and fun' which was 'the boast and attraction of Greenwich merry-making'. But others again, who took no delight in the carnivalesque, deplored the tumbling, the supposedly ungenteel people who indulged in it, and the fact that 'church holidays' were not treated at Greenwich as holy days.[32] It is

the 'rabble of London', remarked Robert Southey with heavy distaste, who climb the hill at Greenwich and then 'roll down its green side, men and women promiscuously'.[33] In a solemn didactic work of 1797, *Tales for Youth, or the High Road to Renown, through the Paths of Pleasure*, a young apprentice begs his master give him a day off on Easter Monday. He and a friend rush to Greenwich, where, though disgusted to find themselves in the company of 'chimney sweepers, brick dust boys, knife grinders, and travelling tinkers', and of women so disreputable the author refuses to describe them, they cannot resist rolling down the hill. They end up, however, 'buried alive by the multitude' and eventually escape minus

Plate 7.14 *(right) Anon*, Greenwich Hill or Holyday Gambols, *etching (London: W. Humphrey, 1740–65), London, British Museum.*

Plate 7.15 *(below) Anon.,* Greenwich Park, *etching (London: C. Sheppard, 1786), London, British Museum.*

Plate 7.16 *(below right) Samuel Rawle after James Nixon,* A View of Greenwich Park on Whitsun Monday, *etching (London: John Sewell, 1802), London, British Museum.*

a gold watch-chain and most of the money they had set aside for this adventure.[34] In the evangelical tract *Easter Monday,* Fanny, an innocent girl from Nottingham, comes down to London to stay with her childhood friend Mary, whom the town has well and truly corrupted. Persuaded against her better judgement to visit the park, she watches in disgust as Mary rolls down the hill, a sight 'Immodest, dang'rous, horrid to behold'; and when a rude stranger drags her too to the top of the hill and insists on her rolling down with him, she only just manages to escape. Fanny is eventually rescued by a benevolent lady of eighty who happened to be passing in her coach and four, and who nurses her through a prolonged high fever, occasioned by her insulted sense of propriety, which actually 'threaten'd her life'.[35]

In the 1850s the moral reformer C. F. S. Money would attack the Greenwich fairs as 'a Nursery for Crime', the 'focus of London iniquity', a 'barbarous relic of a bygone age', and such attitudes would lead in the 1850s to their abolition. And for at least the previous thirty years, most writing about the merry-making in Greenwich Park represents it as engaged in only by the 'rabble' – the 'dregs of the London populace', as J. R. Planché described them after passing through in Easter 1826: 'filth, rags, debauchery, and drunkenness', emanating from 'the slums of the metropolis'.[36] But even allowing for the increasing difficulty in modern commercial London of telling the classes apart on the basis of their dress alone, the comic illustrations tell a different story, one in which

the Easter and Whitsun festivals are enjoyed by, as the commentary puts it, both 'the lower and middle sort', with the former in their best clothes, as good as they could afford.[37] This is especially the case in Pugh's print which, more than any of the others, attempts to convey a sense of the vast numbers, the tens of thousands according to *Modern London,* who come together in the park. The 'lower and middle sort', in Pugh's image, may not interact much, perhaps, but they are prepared, at least on this holiday, to share the same space without either seeming obviously constrained in the presence of the other.

Perhaps more than in Marshall's or Nixon's or Sheppard's prints, however, the lower, not the middling sort are the main characters of the piece. Because we are in Greenwich, sailors are in abundance, not officers but naval ratings. Two of them, beneath the tree on the left, have picked up a pair of prostitutes with particularly festive décolletages, and are canoodling with them in the shade; their companion, apparently fed up to be the odd man out, is left to chat to his pet monkey. Three other sailors, one of a higher rank, perhaps a petty officer, are dancing with a modestly-dressed servant girl and two women who

Plate 7.17 *Anon,* Greenwich Park on Easter Monday, *coloured etching and engraving, (London: John Marshall, 1794), London, National Maritime Museum.*

Plate 7.18 *Thomas Rowlandson,* One Tree Hill Greenwich Park, *coloured etching (no place or publisher, 1811), London, National Maritime Museum.*

may possibly be of a slightly higher station, enjoying the opportunity to mix, perhaps on this day only, with Britain's brave tars. At the foot of the exaggeratedly precipitous hill we can make out a group of tumblers collapsed together on the grass, though too far off to be immodest; higher up, a new wave of half-a-dozen or so young men and women have started their own crazy descent: they will have to weave an intricate, headlong path among the large numbers strolling on the hill with no apparent intention of tumbling down it. Wherever we look, we can see characteristic groups of the low, the middling, and perhaps, in an instance or two, the positively genteel, scattered amongst each other on the lawn, just occasionally perhaps socializing across class divisions.

And, once again, there are children everywhere, far more than in any of the Greenwich series of prints except Phiz's, where some young ragamuffins scramble for oranges thrown by a jovial top-hatted gentleman who has bought them for that purpose from a pretty orange-woman.[38] The sketch illustrates an article in defence of the soon-to-be-abolished fair, which may derive in part from Dickens's famous essay on the fair in *Sketches by Boz*: in the vague distance Phiz has shown a little genteel tumbling, which, in common with Dickens, he represents as involving not the slightest hint of indecency (plate 7.19). But his main point (unlike Dickens) is to show that the abolition of the fair would put an end to the innocent amusements of children who had few enough opportunities to enjoy such good clean fun in such healthy surroundings. Like Phiz's, the children in Pugh's print

are in the main of the 'lower' sort, on holiday from their employment if they have any, but seemingly independent of any adult influence. They play leapfrog, attempt acrobatic circus tricks, and climb trees, from the safety of which, to judge by the gestures and expressions of the angry old couple on the left, they insult the people below. One is the companion of another fiddle-playing, peg-legged beggar, a former sailor we would guess in this place and company. In the distance a few other children can be discerned in the company of parents apparently of the middling sort, but they are far from stage front. The contrast between them, and the street children in the foreground, as between those street children and the other children with families in Hyde Park or Horse Guards Parade, adds a new dimension to Pugh's attempts to portray social difference and social interactions in modern public space in London.

Not all of the designs Pugh contributed to *Modern London* are as intriguing as those I have discussed. Some are views of buildings, interiors as well as exteriors, in which people are much less prominent, or at least much less various in their looks and behaviour. The views of St Paul's and the West India Docks, the illustrations showing the interior of the Bank of England, for example, the Theatre Royal Covent Garden, the Court of King's Bench or the House of Lords are thoroughly competent but seem to have been made without great enthusiasm. A longer chapter, on the other hand, would have lingered over the fine townscape *Westminster from Lambeth*, or the interior of the Drury Lane Theatre, full of those 'characteristic groups' at which Pugh had come to excel. But his images of untroubled social mixing in London, and of parents playing with their children, are unique among all the

Plate 7.19 *Anon, after Phiz,* Whitsuntide in Greenwich Park, *etching, from* The Illustrated London News, *May 21 1853.*

scenes of London life I have come across by his predecessors and immediate contemporaries. It may be a utopian image of London, or it may be that Pugh was observing and depicting something which other artists did not see or chose to ignore. Either way, he makes the occasions when different ranks can come together in a form of social unity, and the close affections of family life as these developed in

the decades around 1800, the defining features of modern life in London. In doing so, he offers us a different and much more benign take on modernity than does the text of *Modern London.* The author, like Pugh, seems untroubled by the sight of social ranks intermingled, but describes a mainly individualist society which derives more from the new science of political economy than from the new culture of sentiment that Pugh finds so much more congenial. Pugh depicts Londoners with a good-humoured and tolerant enjoyment of London life, and in doing so seems to feel as much at home in his adopted city as he was in the Vale of Clwyd.

Notes

1 'Advertisement' to [John Feltham], *The Picture of London* (London: R. Phillips, 1805).

2 *Morning Chronicle*, 25 August 1804.

3 *ML*, pp. iii, 474.

4 A footnote to the history (*ML*, p. 2n.) refers to William Owen of Barmouth, the lexicographer, journal editor and literary scholar, as 'an ingenious countryman' of the author, who I therefore conjecture is the antiquary and historiographer of London David Pugh, who adopted the pseudonym David Hughson.

5 Thomas Seccombe, rev. M. Clare Loughlin-Chow, 'Sir Richard Phillips', *ODNB*.

6 *ML*, pp. 402–6, 465–6 (from Feltham, *Picture of London*, 1802 edn, pp. 125–9, 27–8, and see p. 221).

7 *ML*, p. 359.

8 *ML*, pp. iv, 474; cp. Robert Bage, *Man as he is: a Novel*, 4 vols (London: William Lane, 1792), William Godwin, *Things as they are; or, the Adventures of Caleb Williams*, 3 vols (London: B. Crosby, 1794).

9 For a full account of this incident and its aftermath, see Barrell, *Imagining*, pp. 551–603.

10 *ML*, p. 483.

11 *ML*, pp. 287 (Feltham, *Picture of London*, 1802 edn, p. 29), 326, vi. A few years later Feltham had developed a more optimistic and trusting attitude to the effects of commerce: 'honesty is become, not only a moral virtue, but a political habit, originating in wholesale dealers, but diffusing itself through all ranks' (Feltham, *Picture of London*, 1806 edn, p. 59).

12 *ML*, p. 480.

13 *ML*, p. 480.

14 Alison O'Byrne, 'Walking, rambling, and promenading in eighteenth-century London: a literary and cultural history' (unpublished Ph. D. thesis, University of York, 2003), 133, 157. For other useful works on London parks

in the century, see Neville Braybrooke, *London Green: The Story of Kensington Gardens, Hyde Park, Green Park and St. James's Park* (London: Gollancz, 1959); E. J. Burford, *Royal St. James's: Being a Story of Kings, Clubmen and Courtesans* (London: Robert Hale, 1980); 'Jacob Larwood', *The Story of the London Parks* (London: John Camden Hotten, 1872); Susan Lasdun, *The English Park: Royal, Private and Public* (London: André Deutsch, 1991); Warwick Wroth, *The London Pleasure Gardens of the Eighteenth Century* (1896) (Hamden, CT: Shoe String Press, 1979).

15 Priscilla Wakefield, *Perambulations around London, and its Environs* (London: Darton and Harvey, 1809), quoted by O'Byrne, p. 161.

16 *ML*, pp. 260 (Feltham, *Picture of London*, 1802 edn, p. 66), 458.

17 Just possibly he is snatching them out of the path of the carriage four greys, but he seems too far to the front of the picture for that.

18 *ML*, p. 479.

19 John Trusler, *The London Adviser and Guide*, 2nd edn (London: for the author, 1790), p. 177; quoted by O'Byrne, 156.

20 *ML*, p. 489.

21 *ML*, p. vi.

22 *ML*, p. 489.

23 *ML*, p. 481.

24 *ML*, pp. 402–6 (Feltham, *Picture of London*, 1802 edn, pp. 125–9).

25 *ML*, p. 477.

26 See 'Greenwich Park: or, Whitsun Monday [With a View taken on the Spot by J.N. Esq. R.A.]', *European Magazine*, 41 (May 1802), 386. The poem attributes the image to James Northcote RA, presumably in error. The British Museum attributes it to the gentleman-caricaturist John Nixon.

27 William Hone, 'Whitsuntide at Greenwich', in *The Every-day Book: or, Everlasting Calendar of Popular Amusements*, 2 vols (London: William Hone, 1826), vol. 1, p. 346.

28 *ML*, p. 477.

29 J. Tomlinson, *Contrariety, or a New Broom, for the New House … As performed at the New Theatre, Stafford* (Stafford, N. Boden, 1792), pp. 12, 19.

30 *European Magazine*, 41 (May 1802), 386.

31 See for example his pen-and-ink and watercolours *Greenwich Hill*, at the Fitzwilliam Museum Cambridge, and his print *One-Tree Hill, Greenwich Park* (1811).

32 Hone, *The Every-day Book*, vol. 1, p. 346; 'Greenwich Fair', in *Somerset House Gazette, and Literary Museum*, 2/29 (24 April 1824), 43; *Cheap Repository: Easter Monday* (London: John Marshall, 1795), p. 7.

33 Robert Southey, *Letters from England* (1807), ed. Jack Simmons (Gloucester: Alan Sutton, 1984), p. 410.

34 *Tales for Youth, or the High Road to Renown, through the Paths of Pleasure* (London: William Lane, at the Minerva Press, 1797), pp. 134–6.

35 *Easter Monday*, pp. 6–7.

36 C. F. S. Money, *Greenwich Fair: A Nursery for Crime* (*c*.1856), quoted in Mark Judd, '"The oddest combination of town and country": popular culture and the London fairs', in John K. Walton and James Walvin, eds, *Leisure in Britain, 1780-1839* (Manchester: Manchester University Press, 1983), p. 27; J. R. Planché, *Recollections and Reflections: A Professional Autobiography*, 2 vols (London: Tinsley Brothers, 1872), vol. 1, p. 91; and see Hugh Cunningham, 'The metropolitan fairs: a case study in the social control of leisure', in A. P. Donajgrodzki (ed.), *Social Control in Nineteenth-Century Britain* (London: Croom Helm, 1978), pp. 163–84.

37 *ML*, p. 477.

38 *Illustrated London News*, 21 May 1853, p. 408.

EIGHT *Cambria Depicta*: The History of the Book

I

Cambria Depicta owed its origin, so Pugh tells us in his preface, to a conversation he had with Alderman John Boydell, probably in 1802. It took place at the Shakespeare Gallery in Pall Mall, a favourite meeting place of artists, which Boydell himself had founded. 'ALDERMAN BOYDELL' – Pugh writes his name in awed capital letters[1] – was an engraver, printseller, entrepreneur, former Lord Mayor of London, and a grand London institution; and if he was happy to pass the time of day with an artist as little known as Pugh, this was no doubt because they had one important thing in common. For Boydell, though born in England, had been brought up as a teenager only sixteen miles from Ruthin, at Hawarden, Flintshire, where his father had been land agent to Sir John Glynne.[2] It was Boydell who had published, a quarter of a century ago, the six Welsh views by Richard Wilson which had stimulated Pugh in his first attempt to become a landscape artist.

The subject of this conversation, the landscape of north Wales, was one dear to them both, and in the course of it the prospect arose of a little business to be done between them. 'Mr. Boydell', writes Pugh,

lamented that the landscape painters, whom he had employed in Wales, confined the efforts of their pencils to the neighbourhood of Snowdon: thus multiplying copies upon copies of the same sketches, and frustrating the noble Alderman's intention of publishing a just series of Welsh views. This practice they defended on the ground of the difficulty in which a stranger, unacquainted with the language or the country, involved himself, the moment that he quitted the high roads, and plunged into the intricacies of the mountains.[3]

Unable to ask for directions, unable to make themselves understood at the more sequestered inns where English was not spoken, they rarely ventured off the roads that led from Shrewsbury and Chester to Barmouth and Bangor.

The solution, Boydell suggested, would be for a 'native' – a Welsh-speaker with 'local knowledge' – to write 'a small volume of direction', instructing artists where they might find views worth depicting but not hitherto depicted, and how to find their way to them in safety. This was about the time that Pugh was beginning the series of London views he had contracted to produce for *Modern London*, and he felt unable to volunteer for this task, the more so as the volume at least as Boydell conceived it would be of interest only to a few artists. It was 'not likely to be sufficiently productive', Pugh considered, 'even to pay the expense of the publication'. By the spring of 1804, however, with the drawings for *Modern London* completed, Pugh thought again about this conversation, and soon 'resolved upon a plan, which promised to be serviceable, not only to the artist, but also to the general observer'. If he hoped to sell this idea to the Alderman, he was unlucky, for in December 1804 Boydell died, all but bankrupt.[4] Pugh pressed on, however, and by the summer of 1812, writing from Ruthin where he now lived all year, he told Richard Llwyd that, subject to whatever little improvements Llwyd's 'skilful fist' might like to make to it, the book was finished. 'In my careful reperusal of it . . . I do expect there be little to expunge, and little to alter.'[5]

The path to publication, however, was not smooth. In the same letter, Pugh told Llwyd that he had agreed a deal with Evan Williams, the leading Welsh publisher in London: Williams was to pay him £50 in ready money, apparently on the date of publication rather than on receipt of the manuscript; another £50 the following month; and a final payment of £50 the month after that. If Williams priced the book at 2 guineas, Pugh was to receive in addition 25 free copies; if at 3 guineas, twenty. This seems a slender return on eight years' work and the considerable expense of making several trips round Wales, but Pugh, by now probably very hard up, seems to have been worried that by this arrangement too much of his fee would be deferred, and he was prepared to take even less if more could be paid over immediately, in cash. Perhaps, he muses, he would ask instead for £80 in ready money, plus an additional payment of £55, the free copies and £5-worth of other books which he could not easily get hold of in Ruthin. Or then again, would that be selling himself too cheap? Perhaps he should ask for £20-worth of books, 'and that I do want them is notorious, my library's not worth £4' (see plate 0.15).[6]

By early 1813, however, Pugh may have decided to go ahead without Williams. In January and February we find him announcing in the press his intention 'to publish by subscription Cambria Depicta, or pictures of north Wales, in a quarto volume, with about eighty views, engraved in aquatint, and coloured after nature'.[7] There is no mention of Williams in these announcements. But, as with the six Denbighshire views, the plan to publish by subscription was quickly abandoned. Well before April Pugh must have finally agreed to proceed with Williams, for on the 15th of that month Thomas Cartwright, who had already engraved Pugh's pair of views in Monmouthshire, completed the first eight of the aquatints, with Williams's imprint upon them, intended to be included in Cambria Depicta. Three weeks later Pugh put his final touches to the manuscript and signed the Preface, and, five weeks after that, he died. The manuscript, according to the brief obituary notice in the Chester Chronicle, then became the property of Pugh's mother, and when she died in December 1815, apparently intestate, it would presumably have belonged to her daughter. Perhaps however Williams knew nothing of Mary, and now regarded the book as his own.[8] The last plates are dated February 1815, and in the advertisement leaves of Peter Roberts's Cambrian Popular Antiquities, published early that year, an announcement appeared of the imminent publication, in April, of Cambria Depicta. The announcement included a complete list of the plates, specimens of which were already available to be inspected in Williams's publishing house in the Strand. Subtitled, at this stage, a 'Picture of North Wales', the book was being marketed not as a tour but as a comprehensive topography of North Wales, comprising 'a descriptive Survey of the picturesque Beauties, and the most romantic Scenery, of that Part of the British Empire; with historical Remarks on the peculiar Customs and Manners, Anecdotes of the Inhabitants, commercial Pursuits, Topography, Antiquities, and local History of that beautiful and elevated Country'. For some reason, however – perhaps a delay in colouring the plates, or the need for a longer advertising campaign to drum up interest – publication was held up. The imminent appearance of Cambria Depicta was announced again, in the New Monthly Magazine of December 1815, and again in the Quarterly Review of the following month,[9] but it was the summer of 1816 before the book was finally published. On 4 June of that year the Morning Chronicle carried the following advertisement:

In one volume royal 4to, with 71 Copper-plates, beautifully coloured, price 10 guineas in boards.

CAMBRIA DEPICTA: being a TOUR through NORTH WALES, illustrated with 71 Picturesque Views of that Romantic Country, beautifully coloured from Nature, so as to imitate Drawings. By EDWARD PUGH, a Native Artist.

Printed for E. Williams, Bookseller to the Duke and Duchess of York, No. 11, Strand; where may be had the same work on small paper, in 4to. and Plates not coloured, price five guineas in boards.

The aquatinting of the plates had been completed in February the previous year, and as the coloured versions were published in a separate volume and probably coloured on demand, the delay in publishing the book seems to require some explanation. It may have done Williams's balance sheet no harm that it eventually appeared only after Dorothy Pugh's death, and at a price several times what Pugh and Williams had originally used as the basis of their negotiations.

II

The new plan Pugh had come up with, which he set out in his preface, and which he hoped would make *Cambria Depicta* much more profitable than the little guide to Snowdonia that Boydell had proposed, involved a book that, as well as being luxuriously illustrated, would cover a far wider area of Wales and appeal to a far wider audience than English artists unable to speak Welsh. Artists remained one section of the target readership: Pugh's hope was that his book would

> lead the painter to numberless objects, well worthy of his exertions, in representing them on canvass; whether his genius incline him to the mountain's craggy side, the cwm's solemn profundity, the frightful brink of the cataract, and the rocky margin of the sea; or to the milder features of Nature, observable in the shadowy recesses of the grove, the cultivation of the expanded valley, and the tufted banks of the serpentine *afon*, he will here find frequent and tempting opportunities of indulging and exercising it.[10]

In short, the book was as much concerned with the beautiful (with a glance at Hogarth's serpentine 'line of beauty') as with the sublime, not only with north-west Wales, as Boydell seems to have intended, but with Pugh's native north-east as well.

But *Cambria Depicta* would also address readers with other interests, in history and in the developing science of mineralogy, as well as 'the general observer, whose object is Nature in all her varieties'. 'To the antiquary' it would provide 'frequent occasions of contemplating the magnificent remains of ancient times' – 'the relics of Druidical superstition, the hasty but durable labours of the Romans ... the massive military fortifications of the ancient Britons', the castles of the Middle Ages, the abbeys and monasteries of 'Catholic devotees'. The book offered a 'topographical history' of north Wales, complete with biographical notices of Welsh worthies based on information 'from the most authentic sources', notably Thomas Pennant but many others besides.[11] Richard Llwyd too had supplied some antiquarian or topographical information: the preface to his *Poetical Works* states that 'he very materially contributed several facts of an interesting character' to Pugh's book.[12] The claim that the book, like Arthur Aikin's tour or Pennant's, would be of particular interest to mineralogists was probably going too far, but Pugh did find and describe, if not in great detail, more mines as well as more manufacturing sites than any of the other literary tourists he read in researching his book.

As important to Pugh, however, was the attempt the book makes to vindicate the character and behaviour 'of the different classes of the ancient Britons', while taking care, he hoped, to avoid 'being biased in their favour'. Almost everything the English 'knew' about the people of north Wales in the decades around 1800 came from the many hundreds of written tours by English holidaymakers, written in the period between 1793 and 1815 when, except for a single year in 1802–3 following the Treaty of Amiens, the war with republican France made holidaying abroad, in Paris, or on the grand tour through France and Italy, impossible. Though the great majority of these tours remained unpublished, they were written to be read by family and friends, especially perhaps those preparing their own journeys to Wales. They must have had a huge influence on what the polite classes in England thought they knew about the Welsh, and what came to be passed on in published tours about their supposed manners and character.

English tourists went to north Wales to catch the packet-boat to Dublin, to admire the sublime mountain landscapes or to stay at the new seaside resorts which were much cheaper than those in England. They were not primarily interested in the Welsh people, and they met few of them, because, like the artists, almost all followed the same routes along the two east–west arterial roads from Chester and Shrewsbury. Nevertheless they went there with definite expectations about what the Welsh were like, and they were very ready with their judgements about the Welsh poor. Some who went expecting to find a simple pastoral Arcadia populated by happy singing shepherds, or a hardy and independent mountain race comparable to those in the free cantons of Switzerland, managed to find exactly what they were looking for. Joseph Cradock clearly believed he had arrived among a nation of happy freeholders, paying no rent, desiring no luxuries, and almost delighted by their own poverty. 'How few are the wants of the peasant,' he rhapsodized, 'who dwells in a straw-built hut, on a barren mountain, which the avarice of man has not yet reduced to property, compared with the lord nursed in the cradle of indolence and luxury!' Richard Warner, who chose to believe that the Welsh character was virtually unchanged since the time of the Roman invasions, found something like Arcadia at Mallwyd, and was worried that the new turnpike roads would corrupt the 'simple manners of the people'. John Evans, on the other hand, was certain that

tourists would not find 'Arcadian scenes' in north Wales, but was delighted to find near Moel Siabod 'hardy', clean-living 'mountaineers', content with little, animated by 'a spirit of liberty', and skilled in the tasks of their limited system of husbandry.[13] Most however who travelled with such expectations were disappointed by those they met, and regarded the present inhabitants of north Wales as the degenerate descendants of a once happier race, or as a primitive people stuck at an early stage of economic and cultural development. Even writers who believe they are too enlightened to share this view of the Welsh are liable to adopt it when discomforted by the looks or demeanour of individuals unlucky enough to meet them. 'A savage of the South sea Islands', rasps one generally humane tourist, who elsewhere announces that 'the Welsh are remarkable for their civility'; 'you would scarcely believe her to have been human,' says Evans, on seeing a poor mother 'with a distorted figure at her breast.'[14]

The fact that the Welsh spoke Welsh, not English, was even taken as a defining mark of their ignorance or their primitive state. Cradock, holidaying in north Wales in pursuit of game, complained of the village where he was staying that the local curate 'is the only person in the neighbourhood capable of conversing with me', as though it was a sign of ignorance in the Welsh that they did not speak English, but no ignorance on his part that he could not converse in their language, in their country. Luckily for him, however, his ignorance of Welsh was no barrier to understanding what they had to say. 'If we would view the heart of man without disguise,' he tells us, 'it is among the rude and uncivilized inhabitants of mountains. Too artless to conceal the dictates of their hearts, the tongue reveals the sentiments of the mind. Hence those passions which are concealed

and disguised in more civilized countries, appear here in their native colours.'[15] Thomas Vernon, stopping at an inn near Chirk in 1797 and asking the landlady for dinner, was answered 'in plain English' but was irritated to find that 'the rest of the domesticks gabbled Welch.' Henry Wigstead, in the Vale of Llangollen in the same year, complained that while 'the natives have scarcely understood a word of English', they had taken care to instruct their children to beg; 'and "give me a penny" is to be heard from twenty little surrounding tongues at the same time'. Warner, in Caernarvonshire the following year, found it 'extraordinary' that 'all the women servants at our last two inns were equally unqualified for colloquial intercourse with us'; and in 1799 the painter Robert Ker Porter passed a night at the Cann Office at Llangadfan, an inn where Pugh also stayed. 'The servants cannot speak English,' he complained to his journal, 'which I would pardon, but damn it, they are so stupidly brutish.'[16]

When the English travelled in France or Italy, they were in countries where they frequently spoke and understood the language, or could easily hire a guide who did; in Wales this was not the case, and they were left to make their own unaided judgements of 'the Welsh character', or to adopt those offered them by previous tourists. Many travellers, primed in advance by the tours they had read, expected to find a sullen, unwelcoming, ignorant people, sunk in poverty which was the result of their own ignorance or idleness; and so that was what they did very often find. Here for example is a typical judgement by Porter, visiting Caernarvon: 'The streets seem well enough, and not vastly broad, the houses old and not vastly clean, the people stupid and not very civil';[17] and my notebooks on tours are full of such examples. An exception was James

Plate 8.1 *J. Mitan after Edward Pugh, title-page vignette to the first volume of Theophilus Jones,* A History of the County of Brecknock, *3 vols (Brecknock: G. North, for the author, 1805–9), engraving.*

Plumptre of Norwich, who travelled to north Wales with an unusually open mind, and who gives an idea of how the tourist literature had mis-prepared him for what he found there: 'From the accounts I had received,' he wrote, 'I had formed but an ill opinion of the lower class of people in these parts; but, saving this instance, we found them universally civil and obliging.'[18]

As well as Pennant's tours, which he probably had on his desk as he was writing up his own, Pugh refers to, and had presumably read, all the best-known tours of north Wales written by Englishmen: the chemist and geologist Arthur Aikin, the naturalist the Revd William Bingley, Henry Skrine, a gentleman, the antiquary the Revd Richard Warner, the schoolmaster the Revd John Evans, the poet Samuel Pratt, George Lyttelton, first Baron Lyttelton, a politician and writer, and Edward Lloyd, of whom I know nothing except that he came from Lancashire and that his tour is not worth reading. Apart from Lyttelton and Aikin, these writers are mentioned only to be admonished for their errors; Bingley is especially reproved for wanting to convert Dolbadarn Castle into an inn. Among Pugh's friends or acquaintances was Theophilus Jones, to whose *History of Brecknock* Pugh had contributed a title-page vignette, probably showing the Ely Tower at Brecon. (Plate 8.1).[19] Apparently taking his cue from Jones's magnificently withering article on English tours of Wales published in the *Cambrian Register* in 1796, Pugh tells us that such tours have 'invariably been found defective in their description of the people, their manners, and customs'. This, he suggests, was not at all surprising, for those tours 'have generally been undertaken by complete strangers to these people . . . who, therefore, could not possibly avoid numerous inaccuracies'.[20]

By the end of the preface it is on this aspect of the book, and the illustrations it contains, that he staked his claim for what he had achieved. 'Upon the whole,' he wrote,

If, from my knowledge of the ancient British language, from my intimacy with my native country and its inhabitants, their economy, customs, and character, and from the moderate talent as an artist, which I possess, I may be thought in some degree to have attained the end which I proposed to myself, I shall feel amply recompensed for the fatigue which I experienced for many months, in travelling as a pedestrian, between two and three thousand miles, over one of the roughest districts of Great Britain.[21]

But by the time he had finished writing his tour, he had decided that its unique selling point was to be looked for not in his illustrations, but entirely in the knowledge and understanding it offered of the people of north Wales. The epigraph to *Cambria Depicta* announced as much: among English tourists he now seems to exempt Aikin from the charge of misrepresenting the Welsh, for on his title page is a quotation from Aikin's tour which reads: 'it would have been an advantage, had I been able to give a more copious account of them (the Welsh); but the requisite knowledge of a sufficient number of circumstances from which to deduce a NATIONAL CHARACTER, is not be acquired without long residence, and much intercourse with the inhabitants.'[22] In the very last paragraph of the tour, as Pugh looks back on what he has written, it is the vindication of the character of the Welsh from the aspersions of ignorant Englishman that he emphasizes as absolutely its principal aim, one which his own requisite knowledge, long residence and much intercourse will enable him to achieve. The tour has been an endeavour, he writes, 'to procure as correct information as I could of this portion of the ancient Britons: a people, whose manners, habits, and propensities, have not as yet been faithfully delineated by the pen of any traveller, Mr. Pennant excepted.'[23]

Both Pugh and Theophilus Jones were great, not to say extravagant admirers of Pennant's tour, but unlike both of them, Pennant made barely any attempt to describe the character and customs of the modern Welsh. He mentions several gentlemen who offered him hospitality on his travels, but unless I have missed something it is not until well into the second of the two volumes of *A Tour in Wales* that Pennant acknowledges having spoken to anyone of less than gentle rank, and his solitary paragraph about the character of the inhabitants of north Wales is nearly a hundred pages further on.[24] Pennant of course, unlike Pugh, knew very little Welsh, and partly for that reason he liked to be accompanied on his tours through Wales by the Revd John Lloyd of Caerwys, but if Lloyd's presence opened the possibility of dialogues with the local inhabitants, Pennant's inclinations seem simply not to have led him to attempt them. Lloyd's Welsh was mainly put to use translating manuscripts in the gentlemen's houses where they preferred to stay.[25] Pugh's estimate of Pennant may owe something to his deference to the memory of a local gentleman and scholar, but had not misjudged his own achievement: he was a shrewd, thoughtful and generous observer of modern Welsh life, and what is most delightful and original about his book is the way it represents the people he meets in his wanderings away from 'the repeatedly beaten track'.[26] These animate wonderfully the landscapes that to other tourists might as well have been empty,

for all the notice they took of the inhabitants; and so do the occasional passages in which Pugh seems to be wondering how far he could make his tour, among other things, a 'sentimental journey' through the counties of north Wales, with the wit as well as the feeling of Laurence Sterne.

For there is something 'Yorick'-like in the humour of his page-long account of a stand-off between himself and a bull he meets in a narrow lane, and the dance-like movements by which the bull threatens and Pugh avoids a collision: 'I moved off very gradually towards a gate in the road, in adagio movements, not very unlike those of a French dancing-master in a minuet.'[27] At Chester, before his tour begins, 'a very pretty young lady' makes him a present of 'a very pretty little dog', a black puppy, probably a terrier, who appears alongside Pugh in *The Source of the Severn* (plates 0.4, 0.5), and whom he named 'Miss Wowski', the nickname of the Afro-Caribbean mistress of the Duke of Clarence, George III's third son.[28] This girl reminds us of Sterne's Maria but without the melancholy, the young woman Yorick met near Moulines, who consoled herself for the loss of her lover by the company of a little dog 'tied by her string to a girdle'. His sympathy for the adder he killed with his umbrella, in 'a momentary, but warrantable impulse of cruelty', may recall Yorick's pity for the dead ass he sees near Nampont, or for the caged starling, or even for the dwarf in Paris, whom Sterne 'cannot bear to see . . . trod upon'.[29] Such moments, and there are many more, make Pugh a far different narrator from any other contemporary tourist in Wales, none of whom could make their feelings as present and open to us as he does, when he writes, for example, at the end of his tour, of quitting Ruthin 'with that reluctance which every son must feel on leaving a good and anxious mother in tears'.[30]

Cambria Depicta was anything but a handy guide for tourists to carry round Wales, unless they were travelling by post-chaise. At some 480 pages, exclusive of the folio volume of plates, and nearly 150,000 words, it was far longer than any other tour of north Wales except Pennant's two volumes, published in 1778 and 1781, which, densely packed as they are with information of interest only to antiquarians, no one ever wished longer. The whole tour, as described in *Cambria Depicta*, must have been 850 miles or a bit less.[31] The tourists who travelled 'pent up in coaches', Pugh considered, miss many of the beauties of the landscape; 'and they who ride, fare but little better', for many places in the mountains are impracticable or positively dangerous to riders. But 'to the pedestrian all is free – to him no difficulty or danger is presented, and he may make excursions with the greatest ease.'[32] Apart from a short lift hitched on a barge on the Mawddach estuary, a horse hired in an abortive attempt to ascend Plynlimon, and a twenty-mile ride in a chaise from Oswestry to Shrewsbury at the very end of the tour, Pugh walked pretty well every inch of his journey; but, as if that was not enough, he claims at the end of the book, as we have seen, that he had walked 'between two and three thousand miles'.[33]

These different estimates of how far he travelled are not necessarily incompatible. To satisfy the demands of the *genre*, and to stitch together an unbroken narrative, Pugh describes his 'tour' as one single journey, taking eight months, in 'one of the most beautiful summers ever seen', as it must have been if it lasted from March to October. If we do the arithmetic, however, adding up the days as Pugh records them, then even allowing for some occasional vagueness about how long he stays in a few places along the road, it does not appear to have lasted even four months (Plate 8.2). My guess is that these discrepancies of time and distance are the result of writing up a series of tours (including perhaps several journeys to Anglesey *en route* to Dublin), as one single tour, as Pennant had done, without entirely covering his tracks. *Had* it been one single tour, Pugh may have reckoned, it *would have* lasted eight months, its duration exaggerated perhaps to emphasize what a remarkable feat of stamina it was. But the total length of the various tours and journeys on which the book is based may well have added up to two or three thousand miles.

The same concern to fulfil the demands of a literary *genre* may sometimes explain the prodigious amount that Pugh crammed into single days. Theophilus Jones had scoffed at the 'silly and ridiculous whim of converting pleasure into toil' involved in pedestrian tours,[34] but for Pugh, at least, walking was not a whim but a necessity, which is fortunate for us, as much of what is best about the book is a direct result of his inability to afford the post-chaise or post-horses that would have elevated him above the people he meets. His scanty resources, however, and the long distances between one inn and the next, obliged him often to be pressing on to his next destination, and I hesitate to question the stamina of a man whose pedestrian powers were by any account formidable. He probably found no difficulty in tramping, for example, the twenty hard miles along the old turnpike from Machynlleth to Llanidloes, because he did nothing else that day. But I wonder whether it was

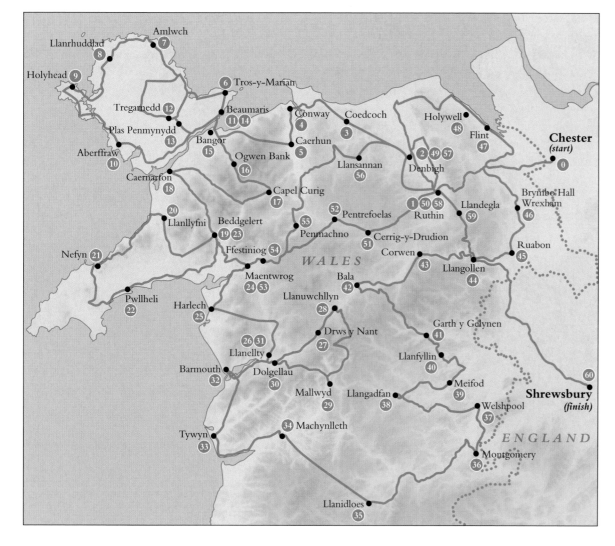

Plate 8.2 *Map of the route of* Cambria Depicta. *The numbers indicate where Pugh spent a night or several consecutive nights; excursions from this route completed within a day, and beginning and ending in the same place, are not marked.*

really possible for him to walk such distances in daylight while pausing to make sketches and to wander repeatedly off piste in search of hidden sublimities. On the nineteen-mile walk from Aberffraw to Beaumaris, for example, he finds time to wander in the grounds of Bodorgan, the country house of the Meyricks, to examine the paintings in the Earl of Uxbridge's house at Plasnewydd, to inspect a pair of cromlechs; to take the ferry to Bangor and back to enjoy a large dinner, and to make a sketch of the creek at Cadnant (Plates 8.3, 8.4), as well as engaging in conversation with two families he met on the road.[35] Perhaps he sometimes strings together places visited on different occasions as beads on a single thread.

The tour begins to look still more like a composite of several different journeys when we stop to ask in what year it is supposed to have taken place. In the preface, Pugh speaks as if he decided in the spring of 1804 to set out on the tour, and to that year he dates one of the two aquatints of the copper mines at Parys Mountain near Amlwch (an earlier image of the same subject is dated 1800, and clearly derives from an earlier journey, perhaps to Dublin). But when visiting Bangor apparently a week and a half after leaving Amlwch, he refers to 1804 as the date of an earlier visit he had made

there, and it suddenly appears to have taken him not ten days but two years to cover the distance between them. It is now apparently 1805 or 1806 – no later, for in Bangor he meets Dr Cleaver, then still bishop of that diocese, who in 1806 was translated to the see of St Asaph.[36]

In the course of writing the book, different time-scales developed, a confusion between the date of first writing an entry and the date of working the MS up into a finished text. On the one hand there are times when Pugh seems to be writing up the tour 'to the moment'. When he says for example that it

Plate 8.3 *(right) Edward Pugh,* Cadnant, *grisaille watercolour for* Cambria Depicta, *Aberystwyth, National Library of Wales.*

Plate 8.4 *(opposite) Thomas Cartwright after Edward Pugh,* Cadnant, *coloured aquatint from* Cambria Depicta, *dated May 1813.*

was 'twelve years ago' that he first saw 'a water-fall on the Trystion', near Corwen, and compares the growth of the vegetation then and now, he is apparently writing in 1805 or 1806 and recalling the walk when he first visited and drew Pont y Glyn Diffwys, a few miles away, which, as we saw in Chapter 4, must have been in late 1793 or early 1794.[37] At Wynnstay too he speaks of having been there twelve years earlier, which, if he means 'earlier than 1805 or 1806', would chime with the visit to nearby Pen-y-Lan when he drew that house as one of the six Denbighshire views.[38] On the other hand, reflecting on the manufacture at Holywell of 'various toys' of brass and copper that used to be exchanged for slaves on the coast of West Africa, he is evidently writing after the abolition of the slave trade in 1807.[39] At the very beginning of the tour he tells us that on the summit of Moel Famau the Jubilee Tower was 'now erecting', dedicated to George III, 'who, on the 26th October, 1810, had swayed the sceptre of Great Britain fifty years'.[40] The final revisions must have been made after that date, but to a manuscript that described a series of journeys that may have been completed and substantially written up by 1806 or not much later.

IV

The pictures, or the 'picturesque embellish-ments', as Pugh described them, were simi-larly of places off the track beaten through north Wales by previous artists. 'I have abandoned the common practice of giving portraits of towns, castles, &c., which have been so often repeated that they now fill every portfolio.' The views in *Cambria Depicta* 'are all of them (as far as I know) new to the public', though he acknowledges a couple of exceptions to this rule, including St Winifred's Well at Holywell, which had appeared in Pennant's tour.[41] As far as I have been able to discover, the great majority of the views are indeed of places which had not before figured in books of views or in loose prints, and in particular, at about one in five, there are surprisingly few images of the famous mountain

scenery of the north west. But there are a few more obvious exceptions than Pugh acknowledged. He includes an aquatint of Conway Castle, for example, well aware that it was an immensely popular subject for artists. He certainly knew the view by Moses Griffiths in Pennant's *Tour in Wales*, and no doubt also the prints after Reynolds, Sandby, and de Loutherbourg, and perhaps Samuel Alken's 1800 aquatint after the Revd Brian Broughton, whom we encountered in Chapter 4; indeed, he had even drawn it himself, and had published his view as one of the series of line engravings by Poole in 1795−6. It is, he writes, 'one of the finest pictures in nature', and 'no wonder that artists annually exhibit pictures of this castle at [the Royal Academy exhibition at] Somerset-place.'[42] Similarly he includes two aquatints of Llangollen, but he may well have known the view of the town published in Wigstead's *Remarks on a Tour to North and South Wales* (1800), and must certainly have been aware of Alken's etching and aquatint of Llangollen, after John 'Warwick' Smith, published in 1794.[43]

Plate 8.5 *(opposite) Edward Pugh,* Paris Mines in 1804, *grisaille watercolour for* Cambria Depicta, *Aberystwyth, National Library of Wales.*

Plate 8.6 *(left) Thomas Cartwright after Edward Pugh,* Paris Mines in 1804, *coloured aquatint from* Cambria Depicta, *dated June 1813.*

Plate 8.7 *(opposite) Thomas Cartwright after Edward Pugh,* Nant Francon, *coloured aquatint from* Cambria Depicta, *dated June 1813.*

Plate 8.8 *(right) Edward Pugh,* Nant Francon, *grisaille watercolour for* Cambria Depicta, *Aberystwyth, National Library of Wales.*

As was probably the case with all the Denbighshire views, the drawings Pugh provided to be aquatinted were – the great majority of them at least – *en grisaille*. A bound volume of sixty-four of them is in the National Library of Wales; the whereabouts of the others is unknown, though as we saw in the Introduction there is a watercolour in a private collection attributed to another artist which is either the original of, or an accurate copy from, an aquatint of which there is no original in the NLW volume. If the attribution of this image should change – and that of course would involve a dramatic reduction in its market value, so don't hold your breath – it would be the only known landscape drawing by Pugh in colour.

A footnote to the preface, added after Pugh's death, tells us: 'He was Ten Years in completing the Drawings for this Volume.' As the images were aquatinted between 1813 and 1815 it may be that Pugh was still producing them for twelve months or more after announcing his original intention to publish by subscription. Most of the aquatints – forty-four in all – were made by Cartwright, who had already aquatinted Pugh's views of Newport and Risca

(see Plates 0.12 and 0.14). He did them in groups of between two and six per month until February 1815, when the job was complete. Sometimes he called in others to help: the well-known artist and engraver John Hassell made one, as did Thomas Bonnor.[44] John Havell supplied no less than eighteen, mainly in the months round Christmas 1813, and in the final month of the job his relation Robert Havell, either the elder or the younger of that name, made another four. Three are unattributed.

Devotee of Pugh as I am, still I find it hard to admire the aquatints as much as I would like. The one review of the book I have found, in the *Gentleman's Magazine* (it was later reprinted by Pugh's publisher, Williams, in the *Cambrian Register*), has nothing but good to say about 'the selection of views, and the number of highly-finished engravings and the excellence of the colouring'.[45] To me, the scenes seem well chosen, and the composition sometimes strikingly well managed; the plates are charming, but charm does not quite compensate for their lack of ambition as compared with the prints by Sandby, for example, or after de Loutherbourg. Those aquatinted by Cartwright, in particular, lose much of the detail and texture of Pugh's original *grisailles*, as if the surface has been carefully sandpapered away. Pugh's watercolour, for example, of the Parys mines in 1804, shows the sublime ruggedness of the cliffs everywhere and a great jagged rent blasted in the mountain (Plate 8.5). All that is tamed and polished into insipidity by Cartwright (Plate 8.6).

The plates were intended to be, as the advertisements say, 'coloured after nature'; the uncoloured plates are often dull, and clearly need colouring; but the coloured plates generally have something off-key, sometimes garish about them. It is unlikely that Pugh, stuck in Ruthin, and dying eight weeks or so after Cartwright finished the first few sets of uncoloured prints, ever had a chance to approve or reject the tinted versions of the plates. Two principal colourists seem to have been employed, and the one who tinted the majority of the plates, especially for Cartwright, uses as his or her default tint for rocks and mountains a rich reddish-brown, which in thinner washes dilutes to an inappropriate pinkish tone. The sunlit meadows are a very yellowy

yellow-green, and the whole effect not unlike some tinted postcards of the 1950s. 'An azure sky', wrote Pugh, 'is unpropitious to an artist in a country like this; and, though the aspect of it be ever so sublime, yet he is not satisfied without a continual succession of clouds, to throw the subjects before him into various lights and shadows.' But in the works tinted by this first colourist, the weather is relentlessly sunny, with occasionally a little regulation white cumulus for variety, whereas the original, monochrome drawings occasionally depict bad weather, or more often, by the softness or paucity of shadow, hint at overcast skies. An extreme case is Cartwright's cheerful view of Nant Ffrancon in sun and shadow (Plate 8.7), based on Pugh's watercolour of a violent downpour (Plate 8.8). The colourist apparently employed by John Havell was a little more respectful of Pugh's text. Of Snowdonia, Pugh remarked that 'gloominess' adds to 'the gravity and grandeur of the place'; an artist will be 'lucky' if he is 'favoured with a murky sky', provided it is 'still clear enough to get the contour of the mountain and rocks'.[46]

Plate 8.9 *(opposite) Edward Pugh,* N East view of Snowdon, *grisaille watercolour for* Cambria Depicta, *Aberystwyth, National Library of Wales.*

Plate 8.10 *(left) John Havell after Edward Pugh,* N. East View of Snowdon, *coloured aquatint from* Cambria Depicta, *dated November 1813.*

Plate 8.11 *(right) Edward Pugh,* A Visit to Cader Idris, *grisaille watercolour for* Cambria Depicta, *Aberystwyth, National Library of Wales.*

Plate 8.12 *(opposite) Thomas Cartwright after Edward Pugh,* A Visit to Cader Idris, *coloured aquatint from* Cambria Depicta, *dated November 1814.*

Havell's colourist responded with the appropriately gloomy 'N. East View of Snowdon', with a charcoal-coloured foreground and a few leaden clouds above the left horizon (Plates 8.9, 8.10). This second artist's default colour for rocky landscapes in shadow is a rich umber, too rich, but still better than the rosy tints of the first.

But it is not the colouring, or the aquatinting, that is the main problem. In setting out to depict pure landscape, with minimal human presence, Pugh was attempting to do something in which his limitations were bound to be exposed, and his main talent left unused. The emblematic, notational style of Pugh's drawing, works well in those of the Denbighshire views – all of them except *Pen-y-Lan* – where the landscape is animated by figures engaged in narratives wonderfully appropriate to the places where they happen. In *Cambria Depicta* only a couple of plates – *A Visit to Cader Idris*, featuring Robert Edwards, the famously eccentric local tourist-guide (Plates 8.11, 8.12) and *Holyhead Wake*, showing 'four lusty lads . . . eating hot hasty-pudding' for prizes[47] – offer anything like the characteristic groups of Pugh's images of London. Elsewhere, the standardized foliage, the repetitive shapes of loose rocks and so on, give the feeling of stage sets after the actors have gone home. As illustrations to the text they are serviceable enough, but they give little of the pleasure of the earlier scenes in Denbighshire or London, energized as those are by intimate local knowledge. They are landscapes that seem to be waiting to be discovered by other artists, with different gifts; they are empty of anything that would allow us to see them also as places.

Pugh's book is a masterpiece, but on account of the text, not the plates. In an excellent paragraph on *Cambria Depicta*, Peter Lord wrote that Pugh, 'although not consistently radical',

was concerned about the condition of the Welsh people, and to that extent his voice is a new one in the field of visual culture. His self-confessed limitations as a draughtsman may have resulted in conventional illustrations, but the text of *Cambria Depicta* represented a profound change of view which would rapidly overtake Welsh intellectual life.[48]

And the first review of the book to appear, in the *Gentleman's Magazine*, judged that

As the writer of a Tour, he is one of the most pleasing we have met with. The style of his narrative is good, his observations just, and he treats his subject with an interest which a lively attachment to it naturally inspires. If he has not the advantage of the learning and the powers of research of a Pennant, he has genius and taste and humour of no ordinary description.[49]

As contemporary reviews go, this is unusually high praise; and anyone who reads *Cambria Depicta* will find its liveliness, humour, and sharpness of observation more than a fair exchange for the antiquarian learning of Pennant.

Notes

1 *CD*, p. iii.

2 See 'Anecdotes relative to the late Alderman Boydell', in W. Bell Jones (ed.), 'An Autobiography of John Boydell, the Engraver', *Flintshire Historical Society Publications*, 11 (1925), 81–7, and Vivienne Painting, *John Boydell* (London: Guildhall Art Gallery, 2005), p. 7.

3 *CD*, pp. iii–iv.

4 *CD*, p. iv.

5 Pugh to Llwyd, writing from Ruthin on 'King George's Birthday' (4 June 1812; letter franked 8 June), NLW MS 9023C.

6 NLW MS 9023C.

7 *Gentleman's Magazine*, 83/1 (January 1813), 40. Similar advertisements appeared in *La Belle Assemblée* (February 1813), 44, and the *European Magazine*, 63 (February 1813), 70.

8 *CCh* 23 July 1813. My assumption that the first tranche of Pugh's fee was to be paid on publication (see previous paragraph) is based on the statement in this obituary that Mrs Pugh owned the manuscript outright when Pugh died; by Mrs Pugh's death, if not before, the manuscript was almost certainly with Williams, who had priced it and was proceeding with the aquatinting of the plates.

9 *New Monthly Magazine*, 1 December 1815, p. 446; *Quarterly Review,* vol. 14 (January 1816), p. 558.

10 *CD*, pp. iv–v.

11 *CD*, pp. v–vi.

12 *Poetical Works of Richard Llwyd, the Bard of Snowdon* (London: Whittaker & Co. et al., 1837), pp. lv–lvi.

13 [Joseph Cradock], *Letters from Snowdon: Descriptive of a Tour through the Northern Counties of Wales* (London: J. Ridley and W. Harris, 1770), p. 68; Warner, *A Walk*, p. 176, and *Second Walk*, pp. 171–7; Evans, *Letters*, pp. 39, 205–9, 215–16; on what basis Evans arrived at this characterization is not clear, but he did not, apparently, engage any of his 'mountaineers' in conversation.

14 Anon., 'Journal of an Excursion', pp. 62, 123; Evans, *Letters*, p. 116.

15 Cradock, *Letters*, pp. 53, 70.

16 Thomas Vernon, 'Journal 1797–1812', DRO NTD/140, p. 3; Wigstead, *Remarks*, p. 17; Warner, *Second Walk*, pp. 311–12; Robert Ker Porter, NLW MS 12651B, unpaginated notes on Welsh inns.

17 Porter, NLW MS 12651B, p. 67.

18 *James Plumptre's Britain*, pp. 37–8.

19 See volume 1 of Theophilus Jones, *A History of the County of Brecknock*, 3 vols (Brecknock: G. North for the author, 1805–9). My thanks to Professor Ralph Griffiths, and to Abigail Kenvyn of the Brecknock Museum and Art Gallery, for their help in identifying the subject of this vignette, though neither felt able to say definitely that the vignette was of the ruined Ely Tower, so neither is responsible for what will be shown as an error on my part if a more convincing candidate is proposed. The Ely Tower nowadays is on private land and shrouded in vegetation. My identification is based on the fact that a title-page vignette of a book with Jones's title might well be expected to show a scene in the county town; on the juxtaposition of the tower, on its (characteristically exaggerated) motte, with the river and bridge; and on a comparison between the construction of the tower in the vignette and the photograph on p. 22 of Griffiths's 'Bishop Morton and the Ely Tower at Brecon', *Brycheiniog*, 34 (2002), 13–30.

20 *CD*, pp. 119n., v–vi; 'Cymro' (Theophilus Jones), 'Cursory remarks on Welsh tours or travels,' in the *Cambrian Register for the Year 1796*, vol. 2 (London: E. and T. Williams, 1799), pp. 421–54. For Bingley's proposal, see his *Tour*, p. 241; for Jones's essay, see Hywel Davies, 'Wales in English Travel Writing 1791–8: The Welsh Critique of Theophilus Jones', *Welsh History Review*, 23/3 (June 2007), 65–93.

21 *CD*, pp. vii–viii.

22 Aikin's sentence continued: 'it is not be gleaned by a hasty excursion through a country, where its language, and the general shyness and suspicion which the natives discover towards the English, or, to use their own word, Saxons, oppose obstacles which only time and endurance can overcome.' Aikin, *Journal*, pp. viii–ix. In his essay in the *Cambrian Register*, Jones italicised the word 'gleaned' (p. 454), to associate Aikin with the essay's attack on Samuel Pratt's *Gleanings through Wales*, which Pugh also attacked (see below).

23 *CD*, p. 463.

24 Pennant, *Tour*, vol. 2, pp. 82, 161–2.

25 R. Evans Paul, 'Thomas Pennant (1726–1798): "the Father of Cambrian Tourists"', *Welsh History Review*, 13/4 (December 1987), 395–417.

26 *CD*, p. vi.

27 *CD*, p. 333.

28 *CD*, pp. 10, 190.

29 Laurence Sterne, *A Sentimental Journey through France and Italy by Mr. Yorick* (1768), ed. Ian Jack (Oxford: Oxford University Press, 1984), p. 114, *CD*, p. 49, Sterne, pp. 38–41, 71–5, 60.

30 *CD*, p. 455.

31 Returning to Ruthin after completing most of the tour, Pugh says he had walked 'many hundreds of miles' (*CD*, p. 398). By the end of the book he has probably walked another 160 miles, and if we follow the entire tour on the map, from inn to inn, it seems to add up to rather less than 650 miles,

with perhaps another 200 miles at most to allow for excursions which begin and end at the same overnight stopping-place.

32 *CD*, pp. 16–17.
33 *CD*, pp. 398, 463.
34 [Jones], 'Cursory Remarks', p. 451.
35 *CD*, pp. 223–4, 67–80.
36 *CD*, pp. iv, 97.
37 *CD*, pp. 295, 297.
38 *CD*, p. 321.
39 *CD*, p. 360.
40 *CD*, p. 15.
41 *CD*, p. vii.
42 *CD*, p. 21.
43 The fact that the drawing of Conway Castle, and one of the drawings of Llangollen, do not appear in the bound volume of Pugh's drawings for *CD* referred to below may suggest that the inclusion of views of these two well-known sites was an afterthought, or may even have been decided upon by Williams after Pugh's death. This possibility is strengthened by the fact that the view of the castle does not appear in the list of plates intended for *CD* in *Cambrian Popular Antiquities.*
44 The date of Bonnor's death is uncertain. The *ODNB* suggests it was between 1807 and 1812, but his aquatint for *CD* is dated 15 July 1813.
45 *Gentleman's Magazine*, 86/ 2 (July 1816), 45, and see *Cambrian Register*, vol. 3 (London: E. Williams, 1818), p. 391.
46 *CD*, pp. 209, 109, and see also pp. 114, 116.
47 *CD*, p. 53.
48 Lord, *Imaging the Nation*, p. 164.
49 *Gentleman's Magazine*, 86/s2 (July 1816), p. 45.

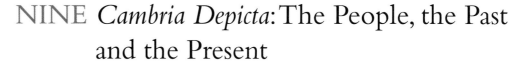

NINE *Cambria Depicta*: The People, the Past and the Present

I

Pugh set out from Ruthin with Wowski at his heels and with a light knapsack containing among other things a 'sandwich-box', a new flageolet he had recently learned to play, the portable edition of John Evans's map of north Wales, and a telescope.[1] He wore a broad-brimmed hat and gaiters, carried an umbrella and, suspended from his right shoulder by broad tape, a small portfolio. Thus equipped, he tells us, he found himself in Bangor mistaken for a Jewish pedlar by three 'black-eyed nymphs' who spoke English with an accent more marked than his own: 'open your bags, Moses,' they ask, 'for we vant some bodkins, sheesors, and oder things.'[2] At Llanllyfni near Beddgelert, and again at Whitford, he is taken for a spy for the French (as George Morland had been on the Isle of Wight[3]), once on account of his portfolio, in which he was supposed to be keeping drawings and plan of suitable sites for an invasion, and once on account of his trousers, which presumably marked him as a sans-culottes. On both occasions his ability to speak Welsh is received as proof of his loyalty to the crown, which suggests that on many occasions he introduced himself in company speaking English.[4]

Pugh enjoys these moments of mistaken identity, and sometimes plays up to them. On a number of occasions he is taken for an Englishman, and sometimes, as at Whitford, he lets the mistake ripen before revealing that he speaks Welsh. On one such occasion, asking directions in English of an old woman who, a monoglot Welsh-speaker, attempts to point out the way by the most extravagant and ludicrous gestures, he eventually reveals that he has understood her all along, and is angrily ticked off for his 'pretended ignorance of her tongue'. When a group of farmers in a pub at Amlwch make him the butt of their humour on the assumption that he cannot understand what they are saying, he so much enjoys their 'unpremeditated wit, so familiar to the Welsh' that he does not disabuse them. But after recounting the incident he gets a little good-humoured revenge by naming for the benefit of posterity one member of the company, whose wit had been more laboured: 'the Rev. Mr. J.....s had better not have shown such promptitude in satirical remarks upon a stranger and his faithful dog, for which his genius was so ill calculated.' If you add up the dots, the name looks to be 'Jenkins'.[5]

Pugh never misses an opportunity to meet and chat with people on the road. Even when he knows his way perfectly well, he frequently asks for directions, so he tells us, 'to have a little confab with my compatriots',[6] and every day is punctuated by such 'confabs'. If on one or two occasions he teases them by pretending not to know Welsh, he always shows his 'compatriots' respect, whatever their status. Irritated that English travellers have rushed to judgement about the manners and character of the Welsh, complaining of their ignorance, their dishonesty, their meanness, their lack of polish, Pugh makes much of his encounters on the road, with the aim and effect of challenging the standard tourist accounts. 'I have but too often seen it observed by tourists', he writes,

> that the Welsh are an 'unpolished and ignorant people;' if at all ignorant, it must be ignorance of those fashionable dissipations, the never-failing promoters of diseases, incident only to the *great* and fashionably *wise*, who take so much pains to secure them.[7]

The wisdom of the north Welsh, he suggests, is manifest in their customary sobriety – unlike the English, they seldom go to the alehouse or brew beer – and in their religious piety.[8] On his tour published in 1795, the English poet Samuel Pratt, on the basis of one unfortunate experience of a kind that might have occurred in any country, had declared the inhabitants of north Wales to be cheats; but though 'necessity', Pugh pointed out, obliged them to be 'cautious and close in their bargains', still 'sincerity, honesty, and charity' were 'the predominant features of the Welsh character.'[9]

A particularly interesting encounter, between Bala and Corwen, is with 'a poor woman, an inhabitant of the neighbourhood, gathering sticks upon the road, with her unfortunate idiotic son, who was confined to his mother's side by means of a string attached to both their waists'. The son, after eyeing Pugh 'with that vacant stare so common to those in a similar condition', otherwise spends his time carefully watching his mother's movements.

When she set forwards, he studiously placed his feet in the prints made by her's, which I suppose he did with precision, as every step seemed to give him great pleasure. He was eighteen years of age, nearly six feet high, and an extremely handsome figure: walked erect, and with a grace unusual to those of his description.[10]

Travellers less at home in Wales, or less careful in their attention to the poor, might have used this meeting as an occasion to reflect on their degenerate state; but where they would have seen degeneracy, Pugh finds only dignity. It is hard to read this passage, and several others in *Cambria Depicta*, without being reminded of the encounters with beggars, 'idiots' and others in Wordsworth, and as we shall see there are other grounds to compare the two writers.

Much of what he learns about the cultural and economic geography of north Wales is derived from conversations with local people. Some is picked up from the people he lodges with. On Anglesey, where he appears to have been on familiar terms with some of the local gentry, he stays as often with them as at roadside inns, and passes on the local information they offer him. But on the mainland his connections are fewer, and nine times in ten he lodges at inns and public houses, striking up cordial and informative acquaintances with a series of innkeepers, both men and women, whom he often takes the trouble to name and to thank for their hospitality and conversation. The Revd John Evans names and converses with innkeepers in his tour too – 'Lloyd', 'Williams', 'Cartwright'; but to Pugh they are 'Mrs Parry', 'Mr. Owen', 'Maurice Roberts', and the difference in respect or intimacy implied in the naming habits of the two tourists suggests a difference, too, in the kinds of conversation they were capable of having with Welsh people below the rank of the gentry.[11]

Pugh derives much information from people he meets on the road, farmers, artisans, cottagers, and so on. But for the most part he records his encounters with them less on account of what they can tell him about their local area than to individualize them, and in doing so to vindicate the inhabitants of north Wales from the criticisms of English tourists. One day, for example, about halfway through the supposed tour, Pugh sets out to walk from the inn at Llanuwchllyn, at the south-west end of Llyn Tegid, to Mallwyd, a distance of some fourteen miles if he had gone by the direct route, but a few steep and muddy miles more as it included an attempt to climb the 2,900-foot Aran Benllyn, aborted when he found it shrouded in mist. His account of that day is packed with information, about the topography, the history (in part legendary) and the economy of the area, with less account than usual of views fit for painters on account of the mist and drizzle. But Pugh devotes most space to the kindness of the strangers he meets on his walk.

A few miles from the inn Pugh stops at a cottage inhabited by an old woman and her daughter, who become involved in a merry conversation about Pugh's dog, and invite him in for refreshments, as do many others he meets.[12] 'Such', Pugh reflects, 'are the sentiments and genuine good feelings of the country poor, that to perform acts of kindness to the stranger, becomes to them a luxury unknown to the haughty rich.' They point him towards Aran Benllyn, and soon he meets a ninety-year-old farmer who insists on his son showing Pugh the way to Llyn Lliwbran, a lake at the north end of the mountain. From there Pugh strikes south, meeting three helpful shepherds on the way who tell him an anecdote about a path to the summit, and keep him company as far as Llyn Dyfi, a lake immediately under the mountain peak. On their advice he abandons the attempt to reach the peak, and attempts to return to the public road by following the Llaithnant rivulet.

After straying off the path and becoming covered in mud he at last reaches the road, where he meets a woman who bursts out laughing at the state of his clothes. In an attempt to judge her attitude to strangers, he addresses her in English, asking the way to Llanymawddwy, and the woman becomes genuinely distressed at her inability to give him directions he can understand. 'This is one of the many instances I have met with on this very journey,' remarks Pugh, 'disproving the assertions of some English tourists, who represent the character of the Welsh to be morose and uncivil.' Shortly afterwards he finds himself in a narrow valley between precipitous mountains on which peat was dug in great quantities, and his description of the complicated and dangerous process of transporting the peat, by sledge, from the tops of the mountains to the valley, derived partly from Pennant, is amplified, as we shall see later, from conversation with the peat-cutters themselves.[13] He next comes across a cottage built so close to the edge of a precipice that he can stare down its chimney to ask directions (which, as often, he did not need) from a young woman roasting lamb at her kitchen-range. After a merry chat with her, Pugh finally reaches Mallwyd, where he meets the innkeeper, 'Mr. David Lloyd', who 'very obligingly' accompanies him next day on a walk round the neighbourhood looking for views suitable for painting.

In the course of his day's walk, Pugh has met and talked to a mother and her daughter, a farmer and his son, three shepherds, a woman on the road, some peat-cutters, a young woman in a cottage and an innkeeper: more local people in a day, innkeepers aside, than most English travellers would speak to in a month's tour, and more time passed with each of them than most tourists would spend with any.[14] Evans, who writes with great confidence about the character and behaviour of the inhabitants of north Wales, believes, like Pugh, that to become acquainted with the Welsh it is necessary to 'deviate from the beaten track . . . traverse the secluded vale' and 'enter the humble roof'. This advice is offered as the preface to a day-long excursion from Mallwyd to Bala and back on which he seems to have made no attempt to communicate with a single soul; indeed, he writes as if he met none.[15] Like Pennant, he rides through a landscape as empty and silent as the Wales through which Pugh walks is populated, lively, and vocal.

In 1799 P. Stampa of London published a print entitled *An Emblem of Wales*, which was also circulated widely as a reverse painting on glass (Plate 9.1). It showed a young woman in a mountainous landscape, wearing a leek in her hair and holding up a coronet bearing the three feathers of the Prince of Wales. Beside her are a putto bearing the same device on his standard, and a billy-goat, solemn and (in the original print) melancholy. The woman wears the classical robes appropriate to an allegorical figure, and only her fashionable blue pumps and carefully curled hair tell us that she is really a modern young lady dressing up – though her hair-style too may be intended as classical. Another, mezzotint emblem of Wales, of English design, was published by P. and J. Gally the following year (Plate 9.2). Wales, here paired with Scotland, is represented by another young woman in a more nondescript British landscape, again wearing classical robes, holding in one hand the coronet with three feathers, a leek in the other, and embracing a rather more cheerful goat than in Stampa's print.

Pugh probably had one of these prints in mind when he designed his own emblem of Wales to be the frontispiece of *Cambria Depicta* (Plates 9.3, 9.4). It shows a young *lady*, for so she evidently is, thoroughly modern and *à la mode* in her red slippers and white muslin dress with puffed sleeves, playing the harp. She sits in a protective bower by a gently running stream; in the distance is a rather tamer view than Stampa had shown, but a more antique one too, for there is a cromlech prominent in the middle distance. The cromlech, 'three, or sometimes more, upright stones, with one large stone placed upon them', is, Pugh tells us, a 'species of druidical remains'.[16] These standing stones stand *for* something: the successful resistance to the romanization of Britain, and, by extension, to the invasion of 'English taste and manners'.

The Welsh harp, Pugh tells us in *Cambria Depicta*, is the 'indigenous musical instrument of the country',[17] the pre-eminent symbol of Welsh national culture. But it is, he complains, falling out of fashion and favour with the gentry, who

> seem to have lost their taste for the instrument; its sounds are no longer heard, except in a few of their houses. The intercourse with England, indeed, has long been so general and so close, and the English taste and manners so incorporated with those of the aboriginal districts, as in a great measure to efface them; and the ancient provincial customs and peculiarities, whether estimable or not, are, in a great measure, discarded. Even the copious and nervous original language of Britain, is, among men of rank and fashion, almost lost and forgotten. Among the peasantry and farmers, however, the harp is yet in some esteem; and, I hope, will thus keep the instrument from total oblivion, till some generous effort be made, in higher life, to revive a regard for simple and pathetic music; when the strings of the harp may again be successfully struck in all parts of the principality.[18]

According to Pugh, his friend Thomas Lloyd, of Marle, near Conway, was thinking of opening a Welsh harp school in a building 'amidst rocks, mountains, woods, and water' on his estate at Tre'r Beirdd, near Mold. It was to be funded by subscriptions from gentlemen who in time would be 'provided with

Plate 9.1 *(above)* An Emblem of Wales, *reverse painting on glass after mezzotint engraving (London: P. Stampa, 1799), private collection.*

Plate 9.2 *(right) Detail from* Scotland. Wales, *coloured mezzotint (London: P. & I. Gally, 1800), private collection.*

Cambria

Plate 9.3 *(left) Edward Pugh*, Cambria, *grisaille watercolour for Cambria Depicta, Aberystwyth, National Library of Wales.*

Plate 9.4 *(below) Anon. after Edward Pugh,* Frontispiece to Cambria Depicta, *coloured aquatint, not individually dated.*

youths of merit' to be maintained as resident harpists in their houses. Whether anything came of this plan, if it ever even became one, I do not know.[19]

Pugh's frontispiece, then, offers a rather more specific, more nuanced idea of the principality than did the two earlier prints. The young musician may be an allegory, an abstraction, but she is also apparently a polite and fashionable one, making precisely the 'generous effort' required of her class if the sound of the harp, and of the language with which its fate seems here intertwined, are to be heard into the future. To my English eyes she looks much as Mary Crawford must have looked when her harp, 'as elegant as herself', was eventually delivered to the parsonage near Mansfield Park, or like Ellen, the eponymous heroine, a very anglicized young Welsh aristocrat, of Anna Maria Bennett's novel of 1794.[20] This may be because of a difficulty I have in imagining that traditional Welsh culture and modernity could inhabit the same space in the decades around 1800, but to Welsh eyes, too, she is certain to appear anglicized. For the harp Pugh has given her is not an 'indigenous' Welsh triple harp, which is played resting on the left shoulder, with the head to the right of the instrument, contrary to the rest of Europe; this is how the blind harpist, probably John Parry, appears in Paul Sandby's *View of the Eagle Tower at Caernarvon* (Plate 9.5), and how Parry is shown in the well-known portraits by his son William in the National Museum and Galleries of Wales.

The instrument that fashionable Cambria is depicted playing is a single-action pedal harp, suggests the harpist and harp historian Ann Griffiths, of the kind made in Paris by Georges Cousineau or Jean Henri Naderman.[21] This cannot be explained simply as a mistake by Pugh, who would have been well acquainted with the Welsh harp, who encountered native harpists on several occasions in his travels, and knew (and stayed with) the celebrated Griffith Owen, the landlord of the Raven in Towyn, 'esteemed the first performer upon the Welsh harp in the kingdom'.[22] So: if at first glance the image appears to celebrate 'ancient provincial customs and peculiarities', on a more careful inspection it may show one of those customs, a symbol of all the rest, being 'discarded'. Or perhaps it suggests that if the harp is once again to shed its music through Cambria's halls, or (to strip away the allegory), if an indigenous Welsh culture is to survive, a compromise may be necessary with the polite, the modern, even the 'improved' culture of Britain in the early nineteenth century. Perhaps the young ladies of Wales would be willing to sound the harp if it was not too visibly Welsh, and would not mark them as provincial if they played it at a fashionable musical evening in Grosvenor Square or Portland Place. Generally, Pugh's vision of Wales is of a modern nation, capable, at ease in the nineteenth century, yet mindful of its distinctive traditions; a coalition of the polite gentry and the traditional 'peasantry', in which the former learn to remember what they are in danger of forgetting, and the latter learn to embrace the future without letting go of what is worth preserving from the past. But that is easier said than achieved, and this frontispiece may speak, presumably with approval, of a gentry not just prepared to compromise with an invasive culture, but perfectly willing to do so. Perhaps, as the frontispiece to the whole book, it concedes or it declares (according to your point of view) that *Cambria Depicta*, written as it is in an urbane English, published in London, is just such a compromise, between a native culture imagined as to a degree archaic (the cromlech), and a modern Wales which might be thought of as polite even by the standards of the British metropolis.

Plate 9.5 *A harpist, and woman knitting stockings as she walks, in Paul Sandby,* View of the Eagle Tower at Caernarvon, *etching and aquatint, plate 1 from* Twelve Views in North & South Wales Set D *(London: Paul Sandby, 1786), Aberystwyth, National Library of Wales.*

III

'Despite his interest in such matters as the precise location of the suicide of Gray's "Last Bard"', writes Lord, for Pugh 'the Welsh were no longer Ancient Britons but also a people who might be expected to sustain a modern culture.' I almost agree. Wherever appropriate, Pugh records in considerable detail the legends, the genealogies and the historical anecdotes deriving from the sources he cites, authors such as Giraldus Cambrensis, David Powel's edition (or one of his editions) of Caradoc's *Historie of Cambria*, Henry Rowlands's *Mona Antiqua Restaurata*, Rowland Vaughan of Caer-gai, Robert Vaughan of Hengwrt, and Edward Lhuyd, as well as English antiquarians, historians, topographers William Camden, William Dugdale, John Leland, John Speed and John Stow. Some of these books may have been hard to get hold of in Ruthin, and my spot-checks suggest that, like many contemporary writers, he was happy to absorb them as filtered through more recent works, Pennant's *Tours*, Llwyd's *Beaumaris Bay*, and *Observations on the Snowdon Mountains* by William Williams of Llandygai. Often however Pugh seems more dutiful than enthusiastic in his commitment to the remembrance of the Welsh past and the information he found in the antiquarian writers. His writing as an antiquary generally lacks the animation, the sprightliness that elsewhere makes *Cambria Depicta* one of the shortest long books ever written.

Occasionally, however, a legend or anecdote seems to offer him the chance to write in a new register, and Pugh will eagerly seize the opportunity. One example will be sufficient. Pennant had described Cwm Idwal, off Nant Ffrancon, as 'infamous for the murder of a young prince of that name, son of *Owen Gwynedd*, by *Dunawt*, son of *Nefydd Hardd* . . . It was a fit place to inspire murderous thoughts, environed with horrible precipices, shading a lake, lodged in its bottom.' In Williams, Pugh found a little more of this legend, together with an alternative account of the naming of the lake and valley, after another Idwal;[23] and he combines, amplifies, and inflates these two passages into something which, after offering a little sensible advice in the manner of a guide-book, becomes more like a paragraph from a Gothic novel:

To visit this with safety, travellers must quit their carriages and horses, and be content to take the foot road. Upon entering this cwm, strangers have stood aghast for the moment, appearing more like fixed statues than animated nature; the mind is instantly filled with thoughts accordant to the horrific gloom and melancholy that pervade the vast profundity of this British Pandaemonium; the awful and formidable black precipices, that nearly surround this dismal pool, forming a wonderful amphitheatre, mysteriously reared by the magic spell of nature, [that] has an irresistible effect upon the nerves of the most gay and airy; and those who have viewed it with such sensations, as the place is so well calculated to inspire, will not wonder when they are told, that in this hollow was foully murdered a young person of the name of Idwal, from whom it derived the appellation of Cwm Idwal . . . Mr Williams of Llandegai gives an account of another Idwal, son of Cadwalader, who, he supposes, retired here from the tyranny of Ivor, who had usurped his father's throne. It is very remarkable that the people in this district continue, from time immemorial, to point out the spot where this Idwal was buried; he is fabled to have been a great giant, or gawr; and the rising ground by the side of the lake, several yards long, is said to be his grave, and precisely the length of his body.[24]

How far in such passages we think Pugh's tongue is in his cheek will depend on our own attitudes to the legendary past of Wales. But certainly there is much in the Wales of legend that Pugh found 'absurd', a favourite term,[25] or irritating, or ridiculous, as he does many of the 'traditional stories' he hears from those he meets on his journey: the reason for the supposed hoof-mark at Carreg Carn March Arthur for example, or the reason why the river Alyn flows partly underground, or the origin of various standing stones and large erratics.[26] Near Capel Curig he amuses himself at one point by making up his own legend to explain one 'immensely large stone, completely formed like a shoe'.[27]

But Pugh is certainly enthusiastic to recall the resistance of the Welsh to invasions by Romans, Saxons, Normans, English, the courage of their leaders, the cruelty, treachery and oppression of the Plantagenet kings. All writers of tours are obliged to pause, when they come to a castle or ancient battlefield, to offer an account of the history of the place. Pugh's accounts, however, are marked by a nationalism which distinguishes them entirely from those of English tourists. He uses these places to follow the careers of the defenders of Wales especially against the Plantagenet kings: at Caergwrle, Llywelyn ap

Gruffydd and his brother Dafydd; at Caernarvon, Madog ap Llywelyn; at Penmynydd on Anglesey, Owen Tudor, whose liaison with Catherine of Valois 'restored the British race to the throne of England'; at Penmaenmawr, Llywelyn ab Iorwerth, and included among the plates is a drawing of his coffin at Llanrwst.[28] When he reaches Glyndyfrdwy, by tradition the birthplace of Owain Glyndwr, he pays sincere and respectful homage to the 'defender of the liberties of his country'; when he visits Caernarvon Castle, he records how Edward I had 'duped' the Welsh in promising them a prince born in Wales and speaking no word of English.[29] On some days in the course of his journey, like the walk from Mold to Flint, this story of Welsh resistance becomes the main preoccupation of the tour: at the Bailey Hill, how Owain Gynnedd and later Llywelyn ab Iorwerth captured the castle from the kings of England; at Maes Garmon, the defeat of the Saxons; at Ewloe Castle, the defeat of the army of Henry II; the capture of Hawarden Castle by Dafydd, the brother of Llywelyn ap Gruffydd; and at the simultaneous capture of Flint by Llywelyn himself.[30]

By the time he gets to Rhuddlan Marsh, his blood is well and truly up, as, following Pennant at his most patriotic, he recalls the defeat of '*our* monarch Caradog', by '*our* enemies', Offa's Mercians.[31] He had written thus once before, on Yr Eifl near Nevin: 'the greatest British military works in the principality', from the amazing solidity of which 'the traveller may form a juster notion of the persevering spirit of *our* ancestors in the defence of their country, than he would from volumes of histories

of the ancient Britons' (my italics throughout).[32] In these passages especially, Pugh is writing against the accounts of Welsh history he found in the writings of some English tourists, Bingley in particular, for whom Glyndwr was just a 'turbulent chieftain', a troublemaker, and Dafydd ap Gruffydd a traitor, not when he turned against his elder brother, but when he 'insidiously took up arms . . . against his former benefactor' Edward I.[33]

Here more than anywhere we discover Pugh's pride in his Welshness, in being 'a native artist', as he invites his compatriots to share his pride in 'the spirit of a martial people',[34] and announces to his English readers that he is not one of them. And though he has clearly picked up this 'we', and this patriotic tone from Pennant, Pugh is announcing his Welshness more emphatically than his genteel predecessor had done. For one of the many ways in which Pennant tempers his patriotism with urbanity is the generosity with which he describes the enemies of Wales, especially Edward I, whose various oppressive measures for 'curbing' those he had conquered are, for Pennant, no more than those of a 'judicious warrior'.[35] Pugh has no more ambition than Pennant to fight over again the wars with the Plantagenets, except in prose, but he is not willing for them to be appropriated into a pageant, a national romance with heroes of equal virtue on either side. 'The cruel disposition of Edward', he retorts to Pennant, 'is now made a subject of doubt: but what is to become of the many historical facts; the piteous lamentations of the sufferers, and the testimony of Sir John Wynn, who wrote from MSS of undoubted authority?'[36]

IV

As we shall see, however, there are limits to Pugh's nationalism, and in particular there are clear limits to his sense that the separate identity of the Welsh can be sustained by repeated appeals to their martial past. He is considerably more interested in the present state and future development of Wales and in observing the signs of economic health, decay and regeneration as he encounters them in his walks. Carefully recording the scenes of industry he passes on the road, he comments for example on new lead mines near Machynlleth, Llanidloes, Llansannan, opened at a time when the price of lead was not high, but likely, he believes, to be productive. Of another new mine in Nant-y-Ffrith near Wrexham, he tells us the yield is so disappointing that 'the shafts are never entered but by the poor people of the neighbourhood, when unemployed in their regular course of labour.' He visits some equally unprofitable older lead mines, one, now nearly worked out, near Llangynog, and the 'once-great' Grosvenor mines at Llanferres, now made unprofitable by the difficulty of extracting the ore. He notices how much the prosperity of Holywell is boosted by the sale of food and clothing to those working in the 'great lead-mines' at Halkin.[37] At the vast copper mines at Parys near Amlwch he is fascinated to see how much of the mountain has been blasted away, its shape changed entirely, since his previous visit four years earlier (see Plate 8. 5). 'It is still sufficiently grand,' however, and so 'sublime' that 'nothing can impress upon the mind a greater awe'; and yet this is not the work of nature but 'all produced by manual labour of thirty years'. He discusses the rapid vicissitudes in the fortunes of yet another copper mine near Dolbadarn Castle, and wonders at the huge yield that will be necessary to make the copper mined on Snowdon profitable, on account of the great expense 'of conveying the ore over the rough sides of this mountain'.[38]

The problems of moving minerals through mountainous landscapes become a topic of particular interest for Pugh. The huge quantity of slates stacked up at Port Penrhyn, waiting to be shipped to London, Dublin, Liverpool and elsewhere, leads him to investigate the different means by which they are conveyed to the coast: from Dolbadarn, along the lake and then by wagons to Caernarvon; or from Ffestiniog by road alone to Maentwrog, a 'tedious and expensive' journey in thirty carts 'which, certainly, do not *improve* this public road'. Far more efficient is the method employed at the great quarry in Nant Ffrancon, to convey the slates first 'from the beds, along the narrow ridges that hang over the frightful precipices', and then down to the coast, a fall of 300 feet: 'a man conducts a four-wheeled barrow loaded along these edges, on a narrow rail-road. When a sufficient number are ready, the slates are conveyed to Port Penrhyn, in eight or a dozen of these little barrows, and thus one horse will draw many tons.' On the basis of information probably derived from a conversation with William Williams of Llandygai, who was a retired quarry-manager as well as a noted antiquary, Pugh reports that by turning from road to rail, Lord Penrhyn has reduced the cost of carrying his slates to port from 5s. a ton to 1s., and can now convey no less than 100 tons every day![39] He is equally fascinated, as were other travellers, by the much more low-tech means of shifting peat from the hills north of Dinas Mawddwy, by means of sledges made from hazel hurdles, guided downhill at 'a velocity hardly credible'. These were remarked upon by a number of other travellers, but only Pugh had enquired about the making of these sledges and described them in such detail that, following his instructions, anyone might make one.[40]

Similarly with manufacturing, Pugh is eager to record the mills and factories he passes on the road and sometimes takes the time to visit. He is as impressed by the industrial sublime of John Wilkinson's great ironworks at Bersham as he had been at Parys: 'These works are immense,' he gasps, 'displaying such a profusion and tumultuous medley of machinery, as to leave the mind not a little astonished at the sight of it . . . I have never beheld a work of this kind half so wild, half so picturesque.' Like many travellers he was fascinated by the natural economy of St Winifred's Well, which leaves the Gothic shrine in which it rises to power, successively, a corn mill, 'several grand and extensive cotton-mills', until eventually it 'gives motion to several copper, brass, and lead mills', perhaps still as many as the twenty-three which Edward Lloyd had counted in 1780.[41] He visits and describes the architecture of the famous bleach-works at Lleweni, designed by Thomas Sandby, and puzzles over a shipyard at Llanelltyd, twelve miles from the sea at low tide, so that the ships building there seem to be growing 'amidst woods and meadows', and Pugh wonders 'how such hulks could be made to float, in a place seemingly land-locked'.[42] Again like other tourists, he admires the ceaseless labour of the outworkers, tirelessly knitting woollen stockings around Bala (see Plate 9.5), who always, even while walking to market and back, are 'busily at work with their knitting-needles;

and no conversation, or any slight occurrence, can divert them from this object of their industry'.[43]

As we saw in chapter 1, for a tourist like Joseph Hucks, the whole point of touring in north Wales was to seek out views 'unmechanized by the ingenuity of man';[44] and though other travellers, John Evans for example, or William Bingley, show considerable interest in the industries of the region, and describe some individual sites in greater detail than Pugh, none observe or describe as many as he does.[45] Once or twice he worries about the adverse effect of industry on the landscape, most notably at Llangollen, where a new factory 'stares one in the face so much, as to be a great offence to the eye of a follower of the arts'. Its construction gave rise to 'violent opposition . . . by many gentlemen in the neighbourhood', who ought instead to have reflected on the advantages it would bring to the area, certainly sufficient to 'palliate the disagreeable effect of it in a landscape'. It would strengthen trade, 'countervailing the efforts making on the continent to supplant us in foreign markets', but more immediately it would provide 'a source of employment to a number of children, who, otherwise, would have been a burden to the parish'.[46]

There is nothing sentimental about Pugh's attitude on such questions. To him, the task of educating the children of the poor was to teach them 'to know their duty as good servants and good subjects',[47] and all successful industrial and infrastructural ventures, however unpicturesque, were 'improvements', and not less so if they depended upon child labour. Above all, on his travels through Wales, it is 'improvement', the buzzword of the decades around 1800, that he sets out to record, applaud and promote. As Lord puts it, Pugh's 'patriotic feelings involved him less often in vacuous praise of the virtues of his people than in pointing out their need for improvement'.[48] Pugh is extravagant in his praise of William Maddocks for the 'improvement' of his estate achieved by the reclamation of Traeth Mawr, and of Lord Penrhyn for the turnpiking of the new Irish road from Shrewsbury to Bangor, 'one of the greatest improvements the country ever saw'.[49] These endeavours are a model of what could be achieved in Wales by 'public spirit': Maddocks and Penrhyn in particular have shown that 'the improvement of their estates' was not 'a doubtful speculation; but a safe and certain profit, which, whilst it advances the income of the improver, betters the condition of the country'. Pugh explicitly 'challenges,' as he puts it, 'the patriotism of the rich landed proprietors', urging them to stop wasting their fortunes on prize-fighters, race-horses, game-cocks, and to take up 'the more rational, honourable, and useful employment of their talents and fortune, in ameliorating the condition of their landed property'.[50]

More than that, the gentry should actively encourage the improvement of the 'lower', mechanical arts in north Wales, which, with the exception of shoemaking, 'are not above mediocrity'. This is partly the result of the failure of the Welsh to develop the division of labour, the advantages of which are reinforced by learned references to Xenophon, Plato, James Harris and Adam Smith, so that 'it is common here for a mechanic to blend his own immediate business with various others', a custom 'highly prejudicial to the acquisition of accurate skill'. As a result, in north Wales, 'solidity seems to be the only aim of every mechanic, forgetting the recommendatory quality of neatness of finishing.' The only exceptions are the productions of artisans 'whose laudable desire of improvement incite to the measure of visiting London', and Pugh proposes that in each county 'a society of gentlemen' should be established, 'to reward such men as, on the completion of their apprenticeship, spend a few years in London for their advancement in their different occupations'.[51]

'The spirit of improvement, now so prevalent', is both cause and effect of the increase of trade and population in the 'bustling towns' he discovers, Wrexham and Holywell in particular, but everywhere in north Wales, and in the increased 'energy of mind' he sees as the great effect of canal construction and other improvements to the transport infrastructure.[52] The forward march of improvement is apparent too in the greater number of visitors attracted there, and the effect they are having especially on architecture and manners in seaside towns. A new 'spirit of building' at Pwllheli means that 'there is little doubt of the place soon becoming very respectable'. Caernarvon has become 'a fashionable bathing-place,' thanks partly to the new hotel built by Lord Uxbridge, more like 'a gentleman's seat' than an inn; it now boasts an 'evening and Sunday promenade . . . on a beautiful terrace on the north-west side of the town, where the beaus and belles taste the refreshing breezes that skim the briny flood'. Barmouth has become 'one of the pleasantest water-places in the kingdom', and 'the number of very handsome houses that have been lately built, and are now building, is an indisputable proof of the great influx of strangers to this place.' Even humble Bala, 'within these twenty years, has been much improved', mainly in response to 'the frequent unfavourable notices' of tourists. 'The principal street is *now* kept very clean; and, in consequence of the example of the better sort, the poor people vie with each other in the repair and decorations of their houses.'[53]

Why the same trickle-down process of improvement has not come about in Ruthin is not clear, but Pugh uses the fact that his book may be read more carefully there than anywhere else in Britain to protest at the rubbish left in the streets and the permission given to pigs 'to wander about the town, and in droves to perambulate the streets, by night and by day'. 'The *swinish multitude*', he submits, must 'be restrained within legitimate bounds; and be taught, that they are not to encroach with impunity on the decencies and conveniences of civil society.' The real swinish multitude, however, in the sense that Burke intended, the ignorant poor, have certainly undergone a process of improvement at Ruthin, as they have throughout north Wales, by the decline of 'wakes'. Thirty years ago, Pugh remembers, they were attended by 'such scenes of barbarity and disgrace, as the better instructed inhabitants would now be ashamed of', almost as violent, he reckons, as the rioting of students at Oxford and Cambridge; but in north Wales, at least, 'these outrages . . . are now heard no more.'[54]

V

Pugh has rather less to say about improvements in agriculture. English tourists repeatedly notice what they believe to be poor farming practice in the north west, John Evans especially, who in his tour offered a ten-page critique of the hill farmers of Wales, predicated on the unspoken assumption that they had all the capital necessary to follow his detailed recommendations.[55] Pugh occasionally does the same, though it is not likely that he had much knowledge of farming. Of the mountains around Beddgelert, for example, he remarks that the land is 'cold, poor, and boggy', and 'produces very little of any sort of grain or other esculents'. This unproductiveness, however, turns out to be not much to do with the nature of the soil the farmers have to contend with, but 'arises either from their obstinacy in persevering in the old injudicious system of managing their lands, or from an ignorance of a better system of culture'. They should irrigate their meadows better, to produce more hay; they should sow earlier, to ensure an earlier harvest. But this, Pugh's longest criticism of farming methods in Snowdonia, quickly gives way to a much longer passage in praise of the healthy diet, hardiness, frugality and sobriety, of the 'mountaineers', as if Pugh would not wish them better farmers, in case their natural virtue was corrupted by greater comfort.

If Pugh was relatively silent about agricultural 'improvement', this was because he was altogether more uncertain of its beneficial effect. When the 'rich landed proprietors' did as Pugh urged them and decided to improve their agricultural estates, Pugh did not much like the results. Where farming was concerned he was an altogether more cautious advocate of modernity, whether in the Vale of Clwyd or further west. Very early in the book he passes 'several fertile farms' and a 'neat small farmhouse', and goes out of his way to praise the kind of benevolent landlord whose 'gratification' it was 'to make his tenants happy'. He did this by ensuring that their farmhouses were 'neat and comfortable' and their rents 'easy', and by adhering 'to the good old system' of '"not adding farm to farm"'.[56] The phrase in quotation-marks is one of the catchphrases of those who wish to arrest the destruction of the 'moral economy' by the march of 'improvement'. 'The dearness of provision', the *Gentleman's Magazine* warned in 1765, 'is caused, in great degree, by landholders adding farm to farm, and letting very large tracts of ground to one tenant'; 'adding farm to farm, leaves great numbers of poor unemployed, who, if the great farm of a thousand a year, was divided into twenty of £50 each, would be employed in cloathing the naked, and feeding the hungry.'[57]

In fact the aggregation of farms, a practice intended to attract tenants with larger capitals who, by means of economies of scale and more sophisticated farming methods, would be able to pay higher rents, was blamed for far more than this: as well as raising rents, increasing the cost of provisions and causing unemployment, 'adding farm to farm' prevented farm servants from marrying, depopulated the countryside, led to overcrowding in cities and widened the gulf between the rich and the poor.[58] At Llanfyllin Pugh was impressed by the number and generosity of the charities recorded on boards in the church, regretting that 'the spirit of divine charity', was now too rare among the rich, now so reluctant to divert their 'super-abundant wealth' from degrading pleasures to acts of benevolence.[59] Near Caerhun he was delighted to come across 'a great number of cottages' whose owners appeared to be safe from the perils of improvement. They were apparently owned outright by the local 'peasantry', who 'enjoy them free of all demands or molestation'. Near Llanidloes, on the other hand, he was shocked to come across a deaf old shoemaker obliged to pay 'a most exorbitant rent, £4 10s.', apparently the going rate in the area, 'for a hut, infinitely inferior to many a pig-stye'. But as we shall see, Pugh's objections to agricultural improvement were as much those of an artist as of a defender of the moral economy, the 'good old system'.

'Improvement' for Pugh is a more difficult topic than my discussion of it has so far suggested. At one point he remarks on 'the gradual improvement in cultivation' that a traveller will notice as he moves across the country from west to east – a gradual improvement in the soil and climate, he might have added. As far as farming is concerned he leaves the matter there, comparing instead the 'melancholy and gloomy aspect' of farmhouses in the west, with the 'modern, gayer buildings' in the counties bordering on England, which, when he saw them again, returning from the mountains, 'exhilarated my spirits'.[60] 'It might be noticed', he continued,

> that the most sprightly parts of Wales are those bordering upon the English countries; as their immediate converse and traffic with England, have made even the common people equally civilized with their neighbours: and an English man will be surprised to find his language as well spoken thirty miles from his own country, as it is in it.[61]

It is in this passage, little more than an aside, that we see most clearly the difficulty for Pugh of balancing his nationalism and his commitment to improvement, to modernity. Modernity for him is something English, and it is the modern culture of England which has improved him, by providing him with a professional identity and the opportunity to adopt the manners of a gentleman. As an individual he seems to wear easily the double identity of cultured Londoner and native Welsh patriot, but the question of whether the country can wear it so easily nags away at him as persistently as it has so many Welsh people in his situation. Does he really want to argue, and if so in what sense, that the north-west Welsh are relatively 'uncivilized', and that their improvement can come only from the increased influence of English culture? How would this square with his anxiety at how the language and culture of the 'aboriginal districts' of Wales are being 'effaced' by 'English taste and manners'?[62]

He observes the economic invasion of Wales with anxiety but also with a utopian hope for independence. When he considers 'the handsome and stupendous cotton factory' at Mold, 'lighted by about two hundred and twenty windows', he regrets that it belongs to 'some merchants in Manchester'; but of the fulling mills and factories processing wool and weaving flannel throughout Merionethshire and Montgomeryshire,[63] he notes with approval that in the latter county 'the manufactories and other commercial works . . . belong to, and are conducted by, the natives.'[64] If only the rich gentry of north Wales would invest in north Wales, the economic destiny of the country would be in its own hands, not in those of entrepreneurs from Lancashire with surplus capital. But it is that same gentry, anglicized as it is, that is effacing the traditional culture of Wales, and though Pugh proposes some measures by which they might arrest that process – the school for harpists, for example – it is not always clear how much he wants it arrested, or where: west of Offa's Dyke, or west of the river Conway?

Notes

1 *CD*, pp. 17, 81, 171, 250, 14.

2 *CD*, pp. 87, 17, 49, 99.

3 William Collins, *Memoirs of a Painter* (London: H. D. Symonds, 1805), pp. 107–11; George Dawe, *The Life of George Morland* (London: Vernor, Hood, and Sharpe, 1807), pp. 160–1.

4 *CD*, pp. 134–5, 370, 194.

5 *CD*, pp. 243–4, 47.

6 *CD*, p. 243.

7 *CD*, p. 53.

8 *CD*, pp. 131, 182.

9 *CD*, pp. 131–2; Pugh may be paraphrasing here p. 427 of Theophilus Jones's essay in the *Cambrian Register*, discussed in chapter 8.

10 *CD*, pp. 287–8.

11 Evans, *Letters*, pp. 54, 82, 127; *CD*, pp. 197, 188.

12 See for example *CD*, pp. 133, 190.

13 Pennant, *Tour*, vol. 2, pp. 79, 81.

14 *CD*, pp. 189–96.

15 Evans, *Letters*, pp. 60–80.

16 *CD*, p. 71.

17 *CD*, p. 94.

18 *CD*, pp. 94–5, and see pp. 210–11.

19 *CD*, p. 95; for the friendship of Pugh and Lloyd, see Pugh's letter to him, 10 March 1809, NLW MS 1562C.

20 Anna Maria Bennett, *Ellen, Countess of Castle Howell*, 4 vols (London: William Lane, 1794); see Sarah Prescott, *Eighteenth-Century Writing from Wales: Bards and Britons* (Cardiff: University of Wales Press, 2008), esp. p. 143.

21 My thanks to two harpists, Ffion Mair Jones and Rhys Jones, for helping me to this point, and to Williams for consulting Ann Griffiths about the instrument Cambria is playing.

22 *CD*, p. 218.

23 Pennant, *Tour*, vol. 2, p. 154; William Williams, *Observations on the Snowdon Mountains* (London: E. Williams, 1802), pp. 81–3.

24 *CD*, pp. 107–9.

25 See for example *CD*, pp. 27, 170.

26 *CD*, pp. 11, 170.

27 *CD*, p. 116.

28 *CD*, pp. 337 (Caergwrle); 123 (Caernarvon); 89 (Penmynydd); 28 (Penmaenmawr); 421–2 (Llanrwst).

29 *CD*, pp. 300–2, 122.

30 *CD*, pp. 346–7 (Bailey Hill, Mold); 347 (Maes Garmon); 349 (Ewloe); 351 (Hawarden); 355–6 (Flint).

31 *CD*, p. 375 (my italics), and compare Pennant, *Tour*, p. 14.

32 *CD*, p. 138 (my italics).

33 Bingley, *A Tour*, pp. 318, 407; by contrast, Warner's liberal politics enable him to sympathize with the struggles of the Welsh to maintain their liberty (Warner, *A Walk*, pp. 136, 164), as does Evans's vestigial Welshness (see for example his account of Glyndŵr, *Letters*, pp. 297–308).

34 *CD*, p. 31.

35 Pennant, vol. 2, p. 214.

36 *CD*, pp. 306–7.

37 *CD*, pp. 223, 226, 423 (Machynlleth, Llanidloes, Llansannan); pp. 331, 263–4, 429 (Nant-y-Ffrith, Llangynog, Llanferres); p. 366 (Halkin).

38 *CD*, pp. 46–7 (Parys Mountain); p. 120 (Dolbadarn); p. 157 (Snowdon).

39 *CD*, p. 99 (Port Penrhyn); p. 120 (Dolbadarn); pp. 167–8 (Ffestiniog to Maentwrog); pp. 104, 100 (Nant Ffrancon to Port Penrhyn). There is an account of Penrhyn's railroad in Williams's *Observations*, pp. 129n.–130n., but Pugh provides more detailed information than is in that book.

40 *CD*, p. 195; compare Evans, *Letters*, pp. 62–3, who gives a rather different though equally detailed account of how the sledges are brought down the mountain, but only a vague account of their construction.

41 Lloyd, *A Month's Tour*, p. 10.

42 *CD*, p. 329 (Bersham); p. 360 (St Winifred's Well); p. 395–6 (Lleweni); pp. 182–3 (Llanelltyd).

43 *CD*, p. 189; of numerous other examples, see Pennant, *Tour*, vol. 2, p. 67; Evans, *Letters*, p. 68; Anon, 'Cursory Remarks made in a Tour through different Parts of England and Wales in the months of August and September 1797', NLW MS 1613.3C., p.5; Thomas Martyn, 'An Account of a Tour of Wales' (1801), NLW MS1340C, p. 123.

44 Hucks, *A Pedestrian Tour*, pp. 70, 7.

45 See for example Bingley's account of the 'mills and manufactories' at Holywell (*Tour*, pp. 32–4) or of the Parys and Mona mines (pp. 207–14), or Warner on the same sites (*A Second Walk*, pp. 206–11, 284–95), or Pennant on the Parys mine (*Tour*, vol. 2, pp. 265–71), or Evans's description of the manufacture of flannel at Newtown or webs at Dollgellau (*Letters*, pp. 31–3, 88–9), or Aikin on wool manufactures (*Journal*, pp. 69–84).

46 *CD*, p. 311.

47 *CD*, p. 292.

48 Lord, p. 164.

49 *CD*, pp. 147–9, 111.

50 *CD*, pp. 253, 149.

51 *CD*, pp. 75–6. The learned footnote on p. 76, which includes a line of Greek from Xenophon's *Cyropaedia*,

was perhaps added by the shadowy editor, whose anonymous presence is felt on two or three occasions in the footnotes to *CD*.

52 *CD*, pp. 119, 237, 231.

53 *CD*, pp. 142 (Pwllheli); 127–8, 124–5 (Caernarvon); 210 (Barmouth); 278 (Bala).

54 *CD*, pp. 454, 439–40.

55 Evans, *Letters*, pp. 367–77.

56 *CD*, p. 13.

57 *GM*, 35 (January 1765), 85.

58 See for example the anonymous *An Address to the P–t, in Behalf of the Starving Multitude* (London: R. Baldwin, 1766), where the phrase is many times repeated, and held responsible for all these effects.

59 *CD*, pp. 224, 258.

60 *CD*, pp. 130–1, 230.

61 *CD*, pp. 230–1.

62 *CD*, pp. 94–5.

63 *CD*, pp. 149, 221, 226, 231, 236, 244.

64 *CD*, pp. 253, 345–6

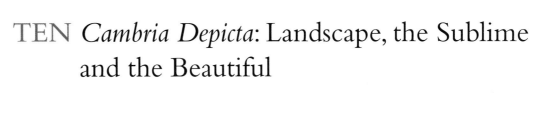

TEN *Cambria Depicta*: Landscape, the Sublime and the Beautiful

I

On one occasion, approaching the north-ern end of Llyn Gwynant, Pugh takes the word 'improved' and stands it on its head. 'The scenery', he writes, 'began to look more wild and improved every step I made'; that is, the land-scape 'improved' from the point of view of the artist, as it became more 'wild' and *un*improved, from the point of view of the farmer or landlord.[1] Elsewhere, however, the more farmland was 'improved', the less picturesque it became, and the less interesting to an artist exploring the byways of Wales for the benefit of those artists who would follow him. In Montgomer-yshire, Pugh found himself in a country where some delightful landscapes in the Banwy and Vyrnwy val-leys were surrounded by tracts of land he thought neither sublime nor beautiful nor picturesque, but certainly improved. After visiting Dolanog bridge on the Vyrnwy he found himself in 'an open space,

that promised me but little for contemplation: but in other respects it was a prospect very pleasing to the landlord and the farmer, as cultivation here appears carried to great perfection' (Plates 10.1, 10.2). Near Meifod he walked 'among the mountains, where the hollows between often exhibited proofs of the able skill of the husbandman; but these, however productive to the occupier, have nothing to recommend them to the artist'. Near Llanerfyl he had to cross a landscape of 'very dull, unpleasant, boggy mountains and dingles, which better agree with the interest of the plodding grazier, than the views of the artist'; and approaching Llangadfan, he found himself on a good new road among boring mountains, a combination better calculated to please 'the commercial traveller' than 'the eye of the painter'.[2] The primary aim of the tour, at least as originally conceived, was

to point out landscapes to the artist; 'improved' landscapes are virtually never recommended, and, with the exception of an unidentified canal scene,[3] the Pontcysyllte aqueduct and (arguably) Parys Mountain, are not to be found among the illustrations to *Cambria Depicta*.

Though Pugh's anxiety to ensure as wide a sale as possible for his book had led him to represent it as a general description, not of the landscape only but of the present state of north Wales and its inhabitants, he remained faithful to Boydell's original conception of it as a guide-book for professional artists. The book is full of information directed at the artist alone; and although, as we shall see, he finds ways of making this aspect of the book as attractive as possible to the non-specialist 'general observer', much of the advice he gives, for example on how to find

Plate 10.1 *(opposite) Edward Pugh,* Dolanog Bridge, *grisaille watercolour for* Cambria Depicta, *Aberystwyth, National Library of Wales.*

Plate 10.2 *(left) Thomas Cartwright after Edward Pugh,* Dolanog Bridge, *coloured aquatint from* Cambria Depicta, *dated April 1813.*

subjects and viewpoints in difficult terrain, is very specialized and delivered in his plainest, most practical prose. 'The artist should desire his guide to shew him the following places: Rhyadr-y-Cwm, Rhyadr Bod-Losgad, Rhyadr-y-Fuwch, and Caenant Llyn-y-Pyscod; all of which will reward his trouble'; 'the following places are worth the toil of clambering to them: the precipices of Cwn Brwynog, Llyn-y-Madrod, and Llwn-Coch.'[4] Sometimes he visits what might have been promising ruins of abbeys or castles only to report that artists should not waste time on them. In Anglesey 'the monastery of Llanvaes . . . holds forth no temptations to the artist'; at Dyserth the castle 'from no point whatever will make a subject for a picture'; at Cymer Abbey 'time and weather have committed great devastation in this monastery; and have left little for the antiquary, and not much for the artist.'[5]

Sometimes he pointedly distinguishes between views that the general traveller should seek out and those more precipitous places to which perhaps only 'the professor of the arts' should venture.[6] On various occasions he seems to be exhorting artists to exert themselves more in search of the original subjects which Boydell had complained they never provided him with. 'No artist', he declares, more as a challenge than as a statement of fact, 'will ever think it too troublesome to walk up the heights' near Llanderfel. 'The allurements of Nant Nanhwynen', he tells us, 'are already well known to the painters: but it may not be improper to notice a neglect of which some are guilty in not ascending to the heights on the south-east side of the vale.' And if Pont Aberglaslyn is now a 'much hackneyed' subject, it is probably because artists are so unwilling 'to bear much toil', so anxious 'to avoid the fatigue of climbing the steps here'. As a result 'the numerous prints of this spot,

already published, are nothing but mere duplicates: the bridge and the bed of the river, constantly introduced into the foreground.'[7]

Pugh is always looking round for good 'subjects' to recommend: here, the artist will find 'an excellent subject'; here, he may find 'subjects to employ him for a considerable time'; there, on one side of a cliff, is 'a subject for the pencil', but not on the other.[8] Once a subject has been located, he searches for the 'points' from which it will appear to the best advantage. Lord Penrhyn's slate mine, he tells us, 'is of considerably less value to the artist than the Paris mines; yet . . . by getting to some happy points, he may be highly gratified.' Good viewpoints, Pugh makes clear, are by no means easy to find, and the artist must often take some trouble to seek them out. In some places, above Beddgelert for example, the 'important points' are so 'various' that the artist cannot miss them; by Llyn Ogwen, he must search the heights to the north side of the lake 'till he can suit himself with points'; on the Vyrnwy, 'the artist must prepare himself for crossing the river frequently; and he will easily find fords and other conveniences, which will enable him the better to choose his points.'[9]

In Pugh's vocabulary, a 'subject', seen from an appropriate 'point', becomes a 'picture', and a 'picture' is discovered where apparently randomly arranged objects can suddenly be grasped, from *this* point but not from *that*, as a composition, a landscape. Sometimes these arise in profusion, so that he finds himself moving as if through a gallery of potential paintings. The scenery of cliffs under Holyhead Mountain 'does not exceed two miles, yet it embraces a great many sublime pictures'. South of Ruthin, however, towards Eyarth Rocks, 'the pictures are not very numerous, yet they are good.'[10] Pugh is committed to an ethic

of landscape art by which, though it appears to be the duty of the artist to exert himself in search of 'points' if he is to avoid producing mere 'duplicates' of pictures already painted, it is not legitimate for him to create 'ideal' pictures by entirely reorganizing what he sees, by shifting hills and diverting streams in the manner positively recommended by William Gilpin. It is, he says, 'an allowed liberty' for the painter to ignore what is immediately in front of him, and 'to compose a foreground of his own'; which is to say, he is *not* at liberty to compose his own middleground, or third, or fourth distance.[11]

What Pugh did learn from Gilpin and other 'connoisseurs', gentlemen students of the aesthetics of the picturesque, is a habit of making judgements on landscapes, and criticizing them when they fail to come up to snuff, in the manner Wordsworth attacks in *The Prelude* as 'a strong infection of the age':[12]

> even in pleasure pleased
> Unworthily, disliking here, and there
> Liking; by rules of mimic art transferred
> To things above all art;[13]

We have already seen him use the fastidious tone of the picturesque theorist in his judgement on Lord Penrhyn's slate mines. We hear it too, when, near Llanelltyd, he comes across 'rather a good waterfall, but too low to excite much interest'; or near Corwen, where the landscape 'with respect to the picturesque, does not come up to mediocrity'; or at Montgomery, where 'the ruins of the castle are too poor and insignificant for description'; or in his almost personal attack, near Newtown, on hills 'destitute of character, and devoid of every thing that can be termed grand' – if hills could speak, these would cry 'ouch!'[14] Yet sometimes such judgements develop into something much more interesting, a way of developing the rather professional manner in which Pugh rates landscape for the benefit of painters into a way of evaluating the landscape of more interest to the 'general observer'.

One of the best examples of this is his description of the 'noble cascade' in Penmachno, which, despite being twenty yards wide, and falling 'in one continued unbroken sheet' down an inclined plane over a distance of a quarter of a mile, 'nevertheless does not possess those requisites that would recommend it to the notice of a painter for imitation: the grounds about it are tame, spiritless, and without a feature of what can justly be called the picturesque.' But no matter: 'it ought not to suffer the least diminution of character' from this description; 'for it has so much sublimity, as to render it a most interesting subject for contemplation'. On this showing, it seems that for Pugh, some landscapes are picturesque in the sense of being fit for representation in a drawing or painting; others may perhaps be too grand for the artist, too sublime, and able only to be contemplated, by amateurs of landscape whether artists or not. A few may do for both: Llyn y Gafr for example, on Cader Idris, makes 'as fine a subject for contemplation as it does for the skill of the painter', and the 'general observer' has as much business there as the professional artist.[15]

But Pugh's main resource to ensure that his general observers stayed with him in passages aimed especially at professional artists, is the expressive power with which he described so many of the landscapes he led them through. We have already had some taste of this, in his description of the waterfall at Pont y Glyn Diffwys in chapter 4. Elsewhere, Pugh embarks on large-scale descriptions of some of the most famous landscapes in north Wales – the views from Snowdon or Moel Siabod, for example – and makes of them bravura pieces. On Moel Siabod he witnesses a sublime sunset, and describes it in an intense fusion of narrative and description as he contrasts its effect on the views to the east and west. Eastward, over to the Clwyd range:

> it was a grand and novel sight, the sun strongly shining upon those distant objects, and on most of the intermediate varieties of hills, rock, and water; with a dark cloud forming a gloomy canopy above me, throwing a shade and obscurity all around, which contrasted grandly with the splendour of the eastern distance.

Turning westward, Pugh finds that Snowdon

> was likewise involved in an almost impenetrable cloud, from the body of vapours that sluggishly moved along . . . The sun was now sinking towards the horizon, and tinged the whole atmosphere with his setting colour. I anticipated the glowing exhibition, and prolonged my departure from the mountain till his rays had lost their influence on our hemisphere. In about half an hour the whole had attained a depth of red, that must be incredible to any, but to those who have been the eye-witnesses. Snowdon seemed a dreadful mass of fire, and the clouds which hovered upon his top, and about his base, the consequence of it: the utmost fury of the burning Etna . . . could never have displayed a scene more sublime.[16]

The view from Snowdon was more of a set-piece for tourist writers, and the standard set by Pennant and by the poet William Sotheby, for example, was very high. In Pugh's magnificent version, especially in his

Plate 10.3 *John Havell after Edward Pugh,* View in Nant Nanhwynen, *coloured aquatint from* Cambria Depicta, *dated November 1813.*

account of the sudden revelation of the scene below through an 'impenetrably thick mist', first in flashes, then in clear sunlight, we seem to hear distinct echoes of Wordsworth himself, though the unpublished *Prelude*, and its superb lines on that view, were of course unknown to Pugh.[17]

But Pugh's remarkable talent for descriptive writing is evident not only in these set-piece descriptions of the most famous views, but in briefer, more unassuming passages of narrative, here for example near Beddgelert (we have glanced at its first sentence already):

> The scenery began to look more wild and improved every step I made, till I reached the end of Llyn Gwynen, or Gwynen lake; where was exhibited a rude and most disorderly assemblage of water, rocks, woods, and mountains. The great and stupendous cliffs, appendages of Snowdon, continually varying in form, with others of very fantastic shape dropping from the opposite heights, and meeting so as apparently to deny the traveller a passage, have a noble effect; which is still heightened by the addition of hills in the mid-ground, and others receding finely into the distance.[18]

Compared with some descriptive passages in *Cambria Depicta*, this does not call attention to itself, but it is a sophisticated piece of writing, which makes use of a turn of rhetoric associated with the pioneer of landscape description, the Scottish poet James Thomson, author of *The Seasons* (1726–44),

which at the time Pugh was writing was still the most popular and most admired nature poem in English. What Thomson liked to do, and what Pugh does here, is to announce that he is confronted by a landscape in which it is apparently beyond the power of the artist or writer to discern any structure, any possibility of composition; and then, in the process of describing its disorderly wildness, to discover a structure within it. To begin with, this place appears just a chaos of unorganized things, a shapeless aggregate of 'water, rocks,

woods, and mountains'; by the end, those cliffs 'of fantastic shape', 'continually varying in form', have come together into a structure in which opposite masses answer each other, framing a middle distance of hills; while beyond them, more distant hills, less distinctly seen, close the view. Compared with John Havell's neat, attractive, tranquil aquatint of this scene (Plate 10.3). Pugh's description communicates a sense of the dynamic interchange between artist and landscape that is involved in the process of composition.

II

Pugh's original aim in visiting Snowdonia was of course to look out for little-known views that would be of interest to artists and print-sellers, views which offered the experience of the 'sublime'. According to Burke, 'a mode of terror, or of pain, is always the cause of the sublime,' terror itself being a variety of pain.[19] As we saw in chapter 4, to go in search of the sublime was to look for experiences which were frightening, but not so much so that they could not be enjoyed as offering, as Burke put it, 'a sort of delightful horror, a sort of tranquillity tinged with pleasure', which arises when the terror is not the result of actual, but only of apparent danger; when, as he put it, the danger did not 'press too nearly'.[20] In mountain country, the most obvious source of sublime experience was 'looking down from a precipice' and experiencing the fear of falling from it, but without actual risk.[21]

When Pugh stands on the south side of the summit of Moel Siabod, he tells us that 'the view of the precipice from its brink, is enough to stupefy the senses, and almost to petrify the whole animal system, so that I found it necessary to keep aloof.' The danger went beyond what could be experienced as delightful, except perhaps in retrospect, or by the reader who experiences Pugh's fear comfortably at second hand, and so he turned instead to describe the sublime views in other directions which could be enjoyed without the risk of vertigo. But for the most part he seems fairly untroubled by the actual fear of falling. To reach the summit of Snowdon, he reports that it was necessary to walk for a few hundred yards along a narrow ridge, 'on each side of which is a headlong fall, a quarter of a mile in depth; a terror to many, unaccustomed to such situations, but which however may be ascended with ease and safety'. Descending Cader Idris, he takes 'the Fox's Path', which, he tells us, is 'nearly perpendicular', and 'seldom attempted but by shepherds', few tourists choosing to take it. He found it, however, 'perfectly safe; the tread upon loose soil, intermingled with stones, rendering it, indeed, somewhat troublesome, but not dangerous'.[22] On such occasions he could enjoy, and recommend, the delightful horror offered by mountain landscape.

Throughout the time he spent among the mountains, however, Pugh was frequently attacked by a fear which he could not modify into 'a tranquillity tinged with pleasure'. Burke considered that being on top of a precipice looking down had more 'sublime force' than being beneath one looking up, though he acknowledged that he was not 'very positive' about this.[23] Pugh was perfectly sure that the opposite was true. Despite the vertigo he had felt on Moel Siabod, he was much less frightened at the top of steep mountains than at the bottom, where he could never rid himself of the fear, either of being crushed to death himself by falling stones, or that houses at the foot of mountains, with whose inmates he empathized, would be overwhelmed by loose rocks and landslides. Other travellers of course mention from time to time the danger of falling rocks, but with Pugh it became, in the course of his tour, a major preoccupation. Before he entered Snowdonia, he had already noticed, though with no great anxiety, the 'immense and numberless blocks of stone' that had fallen off the mountain at Rowen,

Plate 10.4 *Edward Pugh*, A Fall of Rocks, *grisaille watercolour for* Cambria Depicta, *Aberystwyth, National Library of Wales.*

near Caerhûn, and had remarked on the danger of falling rocks, at Parys Mountain and while sailing off the cliffs near Holyhead.[24] It was not until he had walked up Nant Francon, and entered 'the most sublime and magnificent scenery in this island', that he began to be gripped by this terror.[25]

On the way down from visiting Llyn Bochlwyd, he 'passed some frightful jutting rocks and stones, several of which, I have no doubt, weighed some hundreds of tons, lying upon each other in rude order; my road led me under some of them, and I was not without apprehension . . . lest the least motion of my body should bring them down upon my head.' To recover his nerve, he sat on a large rock, weighing, he estimated, four or five tons. 'It slipped about a yard and a half, but was checked in its approaching a precipice only by a few smaller stones directly in its track.' He counted himself fortunate that he had not 'fallen a sacrifice'.[26] A few days later, leaving Capel Curig for Caernarvon, walking under Glyder Fawr, he has sufficiently recovered to describe with an artist's eye 'the amazing projecting rocks' on the mountain side, 'wonderfully grand, and finely broken'; but in the next sentence his apprehension returns: 'some of these great rocks project most frightfully,' he writes, no doubt with a trembling hand, 'and from the loose manner in which they are supported and propped up, the passenger goes by with dread, and great uncertainty of their remaining safe . . . till he is out of danger.'[27] A few days later again, visiting Tan-yr-Allt, the house of William Maddocks near Tremadoc, he wonders how the owner can possibly sleep there at night: 'the nocturnal rest of any person, not possessed of strong nerves, might easily be disturbed by the thoughts of the impending fragments that seem to threaten immediate destruction to this house.'[28]

Approaching Aberglaslyn a few hours later, he tries to talk himself out of this fear. He points out the rough, shattered rocks on the cliffs above the road, and reflects that 'the stranger to such scenes of wildness' (as he is of course himself) 'if he loiter on his way, will be seized with some apprehension of danger.' And indeed, he tells us, 'there are several instances of the falling of rocks in this country.' He must have found a safe place to sit, however, for at this point he made a drawing of 'a prodigious stream of stones, which may give the reader an idea of the danger to travellers, if often repeated'; and as if to show himself that he could overcome his terrors, he added himself into the image, perky, insouciant, perched on one rock, his feet on another, sketching while Wowski looks on (Plate 10.4). Committing the cause of his fear to cartridge paper seems to help him rationalize it away, for suddenly it appears that there is almost no chance at all of actually encountering a landslide. 'Very few examples of this kind', he reassures us, and himself, 'occur in a century,'[29] and for the rest of his tour through Snowdonia he is untroubled by the fear of falling rocks.

Then suddenly, at Llanegryn near Towyn, the old fear returns. Pugh comes across a few cottages 'situated under horribly looking, high craggy rocks', which he is convinced 'threaten instant destruction to the whole. Should high winds, lightning, or any casual misfortune, dislodge some of the heavy masses of stone from their sockets, some fatal event must ensue.' Thereafter this fear keeps coming back until he is safely into lowland country again. At a mine near Llangynog he finds a slate quarry where the workmen 'have so undermined the rock, as to leave it beetling over their heads in a frightful manner . . . it requires no penetration to foresee some dreadful accidents if the work should

Plate 10.5 *(top right) Edward Pugh,* Carreg Diddos, *grisaille watercolour for* Cambria Depicta, *Aberystwyth, National Library of Wales.*

Plate 10.6 *(bottom right) J. Havell, after Edward Pugh,* Carreg Diddos, *coloured aquatint from* Cambria Depicta, *dated November 1814.*

be continued.' By Llyn Tegid, contemplating the strangely-formed rock known as Carreg Diddos, he speaks of his dread that 'a puff of wind' might 'hurl it down this nearly-upright precipice, and shatter to pieces the houses at the bottom'. As if to mock and overcome his fear, his drawing shows one man who has scaled the rock and demonstrates his *sang-froid* by adopting an exaggeratedly fashionable pose, while beneath him another makes an equally exaggerated gesture of alarm (Plates 10.5, 10.6).[30] Near Glyn Ceiriog he hears of an 'immense block of stone, of many tons weight', which

> came down the mountain with great velocity; a house was exactly in its way, but, happily for the inhabitants, who were all at home, it was prevented doing them mischief, by other stones which lay in the same line. It bounded horribly, attended by a loud crashing noise, that called forth the attention of the people, and the last bound that it made, was into the midst of these stones.[31]

Burke's treatise on aesthetics is an enquiry into 'our Ideas of the Sublime and Beautiful', and he represents the beautiful as in all respects the opposite of 'great', the 'sublime'. 'Great', or sublime objects, he writes, 'are vast in their dimensions, beautiful ones comparatively small; beauty should be smooth, and polished, the great, rugged and negligent.' The sublime may be characterized by sudden, strong deviations of surface or outline, the beautiful by 'gradual variation'. Beauty 'should not be obscure; the great ought to be dark and gloomy'.[32] The sublime is gendered as masculine, beauty is associated with femininity, and also with the social feelings and society; the sublime may be experienced in solitude, or as a privation of the social pleasures.[33] And as we saw at the start of our consideration of *Cambria Depicta*, the sublime is to be looked for in the empty and rugged northwest of Wales, the beautiful in the more populated, more sociable north-east. If Nant Ffrancon was the entrance to 'the most sublime and magnificent scenery in this island', 'the scene of the greatest beauty in the world' is, according to Pugh, the Vale of Clwyd.[34]

Impressed and awed though he is, as well as terrified, by the sublime landscapes of the mountains, there are continual reminders while he is among them that he does not belong there. 'The native poor' who live around Llanllyfni', Pugh tells, by way of explaining why they took him for a spy, 'scarcely ever travel beyond the circuit of a few miles from home.' They have, he explains, 'a sort of adhesive quality in them, a strong attachment to their native soil.[35] For all Pugh's travelling through England and Wales, for all his familiarity and apparent affection

for life in London, he seems in *Cambria Depicta* to have the same adhesive quality. The entire book asks to be read as the account of a man who, wherever he finds himself at any time during his tour, cannot help remembering where he is *not*: in Ruthin; in the Vale of Clwyd.

His first glimpse of the vale, as he travels homeward from Chester at the start of the book, is from the bwlch marked by the road climbing eastward from Ruthin in the view of Llanfwrog which is the subject of chapter 2. Though the prospect was as 'familiar' to him as could be, he tells us, he could still discover 'fresh assemblages of beauties in the noble Vale of Clwyd'.[36] Two pages later he retraces his steps in order to climb Moel Famau, and offers a first extended description of the vale, that 'beautiful expanse of country', 'highly cultivated', 'with a prodigious number of gentlemen's seats, farm-houses, and cottages scattered about', as well as the towns of Ruthin, Denbigh and St Asaph, all linked by 'the small, but pretty meandering river Clwyd'; an 'assemblage', in short, of what Pugh had called in his Preface 'the milder features of Nature', including 'the cultivation of the expanded valley', and the 'serpentine *afon*'.[37] In the mountains, 'the gay and flowery vale of Clwyd' is always on his mind. His first glance, on climbing Moel Siabod, is not westward to Snowdon, but eastward to 'the ridge of mountains in the vale of Clwyd'; on the summit of Snowdon, the first thing he searches for are 'the high mountains in the Vale of Clwyd'; and there is something touchingly loyal about this as a description of the Clwyd range seen from a mountain all but twice the height of its highest hill.[38]

As he walks through Montgomeryshire, the beauty of his native vale becomes the touchstone by which he assesses the beauty of the countryside. Of the valley stretching north of Montgomery towards Welshpool, and 'bespread with a great many houses, looking most hospitably', he says that it 'seems to vie with the vale of Clwyd, as seen from Ruthin'. At Pennant Melangell it is 'impossible', he declares, 'to admire too much this paradisiacal spot; it is the Vale of Clwyd in miniature'; and to the Vale of Meifod, he offers the highest praise possible: 'the situation is the most desirable of any which I have met with in my journey, nor do I think that the vale of Clwyd excels it, but in the circumstance of its commanding a view of the sea.'[39]

As he approaches nearer to Ruthin, an intriguing pattern emerges. He praises continually the 'beauties', 'the amazing richness and abundant luxuriancy of the unrivalled Vale of Clwyd', its 'beautiful maids', 'the loyalty and patriotism', the 'cordial sincerity and friendship' of the local gentry; and he tells us continually of places where he catches a glimpse of his favourite vale, or sees it at large.[40] But even

where he has the opportunity to offer extended descriptions of the vale, he holds back from doing so, rather as he avoided showing us more glimpses of it in the *Six Views*. Thus, at Nantglyn, 'from various points may be had some fine peeps into the Vale of Clwyd,' and just north of Denbigh the pedestrian can enjoy 'some agreeable peeps at the vale'. From Denbigh itself, the view of the vale 'is a little confined, and does not embrace all those beautiful objects, the sea, &c., as when seen from Ruthin or St. Asaph'; but when, from the tower of St Asaph's cathedral, there is a 'superb view of the vale', Pugh withholds it from us, promising that if the reader will continue to accompany him on his journey, he will lead him 'to a point, from which may be seen, to yet greater advantage, the various beauties of this enchanting spot'.[41] These moments appear intended to excite our anticipation of the view as the great and fitting climax to the tour and the book, but equally we may read them as the expression of an anxiety, that his account of the view, when finally it comes, will somehow fall short of being all that he has promised it will be.

IV

To his lost painting *The Vale of Clwyd*, exhibited at the Academy in 1808, Pugh had attached what was probably the first and, at the time, probably the best-known description of the vale, from *The Worthines of Wales*, by the Elizabethan soldier and poet Thomas Churchyard:

> This vale doth reach, so farre in vewe of man,
> As he farre of, may see the seas in deede:
> And who a while, for pleasure travayle can
> Throughout this vale, and thereof take good heede,
> He shall delight, to see a soyle so fine,
> For ground and grasse, a passing plot devine.
> And if the troth, thereof a man may tell,
> This vale alone, doth all the rest excell.[42]

At least since Churchyard, the vale, the 'garden' of north Wales as it was described by one contemporary of Pugh's, '*the Eden of North-Wales*' as it was described by another, had been celebrated for its beauty. It was 'Cambria's fair Tempe', claimed Hughes, the poetic headmaster of Ruthin Grammar School.[43] Literary tourists, if they crossed it *en route* to Ireland, Snowdonia, or Barmouth, invariably offered a description of 'the laughing vale', as the poet George Cumberland described it, and of the wealth it apparently displayed. The vale was 'allowed by travellers to be the most beautiful spot in the kingdom',[44] but exactly how to describe its beauty however was not at all straightforward. For Churchyard, what made it a 'passing plot devine' was apparently its extraordinary extent and the richness of its soil, but by the late eighteenth century it was believed that the beauty of landscape had nothing to with mere size, and not much to do with productivity. A rich, fertile landscape might appeal to the moral sense (how pleased we are at the good fortune of the inhabitants!) or to the desire for wealth (how fortunate if it were mine!) but without more abstract qualities to recommend it, it held no attraction for an aesthetic taste, properly so-called, properly disinterested.

In Pugh's time, those whose interest in the vale was primarily economic would continue to find the 'beauty' of the Vale of Clwyd inseparable from its productiveness: for the agriculturalist William Marshall the vale was 'one of the richest, most beautiful, and habitable, passages of country in the island', while the editors of the *Universal British Directory of Trade, Commerce, and Manufacture*, in their entry on Ruthin, were happy to be 'raised into an ecstasy of delight in beholding the variegated labours of the husbandman'.[45] More aesthetically-minded travellers, however, while acknowledging the impact made on them by the view of the vale, found themselves groping for some more sophisticated way to describe it, whether as beautiful, or picturesque, or as both, as a supreme example of 'picturesque beauty'. According to Richard Warner, the vale was not 'picturesque', because 'too extensive to afford scenery of that description:'

> unlike the charming vallies of Llangollen and Conway, where the different objects are brought nearer to the eye, which can thus discriminate them, and dwell separately upon their various beauties, the vale of Clwyd exhibits a picture so immense, and so full of objects, as produces a *confusion*, utterly incompatible with that repose which is a necessary quality of the picturesque. It is, notwithstanding, a beautiful and magnificent scene, and impresses the mind with an immediate animating idea of population, plenty, and unbounded fertility.[46]

Not picturesque, then, and not really beautiful, in aesthetic form or structure, but only as we associate it with ideas of richness and well-being. Corbet Hue, Fellow and Bursar of Jesus College, Oxford, who toured north Wales in 1810, similarly thought the vale remarkable for its fertility and prosperity, but found 'not a single view in the whole valley . . . that I can call picturesque'.

The great theorist of the picturesque was William Gilpin, for whom, approaching in 1773 on the road from Mold to Ruthin, the vale was 'deservedly celebrated by all travellers'. But he clearly had trouble describing it as a landscape, as something more than just a striking view:

> It is chiefly indeed considered as a rich scene of cultivation; but it abounds also with picturesque beauty. It is very extensive; not less than twenty-four miles in length; and six, seven, and sometimes eight, in breadth; and is almost everywhere skreened by lofty mountains, which are commonly ploughed at the bottom, and pastured at the top … Within these bold limits the vale forms one large segment of a circle, varied only in different parts by little mountain-recesses, which break the regularity of the sweep. The area of this grand scene is sometimes open, and extended, affording the most amusing distances: in other parts, it is full of little knolls and hillocks, and thickly planted with wood.[47]

Gilpin acknowledges the richness and remarkable extent of the vale, but he is not a man for extensive views, and his attempt to describe the view as an aesthetic whole – 'one large segment of a circle' is quickly abandoned in search of small-scale scenes and pictures, not the vale itself but bite-sized bits of it, 'little mountain-recesses', 'little knolls and hillocks'. What it lacks, he goes on to suggest, is something to unite foreground, middle ground and background, a broad and winding river such as Claude often employed to articulate his ideal landscapes as the several stages of the eye's journey from foreground to distance. 'The great want it sustains, is that of water. Many little rivulets find their way through it; particularly the Cluyd, from whence it takes it's name; but none of them is in any degree equivalent to the scene. The Cluid itself is but a diminutive stream.'[48]

Joseph Hucks, on the other hand, is one of a number of tourists who attempt to describe and admire the vale as a whole by implicitly admiring the profusion of objects it contains as we may admire them in an extensive landscape by Claude or as described by Thomson in *The Seasons*. This is how Hucks begins his praise of the vale, as what his friend Coleridge would later call a 'burst of prospect'[49] suddenly made visible as we climb to a high viewpoint:

> From Wrexham our road became less interesting; and for ten or twelve miles, presented nothing to recompence the fatigue of a long and tedious walk, until we had ascended a very high hill, when the vale of Clwyd, in all its beauty, unfolded upon the sight: it appeared like a moving picture, upon which nature had been prodigal of its colours. Hamlets, villages, towns, and castles, rose covered

with wood and enclosures; in the midst of it, at a distance of about five miles, the town of Ruthin, partially appeared from the bosom of a most beautiful grove of trees; the vale on each side being bounded by a chain of lofty mountains, and far off, on a bold and rugged promontory, stood Denbigh, with its strong fortress, the undisputed mistress of this extended scene.[50]

The difficulty with this kind of description, which follows fairly closely a pattern that Thomson had popularized, is that it will be read as a mere list, without the order or composition that a view requires if it is to be more than *just* a view. Hucks does his best. His second sentence winds onward, trying to develop from a list into something with structure: the mountains 'bound' the view, in the language of landscape painting and gardening; Denbigh castle offers itself as a final eye-catcher, as if at the end of a garden prospect. But as soon as Hucks stops there, to draw breath, it becomes apparent that he is dissatisfied, not with his own effort but with the vale itself. In the end, his description is defeated by what also defeated Gilpin. 'The great defect of the vale', he announces, 'is want of water; the little river Clwyd, which winds through it, not being perceptible at any distance.' This reflection seems to put him quite out of countenance with the place, and it suddenly becomes much less than the Claudian paradise it had first appeared. 'The land in the vale lying low,' he complains, 'and consequently swampy, is, upon a nearer examination, rather coarse.'[51]

This complaint, that the vale, though beautiful to be sure, lacks any means of being organized into a composed picture, is very common by Pugh's time. Probably it was given its definitive form in the tour of the William Bingley, describing the vale from a hill near St Asaph in 1804. 'The whole scene,' he wrote,

> appeared to the greatest advantage. Towards the south stood Denbigh . . . and on the north, clad in its sober hue, I observed the castle of Rhyddlan. The intervening space was enlivened with meadows, woods, cottages, herds, and flocks scattered in every pleasing direction, whilst the whole was bounded by the sea and the dark retiring mountains. This, from the extent of the picture, is not a scene fitted for the pencil, though its numerous beauties must attract the attention of every lover of nature. When we enter a rugged scene of rock and mountain . . . we are struck with astonishment and awe; but when nature presents us with a scene like this, which seems to abound in health, fertility, and happiness, every nerve vibrates to the heart the pleasure we receive. Here the pencil fails . . . [52]

An artist, it seems, can show us the beauty of landscape forms, but cannot satisfactorily evoke the moral beauty of a prosperous view. With the Vale of Clwyd, therefore, where the beauty is essentially of that second kind, the artist can do nothing. For Bingley this is a mere matter of fact, not a matter for regret – the opposite if anything, for Bingley clearly offers his written description of the vale as a demonstration of what the pen can achieve and the 'pencil', by which he means the paintbrush, cannot.

Bingley thought he had succeeded where others found themselves failing, but his example was of little help to Pugh, who has so much invested in the view, who cannot admit that it is anything less than 'the scene of the greatest beauty in the world', who is committed to describe the vale at much greater length than his predecessors, and who, the more he has raised our expectations, the more he has risked ending his great work on a note of bathos.

V

The full, panoramic view Pugh finally permits us to enjoy, the climax of the whole book, the final clinching moment that will announce the triumph of beauty over sublimity, Denbighshire over Snowdonia, is of the vale as seen from the top of St Peter's Church, Ruthin – a view that was snuffed out in the 1850s when the present broach spire was dumped on top of the old square tower. Like a guide addressing a large train of tourists, Pugh announces with a flourish that those 'who are fond of viewing the varied beauties of nature, will be pleased to follow me to a spot, to which I have long ago promised to bring them, to behold the Vale of Clwyd in its highest splendour of dress'.[53] But his climax has been so long coming, so long deferred, that he suddenly loses all confidence. He worries that he has oversold it, apologises for his 'inability to do justice to it in description', and wonders whether his readers can be trusted to enjoy it as it deserves. 'The stranger,' he warns,

> now supposed on the tower, is so much elevated, as to see the whole of the town, and at the same time to command all the surrounding country, the scene is diversified by such a multiplicity of objects, that it requires great steadiness to contemplate them all, with that degree of pleasure, which they are calculated to produce in the mind of strangers.'[54]

The description that follows, of the views to the north, to the east, to the west, and of the meandering river too quickly lost in trees, is matter-of-fact and oddly interrupted, by an account first of the occasional but, he reassures us, none-too-catastrophic floods in the vale, then of the low cost of living enjoyed by its inhabitants. The paragraphing goes awry. 'All ranks in society may live in this country at the same rate: *i.e.* for about two-fifths less than in London', he claims, and continues, without drawing breath,

> From this tower are discerned innumerable houses; some gentlemen's seats make a figure on the acclivities of the hills; while those in the bottom are but partially seen through the woods. The handsome farmhouses, and the cottages of the peasantry, scattered wide over hill and dale, the many towns and villages in the view, and the sea crossing the end of the vale at right angles, are circumstances which complete a scene of incomparable beauty.[55]

Turning southwards, to describe the prospect 'in the opposite point', Pugh again seems overwhelmed by the difficulty of making the vale live up to all that he has been claiming for it. We learn that 'it is bounded by some noble mountains at the distance of five miles', that, once again, it is 'ornamented with a few gentlemen's houses', that it is 'rich with productive arable and meadow lands', and a little more; but in no time Pugh finds himself retailing, at length, a legend about the magical origin of two strange matching shapes, known as the 'Giant's Legs', two streams which flow side by side and then, both at once, make a short right-angled turn to form the giant's feet, before disappearing from sight.[56] It is a curious performance, longer, more disjointed, and certainly no more successful than the attempts to describe the vale that we have just looked at. But whereas other writers chose to blame the vale for their failure, that of course was not an option for Pugh.

In the end, there is something very touching about these pages. Intended as the great and grand finale of what he appears to know is a remarkable book, devoted to a place that Pugh loves above all other places, and to a description that we have been encouraged to wait and wait for on the understanding that we will be richly rewarded for our patience, its flatness may speak more eloquently of Pugh's adhesive attachment to Ruthin and the Vale of Clwyd than a more flourishing ending would have done. According to Bingley, the vale had to be described in words: 'Here', he wrote, 'the pencil fails.' But when Pugh finally put himself to the test, it was words that failed him; and he was reduced to suggesting that his art might succeed in doing what his writing has not. Soon, he tells us, he will be publishing views of this vale, and of the Vale of Llangollen, 'as large prints; a way in which neither of them has yet been noticed, but which the public may, ere long, I hope, expect to see'.[57] The editor let this sentence stand in *Cambria Depicta*, published three years after death had frustrated Pugh in this act, also, of homage to his native county.

VI

The costly edition in which in 1816 *Cambria Depicta* appeared – large print, on generous quarto pages, lavishly illustrated with labour-intensive hand-coloured plates (though uncoloured copies were available) – was clearly designed to net Evan Williams as large a profit as possible, with the war finally over, and a rise in consumer spending eagerly expected. The book became, in the nineteenth century, a valuable commodity in the second-hand book market. From 1820 onwards copies are advertised in the classified columns of newspapers in Bristol, Chester, London and Oxford, as well as in the *North Wales Chronicle* and the *Wrexham Advertiser*. By the 1870s its reputation had grown, and we find it quoted for its anecdotes of old Wales and its lyrical descriptions.[58] In 1874 a copy of the book was exhibited at Ruthin Town Hall as a desirable rarity at the 'Grand Annual Soirée' of the Literary Institute and Working Men's Club, and later that year Sir Watkin Williams Wynn exhibited his own copy of the book at the Wrexham Museum of Antiquities, in the course of a week of events organised by the Cambrian Archaeological Society.[59] Clearly there were sufficient copies of the book in Wales for those with genteel literary interests to know about it. Its fame did not survive the century, however, and the expense of its original production and thus of reprinting it became a severe handicap to the development of Pugh's reputation as a writer. If *Cambria Depicta* had been published in three small volumes, with small or no engravings, it would have been made available in a cheap edition and its fame would have grown with the growth of the reading public. It would be now regarded as a classic of Welsh literature in English. The impossibility however of any sort of cheap reproduction that would do justice to its illustrations has led to its being forgotten except by a few scholars looking for a quotation or two on the condition of north Wales in the early nineteenth century.

For a different reason the achievement of Pugh's *Six Views* has also been overlooked. Richard Wilson aside, accounts of landscape art in Wales in the eighteenth and early nineteenth centuries have concentrated almost exclusively on the works of non-native artists, most of them Englishmen: Paul Sandby, Philippe de Loutherbourg, J. M. W. Turner and so on. The quality of their work has set an agenda in terms of which what Pugh was doing cannot be considered or recognized. Those great artists, once over the border, headed for the hills and mountains of Snowdonia; the images they made of landscapes on the way there were probably regarded by them, and have certainly been regarded by us, as incidental to the images of the sublime landscapes that were the goal of their excursions. For the most part they showed as little interest in the local inhabitants of north Wales as did the tourists who ignored or misjudged them. What would constitute Welsh landscape art was defined in London, for a largely English, largely metropolitan public, and as far as eighteenth-century art is concerned that definition has changed very little. An artist like Pugh, concentrating instead on the relatively quiet scenery of his native county, interested in it particularly as a series of places as much as of landscapes, concerned (as he would be also in his London views) with what local people were doing there and with who they were, thus continues to be ignored, even among most historians of art in Wales. This book is an attempt to restore him to his rightful place in the cultural history of Wales. What that is, is of course open to debate, but he certainly deserves better than to be forgotten or ignored.

Notes

1 *CD*, p. 162.

2 *CD*, pp. 253 (Dolanog); 255 (Meifod); 251 (Llanerfyl); 250 (Llangadfan).

3 See Thomas Cartwright's aquatint in *CD* of Caergwrle Castle, and see 'The Ffrwd Branch', *http://www.peter-quita.demon.co.uk/articles/Ffrwd.pdf*.

4 *CD*, pp. 167, 153–4.

5 *CD*, pp. 36, 375, 183, and see p. 235.

6 *CD*, pp. 204–5.

7 *CD*, pp. 290, 162, 150–1, and see p. 158n.

8 *CD*, pp. 37, 116, 40.

9 *CD*, pp. 103 (Penrhyn mine); 130 (Beddgelert); 109 (Llyn Ogwen); 289–90 (Vyrnwy).

10 *CD*, pp. 57, 440.

11 *CD*, p. 113.

12 Wordsworth, *The Prelude* (1805 version), Book 11, line 156.

13 Wordsworth, *The Prelude*, Book 11, lines 152–5.

14 *CD*, pp. 185 (Llanelltyd); 300 (Corwen); 238 (Montgomery); 235 (Newtown).

15 *CD*, pp. 408, 205–6.

16 *CD*, p. 114.

17 *CD*, pp. 152–3; Pennant, *Tour*, vol. 2, pp. 163–4; Wordsworth, *The Prelude*, Book 13, lines 1–62. Behind Wordsworth's description, of course, lie William Sotheby's superb lines on the view from Snowdon, in Book II of 'A Tour through Parts of Wales', in *A Tour*, pp. 34–6, which may well have been known to Pugh also.

18 *CD*, p. 162.

19 Burke, *A Philosophical Enquiry*, p. 136, and for the relation of pain and terror, p. 132.

20 Burke, *A Philosophical Enquiry*, pp. 136, 40.

21 Burke, *A Philosophical Enquiry*, pp. 72, 136.

22 *CD*, pp. 114 (Moel Siabod); 152 (Snowdon); 205 (Cader Idris).

23 Burke, *A Philosophical Enquiry*, p. 72.

24 *CD*, pp. 26, 47, 55.

25 *CD*, p. 106.

26 *CD*, pp. 108–9.

27 *CD*, pp. 116–17; 'finely broken' is a favourite phrase of writers on picturesque scenery, probably following William Gilpin, *Observations chiefly relative to Picturesque Beauty*, 2 vols (London: R. Blamire, 1789), vol. 1, p. 153, and *Observations on the River Wye* (London: R. Blamire, 1782), p. 37.

28 *CD*, p. 147.

29 *CD*, pp. 149–50.

30 *CD*, pp. 215, 264, 282–3.

31 *CD*, p. 309.

32 Burke, *A Philosophical Enquiry*, pp. 124, 114–15.

33 Burke, *A Philosophical Enquiry*, pp. 43, 71.

34 *CD*, p. 15.

35 *CD*, p. 135.

36 *CD*, p. 13.

37 *CD*, pp. 15, iv–v.

38 *CD*, pp. 105, 114, 153.

39 *CD*, pp. 237, 270, 254.

40 *CD*, pp. 397, 432, 406, 383.

41 *CD*, pp. 425, 383, 385, 378–9.

42 Thomas Churchyard, 'Of Wrythen both the Castle and the Towne', stanza 9, from *The Worthines of Wales* (1587) (London: Thomas Evans, 1776).

43 John Fox, *General View of the Agriculture of the County of Glamorgan* (London: B. McMillan, 1796), p. 15; *The Cambrian Directory, or, Cursory Sketches of the Welsh Territories* (Salisbury: J. Easton et al., 1800), p. 133; and see Warner, *Second Walk*, p. 194; David Hughes, 'Lines on my Native Place', in his *Poems*, p.209.

44 'How CLUYDS laughing vale her wealth displays': George Cumberland, *A Poem on the Landscapes of Great-Britain* (London: G. G. J. and J. Robinson, 1793), p. 30; *Universal British Directory*, vol. 4, p. 346.

45 William Marshall, *The Review and Abstract of the County Reports to the Board of Agriculture*, 5 vols (York: Thomas Wilson, 1818), vol. 2, p. 163; *Universal British Directory*, vol. 4, p. 346.

46 Warner, *Second Walk*, pp. 195–6.

47 Gilpin, *Observations on Several Parts*, pp. 105–6.

48 Gilpin, *Observations on Several Parts*, p. 106. The variant spellings of 'Clwyd' are Gilpin's.

49 S. T. Coleridge, 'Fears in Solitude', 1798.

50 Hucks, *Pedestrian Tour*, p. 20.

51 Hucks, *Pedestrian Tour*, p. 20.

52 Bingley, *Tour*, p. 48.

53 *CD*, pp. 444–5.

54 *CD*, p. 446.

55 *CD*, pp. 446–7; for a less favourable view of the cost of living in Denbighshire, see Thomas, *Agriculture*, pp. 9. 42, 52–3; and for a less blasé view of the Clwyd in flood, see Bingley, *Tour*, p. 51, and Pennant, *Tours in Wales*, ed. John Rhys, 3 vols (Caernarvon: H. Humphreys, 1883), vol. 2, p. 218n.

56 *CD*, pp. 447–8.

57 Bingley, *Tour*, p. 48; CD, pp. 448–9.

58 *Berrow's Worcester Journal*, 13 December 1879; *Wrexham Advertiser*, 15 November 1873, 27 June 1884.

59 *Wrexham Advertiser*, 28 February, 29 August 1874.

EPILOGUE

When the first proofs of this book had been corrected and returned to the press, Morrigan Mason, Deputy Director of the Bodelwyddan Castle Trust, sent me a photograph of a watercolour which had been purchased in 1990 by the Clwyd Fine Arts Trust but which, by 1993, had been recorded as missing. It had briefly formed part of a loan scheme that the former Clwyd County Council managed on behalf of the Trust, and although the records of the loans are not currently available, strenuous efforts are being made to trace the picture's whereabouts. The original was signed by Pugh on the verso, where he had added the information that it was 'drawn on the spot'. The image had been made as usual, *en grisaille*, no doubt with the intention of its being reproduced in aquatint, and the phrase 'drawn on the spot' was probably intended to appear beneath the title. The title given to the image is 'The Vale of Clwyd', and that, beyond dispute, is what it represents.[1]

Of all the pictures by Pugh that I hoped might re-emerge as a result of this project, top of the list would have been a panoramic representation of his best-loved landscape. The vale of Clwyd was the subject most conspicuously omitted from the *Six Views, in Denbighshire*; even in the images of Llanfwrog and of Coedmarchan, where Pugh had the opportunity to represent something of the famous vale, he gave us the merest glimpse, no more than a 'peep', to use his own term. A number of writers I quoted in Chapter 10, among them the hugely authoritative William Gilpin, had suggested that the vale, however impressive in its extent, was a confused, formless panorama, overwhelming in the profusion of objects it contained, and to the artist unrepresentable. 'Here the pencil fails', wrote William Bingley.[2] I had more or less assumed that Pugh fell in with this opinion and had backed away from depicting his favourite view. True, the vale was the subject of the small oil painting he exhibited at the Royal Academy in 1808, now lost, but I had assumed that it was too small to have shown more than a view *in* the vale, a picturesque enclave, something like the woodland glade in the only oil by Pugh of which a photograph survives, *A Welsh Landscape* (plate 3.1).

At the end of what I have described in my last chapter as the failure of his set-piece attempt to describe the vale in *Cambria Depicta*, he announced that he hoped soon to publish a view of the vale of Clwyd, taken from 'the hills of Lainwen'. From there, wrote Pugh,

> this beautiful and elegant valley, from a happy point of view, forms an agreeable and interesting contrast to the wild and picturesque vale of Llangollen, from the celebrated Nant y Bela; and both are subjects highly worthy of being published as

large prints; a way in which neither of them has yet been noticed, but which the public may, ere long, I hope, expect to see.[3]

These prints never appeared, and again I had assumed that when Pugh expressed the hope that the public would soon see them, he was hoping, in the first place, that he would succeed in drawing the images from which the prints would be made, to make up for his failure at description. Evidently I was wrong: he made one of the drawings at least, and this photograph is probably of the very drawing for the print of the vale of Clwyd (plate 11.1). The drawing was fourteen inches by twelve, which would have been the dimensions of the aquatint also, making it a 'large' print by Pugh's standards, larger than anything else he had produced apart from his two Monmouthshire landscapes (plates 0.12 and 0.14). It is much too large to be an image intended for, but excluded from, *Cambria Depicta,* for which the largest drawings do not exceed eight inches in width.

In taking on the supposedly impossible task of drawing the whole vale, along its whole extent from the south to Rhuddlan Marsh and the sea, Pugh was obliged to simplify its topography to some degree, but not so as to disturb its main features. In his account in *Cambria Depicta* of the view from Ruthin, Pugh described it as scattered over by 'innumerable houses', among 'the greatest profusion of trees and wood'. To tidy things up, he has demolished the great majority of those houses, and felled most of the trees, apart from those growing in the hedges. The picture nevertheless gives a wonderful impression of the extent of the vale, of the 'handsome, undulating lines' of the Clwydian range, and of the trellis of hedges that still, perhaps more than any other feature, characterises the vale as seen from

above, 'divided', as he described it, 'into beautiful meadows as far as Rhyddlan'.[4]

The viewpoint may be the one Pugh spoke of using, around Lainwen, east of the A 525 at the Nant y Garth pass, some four miles south south-east of Ruthin; but the sightlines work better if we place him a few hundred yards to the west, on the other side of the road. The Clwydian range runs the whole length of the right-hand side of the picture, ending at what must be either Graig Fawr or Y Foel by Dyserth, almost in the dead centre. Left from there we can just make out a settlement, which is probably Rhuddlan itself. Of the hills nearer to us the highest is presumably Moel Famau, and in front of it will be Foel Fenlli, the hill that looms up behind Llanfwrog in Pugh's picture.[5] The settlement nearest to us is Llanfair Dyffryn Clwyd, on a ridge standing a good deal more proud of the surrounding valley than it really does, and surmounted by the tower of the church of St Cynfarch and St Mary. Beyond is Ruthin, marked by the towers of St Peter's and the castle ruins. The dark hill on the right must be Graigfechan, a little south-east of Llanfair; Pugh has given it an exaggeratedly pointed summit, and added perhaps a couple of hundred feet to its height.[6]

Beyond anything Pugh had achieved or attempted in *Cambria Depicta,* this landscape is a work of real ambition. The view of the vale of Clwyd was widely known to be one of the most striking in Britain. But connoisseurs of the picturesque, and artists specialising in publishing prints of tourist destinations in Britain, would have been familiar with Gilpin's claim that the vale, from its southernmost point to the sea, defied visual representation; it could be described but not depicted. This picture announces that Pugh is now seeking to be regarded as a major figure among the producers

of 'views', the first artist, or so he believed, to produce a panorama of the vale along and across its fullest extent. Vast though it is, the view can indeed be composed, Pugh is saying, and proves his point by organising the landscape as a close visual equivalent of Gilpin's description. At 'the end of the vale', wrote Gilpin, perhaps standing on the exact spot where Pugh would later draw his view,

> having ascended the higher grounds, we had a grand retrospect of the whole vale in one vast scene. Its bosom, interspersed with lawns, cottages, and groves, appears winding in perspective between the hills, till every form is lost in an expanse of woody distance; while the hills, on each side, take the several lines which distance gives, one after another, as they retire; till at St. Asaph, the whole landscape unites insensibly with the sea.[7]

It will be remembered that, according to Gilpin, the reason why the vale could not be composed into a properly articulated landscape was that it lacked something to unite the successive distances. It needed a river, grander than the Clwyd, winding from foreground to background. In this description, however, he suggests the 'bosom' of the vale itself does the 'winding', advancing and retiring in response to the hills as they project, one after another, into the vale, marking the distances the eye traverses on its way to the sea. Pugh seems to have taken this hint and used it to compose his picture. He has divided the vale, as panoramic views usually are in landscapes by Claude, into alternate bands of dark and light, from the foreground scrub to the sunlit foreground rocks and trees and so on across the nearby fields and into the distance. The dark cone of Graigfechan serves as a 'repoussoir', a blocking device to direct our eyes towards the

centre horizon, where we can follow the valley to its furthest extent and can even persuade ourselves that we can see the sea. On the right-hand side, as if beneath a sky of patchy cloud, the hills too appear as alternate strips of light and dark, again marking the distances, 'one after another', front to back. The work of uniting those distances into a topographical whole is then done by the left-hand side, where the lines of hedges and of the hills, including Coedmarchan, converge in such a way as to point a way through the landscape, from the fields that lie at our feet, past Ruthin, through to the flatter land beyond.

In another way too the image is more ambitious than anything Pugh had done before. In the bottom right of the picture (plate 11.2), the shapes of the trees seem to have been defined not by drawing their outlines (though no doubt Pugh did sketch a rough outline for them) but by modelling the edge of their foliage in the relatively dark grey wash behind them, leaving the form of the trees themselves as, largely, white paper (though apparently touched, here and there along their tops, with flecks of opaque white, as is the face of the cowman, perhaps to conceal

slight slips of the brush). Something similar seems to be happening elsewhere in that corner, from the 'peasant lolling on a rock', as Gilpin would have described him, to some at least of the rocks themselves, and even to the cow, whose form, beautifully drawn as it is, gives the impression of having been modelled in white paper by the shadows around it. If the natural forms in the foreground – rocks, bushes, trees – seem less stylised, or less simplified, than in Pugh's earlier work, that may be because, by learning to paint in watercolour, instead of continuing to produce 'tinted drawings' as he had in his earlier work,[8] he is developing the confidence to generate such forms in one movement of the brush, or at least relatively freehand. It is intriguing to see Pugh, at the end of his career, developing his technique in this way, even in a work intended to be engraved, not conceived as a work of art in its own right.

Perhaps however, remarkable as this image is, it tells us of something lost as well as of something gained. *The Six Views, in Denbighshire*, perhaps especially *Bathafern Hills from Coedmarchan Rocks*, were suggesting that what to most people were 'landscapes',

'views', were to those who lived or worked in them places: sites of labour, of ownership, of conflict, of traditional customs and values. Ten years of drawing the illustrations for *Cambria Depicta*, largely pictures of places previously unknown to him, and which he experienced as tourist or traveller, had obliged, and perhaps encouraged him to concentrate on turning what were places to their inhabitants into landscapes for his readers. Now back on home ground, in his favourite place, the relative sophistication that he can bring to the arts of composition and drawing, and the wider audience he now seeks to engage, have led him to represent the vale of Clwyd too as very definitely a landscape. Nothing *belongs*, in the intense, enchorial way that people and things belonged to the places depicted in most of the *Six Views*. In *The Vale of Clwyd* the cowman and his cow are simply there, are what art historians call staffage; they could be anywhere; no narrative ties them to this place.

Plate 11.3 *(above) Edward Pugh*, Conway Castle, *watercolour for* Cambria Depicta, *Aberystwyth, National Library of Wales.*

Plate 11.4 *(right) Thomas Cartwright after Edward Pugh*, Conway Castle, *coloured aquatint from* Cambria Depicta, *dated January 1815.*

The figure I have described as a 'peasant' may be a shepherd without his sheep, or a traveller, or the artist himself – the picture does not encourage us to ask. His job is to gaze at the view, and so to confirm that the vale of Clwyd is indeed a 'beautiful and elegant valley', an object of aesthetic interest, not a place but a landscape.

One other late picture, from about 1808–12, and of almost equal importance with *The Vale of Clwyd*, has surfaced since this book was in proof. The watercolour *Conway Castle* (plate 11.3) – the title appears on the back of the drawing in Pugh's hand – would be aquatinted by Cartwright for *Cambria Depicta* (plate 11.4), and is the only coloured watercolour landscape currently attributed to Pugh. There is no grisaille version of the subject in the bound volume of drawings for *Cambria Depicta*, just as there is not in the case of another coloured drawing, mentioned on page 182, which is currently attributed to a more expensive artist and which must be either the original, or a copy, of one of the other aquatints in that book. *Conway Castle* is one of the most confident watercolours left to us by Pugh: for the most part the scene is drawn directly with the brush, using minimal outline, and there are passages – the rock-strewn beach, for example, the two men hauling on the boat, the outcrop where the castle perches – which are more freely rendered than anything else we have seen by Pugh. Where Cartwright uses a stylised notation, say for the advancing waves or for the trees on the headland, Pugh has allowed his brush to be a little disobedient to his will: much more so than in the early grisaille *Careg Carn-March Arther* (plate 1.9), and more too than in many of the other drawings for *Cambria Depicta*. Like *The Vale of Clwyd*, *Conway Castle* gives an idea of how much Pugh's watercolour technique had changed and developed in his final years.

Notes

1   All information about Pugh's *The Vale of Clwyd* is from Morrigan Mason, who tells me she derived most of it from the sales invoice dating from its purchase by the Clwyd Fine Arts Trust.

2   Bingley, *Tour*, p. 48.

3   *CD*, pp. 448–9

4   All references in this paragraph are to *CD*, pp. 446–7.

5   My thanks to Pat Astbury, Arnold Hughes, Bethan Hughes, Derek Jones, 'Tricia Jones and Heather Williams for their advice on the features of this view.

6   In October 2012, the view, with Graig-fechan looming through the mist, could be seen at http://www.google.co.uk/imgres?start=66&num=10&hl=en&biw=1366&bih=608&tbm=isch&tbnid=wOSTfv6ReX_VdM:&imgrefurl=http://www. facebook.com/llysfasicollege&docid=IajPpEF6iDUmQM&imgurl=http://a7.sphotos.ak.fbcdn.net/hphotos-ak-snc7/c0.117.851.315/p851x315/464354_376422385724784_908426434_o.jpg&w=851&h=315&ei=1aNdUJKrIYSr0QXO2YCoCw&zoom=1&iact=rc&dur=3&sig=106051123144497190342&page=4&tbnh=67&tbnw=180&ndsp=27&ved=1t:429,r:2,s:66,i:166&tx=133&ty=36 (accessed 9 October 2012). A sunnier version of the view can be seen at http://www.valeofclwydphotos.co.uk/vale-of-clwyd-no-2 (accessed 9 October 2012), a panoramic photograph by Dennis Bailey, to whom also I am indebted for help in identifying features of the view.

7   Gilpin, *Observations on Several Parts*, p. 166.

8   I refer to the distinction made by W. H. Pyne, discussed in Chapter 6.

BIBLIOGRAPHY

Primary Bibliography

1 TEXTS IN MANUSCRIPT

Anon., 'Cursory Remarks made in a Tour through different Parts of England and Wales in the months of August and September 1797' (NLW MS 1613.3C).

Anon., 'Journal of an Excursion made in the Summer of 1808, through several Counties of North Wales' (DRO DD/DH/228/78).

Anon., 'A Journal of a Tour, 1793' (NLW MS 9854C).

Anon., 'A Tour in England and Wales 1802' (NLW MS 789B).

Anon., 'A Tour in Wales 1804' (NLW MS 1084A).

Anon., 'A Tour in Wales 1810' (NLW MS 7344A).

Anon., 'A Tour in Wales 1810' (NLW MS 7345A).

Anon., 'Tour through Wales, 1797, 1872' (NLW MS 16133C).

Eade, William, 'Journal of a Tour through North Wales', Spring 1802 (NLW MS 22190B).

Eyre, Henry, 'Tours in Wales', vol. 1 (NLW MS 62B).

Hawker, Joseph and Elizabeth, 'Journal of a Tour through North Wales 1812' (NLW MS 64B).

Hoare, Richard Colt, 'Diary of a Fishing Tour in North Wales June 1799' (NLW MS 5370C).

Hoare, Richard Colt, 'Sir Richard Colt Hoare's Sketchbook [1799]' (NLW MS 5370C).

Hue, Corbet, 'Journal of a Tour through North and Central Wales from July to September 1810' (NLW MS 23218).

Jones, Huw, 'Cerdd Newydd i'r Anrhydeddus Ysgwïer Robert Watgyn Wynne o Garthmeilo ac Amryw Fannau', dated 14 January 1771 (NLW MS 2068, 81).

Jones, Huw, 'Cwynfan yr Hwsmon Trafferthus' (NLW Cwrtmawr 39, p. 260).

Martyn, Thomas, 'An Account of a Tour of Wales' (1801) (NLW MS1340C).

Panton, Paul, 'Itinerary of Paul Panton' (NLW MS 66A).

Porter, Robert Ker, 'Journal of a tour in North Wales' 1799 (NLW MS 12651B).

Pugh, Edward, Letter to William Owen, 1802–3 (?) (NLW MS 13224B).

Pugh, Edward, Letter to Thomas Lloyd of Tre'r Beirdd, Mold, 10 March 1809 (NLW MS 1562C).

Pugh, Edward, Letter to Richard Llwyd, 4 June 1812 (NLW MS 9023C).

Robertson, Dr, 'Journal of a Tour' (NLW MS 11790A).

[Shirley, Evelyn], 'Cursory Remarks made in a Tour through different Parts of England and Wales in the months of August and September 1797' (NLW MS 1613.3C).

[Slaney, Plowden], 'A Short Journal of a Tour through the Counties of Denbigh, Merioneth, Cardigan, and Carnarvon, and the island of Anglesea in 1793' (NLW MS 9854C).

Sykes, Christopher, 'A Tour in Wales 1796' (NLW MS 2258C).

Vernon, Thomas, 'Journal 1797–1812' (DRO NTD/140).

Williams, William, 'Tour of Wales, 1796' (NLW MS 23253C).

Yates, Richard, 'Tour Journal 1805' (NLW MS 687B).

2   NEWSPAPERS AND PERIODICALS

Adam's Weekly Courant

Annual Register

La Belle Assemblée

Berrow's Worcester Journal

Cambrian Register

Chester Chronicle

Chester Courant

European Magazine and London Review

Gentleman's Magazine.

Hereford Journal

Illustrated London News

Journals of the House of Commons

Montgomeryshire Mercury.

Monthly Magazine

Morning Chronicle

New Monthly Magazine

North Wales Guardian

Oracle

Philosophical Transactions of the Royal Society of London

Politics for the People

Public Advertiser

Quarterly Review

Shrewsbury Chronicle

Sun

True Briton

Universal Magazine

Wrexham Advertiser

3   PRINTED BOOKS AND PAMPHLETS

An Address to the P–t, in Behalf of the Starving Multitude (London: R. Baldwin, 1766).

Aikin, Arthur, *Journal of a Tour through North Wales and Part of Shropshire; with Observations in Mineralogy* (London: J. Johnson, 1797).

Aikin, John, *A Description of the Country from Thirty to Forty Miles round Manchester* (London: John Stockdale, 1795).

Bagot, Lord [William, second Lord Bagot], *Memorials of the Bagot Family; compiled in 1823* (Blithfield: William Hodgetts, 1824).

Baker, J., *The Imperial Guide, with Picturesque Plans of the Great Post Roads* (London: C. Whittingham, 1802).

Barlow, Percival., *The General History of Europe* (London: printed by and for W. and J. Stratford, [1791?]).

Bennett, Anna Maria, *Ellen, Countess of Castle Howell*, 4 vols (London: William Lane, 1794).

Best, Thomas, *A Concise Treatise on the Art of Angling*, 4th edn (London: B. Crosby, 1798).

Bingley, William, *A Tour round North Wales, performed during the Summer of 1798* (London: E. Williams, 1800).

Borrow, George, *Wild Wales: The People, Language and Scenery* (1862) (London: J. M. Dent, and New York: E. P. Dutton, 1906).

Bowlker, Charles, *The Art of Angling; and Compleat Fly Fishing* (Birmingham: M. Swinney, and London: G. G. J. and J. Robinson, 1786).

Boydell, John, 'Anecdotes relative to the late Alderman Boydell', in W. Bell Jones (ed.), 'An Autobiography of John Boydell, the Engraver', *Flintshire Historical Society Publications*, 11 (1925), 81–7.

Britton, John, *The Fine Arts of the English School* (London: Longman, Hurst, Rees, Orme, and Brown, 1812).

Brookes, R., *The Art of Angling* (London: W. Lowndes, 1793).

[Broster, John], *Circular Tour from Chester through North Wales* (London: printed for Crosby & Co. by Broster & Son, Chester, 1802).

Broughton, Brian, *Four Picturesque Views in North Wales, engraved in Aquatinta by Alken, from Drawings made on the Spot by the Rev. Brian Broughton, M.A. Fellow of New College, Oxford: with Poetical Reflections on Leaving that Country* (London: W. Clarke, 1798).

Broughton, Brian, *Six Picturesque Views in North Wales, engraved in Aquatinta by Alken, from Drawings made on the Spot: with Poetical Reflections on Leaving that Country, by the Rev. Brian Broughton, M.A. Fellow of New College, Oxford* (London: for J. Mawman, 1801).

Burke, Edmund, *A Philosophical Enquiry into the Origin of our Ideas of the Sublime and Beautiful* (1757), ed. J. T. Boulton (London: Routledge and Kegan Paul, 1958).

Burn, John, *The Justice of the Peace, and Parish Officer*, eighteenth edn, 4 vols (London: T. Cadell, 1793),

Byng, John, *The Torrington Diaries*, ed. C. Bruyn Andrews, 4 vols (London: Eyre & Spottiswoode, 1934).

The Cambrian Directory, or, Cursory Sketches of the Welsh Territories (Salisbury: J. Easton et al., 1800).

Cary, John, *Cary's New Itinerary; or, an Accurate Delineation of the Great Roads, both Direct and Cross, throughout England and Wales* (London: John Cary, 1798).

Cheap Repository: Easter Monday (London: John Marshall, 1795).

Christian, Lieutenant, *Military reflections addressed to the generals and field officers of the British Army* (London: printed for J. and T. Egerton, at the Military Library, Whitehall, 1786).

Churchyard, Thomas, *The Worthines of Wales* (1587) (London: Thomas Evans, 1776).

[Clarke, E.D.], *A Tour through the South of England, Wales, and Part of Ireland: made during the Summer of 1791* (London: Minerva Press, 1793).

Coleridge, S. T., Earl Leslie Griggs (ed.), *Collected Letters of Samuel Taylor Coleridge*, 6 vols (Oxford: Clarendon Press, 1956).

Coleridge, S. T., *Biographia Literaria*, ed. James Engell and W. Jackson Bate, 2 vols (London: Routledge & Kegan Paul, and Princeton: Princeton University Press, 1983).

A Collection of Welsh tours; or, A Display of the Beauties of Wales: selected principally from Celebrated Histories and

Popular Tours, second edn (London: G. Sael, and Chester: M. Poole, 1797).

Collins, William, *Memoirs of a Painter* (London: H. D. Symonds, 1805).

Compton, Thomas, *The Northern Cambrian Mountains, or a Tour through North Wales* (London: C. Corrall, 1817).

Considerations on the Causes and Alarming Consequences of the Present War (London: J. S. Jordan, 1794).

Correct List of the Minority on Mr. Grey's Motions, moved in the House of Commons, Tuesday April 12, 1791, on the Approach of a Russian War (London: J. Debrett, 1791).

The Country Spectator (Gainsborough, Lincoln and and London: Mozeley & co. et al.).

Cowdroy, William, *The Directory and Guide for the City and County of Chester* (Chester: J. Fletcher, 1789).

[Cradock, Joseph], *Letters from Snowdon: Descriptive of a Tour through the Northern Counties of Wales* (London: J. Ridley and W. Harris, 1770).

Darwall, Mrs, *Poems on Several Occasions*, 2 vols (Walsall: F. Milward, 1794).

Davies, Walter, *General View of the Agriculture and Domestic Economy of North Wales* (London: Richard Phillips, 1810).

Dawe, George, *The Life of George Morland* (London: Vernor, Hood, and Sharpe, 1807).

Eaton, D. I., *Politics for the People*. vol. II. (London: D. I. Eaton, 1794).

Eden, Sir Frederic M., *The State of the Poor: or, an History of the Labouring Classes in England*, 3 vols (London: B. & J. White et al., 1797).

Edwards, J., *A Discourse delivered on Friday, April 19, 1793 . . . being the Day appointed by the King for a General Fast* (Birmingham: J. Thompson, 1793).

Encyclopaedia Britannica; or, a Dictionary of Arts, Sciences, and Miscellaneous Literature, 20 vols (Dublin : James Moore, 1790–8).

[Evans, Revd J.], *The Beauties of England and Wales: or, Original Delineations of Each County*, vol. XVII, Part I (London: J. Harris et al., 1812).

Evans, Revd J., *Letters written during a Tour through North Wales, in the Year 1798, and at Other Times*, third edn (London: C. and R. Baldwin, 1804).

Evans, Thomas, *Cambrian Itinerary, or Welsh Tourist* (London: C. Whittinham, 1801).

The Evidence Summed Up; or a Statement of the Apparent Causes and Objects of the War (London: D. I. Eaton, 1794).

Eyton, Edward, *A Letter, addressed to Sir W. W. Wynne, Bart.* (Chester, Shrewsbury and Wrexham: [John Fletcher, 1794]).

Fairfax, J., *The Complete Sportsman; or, Country Gentleman's Recreation* (London: 'the Booksellers', 1795).

Farington, Joseph, Garlick Kenneth, Angus Macintyre, Kathryn Cave and Evelyn Newby (eds), *The Diary of Joseph Farington*, 17 vols (New Haven and London: Yale University Press for the Paul Mellon Centre for Studies in British Art, 1978–98).

Fast Day, as observed at Sheffield . . . February 28, 1794. Being the Day appointed for a General Fast; to which are added a Hymn and Resolutions ('London Reprinted': 1794).

[Feltham, John], *A Guide to all the Watering and Sea-Bathing Places: with a Description of the Lakes, a Sketch of a Tour in Wales, and Itineraries* (London: Richard Phillips, [1812]).

[Feltham, John], *The Picture of London, for 1802* (London: Richard Phillips, 1802); also editions for 1803, 1804, 1805 and 1806.

Ferrar, John, *A Tour from Dublin to London, in 1795* (Dublin: no bookseller named, 1796).

[Firth, William], *Christian Warfare defended and recommended in a Sermon intended to have been preached before the Vice-Chancellor and the University at St. Mary's Church, Cambridge, on 28th of February, 1794, the Day appointed for a General Fast* (London: C. and G. Kearsley, 1794).

Fox, John, *General View of the Agriculture of the County of Glamorgan* (London: B. McMillan, 1796).

Frend, William, *Extract from the Appendix of a Pamphlet entitled Peace and Union* (London: no bookseller credited, 1793).

Frend, William, *Peace and Union recommended to the Associated Bodies of Republicans and Anti-Republicans* (St Ives: for the author, 1793).

Fuseli, Henry, John Knowles, *The Life and Writings of Henry Fuseli, Esq. M.A. R.A.*, 3 vols (London: Henry Colburn and Richard Bentley, 1831).

Gainsborough, Thos., *The Letters of Thomas Gainsborough*, ed. John Hayes (New Haven and London: Yale University Press, 2001).

The Gentleman Angler (London: G. Kearsley, 1786).

Gilpin, William, *Observations on the River Wye* (London: R. Blamire, 1782).

Gilpin, William, *Remarks on Forest Scenery, and other Woodland Views, (Relative chiefly to Picturesque Beauty)* 2 vols (London: R. Blamire, 1791).

Gilpin, William, *Observations, relative chiefly to Picturesque Beauty, Made in the Year 1772, On Several Parts of England; particularly the Mountains and Lakes of Cumberland, and Westmoreland* (1789), 2 vols, third edn, London (R. Blamire, 1792).

Gilpin, William, *Observations on Several Parts of the Counties of Cambridge, Norfolk, Suffolk, and Essex, And on Several Parts of North Wales; relative chiefly to Picturesque Beauty* (London: Cadell and Davies, 1809).

Hancock, Thomas G., *Distracted Complaints of Mr. Fletcher, Printer, upon his reading the "Expostulatory Reply to Edward Eyton, Esqr.'s Letter, addressed to Sir W. W. Wynne, Bart."* (Chester: the booksellers, and Shrewsbury: the author, n.d.).

Hancock, Thomas G., *An Expostulatory Reply to "Edward Eyton, Esqr.'s Letter, addressed to Sir W. W. Wynne, Bart."*

(Chester: the booksellers, and Shrewsbury: the author, n.d.).

Harrison, John, *A Letter to the Rt. Hon. Henry Dundas, M.P.* (London: J. Smith and D. I. Eaton, 1794).

The History of Two Acts (London: G. G. and J. Robinson, 1796).

Hoare, Richard Colt, M. W. Thompson (ed.), *The Journeys of Sir Richard Colt Hoare through Wales and England 1793–1810* (Gloucester: Alan Sutton, 1983).

Hone, William, *The Every-day Book: or, Everlasting Calendar of Popular Amusements*, 2 vols (London: William Hone, 1826).

Hucks, J., *Poems, by J. Hucks, A. M. Fellow Of Catharine Hall, Cambridge* (Cambridge: Benjamin Flower, 1798).

Hucks, J., *A Pedestrian Tour through North Wales, in a Series of Letters* (1795), ed. Alun R. Jones and William Tydeman (Cardiff: University of Wales Press, 1979).

Hughes, David, *Poems, on Various Subjects, in English and Latin* (Denbigh: W. Morris, 1865).

Hutton, William *Remarks upon North Wales: being the Result of Sixteen Tours through that Part of the Principality* (Birmingham: Knott & Lloyd, 1803).

[Jones, Theophilus], 'Cursory Remarks on Welsh Tours or Travels', in the *Cambrian Register for the Year 1796*, vol. 2 (London: E. and T. Williams, 1799), pp. 421–54.

Jones, Theophilus, *A History of the County of Brecknock*, 3 vols (Brecknock: G. North, for the author, 1805–9).

Kay, George, *General View of the Agriculture and Rural Economy of Anglesey* (Edinburgh: John Moir, 1794).

Kay, George, *General View of the Agriculture and Rural Economy of Denbighshire*, (Edinburgh: John Moir, 1794).

Kay, George, *General View of the Agriculture and Rural Economy of Merionethshire* (Edinburgh: John Moir, 1794).

Kay, George, *General View of the Agriculture of Flintshire* ([Edinburgh: printed by John Moir, 1794]).

Lessing, G.E., *Laocoon* [1766], in *Selected Prose Works of G.E. Lessing*, tr. E. C. Beasley and Helen Zimmern, ed. Edward Bell (London: George Bell, 1885).

Lewis, Samuel, *A Topographical Dictionary of Wales* (London: S. Lewis, 1849), *http://www.british-history.ac.uk/report.aspx?compid=47862*.

Lhuyd, Edward, 'Unpublished Letters of Edward Llwyd, of the Ashmolean Library, Oxford', *Cambrian Quarterly Magazine and Celtic Repertory*, 3/10 (April 1831).

Lloyd, Edward, *A Month's Tour in North Wales, Dublin, and its Environs* (London: G. Kearsly, 1781).

Llwyd, Richard, *Beaumaris Bay* (Chester: J. Fletcher, [1800]).

Llwyd, Richard, *Poems: Tales, Odes, Sonnets, Translations from the British* (Chester: J. Fletcher, and London: E. Williams, 1804).

Llwyd, Richard, *Beaumaris Bay: the Shores of the Menai, and the Interior of Snowdonia* (Chester: J. Parry, 1833).

Llwyd, Richard, *Poetical Works of Richard Llwyd, the Bard of Snowdon* (London: Whittaker & Co., et al., 1837).

Lyttelton, George, Baron, 'Letters to Mr Bower', in *The Works of George Lord Lyttelton* (London: J. Dodsley, 1774), 737–51.

Manners, John Henry, Duke of Rutland, *Journal of a Tour through North and South Wales, the Isle of Man, &c. &c.* (London: J. Triphook, 1805).

Marshall, William, *The Review and Abstract of the County Reports to the Board of Agriculture*, 5 vols (York: Thomas Wilson, 1818).

[Mavor, William F.], *A Tour in Wales, and through several Counties of England, including both the Universities, performed in the Summer of 1805* (London: Richard Phillips, 1806).

Morganwg, Iolo, Geraint H. Jenkins, Ffion Mair Jones

and David Ceri Jones (eds), *The Correspondence of Iolo Morganwg*, 3 vols (Cardiff: University of Wales Press, 2007).

[Nash, Michael], *Gideon's Cake of Barley Meal. A Letter to the Rev. William Romaine, on his preaching for the Emigrant Popish Clergy*, second edn (London: J. S. Jordan, 1793).

Newcome, Richard, *An Account of the Castle and Town of Ruthin*, second edn (Ruthin: Royal Victoria Press, 1836).

The North Country Angler, or the Art of Angling as practised in the Northern Counties of England, second edn (Leeds: D. Smith, 1788).

[Oldfield, T. H. B.], *An Entire and Complete History, Political and Personal, of the Boroughs of Great Britain*, 3 vols (London: J. Debrett, 1792).

Osbaldiston, William, *The British Sportsman, or, Nobleman, Gentleman, and Farmer's Dictionary, of Recreation and Amusement* (London: J. Stead for Champante and Whitrow, n.d.).

The Parliamentary History of England, 36 vols (London: R. Bagshaw, T. Longman, 1806–20).

Particulars of Sale … 26th Day of September, 1867 … the Mansion House and Demesne Lands known as "Llantysilio Hall" (no publication details).

Paterson, Daniel, *A New and Accurate Description of all the Direct and Principal Cross Roads in England and Wales*, tenth edn (London: Longman, 1794).

Peacock, W., *Peacock's Polite Repository; or Pocket Companion* (London: Peacocks and Bampton, 1815).

Pen-y-Lan, NLW Sale Catalogue, Denbighshire 399.

Pennant, Thomas, *A Tour in Wales*, 2 vols (London: Henry Hughes), vols 1 (1778) and 2 (1781).

Pennant, Thomas, *The Literary Life of the late Thomas Pennant, Esq. By himself* (London: Benjamin and John White, and Robert Faulder, 1793).

Pennant, Thomas, *Tours in Wales*, ed. John Rhys, 3 vols (Caernarvon: H. Humphreys, 1883).

[Phillips, Richard], *Modern London; being the History of the Present State of the British Metropolis* (London: Richard Phillips, 1804).

Pliny, *Natural History*, Loeb edition, tr. H. Rackham, vol. 9 (Cambridge, MA and London: Harvard University Press and Heinemann, 1984).

Plumptre, James, Ian Ousby (ed.), *James Plumptre's Britain: The Journals of a Tourist in the 1790s* (London: Hutchinson, 1992).

Pückler-Muskau, Hermann Fürst von, *Briefe eines erstorbenen. Ein fragmentarisches Tagebuch aus England, Wales, Irland und Frankreich, geschrieben in den Jahren 1828 und 1829*, 4 vols (Stuttgart: Hallberger 1831).

[Pugh, Edward], *Cambria Depicta: A Tour through North Wales, illustrated with Picturesque Views. By a Native Artist* (London: E. Williams, 1816).

[Pyne, William,], 'Ephraim Hardcastle', *Somerset House Gazette and Literary Museum; or, Weekly Miscellany of Fine Arts, Antiquities, and Literary Chit Chat*, 2 vols in 1 (London: W. Wetton 1824).

Pyne, W. H. and Combe, William Combe, with A. C. Pugin and Thomas Rowlandson, *The Microcosm of London*, 3 vols (London: Rudolph Ackermann, 1808–11).

Radcliffe, Ann, *The Italian* (1797), ed. Frederick Garber (Oxford: Oxford University Press, 1981).

Redgrave, Samuel, *A Dictionary of Artists of the English School: Painters, Sculptors, Architects, Engravers, and Ornamentists*, second edn (1878), reprinted in facsimile (Bath: Kingsmead Reprints, 1970).

Reynolds, Joshua, *Discourses on Art*, ed. Robert R. Wark (New Haven and London: Yale University Press, 1975).

Roberts, Peter, *The Cambrian Popular Antiquities: or, An Account of some Traditions, Customs, and Superstitions, of Wales: with Observations as to their Origin* (London: E. Williams, 1815).

Robertson, Andrew, Emily Robertson (ed.), *Letters and Papers of Andrew Robertson, AM, Miniature Painter* (London: Eyre and Spottiswoode, 1895).

Scott, Thomas, *An Estimate of the Religious Character and State of Great Britain* (London: J. S. Jordan et al., 1793).

Shelley, Mary, 'Life of William Godwin', ed. Pamela Clemit, in *Mary Shelley's Literary Lives*, gen. ed. Nora Crook, 4 vols (London: Pickering and Chatto, 2002), vol. 4.

[Shirley, Thomas], *The Angler's Museum; or, the whole Art of Float and Fly Fishing* (London: John Fielding, [1784?]).

Simpson, W. T., *Some Account of Llangollen and its Vicinity* (London: C. B. Whittaker, 1827).

Skrine, Henry, *Two Successive Tours through the Whole of Wales* (London: Emsley and Bremner, 1798).

Sotheby, William, *A Tour through Parts of Wales, Sonnets, Odes, and other Poems* (London: R. Blamire, 1794).

Southey, Robert, *Letters from England* (1807), ed. Jack Simmons (Gloucester: Alan Sutton, 1984).

Spence, Thomas, *Pig's Meat, or, Lessons for the Swinish Multitude*, 3 vols (London: Thomas Spence, 1794).

State Trials, William Cobbett and T. B. Howells (eds), *A Complete Collection of State Trials*, 30 vols (London: Longman et al., 1816–22).

Sterne, Laurence, *A Sentimental Journey through France and Italy by Mr. Yorick* (1768), ed. Ian Jack (Oxford: Oxford University Press, 1984).

Strange, John, 'An Account of Two Giants Causeways, or Groups of prismatic basaltine Columns, and other curious vulcanic Concretions, in the Venetian State in Italy; with some Remarks on the Characters of these and other similar Bodies, and on the physical Geography of the Countries in which they are found', *Philosophical Transactions of the Royal Society of London*, LXV/1 (1775), 5–47.

Tales for Youth, or the High Road to Renown, through the Paths of Pleasure (London: William Lane, at the Minerva Press, 1797).

Taylor, Samuel, *Angling in all its Branches, reduced to a Complete Science* (London: T. N. Longman and O. Rees, 1800).

Thelwall, John, *Political Lectures (No. I.) on the Moral Tendency of a System of Spies and Informers* (London: D. I. Eaton, 1794).

Thelwall, John, *The Tribune*, 3 vols (London: D. I. Eaton et al., 1795–6).

Thelwall, John, Judith Thompson (ed.), *The Peripatetic* (Detroit: Wayne State University Press, 2001).

Thoughts on the Present War with France (London: J. Debrett, 1793).

Tomlinson, J., *Contrariety, or a New Broom, for the New House . . . As performed at the New Theatre, Stafford* (Stafford: N. Boden, 1792).

Trusler, John, *The London Adviser and Guide*, second edn (London: for the author, 1790).

The Universal British Directory of Trade, Commerce, and Manufactures, vol. 4 (London: for the Patentees at the British Directory Office, and Champante and Whitrow, 1798).

Vancouver, George, W. Kaye Lamb (ed.), *The Voyage of George Vancouver 1791–1795*, 4 vols (London: Hakluyt Society, 1988).

Wake, W. R., *Two Sermons preached in the Parish Church of St. Michael, one on the Fast Day, April 19* (Bath: Bull and Co. et al., [1793]).

Wakefield, Priscilla, *Perambulations around London, and its Environs* (London: Darton and Harvey, 1809).

Walford, Thomas, *The Scientific Tourist through England, Wales, & Scotland*, 2 vols (London, J. Booth, 1818).

Warner, Richard, *A Walk through Wales, in August 1797* (Bath: R. Cruttwell, and London: C. Dilly, 1798).

Warner, Richard, *A Second Walk through Wales . . . in August and September 1798* (Bath: R. Cruttwell, and London: C. Dilly, 1799).

Webb, Daniel, *An Inquiry into the Beauties of Painting; and into the Merits of the most Celebrated Painters, Ancient and Modern* (London: J. Dodsley, 1760).

Wigstead, Henry, *Remarks on a Tour to North and South Wales in the Year 1797 . . . with Plates from Rowlandson, Pugh, Howitt &c.* (London: W. Wigstead, 1800).

Williams, William, *Observations on the Snowdon Mountains* (London: E. Williams, 1802).

Williams Wynn, C. Charlotte Grenville and Rachel Leighton (eds), *Correspondence of Charlotte Grenville, Lady Williams Wynn and her Three Sons* (London: John Murray, 1920).

Wordsworth, Wm., Ernest de Sélincourt (ed.), *The Prelude, or Growth of a Poet's Mind*, second edn, rev. Helen Darbishire (Oxford: Clarendon Press, 1959).

Wyndham, Henry P., *A Gentleman's Tour through Monmouthshire and Wales, in the Months of June and July, 1774. A new edition* (London: T. Evans, 1781).

Yorke, Philip., *The Royal Tribes of Wales* (Wrexham: John Painter, 1799).

Secondary Bibliography

Adamson, Donald and Dewar, Peter Beauclerk, *The House of Nell Gwyn: The Fortunes of the Beauclerk Family 1670–1974* (London: William Kimber, 1974).

Baker, Rosa, 'The Family of Richard Wilson, R.A., and its Welsh Connections', *Flintshire Historical Society Journal* 35 (1999), 85–114.

Baker, Rosa, and Jones, Rosemary, 'The Park and Gardens of Colomendy Hall', *Flintshire Historical Society Journal* 34 (1996), 33–52.

Barbier, C.P., *William Gilpin* (Oxford: Oxford University Press, 1963).

Barrell, John, *The Birth of Pandora and the Division of Knowledge* (Philadelphia: University of Pennsylvania Press, 1992).

Barrell, John, *Imagining the King's Death: Figurative Treason, Fantasies of Regicide 1793–1796* (Oxford: Oxford University Press, 2000).

Barrell, John, *The Spirit of Despotism: Invasions of Privacy in the 1790s* (Oxford: Oxford University Press, 2006).

Barrell, John and Mee, Jon (eds), *Trials for Treason and Sedition 1792–1794*, 8 vols (London: Pickering & Chatto, 2006–7).

Bevan-Evans, M., 'Gadlys and Flintshire lead-mining in the Eighteenth Century: II', *Journal of the Flintshire Historical Society*, 19 (1961), 32–60..

Bevan-Evans, M., 'Gadlys and Flintshire Lead-mining in the Eighteenth Century: III', *Journal of the Flintshire Historical Society*, 20 (1962), 58–89.

Bogle, James, *Artists in Snowdonia* (Talybont: Y Lolfa Cyf, 1990).

Bonehill, John and Daniels, Stephen (eds), *Paul Sandby: Picturing Britain* (Nottingham, Edinburgh and London: Nottingham City Museums and Galleries, National Gallery of Scotland and Royal Academy of Arts, 2009).

Boswell, Percy G. H., 'The Salopian Rocks and Tectonics of the district South-west of Ruthin (Denbighshire), *Quarterly Journal of the Geological Society*, 83/5 (1927–8), 689–710.

Boughton, Peter, *Watercolours of North Wales* (Chester: Grosvenor Museum, 1989).

The Boundary Dispute, educational pamphlet containing primary source materials (Llanferres: Colomendy Centre for Outdoor Education, n.d.).

Bowen, E. G., *David Samwell (Dafydd Ddu Feddyg) 1751–1798* (Cardiff: University of Wales Press, 1974).

Braybrooke, Neville, *London Green: The Story of Kensington Gardens, Hyde Park, Green Park & St. James's Park* (London: Gollancz, 1959).

Burford, E. J., *Royal St. James's: Being a Story of Kings, Clubmen and Courtesans* (London: Robert Hale, 1980).

Cato, Miles Wynn, *Parry: The Life and Works of William Parry A.R.A. (1743–1791)* (Aberystwth: the author, 2008).

Chapman, John, *A Guide to Parliamentary Enclosures in Wales* (Cardiff: University of Wales Press, 1992).

Chapman, John, 'Parliamentary Enclosure in Wales: Comparisons and Contrasts', *Welsh History Review*, 21/4 (December 2003), 761–9.

Chester, *Guide to Chester and North Wales (Northern Section)* (London and Melbourne: Ward Lock, n. d.).

Courtney, W. P. , 'David Hughson: Edward and David Pugh', *Notes and Queries*, new series, iv, 22 July 1911, pp. 70–2.

Cunningham, Hugh, 'The metropolitan fairs: a case study in the social control of leisure', in A. P. Donajgrodzki (ed.), *Social Control in Nineteenth-Century Britain* (London: Croom Helm, 1978), pp. 163-84.

Davies, Hywel M., '"Very different springs of uneasiness": Emigration from Wales to the United States of America during the 1790s', *Welsh History Review*, 15/3 (June 1991), 368–98.

Davies, Hywel M., 'Wales in English Travel Writing 1791–8: The Welsh Critique of Theophilus Jones', *Welsh History Review*, 23/3 (June 2007), 65–93.

Davies, W. Lloyd, 'The Riot at Denbigh in 1795', *Bulletin of the Board of Celtic Studies*, 4 (1927), 61–73.

Davies, Damian Walford and Pratt, Lynda (eds), *Wales and the Romantic Imagination* (Cardiff: University of Wales Press, 2007).

Dodd, A. H., 'The Roads of North Wales, 1750–1850', *Archaeologia Cambrensis*, 80/1 (June 1925), 121–48.

Dodd, A. H., *The Industrial Revolution in North Wales* (Cardiff: University of Wales Press, 1951).

Donald, Diana, *The Age of Caricature: Satirical Prints in the Age of George III* (New Haven: Yale University Press, 1996).

Ebbs, Cris, *Mines & Caves of Loggerheads Country Park* (Llanarmon-yn-ial: Cris Ebbs, 2008).

Edwards, J. B., 'John Jones (Jac Glan-y-Gors): Tom Paine's Denbighshire Henchman?' *Denbighshire Historical Society Transactions*, 51 (2002), 95–112.

Edwards, John Wyn, 'Enclosure and agricultural improvement in the Vale of Clwyd 1750–1875' (MA thesis, University of London, 1963).

Ellis, Bryn, 'The History of Quarrying in the Maeshafn–Llanarmon Area', *Denbighshire Historical Society Transactions*, 43 (1994), 45–65.

Ellis, Bryn, 'Limestone Quarrying in North-east Wales before 1900', *Welsh History Review*, 18/1 (June 1996), 125–39.

Ellis, Bryn, 'Denbighshire Quarter Sessions Rolls in the Eighteenth Century', *Denbighshire Historical Society Transactions*, 50 (2001), 76–97.

Ellis, Bryn, 'Denbighshire Quarter Sessions Rolls in the Eighteenth Century part 2: 1751–1800: Roads, Bridges and Public Buildings', *Denbighshire Historical Society Transactions*, 51 (2002), 80–94.

Ellis, Osian, *Hanes y Delyn yng Nghymru / The Story of the Harp in Wales* (Cardiff: University of Wales Press, 1980).

Evans, D. G., 'The Hope Enclosure Act of 1791', *Flintshire Historical Society Journal*, 31 (1983–4), 161–86.

Evans, Neil., 'Regional dynamics: north Wales, 1750–1914', in Edward Royle (ed.), *Issues of Regional Identity: In Honour of John Marshall* (Manchester: Manchester University Press, 1998), pp. 201–25.

Evans, R. Paul, 'Thomas Pennant (1726–1798): "The Father of Cambrian Tourists"', *Welsh History Review*, 13/4 (December 1987), 395–417.

Fox, Celina, *The Arts of Industry in the Age of Enlightenment* (New Haven and London: Yale University Press, 2010).

Freud, Sigmund, 'The "uncanny", in *Art and Literature*, tr. James Strachey, The Penguin Freud Library, 14 (Harmondsworth: Penguin Books, 1985), pp. 339–76.

Grant, Colonel Maurice Harold, *A Chronological History of the Old English Landscape Painters (in Oil) from the XVIth Century to the XIXth Century*, new revised and enlarged edition, 8 vols (1957–61), vol. 5 (Leigh-on-Sea: F. Lewis, 1959).

Grant, Colonel Maurice Harold, *A Dictionary of British Landscape Painters from the 16th Century to the early 20th Century* (1952) (Leigh-on-Sea: F. Lewis, 1976).

Graves, Algernon, *The Royal Academy of Arts: A Complete Dictionary of Contributors and their Work from its Foundation in 1769 to 1904*, 8 vols (London: Henry Graves and George Bell, 1905–6).

Graves, Algernon, *The British Institution 1806–1807* (1875) (Bath: Kingsmead, 1969).

Green, R. G. and Hawkins, A. Brian, 'Rock Cut on the A5 at Glyn Bends, North Wales, UK', *Bulletin of Engineering Geology and the Environment*, 64/1 (2005), 95–109.

Griffiths, Eric, *Philip Yorke I (1743–1804), Squire of Erthig* (Wrexham: Bridge Books, 1995).

Griffiths, Ralph, 'Bishop Morton and the Ely Tower at Brecon', *Brycheiniog*, 34 (2002), 13-30.

Guest, Harriet, *Empire, Barbarism, and Civilisation: Captain Cook, William Hodges, and the Return to the Pacific* (Cambridge: Cambridge University Press, 2007).

Guldi, Jo, *Roads to Power: Britain Invents the Infrastructure State* (Cambridge, MA and London: Harvard University Press, 2012).

Hague, Douglas B., 'Giler, Cerrig-y-drudion, Denbighshire', *Denbighshire Historical Society Transactions*, 7 (1958), 67–85.

Harper, Charles G., *The Holyhead Road: The Mail-Coach Road to Dublin*, 2 vols (London: Chapman and Hall, 1902).

Hayes, John, *The Drawings of Thomas Gainsborough*, 2 vols (London: A. Zwemmer, 1970).

Herbert, Trevor and Jones, Gareth Elwyn, *The Remaking of Wales in the Eighteenth Century* (Cardiff: University of Wales Press, 1988).

Herd, Andrew, *The Fly* (Ellesmere: Medlar Press, 2003).

Hernon, Paul, *Sir Watkin & Mr. Sandby* (Wrexham: Wrexham County Borough Museum, 2006).

Hill, Draper, *Mr. Gillray the Caricaturist: A Biography* (London: Phaidon Press, 1965).

Howard, Sharon, 'Riotous Community: Crowds, Politics and Society in Wales, c. 1700–1840,' *Welsh History Review*, 20/4 (December 2001), 656–86.

Howell, David W., *The Rural Poor in Eighteenth-Century Wales* (Cardiff: University of Wales Press, 2000).

Howells, M.F., *British Regional Geology: Wales* (Nottingham: British Geological Survey, 2007).

Howson, J. S. and Rimmer, Alfred, *The River Dee, its Aspect and History* (London: J. S. Virtue, 1892).

Hubbard, Edward, *Clwyd (Denbighshire and Flintshire): The Buildings of Wales* (New Haven and London: Yale University Press, 2003).

Hughes, Peter, 'Paul Sandby and Sir Watkin Williams-Wynn', *Burlington Magazine*, 114 (1972), 459–67.

Jenkins, Geraint H., *The Foundations of Modern Wales 1642–1780* (Oxford: Oxford University Press, 1993).

Jenkins, Geraint H., 'An Uneasy Relationship: Gwallter Mechain and Iolo Morganwg', *Montgomeryshire Collections*, 97 (2009), 73–99.

Jenkins, J. Geraint, 'Commercial Salmon Fishing in Welsh Rivers', *Folk Life*, 9 (1971), 29–60.

Jenkins, J. Geraint, 'Fish Weirs and Traps', *Folk Life*, 12 (1974), 5–9.

Jones, David, *Before Rebecca: Popular Protests in Wales 1793–1835* (London: Allen Lane, 1973).

Jones, Emrys, 'The Welsh in London in the Seventeenth and Eighteenth Centuries', *Welsh History Review*, 10/4 (December 1981), 461–75.

Jones, Rod, 'Out of the past: pictures in theory and history', in Tony Curtis (ed.), *Wales: The Imagined Nation. Studies in Cultural and National Identity* (Bridgend: Poetry Wales Press, 1986), pp. 261–85.

Jones, Tim, *Rioting in North East Wales 1536–1918* (Wrexham: Bridge Books, 1997).

Joyner, Paul, *Artists in Wales c. 1740–c. 1851* (Aberystwyth: National Library of Wales, 1997).

Judd, Mark, '"The oddest combination of town and country": popular culture and the London fairs', in

John K. Walton and James Walvin (eds), *Leisure in Britain, 1780-1839* (Manchester: Manchester University Press, 1983), pp. 10-30.

Kenyon, George T., *The Life of Lloyd, First Lord Kenyon, Lord Chief Justice of England* (London: Longmans, Green, 1873).

King, Tony, 'The Boundary Markers of Llanferres', *Clwyd Historian*, 43 (Autumn 1999), 24–7.

King, Tony and Williams, Christopher J., 'The Jubilee Tower on Moel Fama', *Denbighshire Historical Society Transactions*, 58 (2010), 65–109.

'Larwood, Jacob', *The Story of the London Parks* (London: John Camden Hotten, 1872).

Lasdun, Susan, *The English Park: Royal, Private & Public* (London: André Deutsch, 1991).

Leask, Nigel, *Robert Burns and Pastoral: Poetry and Improvement in Late Eighteenth-Century Scotland* (Oxford: Oxford University Press, 2010).

Lerry, George G., 'The Industries of Denbighshire from Tudor Times to the Present Day. Part III: More Tecent Developments (b)', *Denbighshire Historical Society Transactions*, 9 (1960), 146–73.

Lewis, J. B., 'The Cloughs in the North West', *Clwyd Historian*, 27 (Autumn 1991), 16–20.

Lewis, W. J., *Lead Mining in Wales* (Cardiff: University of Wales Press, 1967).

Lin, Patricia, 'Caring for the nation's families: British soldiers' and sailors' families and the state, 1793–1815', in Alan Forrest, Karen Hagemann and Jane Rendall (eds), *Soldiers, Citizens and Civilians: Experiences and Perceptions of the French Wars, 1790–1820* (Basingstoke: Palgrave Macmillan, 2009).

Llangollen, *A Pictorial and Descriptive Guide to Llangollen, Corwen, Bala, and North Wales (Southern Section)* (London: Ward Lock, n. d.).

Llangwm, Conway (part) (Cardiff: CADW, Welsh Historic Monuments, 1998).

Lloyd, J. Y. W., *The History of the Princes, the Lords Marcher, and the Ancient Nobility of Powys Fadog*, vol. 4 (London: Whiting, 1884).

Löffler, Marion, 'Serial literature and radical poetry in Wales at the end of the eighteenth century', in Michael Brown, Catriona Kennedy, John Kirk and Andrew Noble (eds), *United Islands? Multi-Lingual Radical Poetry and Song in Britain and Ireland, 1770–1820*, vol. 2: *The Cultures of Resistance* (London: Pickering and Chatto, forthcoming).

Long, Basil, 'John Warwick Smith (1749–1831)', *Walker's Quarterly*, 24 (1927).

Long, Basil, *British Miniaturists 1520–1860* (1929) (London: Holland Press, 1966).

Lord, Peter, *The Visual Culture of Wales: Industrial Society* (Cardiff: University of Wales Press, 1998).

Lord, Peter, *The Visual Culture of Wales: Imaging the Nation* (Cardiff: University of Wales Press, 2000).

Moore, Donald (ed.), *The Artist's Journey through North Wales: Clwyd: 18th and 19th Century Pictures from the National Library of Wales* (Bodelwyddan Castle: Clwyd Fine Arts Trust, n.d.).

Moore, Donald, 'The discovery of the Welsh landscape', in Donald Moore (ed.) *Wales in the Eighteenth Century* (Swansea: C. Davies, 1976).

Nicholas, Thomas, *Annals and Antiquities of the Counties and County Families of Wales*, 2 vols (London: Longman, 1872).

O'Byrne, Alison, 'Walking, rambling, and promenading in eighteenth-century London: a literary and cultural history' (unpublished Ph.D. thesis, University of York, 2003).

Osborne, Harvey, 'The development of salmon angling in the nineteenth century', in R. W. Hoyle (ed.), *Our Hunting Fathers: Field Sports in England after 1850* (London: Carnegie Publishing, 2007).

Owen, Bryn, *History of the Welsh Militia and Volunteer Corps, 1757–1908. Denbighshire and Flintshire. Part 1: Regiments of Militia* (Wrexham: Bridge Books, 1997).

Owen, Elias, *Welsh Folk-Lore: A Collection of the Folk-tales and Legends of North Wales* (Oswestry and Wrexham: Woodall and Minshall, 1896).

Owen, Geraint, *Old and Present Pubs of Ruthin Town* (no place: Invisus Publications, 2004).

Owen, Hywel Wyn and Morgan, Richard, *Dictionary of the Place-names of Wales* (Llandysul: Gomer, 2008).

Painting, Vivienne *John Boydell* (London: Guildhall Art Gallery, 2005).

Palmer, Arnold N., *A History of the Parish of Ruabon* (Wrexham: Bridge Books, 1992).

Parry, Colonel Ll. E. S. and Freeman, Engineer Lieutenant B. F. M., *Historical Records of the Denbighshire Hussars Imperial Yeomanry* (Wrexham: Woodall, Minshall and Co., 1909).

Payne, Matthew and James, *Regarding Thomas Rowlandson 1757–1827: His Life, Art & Acquaintance* (no place: Hogarth Arts, 2010).

Penford, Alastair (ed.), *Thomas Telford: Engineer* (London: Thomas Telford Ltd, 1980).

Penfold, Alastair, *Thomas Telford 'Colossus of Roads'* (Telford: Telford Development Corporation, 1981).

Pennant Jones, Middleton Pennant Jones, 'John Jones or Glan-y-Gors', *The Transactions of the Honourable Society of Cymmrodorion. Session 1909–1910* (1911), 60–94.

Pitman, Liz, *Pigsties and Paradise: Lady Diarists and the Tour of Wales 1795–1860* (Llanrwst: Gwasg Carreg Gwalch, 2009).

Planché, J. R., *Recollections and Reflections: A Professional Autobiography*, 2 vols (London: Tinsley Brothers, 1872).

Porter, J. H., 'Net fishermen and the salmon laws: conflict in late Victorian Devon', in Barry Stapleton (ed.), *Conflict and Community in Southern England: Essays in the Social History of Rural and Urban Labour from Mediaeval to Modern Times* (New York: St. Martin's Press, 1992), pp. 240–50.

Pratt, Derrick and Veysey, A. G., *A Handlist of the Topographical Prints of Clwyd (Denbighshire, Flintshire and Edeyrnion* (Hawarden: Clwyd Record Office, 1977).

Prescott, Sarah, *Eighteenth-Century Writing from Wales: Bards and Britons* (Cardiff: University of Wales Press, 2008).

Pretty, David A., *Anglesey: The Concise History* (Cardiff: University of Wales Press, 2005).

Pritchard, R. T., 'Denbighshire Roads and Turnpike Trusts', *Denbighshire Historical Society Transactions*, 12 (1963), 86–9.

Quartermaine, Jamie, Trinder, Barrie and Turner, Rick, *Thomas Telford's Holyhead Road: The A5 in North Wales* (York: Council for British Archaeology, 2003).

Roberts, John, Askew *Wynnstay and the Wynns: A Volume of Varieties* (Oswestry: Woodall and Venables, 1876).

Roberts, P. R. , 'The Decline of the Welsh Squires in the 18th Century', *National Library of Wales Journal*, 13/2 (1963), 157–73.

Rolt, L. T. C., *Thomas Telford* (Harmondsworth: Penguin Books, 1985).

Ruthin Parish Registers, 3 vols (Wrexham: Clwyd Family History Society, 1994–5).

Sherratt, Gordon, *An Illustrated History of Llangollen* (Llangollen: Ceiriog Press, 2000).

Snell, K. D. M., *Annals of the Labouring Poor: Social Change and Agrarian England, 16601900* (Cambridge: Cambridge University Press, 1985).

Soldon, Norbert C., *John Wilkinson 1728–1808: English Ironmaster and Inventor* (Lewiston, NY: Edwin Mellen Press, 1998).

Solkin, David, *Richard Wilson: The Landscape of Reaction* (London: Tate Gallery, 1982).

Strahan, Aubrey, *The Geology of the Neighbourhoods of Flint, Mold and Ruthin* (London: HMSO, 1890).

Temple, Nigel, 'Humphry Repton, Illustrator, and William Peacock's Polite Repository 1790–1811', *Garden History*, 16/2 (Autumn 1988), 161–73.

Tennant, Rowland, *A History of Holywell and Greenfield* (Wrexham: Bridge Books, 2007).

Thomas, David, *Agriculture in Wales during the Napoleonic Wars* (Cardiff: University of Wales Press, 1963).

Thomas, Peter D. G., 'Wynnstay versus Chirk Castle: Parliamentary Elections in Denbighshire 1716–1741', *National Library of Wales Journal*, 11/2 (Winter 1959), 105–22.

Thompson, Keith M., *Ruthin School: The First Seven Centuries* (Ruthin: Ruthin School Quatercentenary Committee, 1974).

Toscano, Maria, '"Nature catched in the fact": sperimentalismo e collezionismo antiquario-naturalistico nel Regno di Napoli, Veneto, Gran Bretagna tra XVIII–XIX secolo' (Ph.D. thesis, no date, Università degli Studi di Napoli 'Federico II', *http://www.fedoa.unina.it/777/1/Tesi_Toscano.pdf*.

Wager, David A., 'Welsh Politics and Parliamentary Reform, 1780–1832', *Welsh History Review*, 7/4 (December 1975), 427–49.

Wallace, A. R., *My Life: A Record of Events and Opinions*. 2 vols (London: Chapman and Hall, 1905).

Wedd, C. B., Smith, B. and Wills, L. J., *The Geology of the Country around Wrexham*, Part I: *Lower Palaeozoic & Lower Carbonaceous Rocks* (London: HMSO, 1927).

Williams, C. J., 'The Lead Mines of the Alyn Valley', *Flintshire Historical Society Journal*, 29 (1979–80), 51–87.

Williams, C. J., 'The Lead Miners of Flintshire and Denbighshire', *Llafur*, 3/2 (1980), 87– 96.

Williams, C. J., 'The Mining Laws in Flintshire and Denbighshire', *Bulletin of the Peak District Mines Historical Society*, 12/3 (1994), 62–8.

Williams, C. J., *Metal Mines of North Wales: A Collection of Pictures*, second edn (Wrexham: Bridge Books, 1997).

Williams, Iolo A., 'Notes on Paul Sandby and his Predecessors in Wales', *Transactions of the Honourable Society of Cymmrodorion*, 2 (1961), 16–33.

Williams, Isaac J., *A Catalogue of Welsh Topographical Prints in the National Museum of Wales* (Cardiff: National Museum of Wales, 1926).

Williams, Isaac J., 'Edward Pugh of Ruthin 1761–1813, *Denbighshire Society in London Handbook* (1938–9), 22–34.

Wilton, Andrew, *Turner in Wales* (Llandudno: Mostyn Art Gallery, 1984).

Wroth, Warwick, *The London Pleasure Gardens of the Eighteenth Century* (1896) (Hamden, CT: Shoe String Press, 1979).

Wynne, R. O. F., 'The Wynne Family of Melai and Garthewin', *Denbighshire Historical Society Transactions*, 5 (1956), 74–87.

Zaring, Jane, 'The Romantic Face of Wales', *Annals of the Association of American Geographers*, 67/3 (September 1977), 397–418.

INDEX

Pugh, Dorothy (née Jones), mother of Edward 6, 171, 175, 188 n. 8

PUGH, EDWARD, addresses in London 7, 13–17; annual routine 13; birth 6; in Chester 10–14; death 23, 171; education 6–7; exhibits at Royal Academy 7–8, 10, 13, 16–17, 27; as 'hybrid' artist 4–5, 31; on 'improvement' and modernisation of Wales, *see* Wales; letters 6, 16; letter to Richard Llwyd 22–3, 171; member of Church of England 6, 22; as miniaturist 5–8, 11–13, 15–17; as 'native artist' 3, 198; obituaries 23, 171; and patriotism 22, 27; as pedestrian 7, 22, 176–7; political views 10, 76; possible practice in Dublin 12; prices of Pugh's miniatures 11–13; retirement to Ruthin 16–17, 22, 84; sources for biography 5; volunteers for Armed Association of Artists 15; watercolour, methods and techniques 8; as Welsh speaker 3, 6, 170, 190; and Richard Wilson 2–4, 40–1, 51–2, 170

Works:

　Cambria Depicta 5, 12–13, 16–17, 22–4, 27, 73–4, 83–4, 86–7, 91, 103, 116, 122–3, 130–1, 144, 170–221, 222–3, 226–7; advertisements for 23, 171, 220; conversations, 'confabs' 175, 190–2; date of tour and composition 178–9; description of Vale of Clwyd 219; distance travelled and time taken 22, 176; fear of falling rocks 116, 211–13; as guide-book for artists 22, 170, 172, 206–8, 211, and choosing 'points' and 'pictures' 192, 208; as general topography of North Wales 171, 207; as guide-book for tourists and 'general observer' 171–2, 207, 209; and history of Wales 198; later reputation 220; lodging on walk 191; original title 171; and popular legend 197–8; price 22–3, 171; reviewed in *Gentleman's Magazine* 182, 186–7; size, length of volume 176; and slave trade 22, 179; and Sterne's *Sentimental Journey* 175;

suspected spy for France 27, 190, 214; and vindication of character of the Welsh 22, 172–5, 191–2, 202: *see also* Welsh people; illustrations 23–4, 180, 182; aquatinting and colouring of 185–6; *Cadnant* 177; *Cambria* (frontispiece to *Cambria Depicta*) 193, 196; *Carreg Diddos* 212; *Conway Castle* 181, 188 n. 43, 224–7; *Dolanog Bridge* 206–7; *A Fall of Rocks* 212; *Holyhead Wake* 186; *Nant Ffrancon* 185; *N. East view of Snowdon* 186; *Paris Mines in 1800* 178, 184; *Paris Mines in 1804* 178, 184; *The Source of the Severn* 5, 175; *View in Nant Nanhwynen* 210; *View near the Loggerheads* 46; *A Visit to Cader Idris* 186

　Cambrian Popular Antiquities, illustrations 23–6; (attrib.) *The Fairies* 23–4; (attrib.) *Fives Playing* 26; (attrib.) *Singing to the Harp and Dancing* 26

　miniature portraits *The Cambrian Shakespeare* (Thomas Edwards) 6, 8, 16; (attrib.) *Lady Morris* 7; (attrib.) *Mrs Jones-Parry* 7–8; *Portrait of an unknown lady* 8; other exhibited miniature portraits 8, 15

　Modern London, 150–69; illustrations 5, 15–16, 22, 26, 27, 150–69, 170, 186, and architectural drawing 150; 'characteristic groups' and comic mode 150, 156; representations of children playing 154, 156, 161–2, 167; representations of families with children 154, 156, 162, 167–8; representation of social mixing 155, 157, 163, 166–8; *The Admiralty, the War Office, and the Treasury* 158, 160, 162, 167; *The Bank, Bank Buildings, Royal Exchange, & Cornhill* 159–60; *Drury Lane Theatre* 167; *The Entrance to Hyde Park on a Sunday* 154–5, 158, 167; *Greenwich Park, with the Royal Observatory, on Easter Monday* 158,

163–9; *The Houses of Parliament, with the Royal Procession* 153; *The Promenade in St James's Park* 155, 157; *The Society of Arts distributing its Premiums* 162; *Westminster from Lambeth* 167

　Six Views, in Denbighshire 2, 4–5, 8, 10, 16, 27, 31, 50, 55, 65, 69, 70, 74, 84, 86, 102, 135, 143, 148, 171, 179, 182, 186, 215, 220, 222, 226–7; advertised in Chester newspapers 10, 70, 102; patrons, patronage of 4, 10, 65, 74, 86, 103, 104, 131, 133, 135; reissued after Pugh's death 23; *Bathafern Hills, from Codemarchan Rocks* 3, 84–97, 133, 222, 225; *A Fall on the Dee, near the Vale of Crucis* 3, 127–35; *Foel Famma, from Careg Carn-March Arther* 3, 36–58, 93, 104, 132, 142; *Llanfwrog, Ruthin and Llanbedr* 3, 11, 62–79, 84, 102, 214, 222–3; *Pen-y-Lan, across the Dee* 3, 130, 138, 141–2, 145, 148; *Pont-Newydd over the Ceirw near Corwen* (Pont y Glyn Diffwys) 3, 11, 102, 106–17

　other works *Conway Ferry* 12; *Ely Tower* (?) in Theophilus Jones, *History of Brecknock* 174, 188 n. 19; *Gayton Wake* (lost oil painting) 17; *Newport in Monmouthshire* 19–21; *Pont Ychel Ruthin* 107; *Porth-Ycha, Conway* 12, 188 n. 43; *Portrait of a little boy with his pet dog* 8–9; *Ruthin, Denbighshire* 77–9; *The Vale of Clwyd* (lost oil painting) 17, 83, 216, 222; *The Vale of Clwyd* (lost watercolour) 222–6, and watercolour method 224–6; *The Vale of Clwyd* (projected aquatint) 219, 222; *The Vale of Llangollen* (projected aquatint) 219, 223; *View of a Stone Bridge … at Risca* 19, and copper token based on 19; *A Welsh Landscape* (lost oil painting) 17, 83, 222; vase, designed for Patriotic Fund 15

Pugh, John, three brothers of Edward so named 6

Pugh, Mary, sister of Edward 6, 171